T0305932

The Political Economy of Latin American Independence

Although historians usually trace its origins to the Haitian Revolution of the late eighteenth century, Latin American political, economic, and cultural independence is still very much a work in progress. As new national identities were developed, fresh reflection and theorizing was needed in order to understand how Latin America related to the wider world. Through a series of case studies on different topics and national experiences, this volume shows how political economy has occupied an important place in discussions about emancipation and independence that occurred in the region.

The production of political economic knowledge in the periphery of capitalism can take on many forms: importing ideas from abroad; translating and adapting them to local realities; or else producing concepts and theories specifically designed to make sense of the uniqueness of particular historical experiences. *The Political Economy of Latin American Independence* illustrates each of these strategies, exploring issues such as trade policy, money and banking, socio-economic philosophy, nationalism, and economic development. The expert authors stress how the originality of Latin American economic thought often resides in the creative appropriation of ideas originally devised in different contexts and thus usually ill-suited to local realities.

Taken together, the chapters illustrate a fertile methodological approach for studying the history of political economy in Latin America. This book is of great interest to economic historians specializing in Latin America, as well as those who study the history of economic thought, political economy, and Latin American history.

Alexandre Mendes Cunha is an Associate Professor in the Economics Department and currently the Director of the Center for European Studies at the Federal University of Minas Gerais (UFMG), Brazil.

Carlos Eduardo Suprinyak is an Associate Professor in the Economics Department, Federal University of Minas Gerais (UFMG), Brazil. His research interests include the history of economic thought, economic history, and economic methodology.

Routledge Studies in the History of Economics

The Political Economy of Latin American Independence

Edited by Alexandre Mendes Cunha
and Carlos Eduardo Suprinyak

Routledge
Taylor & Francis Group

LONDON AND NEW YORK

First published 2017
by Routledge
2 Park Square, Milton Park, Abingdon, Oxon OX14 4RN

and by Routledge
711 Third Avenue, New York, NY 10017

Routledge is an imprint of the Taylor & Francis Group, an informa business

British Library Cataloguing in Publication Data
A catalogue record for this book is available from the British Library

Library of Congress Cataloguing in Publication Data
Names: Cunha, Alexandre Mendes, editor. | Suprinyak, Carlos Eduardo.
Title: The political economy of Latin American independence /
edited by Alexandre Mendes Cunha and Carlos Eduardo Suprinyak.
Description: 1 Edition. | New York : Routledge, 2016. | Includes index.
Identifiers: LCCN 2016019002| ISBN 9781138644786 (hardback) |
ISBN 9781315628585 (ebook)
Subjects: LCSH: Latin America–Economic policy. | Latin America–
Economic conditions–1982– | Nationalism–Latin America.
Classification: LCC HC125 .P6445 2016 | DDC 330.98–dc23
LC record available at https://lccn.loc.gov/2016019002

ISBN: 978-1-138-64478-6 (hbk)
ISBN: 978-1-315-62858-5 (ebk)

Typeset in Times New Roman
by Out of House Publishing

Contents

Contributors

Michele Alacevich is Director of Global Studies and Assistant Professor of History at Loyola University, USA. He holds a PhD in Business History from the University of Milano, Italy. He specializes in the history of twentieth-century development institutions and ideas, and international history. Current interests include the history of development, the policies of postwar reconstruction in Eastern and Southern Europe, and the history of social sciences in the twentieth century, with a focus on the linkages between the history of ideas, economic and political history, and the history of economic thought. He has authored two books: *The Political Economy of the World Bank: The Early Years* (Stanford University Press, 2009), and *Economia politica. Un'introduzione storica*, with Daniela Parisi (Il Mulino, 2009). His publications include articles in *Journal of Global History*, *History of Political Economy*, *Review of Political Economy*, *Rivista di Storia Economica*, and *Journal of the History of Economic Thought*.

Andrés Álvarez is Associate Professor of Economics at the University of los Andes in Bogotá, Colombia. His fields of interest are the history of economic thought, with emphasis on monetary theory, and financial and monetary history.

Mauro Boianovsky is Full Professor of Economics at Universidade de Brasilia (UnB). He holds a PhD in Economics from Cambridge University. He has published on the history of economic thought in international journals and collected volumes. His book *Transforming Modern Macroeconomics: Exploring Disequilibrium Microfoundations, 1956–2003*, jointly with Roger Backhouse (Cambridge University Press, 2014), has received the ESHET 2014 best book award. He has been elected president of the History of Economics Society for the period 2016–2017.

Nelson Mendes Cantarino obtained his PhD in Social History from the University of São Paulo, Brazil, and held a post-doctoral fellowship at the Institute of Economics, State University of Campinas (Unicamp), Brazil. He has mainly worked on the following themes: Enlightened reformism; modern colonial empires, their dynamics and structures; modern history,

history of economic thought, and economic history; economic development and the theory of economic development.

José Luís Cardoso is Research Professor and Director of the Institute of Social Sciences of the University of Lisbon. He is author and editor of several books on the Portuguese history of economic thought from a comparative perspective, with special emphasis on the study of the processes of diffusion and assimilation of economic ideas. He has published articles in the main international journals on the history of economic thought. His research interests also include economic history and methodology of economics. He is the general editor of the series *Classics of Portuguese Economic Thought* (thirty volumes), co-founder of the *European Journal of the History of Economic Thought*, and co-editor of the *e-journal of Portuguese History*.

Maurício C. Coutinho is Full Professor of Economics at the State University of Campinas (Unicamp), Brazil. His research focuses on the history of economic thought, especially the following themes: eighteenth-century monetary economics (including Cantillon, Hume, Galiani, Turgot, Steuart, Smith, Harris), and Portuguese-Brazilian late colonial economic thought. Currently, he is studying the arguments elaborated by economists concerning slavery.

Alexandre Mendes Cunha is Associate Professor in the Department of Economics and currently Director of the Center for European Studies at the Federal University of Minas Gerais (UFMG), Brazil. He obtained his PhD in History from the Fluminense Federal University (UFF), Brazil, spending a period as a visiting researcher at the Technical University of Lisbon. His research interests include the history of economic thought, intellectual history, and economic and political history. He has published two edited books and several peer-reviewed articles (including in journals such as *History of Political Economy* and *The Review of Radical Political Economics*) and book chapters.

Luiz Felipe Bruzzi Curi is a doctoral student of Economic History at the University of São Paulo, Brazil, currently spending a period as a visiting research student at the Universität Hohenheim, Germany. His research interests include the history of economic thought, economic history, and the history of Republican Brazil.

Thiago Fontelas Rosado Gambi has a PhD in Economic History from the University of São Paulo, Brazil, and is Associate Professor at the Institute of Applied Social Sciences, Federal University of Alfenas (Unifal), Brazil. His main fields of research are banking history and Brazilian economic thought in the nineteenth century.

Anthony Howe is Professor of Modern History at the University of East Anglia, UK. His publications include *Free Trade and Liberal England,*

1846–1946 (Oxford, 1998), and a four-volume edition of *The Letters of Richard Cobden (1804–65)* (Oxford, 2007–2015). He is currently engaged on a global history of free trade from Adam Smith to the WTO.

Jimena Hurtado is Associate Professor at the Economics Department, University of los Andes, Colombia. Her research focuses on economic philosophy and the history of economic thought, especially during the eighteenth and twentieth centuries. Recently, she has worked on political philosophy, including recognition in the social interactions economics analyzes, and the origins of economic thought in nineteenth-century Colombia.

Joseph L. Love is Professor Emeritus at University of Illinois, Urbana-Champaign, USA. He is interested in the history of economic ideas, policy, and performance in Brazil and in Latin America as a whole. Earlier, he studied regionalism in Brazil. He is the author of *Rio Grande do Sul and Brazilian Regionalism, São Paulo in the Brazilian Federation, Crafting the Third World: Theorizing Underdevelopment in Romania and Brazil*, and *The Revolt of the Whip* (all with Stanford University Press). In addition, he has authored some eighty scholarly articles and essays, and has co-edited four books.

Stephen Meardon is Associate Professor of Economics at Bowdoin College, USA. He received his PhD in Economics from Duke University, USA. His most recent research examines how economic doctrines of free trade and protection treat the problem of "reciprocity." He aims to show how new economic ideas, and new alignments of free-trade and protectionist doctrines with kindred causes (e.g., peace, international copyright, opposition to slavery, territorial expansion), have been forged in circumstances where the correct application of the doctrines is ambiguous or seemingly inexpedient.

Milena Fernandes de Oliveira is Associate Professor at the Institute of Economics, State University of Campinas (Unicamp), Brazil. She obtained her PhD in Economic History from the same institution, with a doctoral internship at the École des Hautes Études en Sciences Sociales, Paris. She is currently working on the historiography of economic history and its interfaces with some long-standing issues, such as consumption and the nation, as well as intellectual history and the history of economic ideas.

Claudio Robles Ortiz received his PhD in History from the University of California, Davis. He studies the economic, social, and political history of Chilean rural societies from the 1850s to the present, and his research examines technological innovation and economic growth in agriculture, the transition of the *hacienda* system towards agrarian capitalism, and agrarian interests in economic policy debates. In the area of political history, he studies the agrarian reform of the 1960s and 1970s and its impact on local and national politics. His publications include the books *Hacendados progresistas y modernización agraria en Chile Central, 1850–1880* (Universidad de los Lagos, 2007), and *Jacques Chonchol: Un cristiano revolucionario en la política chilena del siglo XX. Conversaciones con Claudio Robles Ortiz* (Universidad Finis Terrae, 2016), and a number of articles in Spanish and English.

Carlos Eduardo Suprinyak is Associate Professor of Economics, Federal University of Minas Gerais (UFMG), Brazil. He obtained his PhD in Economics from UFMG, and spent one year as a visiting research student at Goldsmiths College, University of London. His research interests include the history of economic thought, economic history, and economic methodology. He has published a book on the market for beasts of burden in nineteenth-century Brazil (*Tropas em Marcha*, Annablume, 2008), and several peer-reviewed articles on the history of economic thought and economic history. He is currently chief-editor of *Nova Economia*, and co-editor of *Research in the History of Economic Thought and Methodology*.

Alvaro Grompone Velásquez is a junior researcher at the Instituto de Estudios Peruanos. He holds a Master's Degree in History from the Pontificia Universidad Catolica del Peru (PUCP), after concluding his studies in economics at the same university. He is interested in Peruvian economic ideologies since the mid-nineteenth century, now focusing on the last fifty years.

Foreword

Joseph L. Love

As the editors make clear in their introduction and in Chapter 1, "emancipation" leading to full independence is understood in this volume as an ongoing process. The national states of Latin America, excepting Cuba, formally declared their independence from Spain and Portugal in the first quarter of the nineteenth century, but the relative autonomy of those states in the international system remains limited today. According to one of the contributors, Mauro Boianovsky, nationalism in the region only attained its full development in the early postwar period, contemporaneous with the appearance of "economic development" as a distinct subfield of economics. Boianovsky further argues that the national identities being created are not economic alone, but are evolving "cultural-economic structures" implied in the word "formation" (*formação*), a term that refers both to a process and to a concrete entity.

The nations of the region differ from other Third World areas in a very important respect: They are much more fully Westernized. Latin America's legal systems, its predominant religion, its two great languages, and much of its gene pool are European-derived. This, not only because Europeans filtered or streamed into the region over a 500-year period, but also because Old World diseases, Iberian-imposed labor systems, the forced movement of native populations, and Spanish disturbances of ecological patterns destroyed the large majority of native populations over the sixteenth and early seventeenth centuries. Native peoples were in part replaced by European settlers and Africans who were brought to the New World as slaves. Furthermore, Latin America was directly under European rule for three hundred years – far longer than most colonized regions of Africa, Asia, and the Middle East. Finally, from the beginning the economic systems of Ibero-America were deliberately designed to complement those of Europe as a supplier of precious metals, sugar, and raw materials.

Given these brutal facts, it is hardly surprising that Latin America's cultural products, including its ideological and theoretical projects, would reflect European models, even as they were adapted to local circumstances. This is no less true in economics than in other fields of intellectual endeavor.

Economic theory in Latin America developed slowly partly because of cultural traditions that emphasized the essay as a medium of intellectual communication rather than monographic research. The region's universities did not offer research degrees (PhDs), as opposed to professional programs in law, medicine, and engineering, until the 1960s or later. Moreover, the systematic collection of economic data was scant outside the areas of foreign trade and finances until World War II. This effort was led by national banks founded in the interwar years or later, and by the UN Economic Commission for Latin America, established in 1948. These various agencies gathered, ordered, revised, and published economic and social data on the world region.

In the nineteenth century, the prevailing European economic ideology was of course liberalism, a doctrine that assumed market-determined movements of capital and labor, as well as certain civil rights to all citizens. Latin American liberals stressed the values of rationalism, materialism, and pluralism as against authoritarianism in politics and the exclusion of non-Catholic religions in confessional matters. In the words of Charles Hale, a leading student of nineteenth-century liberalism in Latin America, liberalism passed from an embattled ideology in the years *c.* 1825–1875, a half-century in which it achieved victories that were frequently reversed, to a triumphant one in the last quarter of the nineteenth century.

In economic theory and doctrine, Latin Americans were eclectic in their choice of liberal European thinkers, and, though British writers tended to prevail, the New World theorists were also influenced by French and German economists. The Latin Americans' basic problem in the nineteenth century was applying and adapting the liberal doctrines of classical economic theory to national economies in which labor systems were coercive and often precapitalist. This was the case of chattel slavery in Brazil, but also that of labor systems in other countries that bound peasants to their estates through debt servitude or other forms of dependence. Furthermore, state-sanctioned monopolies inherited from the *ancien régime* continued in some countries, and landed estates controlled by the Church were often held in mortmain, a medieval legal institution that prohibited the sale of such properties. Liberals, at least in theory, opposed monopoly and sought to move all real property into the market, in the process abolishing mortmain, primogeniture, entail, and other centuries-old European institutions that prohibited or impeded the formation of a market in real property.

The chapters in this collection seem to show that Ibero-American theorists and statesmen, including the reformers, were primarily interested in state-building in the nineteenth century – because order had to come first – and nation-building and nationalism in the twentieth; yet both processes transpired in both centuries. Following the European and North American trends after 1914, classical liberalism, with its laissez-faire orientation, yielded to state intervention in economy and society.

David Ricardo's exposition of the theory of comparative advantage and his prescription of free trade "justified" Latin America's traditional orientation toward exporting precious metals and sugar. Other exports were added to the list in the nineteenth century – industrial minerals (e.g., copper and nitrates) and new foodstuffs (e.g., beef and wheat), as European demand advanced for consumables for its burgeoning urban masses and inputs for its new manufactured products.

Like Boianovsky, the editors of this collection, Alexandre Mendes Cunha and Carlos Eduardo Suprinyak, stress that independence is a complex and multi-dimensional process involving not only economic, but also political and cultural dimensions as well, evolving over the last two centuries. Economic ideas and policies, adapted from European prototypes, were integral to the search for development. The studies in this book examine not only the European originals, but also the selectivity, adaptations, misunderstandings, and failed attempts to effectively deploy European theories. The editors' chapter is followed by that of José Luís Cardoso, who elaborates the examination of selecting, translating, diffusing, adapting, and sometimes transforming ideas borrowed from European political economy. Most fundamental, he holds, is the mimetic process itself, through which all imitators must pass.

A sweeping bird's-eye view of economic nationalism in different contexts is that of Michele Alacevich. He compares Latin American economic nationalism with that of Eastern and especially Southern Europe, paying special attention to protectionist policies that Latin Americans favored but Southern Europeans did not.

Turning to the nineteenth century, we find that Britain's efforts to bring independent Latin America into its trading orbit, though successful, affected both theory and practice in the metropolis itself. This was especially the case as Britain experimented with trade in Brazil at the opening of the nineteenth century and moved to a position of free trade by the 1840s. (See chapter by Anthony Howe.) In the following century, as Stephen Meardon shows, the United States replaced Britain as the "center" of the Latin American economy. By the early 1890s, US Secretary of State James Blaine was able to coordinate bilateral trade treaties with the independent states of Latin America and at the same time to create an American-dominated trade zone formed by the member states of the newly created Pan American Union. A half-century later, Secretary of State Cordell Hull and his Assistant Secretary for Latin America, Sumner Welles, used the Reciprocal Trade Agreements Act of 1934 to create a more liberal policy through bilateral tariff reductions. As Meardon concludes, the same trade policy instruments could serve to further either a free trade or a protectionist agenda, depending on the purposes of those responsible for using them.

Although dominant, Ricardo's "scientific" justification of Latin America's specialization in primary goods in world trade did not go unchallenged. Friederich List's case for industrialization and the protection of nascent manufacturing enterprises in agricultural countries (1841) emphasized the importance of developing productive forces in nation-building. His position was complemented by John Stuart Mill's infant industry argument (1848), though Mill more than List emphasized the conditional and temporary validity of protection. List was discovered and championed by a number of Latin Americans in the latter years of the nineteenth century. Among the earlier defenders was Julio Menadier, a Chilean who, in the words of Claudio Robles, would "creatively adapt" List's argument so as not to antagonize Chile's dominant agricultural elite. Another chapter by Luiz Felipe Bruzzi Curi establishes that German theorists – and not List alone – were known in Brazil as well. Bruzzi focuses on figures in two generations – the statesman Rui Barbosa in the 1890s and the politically influential industrialist Roberto Simonsen in the 1930s.

The chapter by Milena Fernandes de Oliveira and Nelson Mendes Cantarino deals with the broad issue of trying to reorder the Luso-Brazilian Empire without structural transformations. The Portuguese statesman Rodrigo de Souza Coutinho signed treaties with Britain's Lord Strangford, giving preference to Britain in customs duties, even though Britain had out-lawed the slave trade in 1807, a traffic of vital interest to Portuguese impe-rial statesmen. Britain subsequently forced Portugal to recognize Brazilian independence in 1825. Mauricio Coutinho considers the case of José da Silva Lisboa, Visconde de Cairu, a high official in newly independent Brazil. Cairu opened the ports of Brazil to international trade and ended the prohibition on manufacturing in the country. He recognized the economic superiority of free labor, but viewed slavery as an inevitable mainstay of the Brazilian economy of his day. Cairu adapted or distorted the writings of European economists to fit Brazilian realities. A third chapter on Brazil by Thiago Fontelas Rosado Gambi concerns Joaquim José Rodrigues Torres, Viscount of Itaboraí, minis-ter of finance of Brazil in the middle of the nineteenth century and president of the second Bank of Brazil. Gambi shows that Itaboraí subscribed to the monetary theories and policies of British economists, especially those of John McCulloch. In principle Itaboraí championed the convertibility of Brazilian currency. Like the other nineteenth-century Brazilian economists, however, Itaboraí was forced to tailor the application of British ideas to the realities of Brazil's weak national finances and its slave-based economy.

Alvaro Grompone Velásquez chapter indicates the prestige that economic liberalism had achieved by the mid-nineteenth century in Peru. Liberals in that country sought to define an economic identity for their nation, and drew upon European political economy as a source of scientific authority.

Jimena Hurtado's chapter on nineteenth-century Colombia shows that the market-driven and secular propositions of British economists were less accept-able to Colombian liberals than the socially conservative moral doctrines of Jean-Baptiste Say. His views were seen as more compatible with traditional Christian values. Liberalism had to be "embedded," as Polanyi would later put it, in the protective networks of traditional society based on Christian values. But Catholic dogma would be eliminated from social discourse.

Another study on Colombia by Andrés Álvarez concerns the effort by the nation's statesmen to develop a national bank over the course of the nineteenth century. Álvarez establishes that Colombian economic theorists were thoroughly versed in the procedures required to establish a national bank, citing examples from France, Britain, and the United States. But the relation between government and private capital in Colombia was hotly disputed. At the level of practice, President Rafael Núñez's attempt to establish a national bank simultaneously serving the country's monetary, credit, and fiscal needs ended in failure.

In the mid-twentieth century, a regional school arose that challenged development based on traditional international trade patterns. The school, led by the Argentinean Raúl Prebisch, presented a formal economic argument supported by long-term economic data showing that countries producing primary goods were engaging in "unequal exchange" with their manufactures-exporting trading partners. An autochthonous body of theory thus arose in the Economic Commission for Latin America, whose doctrines came to be known as Structuralism. Justifying state-led industrialization, Structuralism indirectly promoted the development of Latin America's national bourgeoisies. (See chapter by Joseph L. Love.)

Acknowledgments

This book gathers contributions originally presented at the 4th ESHET Latin American Conference, hosted by the Federal University of Minas Gerais (UFMG), in Belo Horizonte, Brazil, on November 19–21, 2014. The highly stimulating academic environment that permeated the conference, and the effort and dedication of all the contributors, who since then have extensively reworked their chapters, caused the volume to gain much in terms of internal coherence and articulation. Accordingly, it is to our fellow authors that we first need to extend our gratitude. We would also like to thank the several institutions that financially supported the conference – CNPq, CAPES, FAPEMIG, IPEAD, and INET – and thus created the conditions for this project to become a reality. Likewise, we thank the other scientific committee members, who shared with us the planning and managerial duties created by the event: Mauro Boianovsky, Maurício Coutinho, José Luís Cardoso, and Maria Cristina Marcuzzo. To the European Society for the History of Economic Thought, and its president at the time, José Luís Cardoso, we express our gratitude for supporting the initiative, and for nurturing the interaction among European and Latin American scholars dedicated to the history of economic thought.

Special thanks are also due to Maria Cristina Marcuzzo, for conceiving this precious space for the interlocution of Latin American historians of economics, which eventually led to the creation of the Latin American Society for the History of Economic Thought (ALAHPE) in Santiago, Chile, in November 2015. The Belo Horizonte conference was preceded, in 2013, by the international workshop "The History of Economic Thought in Latin America," sponsored by UFMG's Center for Latin American Studies. The colleagues who joined us on that occasion – Andrés Álvarez, Jimena Hurtado, José Edwards, Maurício Coutinho, Mauro Boianovsky, and Ricardo Solís – convinced us beyond doubt that the history of Latin American economic thought can be a rich, fruitful, and fascinating subject. We thus salute them in the hope that these may be only the first steps in a long journey.

Our thanks go also to other colleagues who gave valuable contributions to different parts of this volume: Guilherme Pereira das Neves, Harald Hagemann, Keith Tribe, Lars Magnusson, Marco Cavalieri, Maria Pia

Paganelli, Sandra Peart, and Simon Hupfel. We take this opportunity as well to publicly express our appreciation for Joseph Love, who not only contributed one of the chapters, but also generously accepted our invitation to preface the volume.

We warmly thank the Routledge editorial team, in particular Emily Kindleysides, who believed in the project from the very first moment, and Laura Johnson, for her support during preparation of the manuscript.

Finally, we would like to thank our home institution, the Federal University of Minas Gerais, and in particular the Center for Development and Regional Planning (Cedeplar), whose director, Cássio Maldonado Turra, has provided decisive institutional backing for this project since its inception.

Alexandre Mendes Cunha would further like to express his personal gratitude to his wife, Tarsila Ortenzio Velloso, for her patient and constant support throughout this and so many other projects.

Editors' introduction

Alexandre Mendes Cunha and
Carlos Eduardo Suprinyak

This is a book about the history of Latin American political economy. As such, it seeks to offer a reflection on the specific character of the economic thought produced in Latin America, exploring in particular how traditional labels such as 'original,' 'adapted,' or 'critical' should be qualified and reinterpreted in order to make sense of the concrete intellectual endeavors pursued in the region. The chapters that comprise this volume were originally presented at the 4th ESHET Latin American Conference – hosted by the Federal University of Minas Gerais (Belo Horizonte, Brazil), on November 19–21, 2014 – and subsequently further elaborated by their authors. The theme chosen for the conference was "Originality, Adaptation, and Critique: the place of Latin America in the History of Economic Thought," through which the conveners hoped to explore questions such as the following: What do we mean when we talk about Latin American economic thought? Are the works of any Latin American economist apt to be thus qualified, or should the term be reserved for ideas and theories which seek to explain economic themes peculiar to the region? Does 'original thought' necessarily involve abstract and far-reaching theoretical constructs, or is there also originality in the adaptation of foreign ideas to local realities? To what extent has the need to criticize the 'universalist' aspirations of economic theory defined the character of Latin American economics?

Scholarly interest in the history of economic ideas in Latin America has increased markedly in recent years, but when compared to more traditional themes and approaches, the field still remains largely uncharted. The conference's purpose was precisely to serve as a forum for exploring the multiple analytical dimensions and avenues for inquiry that could lead to a richer, more illuminating historiography of economic thought in and about Latin America. The present volume further develops this perspective by focusing on a specific subject: the role of political economy in the reflection about Latin American independence. The latter concept is central for the approach we propose. As further explored in Chapter 1, although Latin American nations became politically emancipated from their colonial metropolises in the early nineteenth century, their struggle for independence – political, cultural, economic – has involved a much longer process, extending throughout the nineteenth and twentieth centuries to the present day. The chapters that follow illustrate how political economy and the quest for independence have been concretely intertwined in Latin America since its political emancipation.

The volume also stimulates dialogue with debates that transcend the history of economic thought as a disciplinary subfield. The dichotomy established in Latin American scholarship, during the course of the twentieth century, between intellectual history, on one hand, and the history of ideas on the other, provides an important point of reference, as it helps to situate the methodological perspective that guides the studies here presented.

Scholarly investigation about the history of ideas in Latin America reached professional and institutional maturity in the 1940s, specially through the works of Francisco Romero in Argentina and José Gaos in Mexico – the latter of whom served as a mentor to Leopoldo Zea, who would soon become one of the foremost authorities on the subject. Zea was the central figure behind the creation of a continental network of scholars dedicated to the history of Latin American ideas, which produced a series of monographic studies on Argentina, Uruguay, Brazil, Chile, Bolivia, Peru, Ecuador, Colombia, Venezuela, and Cuba. His widely known book, *Dos etapas del pensamiento en Hispanoamérica: del romanticismo al positivismo*[1] (1949), became a seminal reference for other works in the field. Nevertheless, the approach favored by Zea tended to privilege philosophical ideas to the detriment of other intellectual currents. Although the tradition thus formed underwent changes due to the influence of dependency theory during the 1960s, and later of poststructuralism in the 1980s, it remained attached to a somewhat restrictive view of nuclear ideas that defined given historical eras. As pointed out by Horacio Tarcus (2015, pp. 11–15) in a recent historiographical survey, this came to be challenged with the publication of Juan Marichal's *Cuatro fases de la historia intelectual latinoamericana (1810–1970)*[2] (1978). In this book, Marichal developed an intellectual history in which concepts, doctrines, and the logic-historical mechanisms connecting them figured less prominently, in order to bring forward the political and cultural contexts, the relevant intellectual communities and institutional environments surrounding the production of ideas – in other words, how the intellectual matrices coming from Europe would be rethought in Latin America, "not as imperfect copies, but rather as original refractions" (Tarcus 2015, pp. 11–15).

Even if our focus in the present volume lies in the history of political economy, the comparison with studies of philosophical ideas seems appropriate in order to illustrate how the analytical perspective we propose may transcend the abovementioned dichotomy between intellectual history and the history of ideas. To a large extent, the investigations on the history of Latin American political economy in the chapters that follow seek to explore precisely the articulation between the history of doctrines, theories, and concepts, on one hand, and the history of practices, of the concrete manifestations of such ideas in specific socio-political contexts, on the other. Moreover, we wish to emphasize how the latter may, and usually do, influence the way in which economic ideas are adapted and criticized outside of their context of origin, and how this may provide a benchmark for a more fruitful discussion of intellectual originality.

One way of approaching the problem of originality is through the concept of identity. To reflect on national or regional identities is different from recognizing local realities, or even from reasoning critically about one's specific place within a larger order. In the words of Richard Morse,

> identity, which implies linkage to or manifestation of collective conscience, is not the same as "reality" ... Both terms fluctuate between a descriptive, empirical meaning and a prospective or promissory one. ... Reality starts with environment, identity with tacit self-recognition.
>
> (1995, p. 1)

Such a prospective perception, which projects self-awareness about national or regional specificities, would gain strength in Latin America from the 1920s, giving rise to indigenous artistic movements, and to narratives about the nature and consequences of the peculiar ethnic-racial heritage of local societies. It also found echo, however, on economic reasoning, initially as part of an anti-imperialist discourse, and later within the context of debates on industrialization, which would mature into the analysis championed by CEPAL in the 1950s. In this sense, one could interpret the history of political economy as an integral part of the process through which national and regional identities were constructed in Latin America.

The contributions to this volume offer a variety of perspectives from which these issues may be explored in connection to specific topics and experiences. These are organized in five parts, each covering a different set of aspects within the general theme. Part I discusses some methodological issues involved in the analysis of the international diffusion of economic ideas, with special emphasis on the appropriation of political economy as a relevant discourse in the struggle for Latin American independence. In Part II, the focus will be on nineteenth-century debates about trade policy, putting in evidence how clear-cut doctrinal precepts such as 'free trade' or 'protectionism' were subject to varying interpretations when transposed to Latin American contexts. Part III then discusses episodes when economic ideas from abroad were explicitly introduced in Latin America, highlighting how they have been subsequently adapted and transformed in order to fit local realities. Part IV analyzes the challenges and possibilities inherent in the production of indigenous brands of political economy in the region, and how this often involved the creative appropriation of ideas developed elsewhere. Finally, Part V tries to situate the concepts of nationalism and economic development as essential elements in the creation of a specifically Latin American economic discourse, closely related to the construction of national and regional identities.

Notes

1 In English, *Two Stages of Thought in Latin America: from romanticism to positivism*.
2 In English, *Four Phases of Latin American Intellectual History (1810–1970)*.

References

Morse, Richard M. 1995. The multiverse of Latin American identity, c. 1920–c. 1970. In: Leslie Bethell (ed.) *The Cambridge History of Latin America*. Cambridge: Cambridge University Press, Vol. 10.

Tarcus, Horacio. 2015. "Una invitación a la historia intelectual. Palabras de apertura del IIo Congreso de Historia Intelectual de América Latina." *Revista Pléyade* (15): 9–25.

Part I

International dissemination of economic ideas

1 Political economy and Latin American independence from the nineteenth to the twentieth century

*Alexandre Mendes Cunha and
Carlos Eduardo Suprinyak*

Emancipation, independence, and political economy

The political emancipation of Latin America is a historical phenomenon charged with symbolic meanings, closely related as it was to some of the most consequential events in modern history, such as the French Revolution, the ascent of British hegemony, and the collapse of the *ancien régime*. As usual in cases of this nature, we tend to create an image of the process leading to the celebrated outcome that is characterized by pivotal events, crucial dates, and designated heroes, as if the future implications of a given incident had been instantly settled, once and for all. This, of course, is a rationalization of history, as abundantly evident in the case of Latin American independence movements. For Spanish American nations like Mexico, Venezuela, Argentina, and Colombia, political emancipation was a protracted process above all else, and a number of episodes and characters could have a claim to being deemed the 'defining moment' – all equally arbitrarily. In the case of Brazil, while the unraveling of events was more linear than in neighboring Spanish America, their nature and significance were also far from clear. After all, the Brazilian independence movement revolved around the heir to the Portuguese throne, who was proclaimed Brazilian Emperor only to abdicate in favor of his son less than a decade later, alleging that his subjects saw him as a Portuguese (Bethell and Carvalho 1985, p. 692).

If there are obvious challenges to a precise historical characterization of the political emancipation of Latin American nations, the issue is further complicated when we take into account that the political dimension, in isolation, does not exhaust the problem. Here it may be useful to draw a distinction between 'emancipation' and 'independence.' As a more formal, politically determined phenomenon, 'emancipation' can be situated at the moment when the sovereignty of a given nation is successfully affirmed and/or recognized before other nations. 'Independence,' by contrast, has to do with the capacity to formulate and pursue her own national agenda, without being systematically constrained by external factors arising out of asymmetrical power relations. A nation may thus be formally 'emancipated,' while remaining under the tutelage of other political actors more powerful than herself; in this sense, she will not be 'independent.' To put it in other words, whereas emancipation may be at least approximately characterized as a *moment*, independence should be seen as a *process* – and for most Latin American nations, still a work in progress.

Such tutelage, of course, may come under several guises: political, intellectual, cultural, and, last but not least, economic. The latter was a particularly relevant element in the post-emancipation experience of the former Latin American colonies, since they had long been integrated, in a subordinate position, within the international economic order. The difficulties involved in escaping the fetters of political domination paled in comparison to the task of achieving economic self-determination, as became apparent when the former colonial rule was quickly replaced by the less explicit, but equally pervasive dictates of a new metropolis, whose power was asserted mainly through international trade and industrial production. The political agenda of the young Latin American nations thus necessarily gravitated towards the economic role they should perform in the new emerging world order – a role that, it was hoped, could reinforce their claims to national autonomy. A political economy of independence was in order.

If the heritage of political and economic subordination did not cease to affect Latin America after the conclusion of the independence movements in the region, the same of course was also true in the intellectual domain. It was only natural, therefore, that those who aspired to the role of leaders in these new societies would turn for inspiration to the established centers of intellectual production in the Western world: Britain, France, Germany, and, to a lesser extent, the United States. The sources were varied, as were the uses to which they were put. Beneath the disparity of influences and outcomes, however, lay an expanding channel for the international diffusion of ideas, with political economy as one of its most profuse streams.

It is tempting to downplay the intellectual relevance of the knowledge produced through such a process of diffusion. Insofar as Latin Americans merely took ideas developed elsewhere, and adapted them to suit their local reality, one could argue that no legitimate claims to doctrinal or theoretical originality could be made on their behalf. Conversely, it was only when Latin American intellectuals began to adopt a critical attitude towards ideas received from abroad, and thus question their adequacy to the specific problems faced by their region, that a truly indigenous Latin American thought could finally emerge – as evidenced, in the case of political economy, by the rise of the 'structuralist' approach associated with CEPAL (ECLAC) during the postwar era.

To do so, however, would be to ignore the profoundly creative process that lies behind the successful adaptation of ideas to historical contexts different than those in which they were conceived, therefore posing problems they were not originally designed to address. In order to capture the nature, the possibilities, and the limits inherent in such attempts to transpose ideas across social, institutional, and cultural borders, one should not think of them as passive absorptions, or even mechanical adaptations. Rather, as José Luís Cardoso (this volume) argues, what is at stake is an act of *appropriation*, where active and purposeful subjects identify ideas that could serve their intellectual aspirations, and subsequently infuse them with a host of meanings that were not part of their original make-up. Although usually left out from canonical accounts of the evolution and consolidation of theoretical constructs, scientific or otherwise, the fruitfulness of these various appropriations is a crucial element behind the relative success or failure of a given idea in establishing itself as a powerful doctrinal influence.

Besides throwing light on the specific features that allow an idea to be successfully appropriated in different contexts, this approach also offers a different perspective from which to investigate the role of the 'recipients' in the process of intellectual diffusion. If appropriation is a creative endeavor, the collective appropriation of a set of ideas within a specific sociohistorical context could plausibly be construed as the creation of an intellectual tradition peculiar to that context (Cardoso 2003). More to the point of the present chapter, the repeated appropriation of economic ideas from abroad that figured so prominently in the former Iberian colonies, both during and immediately after their emancipation, could be regarded as the birth of a truly Latin American political economy. Far from being derivative or merely reflexive, this political economy of Latin American independence has as much claim to doctrinal originality as any of its more prestigious counterparts.

One consequence arising out of this historiographical perspective is that economic ideas, policies, and ideologies cannot be easily separated when tracing out the formation of indigenous strands of political economy in Latin America. Since the appropriation of foreign ideas was, more often than not, guided by the search for solutions to concrete problems faced by the young and politically inexperienced nations, the interplay between theory and policy was simply inescapable. To separate 'pure' ideas from the political use made of them would thus mean introducing an artificial division that obscures, rather than illuminates, the relevant motivations, constraints, and challenges at stake. Similarly, since the outcomes of intellectual activity were typically used as weapons in the social and political struggle to legitimate given norms and values, political economy kept the frequent company of economic ideology (Meek 1967; Love 1995). None of this, however, should be seen as in any way diminishing the significance, or else denigrating the 'purity' of the economic ideas produced in the region. Rather, it helps bringing into sharp relief the close and pervasive ties that everywhere connect politics, society, and economic thought, and which are frequently obscured in accounts that discuss economic ideas as they stand in relation to an abstractly conceived set of problems, instead of the crude realities on which they are brought to bear.

In what follows, we will attempt to illustrate concretely how this approach can be used to understand some of the specific features that have historically characterized the economic thought coming out of Latin America. Before that, however, it seems appropriate to present an overview of the concrete features that characterized political emancipation in the region, and to show how they tended to reinforce preexisting ties of economics dependence. This will set the stage for analyzing how economic ideas were appropriated, how they gained concrete expression, and where would lie the basis for the emergence of a more autochthonous discourse.

Political emancipation and economic dependence

The movements of political emancipation in Latin America occurred basically during the first half of the nineteenth century. Nevertheless, the analysis of the specific trajectories of the various countries in the region presents us with an eminently more complex picture, one in which independence cannot be summarized by a restricted set of political events, considered in themselves. Rather, it is necessary to consider a long process that effectively began in the late eighteenth century, and further proceeded well into the twentieth century. In order to investigate independence as an ongoing process, our purpose is to jointly analyze the issue of political emancipation from colonial tutelage, on one hand, and the establishment of new patterns of economic dependence, on the other – an approach that further extends and complicates the inquiry, since economic dependence is a phenomenon that arguably afflicts the region until the present day.

Thus, albeit in a somewhat brief and schematic manner, we will refer to a broad framework of political and economic transformations that took place in the region from the late eighteenth to the mid-twentieth century, without concerning ourselves with describing the specific trajectories of individual countries. Furthermore, since our interest lies mainly on the ideas connected to these political and economic processes, we will only offer very brief descriptions of the political events themselves.

The main catalyst for the political emancipation of Latin American nations was the Peninsular War that followed the occupation of Spain and Portugal by Napoleonic troops between 1807 and 1808.[1] This led Joseph Bonaparte to be crowned as king of Spain, a move followed by the creation of several local government boards (*juntas*) with the goal of preserving sovereignty, even with French occupation, in both the Spanish kingdom and its American possessions. In the Portuguese case, this led to the unprecedented situation of a European monarch leaving his kingdom of origin in order to settle in one of his colonies, with the purpose of safeguarding his American empire. As tensions deepened between Spain and its colonies, this led to armed struggles between local forces and royal armies in most of the Spanish American territories, beginning around 1810, and culminating in the political emancipation of a host of new Latin American nations in the 1820s.

On the eastern side of the continent, with the arrival of the Portuguese royal family in Brazil in 1808, and the effective transfer of several major metropolitan institutions to the new court in Rio de Janeiro, the traditional roles of colony and metropolis were somehow reversed, with the Portuguese state apparatus starting to operate from Brazil. This was ratified with the establishment, in 1815, of the United Kingdom of Portugal, Brazil, and the Algarves, which had its capital in Rio de Janeiro. These political displacements eventually precipitated conflicts in Portugal. In 1820, in the middle of a liberal revolution in Oporto, the Portuguese demanded the return of their king to Europe. João VI complied with the request the following year, thus leaving his son, Prince Pedro de Alcântara, to become Regent of the Kingdom of Brazil. Growing conflicts between Brazilians and Portuguese led, in 1822, to the creation of the Empire of Brazil, politically separated from the Portuguese kingdom, but ruled by a Portuguese prince turned emperor, under the title of Pedro I. Unlike its Latin American neighbors, the political emancipation of Brazil thus occurred within a monarchical regime that remained in place throughout the nineteenth century, only ending after an 1889 coup, headed by the military, which deposed Pedro II (the son of the first emperor) and finally established a federalist republic.

If the Brazilian process of emancipation from Portugal was (at least apparently) more peaceful, and managed to preserve the territorial unity of the former colony, the case of Spanish America, on the other hand, was marked by open conflict and territorial fragmentation. The wars of independence – which often featured elements of civil conflict due to opposition between local groups – took place along two main fronts, one in the south and another in the north. Northern South America experienced a more intense conflict, one which was directly monitored by Spain. The struggle began in Venezuela, where the Board of Caracas declared its independence in 1810, and from thence expanded to New Granada, Quito, and Guayaquil, under the leadership of Simón Bolivar. In the southern end of the continent, the movement had its origins in Argentina, which formed a new government in 1810, and subsequently declared its independence from Spain in 1816. The Argentinian campaign advanced over the *pampas* under the leadership of José de San Martín, who led his troops across the Andes towards Chile, and in a joint effort with the army led by Bernardo O'Higgins managed to defeat the Spanish forces. The point of convergence for the two war fronts would be Peru, where stood the largest remaining royalist army, finally defeated in the celebrated battle of Ayacucho in 1824. In Mexico, a failed social revolution during the 1810s had led to a prolonged royalist reaction, but by 1821 the country had already secured its political emancipation. Spain had effectively lost its American empire, although it managed to preserve dominions in the Caribbean such as Cuba and Puerto Rico – a situation that would last until the 1898 Spanish–American War, which turned the two islands into US protectorates. Cuba became a republic shortly thereafter (1902), but the effects of the 'Platt Amendment' to the Cuban constitution continued to limit the political sovereignty of the country for several decades (Lynch 1973; Lynch 2001, pp. 74–5).

The marked contrast between the fortunes of Spanish and Portuguese America offers us a first essential element for our analysis. However, it should be noted that the Brazilian political framework outlined above was not as static as the life span of the Brazilian Empire might suggest. The effort to preserve the unity of so large and disparate a territory brought about many conflicts. Even before the proclamation of independence, there were political movements that pursued different paths to political emancipation, such as the so-called Pernambucan Revolt, which in 1817 installed a provisional republican government in northeastern Brazil, or else the 1824 Confederation of the Equator, a separatist movement also rooted in the northeast, inspired by the Colombian republican constitution.[2] Undoubtedly, however, the moment of more intense political turmoil in the imperial era occurred during the Regency period,[3] in the 1830s, when a series of riots broke out inspired by separatist republican campaigns. Some of these movements even incorporated important popular elements, managing to congregate blacks and Indians around a political cause – as in the case of the *Cabanagem* revolt that shook the province of Grão-Pará, in northern Brazil, between 1835 and 1840.[4]

Another important qualification must be added regarding the political fates of Spanish and Portuguese America after their emancipation. In practice, the republican forms of government adopted by Hispanic nations did not necessarily make them more 'independent' in any concrete sense, when compared to the former Portuguese colony that remained attached to a monarchical regime. The dependence of Latin America vis-à-vis Western Europe throughout the nineteenth century was primarily of an economic nature, even though the weight of external pressure on domestic political frameworks was strongly felt at the time. Despite the controversy over whether Latin America was part or not of the so-called British 'informal' Empire,[5] there remains little doubt that, as pointed out by Leslie Bethell (1995, p. 271), the nineteenth century was, for Latin America, an "English century." Even allowing for the growing presence of the US in the region, under the auspices of the Monroe Doctrine and its slogan 'America for Americans,' since the Napoleonic Wars and until the outbreak of World War I the weight of British influence was felt in multiple areas, and assured when necessary by 'gunboat diplomacy.' Britain became the main trading partner, the main investor, and the main creditor for Latin America. The strength of its economic influence assumed many forms, such as the supremacy of its merchant navy – British vessels carried most of the trade between the region and world markets – or its position as key supplier of manufactured goods and capital flows, with the City of London providing the funds for investment in infrastructure, agriculture and mining (Bethell 1995, pp. 271–2).

Regardless of whether this resulted from informal imperialism or not, in practice Latin America remained broad and unambiguously connected to British interests throughout the nineteenth century. It is important to highlight, however, how the relationships established by Spain and Portugal with Britain by the end of the colonial era sealed different paths for each kingdom and their American colonies – and also how, as pointed out by José Luis Romero (1977, p. xi), we can draw implications from this breach for the history of ideas in the region. Portugal had followed, at least since the Methuen Treaty of 1703, a path of progressive (albeit hesitant) alignment with British mercantile and foreign policy. Spain, on the other hand, in line with its dynastic ties to Bourbon France, and later due to the pact signed between the two nations in the aftermath of the French Revolution, found itself in an increasingly fragile international position, especially in light of the overwhelming British maritime supremacy, which created obstacles for the maintenance of Spanish overseas dominions.

The political emancipation of Latin America was historically superposed over the process through which the Iberian colonial order was overcome in the region. In this sense, the dilemmas faced by both kingdoms around the turn of the nineteenth century, as illustrated by their different foreign policy alignments, constitute the pre-history of the emancipatory movements.

We can here recall how the economic weakness of Spain and Portugal imposed limits to the growth of their American colonies, and consequently how, particularly in the Portuguese case, the metropolis gradually came to become dependent on its own colonies. Two very influential scholarly accounts can help clarify this process. John Lynch (1985, p. 3) has argued that Hispanic Americans were gradually becoming conscious of their condition as "a colonial economy dependent on an underdeveloped metropolis." What characterized the metropolitan power, as much as its colonial empire, was the exportation of primary products, the dependence on a foreign merchant navy, and the ascendancy of a noble elite with scarce any inclinations for overcoming the traditional order. During the late eighteenth century, Bourbon Spain tried to pragmatically face these challenges in an attempt to modernize its economy, society, and institutions through an eclectic reform program informed by 'enlightened' ideas – including a more strict control of the colonies in order to increase crown revenues.[6] Such reforms, nevertheless, did not change the overall picture: Spain was still, in essence, an agrarian economy, for which maritime trade was above all an outlet for domestic agricultural production. Its economic relations with the colonial dominions were thus characterized not by complementarity, but rather by harmful similarities. While the reformist effort collapsed amidst the panic caused by the French Revolution, the tensions between the metropolis and its colonies were aggravated during the 1790s due to the political inability of Manuel Godoy, the first secretary to the new monarch, who treated Spanish America as little more than a source of precious metals and tax revenue (Lynch 1985, pp. 3–7).

With respect to the case of Portuguese America, Fernando Novais (1979) has famously discussed the crisis of the Portuguese 'old colonial system' as part of the process of primitive accumulation of capital that would lead to the rise of industrial capitalism, and thus to a new form of exploitation of peripheral areas. Novais showed in detail how Portugal, around the turn of the nineteenth century, deepened its trade deficit with the Brazilian colony in order to preserve its surplus position against other trading partners. Brazil thus grew disproportionately in importance vis-à-vis the other Portuguese colonies in

Africa and Asia, and the reformist program implemented in particular during the 1790s was informed precisely by this development. The reforms served to highlight the crucial importance of Brazil for the survival of the Portuguese kingdom, eventually leading to the transfer of the Portuguese court to Brazil in 1808 – an event which, although dissociated from political emancipation, in practice signified the end of the colonial system.

To Novais (1979, p. 301), Portugal needed the Brazilian colony more than ever as a "protection currency" to be traded with England amidst the European conflicts, but also knew this could result in the transfer of commercial advantages to its ally. In order to profit from the boost offered to its economy by the exploitation of colonial resources, Portugal needed to become a developed nation, which resulted in proposals for integration and increased complementarity between colony and metropolis. At the same time, however, this came up against deeply rooted structural barriers, and further modernization in the domestic political arena could have potentially revolutionary implications.

The backwardness and attempted reforms in the Iberian monarchies, changes in the international context, and the different political strategies adopted by Portuguese and Spanish ministers, all resulted in distinct dynamics for the American colonies. On the Spanish side, there was a progressive worsening of tensions as Spain came to be seen as a hindrance to the growth of the colonies, which contributed to the emergence of conflicting attitudes between the *criollo* elites and the *peninsulares*,[7] in turn resulting in increased monitoring and strict supervision by the metropolis. The conflict of interests between the metropolis and its colonies was also striking, as illustrated by the regulations collectively known as '*comercio libre*,' first instituted in 1765 and further expanded in 1778. Despite their name, the measures sought to reorganize colonial trade with the purpose of securing exclusive returns to Spain, and generally strengthening the links connecting the colonial economy to the kingdom. The Spanish enlightened economist Gaspar de Jovellanos hailed the legislation at the time, insisting that "the colonies are useful as they provide a secure market for the surplus production of the metropolis" (Lynch 1985, pp. 15–16).

In the Portuguese case, political action involved a relatively successful renegotiation with local colonial elites, as part of a response by the metropolitan administration to the threats posed by the revolutionary mood prevailing in the United States and Europe – which could, as in the case of the frustrated *Inconfidência Mineira*,[8] be transposed to the Portuguese dominions. The cooptation took the form of progressive incorporation of local elite members into important administrative positions, and even at the very core of Portuguese Enlightened reformism, as represented by the intimate circle around the powerful minister Rodrigo de Souza Coutinho, the primary responsible for designing the transfer of the Portuguese court to Brazil. Kenneth Maxwell (1973b) named this group of native Brazilians, all of them graduates from the University of Coimbra, as the "Generation of the 1790s."

It was precisely with this generation that Enlightened reformism, filled with liberal undertones, but also carefully purged of any forms of political radicalism or subversion, would make its way into Portuguese America. It became, in this sense, a guide for the initial political activities of men who would later play important roles in the independence movement of 1822 – as, for example, José Bonifácio de Andrada, one of the 'founding fathers' of the Brazilian nation, and a typical representative of the Generation of the 1790s. Andrada's plans for the new nation forcefully illustrated the confluence of economic (and even social) liberal ideas with conservatism and political centralism.

There is here some common ground among the emancipatory experiences throughout Latin America, in the sense that different movements all strove to promote a kind of 'conservative revolution,' with the predictable exclusion of the lower orders. As pointed by David Ruiz Chataing (2005, p. x), when the term '*pueblo*' appeared in independence documents, the reference was always to those able to exercise an active citizenship, which meant, albeit with distinctions, men who could read and write, exceeded a threshold of wealth, or else exercised a liberal profession, with typical restrictions on social origins that included a previous servile condition. However, when the term '*pueblo*' was meant to include people of humble origin, it was in order to highlight the risks associated with their intervention in public affairs. The board established in Caracas in 1810 expressed this emphasis in its founding charter, stating it was created "because they sensed the dangerous fermentation that took over the people with the spreading news, and given the fear that by mistake or under force they were induced to recognize an illegitimate government" (Chataing 2005, p. xi). The notion that the 'people' needed to be tutored and guided exemplifies in a very concrete way the conservative nature of Latin American independence movements, as built on the selective absorption of a liberal ideology.[9]

In the several new nations blossoming in Spanish America, particularly because of English support and influence, the first economic measures invariably included the abolition of monopolies, trade liberalization, suspension of the slave trade, and the elimination of Indian bondage – the latter, however, with more symbolic than practical effect in most countries (Chataing 2005, p. xiii). The opening of the Brazilian ports "to friendly nations" (i.e., England) was proclaimed even prior to the arrival of the royal family in Rio de Janeiro, as the first act of the Portuguese monarch in Brazilian territory after landing in Salvador de Bahia on January 28, 1808.[10] However, in spite of strong British pressure, the abolition of the slave traffic was not enforced at this moment, nor for a long time after the emancipation from Portugal. The Brazilian constitution, approved in 1824, openly drew its inspiration from contemporary European liberal and constitutional ideas – but it remained largely silent on the issue of slavery.

We wish to stress how the influence of liberalism in nineteenth-century Latin America could be readily absorbed in the economic domain, while having a limited impact in terms of its broader political meanings. This brand of conservative liberalism was shared by many prominent characters at the time, as in the case of José da Silva Lisboa, highlighted by Maurício Coutinho in his contribution to this volume. Milena Oliveira and Nelson Cantarino, in another of the following chapters, show how the trade agreements signed between Portugal and Britain in 1810 reveal the ambiguities inherent in Luso-Brazilian liberal thought, demonstrating how it was closely associated with the Portuguese Enlightened reformism from the late eighteenth century, which served as a benchmark for trade policy discussions after the arrival of the royal family in Brazil.

A conservative logic thus permeated Latin American emancipatory movements, leading to a highly selective appropriation of the intellectual legacy of the Enlightenment, and of liberalism in general. This phenomenon contributed significantly to the reproduction of unequal economic and social structures in most countries of the region. Let us thus finally address the theme of economic dependence, with due attention to associated political aspects.

Although the initial struggles of the young Latin American nations took place in the field of politics, in connection with efforts to establish a state apparatus and stable governance structures, the patterns of economic development verified in the region throughout the nineteenth century increasingly turned the subject of economic emancipation into a concrete political agenda. This would become prominent in the explicitly nationalistic character of the debates on industrialization, especially during the 1930s. It was only from this moment onwards that a critical reflection on the issue of economic dependence began to take shape, later gradually assuming the character of a developmentalist ideology, and finally culminating, in the 1960s and 1970s, in the so-called dependency theory.

The timeline of Latin American industrialization established by economists associated with CEPAL – in particular Celso Furtado and Osvaldo Sunkel – for apprehending underdevelopment within a historical-structural framework offers an interesting perspective on the problem of economic dependence. According to this interpretation, the process began in the later decades of the nineteenth century as a result of export-induced growth in the major economies of the region, being closely related to the dynamics of the primary export sector. This stage was followed by import substitution industrialization (ISI) after the crisis of 1929, which dominated economic policy in Latin America until the 1960s, when mounting problems finally raised doubts concerning the possible further extension of ISI. The dual nature of reflection in the latter period offered the background for debates on dependency theory.

With the publication in 1969 of Celso Furtado's *Formação Econômica da América Latina*,[11] the Brazilian economist attempted to synthesize and interpret the historical dynamics of the Latin American economy, based on his own monograph on Brazilian economic history (*Formação Econômica do Brasil*, 1959), and on several other country-specific studies produced by authors linked to CEPAL. Furtado described three types of export economies that summarized, in his view, the paths open for Latin American participation

in the expansion of international trade during the 1840s: a) countries exporting temperate agricultural commodities; b) countries exporting tropical agricultural commodities; and c) exporters of mineral products (Furtado 1970
[1969], p. 32). In this context, an expansion of the global demand for raw
materials, by also increasing and diversifying domestic demand, tended to
jump-start the first stage of Latin American industrialization. Furtado
insisted on how the same process produced different outcomes in countries
belonging to each of the three groups, which made this one of the most interesting aspects behind the dynamics of underdevelopment in the region (p. 75).
As noted by Sunkel and Paz (1970, p. 7), there were many common features
underlying the economic history of Latin American nations throughout the
late nineteenth and early twentieth centuries, such as the massive inflow of
British capital, a significant absorption of the workforce, the creation of specialized export sectors, the establishment of new trade routes, and important
changes in the social and political structure that favored the liberalization of
the economy. These elements, however, assumed very different forms in each
country. In this sense, typologies such as the one presented by Furtado can
offer an analytical approach to the general problem without completely oblit-
erating the crucial differences.

The crisis of 1929 introduced an important turning point in the economic
dynamics of the region. The international crisis sharply reduced global
demand, and thus led to structural tensions that produced currency devaluation, government deficits, and increased stocks of export commodities.
The resulting inflationary pressures ended up raising the relative prices of
imported industrial products, and thus stimulating domestic production. This
process, which mostly favored countries that had already began to industrialize in the previous stage, provided the basis for import substitution industrialization. This was, however, a phenomenon essentially motivated by the 1930s
depression and the subsequent war period, in which the reduced ability to
import enabled an intensive use of the existing industrial capacity. In order to
proceed further, the creation of basic industries was required, and this came
about as a direct result of state action, which ushered in a new stage of Latin
American industrialization (Furtado 1970 [1969], pp. 82–92).

The exhaustion of ISI in the most advanced economies in the region from
the 1950s onwards made room for an agenda of industrialization directly
induced by state action, which in turn introduced problems of a different
order. The analytical framework proposed by dependency theory at the time
tried to put in evidence the structural limits to national industrialization.
Insistence on a state-led model in countries such as Argentina and Brazil
tended to produce typical examples of "modernization at the cost of growing authoritarianism and continuing poverty typical of 'development with
marginal population'," as diagnosed by Cardoso and Faletto (1979 [1971],
p. 153). To Furtado, the stage that followed ISI sanctioned a specific type of
international positioning, and a corresponding economic structure defined
by the emulation, within the periphery, of consumption patterns generated in

central economies, thus reinforcing technological dependency and inadequate productive structures (Furtado 1983 [1978]). Dependency theory thus insisted that even if Latin American countries had obtained political emancipation from their former metropolises, they still occupied a subordinate position in the structural dynamics of the world economy, being subject to the foreign policy interests of the dominant centers – as strikingly illustrated, for example, by US support for authoritarian regimes in the region. The structural transformations underlying Latin American industrialization tended, in each successive stage, to reiterate the conditions of economic dependence, which in turn limited the possibility of full political independence.

As pointed out above, political emancipation from the colonial metropolises should be understood as only one point in a long process towards independence. Since economic dependence remained a striking common feature of the new Latin American nations, it thus offered a critical focus for thinking about the historical dilemmas faced by them. An autochthonous reflection on these issues, however, would have to wait for a more mature debate about the political, cultural, social, and economic identity of the region, which only effectively gained ground during the first decades of the twentieth century.

Before finally moving to a classification of the types of political economy originating in the region, it seems opportune to reinforce some of the salient features of Latin American economic and political ideas as developed during the nineteenth and twentieth centuries. First, one must bear in mind that the liberal ideology that inspired political emancipation in the region was absorbed, first and foremost, in its economic aspects, and only very selectively in its political implications, thus resulting in a sort of conservative liberalism. From the late nineteenth century onwards, the influence of romanticism, as well as the progressive consolidation of Latin American nation-states, resulted in a rise to prominence of nationalist ideas in several countries. Combined with positivism, such ideas would become an influential ideology of modernization, which in many respects corresponded, in Latin America, to the transforming impulse represented by the Enlightenment, in Europe, more than a century before. As this ideology of modernization matured, it led to growing reflection about the specificities of Latin American political and economic dependence – in other words, an analysis of the conditions of underdevelopment engendered by the capitalist economic order itself, and the associated agenda of structural changes needed to overcome them. Having its roots in the 1930s debates on industrialization and economic planning, this developmentalist ideology would be catalyzed and amplified by CEPAL since the end of the 1940s, laying the groundwork for the articulation of dependency theory many years later.

Types of Latin American political economy

Given that the appropriation of economic ideas in Latin America has been typically intertwined with considerations of economic policy and ideology, it would be a futile exercise to pass judgment on the variants of political economy developed in the region on the grounds of their doctrinal consistency. Acts of intellectual appropriation, by their very nature, often imply a *selection* of specific elements found in the original doctrine that may serve one's particular purposes; an *adaptation* of those elements that do not easily translate from one sociohistorical context to another; and an *extension* of the doctrine's domain of application to include problems and phenomena that were not part of its original intent. It is in the concurrence of these three processes – selection, adaptation, and extension – that the true originality of Latin American political economy will be found. This was political economy in the strictest sense of the term: a set of economic ideas designed to address concrete political issues.

Moreover, one needs to bear in mind that ideas possess specific chronologies in their context of creation, related to the problems and debates to which they intended to contribute. However, when these ideas are appropriated in other contexts, chronologies become superposed: different doctrinal sets are simultaneously brought to bear on a given subject, as if they were contenders in the same intellectual arena, or even complementary aspects in a more encompassing approach. This explains in part the often 'eclectic' nature of Latin American debates about political economy. As the context-specificity of the source ideas is lost, they come to seem more malleable and versatile than they initially were, leading to the coexistence of perspectives that, within their original chronologies, were all but incompatible.

In the remainder of this chapter we present a typology of the strands of political economy developed in Latin America from the immediate aftermath of the independence movements to the postwar era. The three main currents identified – liberalism, nationalism, and developmentalism – should not be seen as coherent doctrinal bodies to which supporters consistently adhered, or even as alternative perspectives standing in direct confrontation with one another. Rather, they are more in the nature of Weberian 'ideal types,' that is, clusters of ideas (both political and economic) that exhibit some degree of internal stability and recurrence, while in practice being typically intermeshed with other alien and/or contradictory notions. It is thus common to find the same individual or group resorting to one of these clusters when discussing a specific issue, and then to another after shifting to a different topic. Consequently, the attempt to identify doctrinal 'eras' in Latin American economic thought should be qualified in important respects. One can see a given set of ideas temporarily occupying a predominant position, and thus marshalling discussion in a certain direction, but the close proximity between economic thought and practical political considerations virtually guaranteed that other strands could always coexist within the same context. The potential usefulness of the proposed constructs lies precisely in their capacity to bring into focus the common intellectual origins behind a cluster of ideas, while not losing sight of the intricacies involved in selecting, adapting, and extending these ideas to fit a different reality.

Liberalism

With the benefit of hindsight, it may be easy to associate economic liberalism in nineteenth-century Latin America with the consolidation of asymmetrical relations between Great Britain and the new countries emerging in the region – the abovementioned British 'Informal' Empire – where the latter increasingly found themselves in a position of dependence towards the new hegemonic metropolis. In the context of post-emancipation Latin America, however, few banners sounded as radically liberating as 'free trade.' For societies that had lived for centuries under the sway of colonial exclusiveness, and whose economic cast had been decided mostly by the fiscal needs of the Iberian metropolises, the promise of self-determination inherent in the freedom to engage in commercial transactions with any partners whatsoever seemed to hold the key to a bright future. As seen above, the relaxation of trade restrictions had actually been one of the main sources of dispute and unrest in the Iberian colonies during the decades leading to their independence.

The teachings of British political economy seemed to corroborate these aspirations. Adam Smith, after all, had offered a thorough critique of all misguided forms of mercantile restriction and economic privilege, of which colonial rule was a glaring example. With political subordination buried in the past, Latin America was now finally free to find its proper place in the international division of labor, and thus partake in the "universal opulence" of mankind adumbrated by Smith. Under the influence of both colonial experience and political economy, trade restrictions and monopolistic practices came to be naturally associated with the obnoxious remnants of the *ancien régime*.

Political and economic liberalism were brought into Latin America as part of the same ideological program, and the enthusiasm for free trade and the abolition of corporate privileges had its counterpart in the attempts to implement a constitutional republican model in several of the new nations. The intellectual appeal of the works of Montesquieu, Constant, and Tocqueville, however, was soon counteracted by the challenges inherent in applying their ideas to the peculiar political culture deeply ingrained in the former Iberian colonies. The most salient obstacles to any such endeavor were, of course, the conspicuous class divisions separating *criollos*, *mestizos*, blacks, and Indians, which virtually precluded all but the most innocuous campaigns towards more extensive representation. The persistent political instability across the region in the aftermath of emancipation thus led to a gradual abandonment of the more radical forms of political liberalism in favor of alternatives that could cater more naturally to the prevailing local notions of legitimacy and social order – such as Manuel Belgrano's proposal of a constitutional monarchy headed by an Inca sovereign (Safford 1985, pp. 355–62).

Economic liberalism in Latin America suffered a similar fate. The general principles established by Adam Smith, Jean-Baptiste Say, and David Ricardo were hailed as the key to a prosperous future freed from abhorrent restrictive policies, but in practice they were often stretched, and even solemnly ignored, in the face of thorny concrete problems. The dismal economic performance of the region in the two decades immediately following emancipation led people of all political persuasions to advocate some measure of protection for local manufactures, in an attempt to mitigate the adverse effects of mounting trade deficits. Conversely, when the demand for Latin American exports rose consistently in international markets during the 1850s and 1860s, the bulk of opinion turned once again favorable to free trade – not because doctrine had somehow established itself more firmly, but rather because reality now seemed to endorse doctrine.

As the political battlefield throughout the region coalesced around Liberal and Conservative parties, one would be hard pressed to identify specific alignments on the basis of economic policy prescriptions. Whereas liberals and conservatives tended to agree, under normal circumstances, on the virtues of free enterprise, this did not prevent the emergence of unexpected coalitions. In Venezuela, for instance, the Liberal Party grew out of complaints made by the coffee planters against measures that had abolished usury laws and authorized the liquidation of landed property as collateral for outstanding debts. The conservative faction, in its turn, stuck to the defense of creditors' rights based on the principles of economic liberalism (Safford 1985, pp. 386–7). In Brazil, Bernardo Pereira de Vasconcelos, a former liberal who became one of the country's most prominent conservative statesmen by the mid-nineteenth century, was characterized in the press as a follower of Bentham, who believed that material interests were the only source of morality (Bethell and Carvalho 1985, pp. 711–13). More generally, the rise of a new generation of liberal politicians in the second half of the century relied, at first, on the support of urban craftsmen and manufacturers – precisely the economic groups most adversely affected by the free trade policies adopted over recent decades. In Nueva Granada, this marriage of convenience lasted only until the liberals reached power and failed to apply protective tariffs for domestic manufactures, thus bringing about an artisan rebellion of radical overtones, which was suppressed by an alliance between liberals and conservatives (Safford 1985, pp. 391–2).

The discussions on Indian communal land provide an interesting example of how liberal economic ideas were extended in Latin America to cover topics they were not originally designed to explain. In the eyes of the elite groups that contributed directly to post-emancipation institutional reforms, communal property was contrary to the principles of economic liberalism, since it inhibited the expression of individual interests. Consequently, the proper integration of Indian communities within Latin American society required the division of their land possessions, and the attribution of individual property titles. The implications of such policy for the cultural heritage and lifestyle of the several Indian groups spread across the region scarcely raised any concerns until, decades later, the consequences of failed Indian assimilation began to be felt (Donghi 1985, pp. 323–5).

When it reached Latin America, however, economic liberalism was not only extended to uncharted territories; it was also selectively appropriated to fit local conditions. The most striking illustration of this process was the treatment dispensed to the question of slavery. Where slavery was not abolished immediately after emancipation, governments of liberal and conservative persuasion alike devoted very little energy to measures that pointed in this direction, while often actively defending the institution as vital for the economic welfare of their nations. In Brazil, the last of the Latin American countries to abolish slavery, the exclusion of slave labor from the domain of phenomena that could be elucidated by economic liberalism became even more evident as Britain incorporated an anti-slavery campaign into the core of its trade diplomacy (Howe, this volume). A convicted disciple of Smith and Say such as José da Silva Lisboa, while recognizing the superiority of free labor, rationalized the persistence of slavery in Brazil arguing that the specific conditions of an economy specializing in tropical agriculture required "particular," instead of "general" principles of political economy (Coutinho, this volume).

Similar processes were also at play in Spanish Latin America. The educational reforms implemented in Colombia after the country's political emancipation sought to introduce radical liberal elements in the curricula for higher education, with the purpose of cultivating a "rational and illustrated citizenry." The use made of the works of Bentham, Say, and Destutt de Tracy, however, sought to appeal to local traditions by making them seem compatible with Christian values (Hurtado, this volume). The history of trade agreements between Colombia and the US also illustrates how the very same policy principles, supported by similar institutional arrangements, could be reconstructed in order to support either free trade or protectionism, depending on the context of their application (Meardon, this volume).

In conclusion, there is no question that economic liberalism exerted a powerful influence over economic and social ideas in Latin America during the nineteenth century, but its incorporation into the doctrines and ideologies developed in the region was far from orthodox. Liberalism was used to legitimate unusual claims, and bent almost beyond recognition in order to accommodate recalcitrant reality. Even so, as the century progressed, liberal discourse came to be more and more associated with the defense of abstract, universal, and ultimately hollow principles. Accordingly, conservative opinion started looking elsewhere for the elements with which to support its case.

Nationalism

Attempts to create a shared sense of national identity were an important constitutive element within the independence movements that gained strength in Latin America during the early decades of the nineteenth century. By that time, such efforts were not new. They went back at least to the late-eighteenth-century works of Jesuit expatriates like Juan Pablo Viscardo, who extolled his fellow Spanish Americans to embrace the New World as their motherland, and found concrete expression in political movements such as the Túpac Amaru rebellion, in Peru. Even though they strove to obtain support among indigenous Americans, these early displays of nationalism essentially embodied the values of *criollo* culture, the attitudes and aspirations of European descendants who had come to regard America as their home (Lynch 1985, pp. 40–2). As with most other elements in the intellectual landscape of modern Latin America, the nascent ideal of nationhood had a European, not a local pedigree.

Moreover, in the immediate aftermath of political emancipation, free trade and the defense of national interests were not seen as antagonistic principles, but rather the opposite. Freed from the artificial restraints of the colonial regime, the new Latin American nations were faced with the challenge of carving their place in the world order. In the economic domain, this meant securing a solid position in the international division of labor. Free trade thus could, and indeed was, rationalized as part of the process leading to the strengthening of national identities (Velásquez, this volume). In this rather loose sense, therefore, one could argue that nationalism – political, economic, and otherwise – has been a constant feature of Latin American history since the early moments of its emancipated existence.

As the nineteenth century progressed, however, the meaning attached to nationalistic ideology underwent significant changes. Although the later decades of the century witnessed a more complete integration of Latin America within the world economic order, and consequently brought about stability and material prosperity on a scale hitherto unknown in the young nations, the influence of liberal ideas in the region receded as political conservativeness gained ground almost everywhere. In strictly political terms, this meant increasing government centralization, as opposed to the republican and federalist ideals that populated the emancipation era. Even in Brazil, where republicanism had never reached the same level of public support it enjoyed in other Latin American nations, a strong push towards centralization became visible after the rise to power of the so-called '*Saquarema* cabinet' in 1848 (Graham 1985, pp. 779–81). Charles Hale (1986, p. 369) has argued that, from the 1870s onwards, liberalism came to represent a "unifying myth" in Latin American ideology – a set of hollow slogans about individual freedom and autonomy that covered the most blatantly anti-liberal elements, inherited from the colonial order, that still permeated these societies. Besides once again calling attention to the malleable nature of ideas, especially when removed from their context of origin, this characterization also indicates how apparently contradictory doctrines can often peacefully coexist within the same intellectual environment.

The new facet of Latin American nationalism echoed the growing prominence of romantic and historicist philosophies in Continental Europe. Against the abstract rationalism of both natural law philosophy and utilitarianism, there was a shift in emphasis towards the cultural specificities of each people, as embodied in national formations. Human societies, instead of the concrete manifestations of universal principles of nature, came to be seen as organisms that evolved according to their own particular set of rules and constraints, which singled and distinguished each of them from all the others. To the extent that it preserved its ideological influence, republicanism became a template for centralized, stable, and efficient administration, with due attention to the peculiar traits of each national culture. In other words, it became the political philosophy of 'order and progress,' as proclaimed in 1867 by the Mexican Gabino Barreda, and later inscribed in the Brazilian republican national flag. An important part of 'progress,' of course, meant economic progress, and the political pragmatism of the era accordingly replaced the moral niceties of constitutionalism with the down-to-earth knowledge of economic matters (Hale 1986, pp. 369–77).

As often stressed in the literature, the ascension of nationalism in late-nineteenth-century Latin America was firmly rooted in positivist philosophy. In its Comtean variant, positivism portrayed society as a living organism whose laws of motion and evolution could only be understood through the study of history. In this sense, it reinforced the tendency to focus on the specific conditions surrounding the institutional development of Latin American countries, along the lines of the approach favored by the German historical school of jurisprudence. The influence of positivism in Latin America was concretely felt, in particular, in a series of projects for educational reform, which sought to substitute 'scientific' training for the traditional humanistic curricula. Behind such efforts lay the desire for providing education that could be of direct service in the transformation of society. The government apparatus was, of course, the natural instrument for implementing these goals, and the spread of positivism in Latin America accordingly went hand-in-hand with political secularization and the ideal of a 'strong state.' When coupled with the overall technocratic bias of positivist-inspired education, this led to the emerging notion of 'scientific politics,' in which centralization, and even some forms of authoritarianism, could be construed as rational intervention based on expert knowledge, and thus appeal to liberals and conservatives alike (Hale 1986, pp. 382–91).

As in the case of Comte, the English philosopher Herbert Spencer and his 'Law of Progress' also enjoyed enormous influence in Latin America. The famous Argentine politician and intellectual Domingo Faustino Sarmiento, who came to entertain positivist ideas by the end of his life, recognized in Spencer a clear expression of his own convictions, stating that his philosophical system "should provide the way to express the longing for progress of his whole generation" (Hurtado 2008, p. 99). As mentioned above, positivism gave effective expression to aspirations for modern statecraft in Latin America. In this sense, it provided an ideology of progress and modernity, upheld by the principles of order and evolution, and dedicated to the problem of nation-building (Molina 2005, p. 18).

As in the case of liberalism discussed above, nationalism also did not provide a definite set of doctrinaire prescriptions capable of solving concrete problems, but rather a diffuse template that could be mobilized and interpreted in very different ways. In Brazil, for instance, the conservative and centralizing *Saquarema* administration passed a series of reforms in the 1850s that put the Brazilian economy significantly more in tune with contemporary liberal capitalism, such as the abolition of slave traffic and the new law on landed property titles (Graham 1985, pp. 779–80). Joaquim José Rodrigues Torres, the

Saquarema expert on economic and financial matters, while doctrinally committed to the monetary orthodoxy of the British currency school, conceded to using the national Bank of Brazil, under his administration, to "promote credit and national wealth" (Gambi, this volume). In Colombia, conversely, the creation of a national bank had been regarded, since the early days of emancipation, as a constitutive element in the process of nation-building, being closely related to the administration of public finance. This idea culminated, by the end of the nineteenth century, in the pleas of president Rafael Núñez – a former liberal turned conservative nationalist – for a paper money system that could be used as a political weapon (Álvarez, this volume).

The influence of German ideas in Latin American political economy was also multiform. In Chile, the Prussian immigrant Julio Menadier introduced the nationalist and protectionist ideas of Friedrich List in a full-fledged program for the defense of *agrarian* interests. He did this by portraying agriculture as the "mother industry" of the Chilean economy, and thus forging an unstable alliance between the landed classes and the national metal-mechanic industry, which could provide agriculture with the machines and implements necessary for its modernization (Robles, this volume). More generally, Latin American thinkers who appropriated Listian protectionist ideas during the late nineteenth and early twentieth centuries have tended to ignore the author's view of tropical areas as unsuitable for industrialization (Boianovsky 2013). The concept of *Volkswirtschaft*, as developed in the works of German historical economists such as Adolph Wagner, was repeatedly translated into the Brazilian political economic debate, but the specific meaning attached to it was context-dependent: in the hands of Rui Barbosa, the Finance Minister for the newborn Brazilian Federalist Republic, *Volkswirtschaft* became 'social economy'; for Roberto Simonsen, the leading industrialist of the interwar period, it meant 'national economy' (Curi, this volume).

By the early twentieth century, nationalist ideology in Latin America had come to acquire a host of different meanings that made tensions with liberalism become more evident. Racial theories imported from Europe increasingly stressed the problems associated with the heritage of ethnic miscegenation prevalent in the region, giving rise to an anthropologically inspired pessimism regarding the prospects of Latin American civilization. Political instability, and other typical local phenomena such as the *caudillos*, could be construed as reflections of the cultural and moral inclinations typical of a certain racial pattern, thus highlighting how the principles derived from liberal ideology were incompatible with Latin American societies. One of the reactions to these and similar ideas was a revival of idealist philosophy, which sought to associate the fate of the region to the fulfillment of an indigenous character. By the interwar period, therefore, positivism no longer reigned supreme, and nationalism had become inextricably mixed with metaphysical theories of cultural determination, which alternately featured elements of socialism, agrarianism, and corporatism (Hale 1986, pp. 414–41).

Developmentalism

While liberalism and nationalism were doctrines imported from Europe into Latin America, the set of theories and policy prescriptions commonly referred to as 'developmentalism' is often regarded as an indigenous intellectual product – an original contribution springing from Latin America to enrich the common stock of economic knowledge. Precisely because of its status as a 'truly original' Latin American brand of political economy – in particular its early manifestations, most closely associated with the work of CEPAL – developmentalism has been the subject of repeated surveys and scholarly exegeses, both critical and celebratory.[12] Accordingly, it will not be our purpose here to recite once again the main features and characters, the successes and failures associated with the Latin American developmentalist agenda. Rather, we will focus on the elements that distinguished developmentalism from the economic ideologies that preceded it, and also on its points of contact with intellectual currents generating outside the region.

There has been some debate regarding whether developmentalism should be seen as an outgrowth of the positivist and nationalist doctrines that prevailed in Latin America during the late nineteenth century, or rather as a new phenomenon that bore the distinctive marks of the interwar experience.[13] These and other difficulties associated with pinpointing the precise origins of developmentalism only reinforce how fluid are the boundaries that separate different economic ideologies. There were obviously several elements within nationalism that could be used to foster a developmentalist approach: the emphasis on the historical experience of each nation, the technocratic use of socioeconomic knowledge, the central role of the state, among others (Boianovsky, this volume). In its purest forms, however, nationalism was self-centered to the point of isolationism, stressing the fulfillment of cultural destinies and the development of autochthonous social and institutional forms. Developmentalism, on the other hand, was only rarely autarkic, and usually reverted to the traditional liberal aspiration of securing a solid and stable position within the international economic order – although the path to this goal was no longer seen to rest on static comparative advantages, but rather on conscious emulation of the successful experiences of industrialized nations.[14] As an economic ideology, it could occasionally cater to either liberal or nationalist sensibilities, but it might also, just as well, alienate both.

The ascent of developmentalism in Latin America also parallels the consolidation of the neoclassical paradigm in economic theory during the second quarter of the twentieth century. As the traditional concern of nineteenth-century political economy with matters of growth and institutional development was replaced by the static analysis of abstract economic models, development economics emerged as a disciplinary sub-field where the peculiar problems afflicting 'backward' nations could be discussed. Here, however, the malleability of economic ideas once again comes to the fore, since developmentalism could draw inspiration from manifold sources: the German Historical

School, for Brazilian industrialist Roberto Simonsen (Curi, this volume); interwar business cycle theory, in the case of Raúl Prebisch (Perez Caldentey and Vernengo 2012; Sember 2012); or else Celso Furtado's appropriation of Keynesian-inspired macroeconomics and growth models (Boianovsky 2010; Coutinho 2015). For all its undeniable originality and attention to regional specificities, Latin American developmentalism incorporated a broad amalgam of foreign intellectual influences, including authorities as diverse as Walt Rostow, Michal Kalecki, Ragnar Nurkse, Charles Kindleberger, W. Arthur Lewis, François Perroux, Nicholas Kaldor, and Karl Marx.

Moreover, although its Latin American incarnation possessed unique and distinctive features, the phenomenon of developmentalism was not exclusive to the region. As Joseph Love (1996) has shown, the economic discourse of industrialization and protectionism developed in the 'backward' economies of Central and Eastern Europe during the interwar years constituted one of the crucial sources of influence for Latin American structuralism, especially through the works of Rumanian economist Mihail Manoilescu. Latin America was not, however, the only place where Eastern European economic nationalism found fertile ground. In Southern Europe, another region afflicted by problems of unequal development and economic backwardness, a discourse of national economic development also came to occupy a prominent public position, especially due to the influence of Polish economist Paul Rosenstein-Rodan. The results produced in each region, however, were very different. Whereas in Southern Europe, under the Marshall Plan and postwar reconstruction, economic nationalism coexisted with openness to international trade, in Latin America, the dawning awareness of belonging to the 'periphery' of postwar capitalism led to protectionism and import substitution industrialization (Alacevich, this volume).

The history of developmentalism in Latin America also illustrates some of the other aspects we have been emphasizing in this chapter. Although it reached a higher level of theoretical sophistication than either liberalism or nationalism, developmentalism was always very closely related to political action – it was policy first, and theory only later (Love, this volume). Additionally, as the concrete application of developmentalist ideas during the postwar era failed to produce the expected results, the doctrine was expanded in unexpected directions in order to account for the specific features of Latin American historical experience. The frustration produced by abortive industrialization processes everywhere in the region pushed developmentalism towards dependency theory, an often bleak statement about the obstacles inherent in the structure of peripheral economies that prevented the successful emulation of the model offered by advanced capitalist nations. Developed in the 1960s and 1970s both as a critical theoretical approach, and as an unfolding of ideas originally developed by CEPAL, dependency theory thus became yet another important focus for the articulation between economic and political concerns. The intellectual trajectory of a prolific economist like Celso Furtado, who lived through the rise and decline of developmentalist ideology in Latin America, and eventually developed his own dependency approach, strikingly reveals how a core set of doctrinal beliefs can manifest itself in multiple forms, following changes in the relevant context of application.

Concluding remarks

Political economy provides one of the essential playing fields where the fate of Latin American nations, and the problems associated with their independence – political, economic, and otherwise – have been critically discussed and intellectually negotiated. When dealing with the political economic discourse produced in the region, one must heed not to dismiss particular contributions on the grounds of their inconsistency or eclecticism. Rather, the originality of Latin American economic thought should be sought in the creative appropriation of ideas produced elsewhere, and thus usually ill-suited to specific local conditions. This means expanding the domain of application of certain doctrines and theories, but also choosing to ignore other potentially troublesome aspects, or at least to change their meanings in significant ways. It also means creating intellectual spaces where ideas originally developed in separate contexts will be made to coexist, either as conflicting arguments or eclectic perspectives. In this expanded sense, the history of Latin American political economy can hopefully shed much light on what is distinctive about the recent historical experience of the nations that comprise the region.

Notes

1 The Peninsular War (1807–1814) was a military conflict for control over the Iberian Peninsula that opposed the French and Spanish empires, on one side, and an alliance between Great Britain and the Kingdom of Portugal, on the other. The conflict began when French and Spanish armies invaded and occupied Portugal in 1807, and gained new contours in 1808 after France, having now broken its alliance with Spain, occupied the whole Peninsula. The war lasted until the defeat of Napoleon in 1814.
2 See Mello (2004) and Silva (2006).
3 The Regency was a period in Brazilian political history that began in April 7, 1831, when Emperor Pedro I abdicated the Brazilian throne in favor of his son, Pedro II, who had just turned five years old. According to the Constitution of 1824, when a monarch could not perform his full political functions, a three-person Regency should be appointed to rule. Since 1834, a Regent was to be elected to a four-year term by censitary vote. The elections, and consequent alternation in executive leadership between 1835 and 1840, allowed for a proto-republican experience in Brazil. On July 23, 1840, the Brazilian parliament formally declared Pedro II emancipated, at his 14 years of age.
4 See Bethell and Carvalho (1985) and Harris (2010).
5 In contrast to the interpretation advanced by dependency theory, Bethell (1995) argues forcefully that the Paraguayan War (1864–1870) – which opposed Paraguay and the Triple Alliance of Argentina, Brazil, and Uruguay – should not be understood as an instance of British imperialism in Latin America.
6 Two main expedients were adopted by the mid-eighteenth century: the granting of monopolies on an increasing number of goods, and the imposition of direct

government collection of taxes, in lieu of the traditional leases to private contractors (Lynch 1985, p. 12). On the Enlightened reformism in Spain, see also Paquette (2008).

7 '*Criollo*' is a reference to a social class in the hierarchy of Hispanic American colonies, comprising the locally born people of confirmed European (primarily Spanish) ancestry; '*peninsular*,' on the other hand, refers to the Spanish-born people residing in the New World.

8 The '*Inconfidência Mineira*' was an unsuccessful separatist movement, directly inspired by the independence of the British colonies in North America, which occurred in 1789 in Minas Gerais, the most important mining area of the Portuguese empire (see Maxwell 1973a).

9 The scholarship on the processes of political emancipation/independence in Latin America has only gradually abandoned a 'homogeneous' view of the examined societies and began to differentiate the groups and interests involved. As pointed out by Chust and Serrano (2007, pp. 10–25), until the 1950s there was a predominance of nationalist-inspired readings of the wars of independence, reflected in the cult of heroes and of the fatherland, and in a homogeneous idea of 'the people.' In the 1970s, this view was largely replaced by a new research agenda, inspired by dependency theory and Marxism, which gave more attention to notions such as classes and interest groups, while at the same time exhibiting more professional historical scholarship. More recent decades, in turn, were marked by multiple research emphases and a de-politicization of the debate, escaping from simplistic dualisms and anachronisms that were typical of certain readings influenced by dependency theory.

10 See Cardoso (2001).

11 The title was translated as *Economic Development of Latin America* in the 1970 English edition.

12 See, for instance, Bielschowsky (1988), Sikkink (1991), Bresser-Pereira (2011), Malta and Ganem (2011), Fonseca and Mollo (2013), and Dathein (2015).

13 For an illustration of these contrasting perspectives with regard to the specific case of Brazil, see Bielschowsky (1988) and Fonseca (2015).

14 As argued by Valdés (1997, p. 342), many elements that would later occupy a prominent position in the CEPAL approach, such as the pivotal role of industrialization and the perception of deteriorating terms of trade, had been used before as part of a discourse for national autonomy. However, it was only when they became associated to the problem of economic growth that an effective development theory came to light.

References

Bethell, Leslie. 1995. "O imperialismo britânico e a Guerra do Paraguai." *Estudos Avançados* 9(24): 269–85.

Bethell, Leslie; Carvalho, José M. de. 1985. Brazil from Independence to the middle of the nineteenth century. In: Bethell, Leslie (ed.). *The Cambridge history of Latin America*. Cambridge: Cambridge University Press, Vol. 3.

Bielschowsky, Ricardo. 1988. *Pensamento econômico brasileiro: o ciclo ideológico do desenvolvimento*. Rio de Janeiro: IPEA/INPES.

Boianovsky, Mauro. 2010. "A view from the tropics: Celso furtado and the theory of economic development in the 1950s." *History of Political Economy* 42(2): 221–66.

Boianovsky, Mauro. 2013. "Friedrich List and the economic fate of tropical countries." *History of Political Economy* 45(4): 647–91.

Bresser-Pereira, Luiz C. 2011. From Old to New Developmentalism in Latin America. In: Ocampo, José Antonio; Ros, Jaime (eds.). *The Oxford handbook of Latin American economics.* Oxford: Oxford University Press.

Cardoso, Fernando Henrique; Faletto, Enzo. 1979 [1971]. *Dependency and development in Latin America.* Berkeley: University of California Press.

Cardoso, José L. 2001. *A economia política e os dilemas do império Luso-Brasileiro, 1790–1822.* Lisboa: Comissão Nacional para as Comemorações dos Descobrimentos Portugueses.

Cardoso, José L. 2003. The international diffusion of economic thought. In: Samuels, Warren; Biddle, Jeff; Davis, John (eds.). *A companion to the history of economic thought.* Oxford and New York: Blackwell.

Chataing, David R. 2005. Presentación. In: Miranda Bastidas, Haidee; Becerra, Hasdrúbal (eds.). *La independencia de Hispanoamérica: declaraciones y actas.* Caracas, Venezuela: Biblioteca Ayacucho.

Chust, Manuel; Serrano, José A. 2007. Un debate actual, una revisión necesaria. In: Chust, Manuel; Serrano, José A. (eds.). *Debates sobre las independencias iberoamericanas.* Madrid/Frankfurt am Main: AHILA/Iberoamericana/Vervuert.

Coutinho, Mauricio C. 2015. "Subdesenvolvimento e Estagnação na América Latina, de Celso Furtado." *Revista de Economia Contemporânea* 19(3): 448–74.

Dathein, Ricardo. 2015. *Desenvolvimentismo: o Conceito, as Bases Teóricas e as Políticas.* Rio Grande do Sul: Editora UFRGS.

Donghi, Tulio H. 1985. Economy and society in post-Independence Spanish America. In: Bethell, Leslie (ed.). *The Cambridge history of Latin America.* Cambridge: Cambridge University Press, Vol. 3.

Fonseca, Pedro C. D. 2015. Desenvolvimentismo: a construção do conceito. In: Dathein, Ricardo (ed.). *Desenvolvimentismo: o Conceito, as Bases Teóricas e as Políticas.* Rio Grande do Sul: Editora UFRGS.

Fonseca, Pedro C. D.; Mollo, Maria L. R. 2013. "Desenvolvimentismo e novo-desenvolvimentismo: raízes teóricas e precisões conceituais." *Revista De Economia Política* 33(2): 222–39.

Furtado, Celso. 1970 [1969]. *Economic development of Latin America: a survey from colonial times to the Cuban revolution.* Cambridge: Cambridge University Press.

Furtado, Celso. 1983 [1978]. *Accumulation and development: the logic of industrial civilization.* New York: St. Martin's Press.

Graham, Richard. 1985. Brazil from the middle of the nineteenth century to the Paraguayan War. In: Bethell, Leslie (ed.). *The Cambridge history of Latin America.* Cambridge: Cambridge University Press, Vol. 3.

Hale, Charles. 1986. Political and social ideas in Latin America, 1870–1930. In: Bethell, Leslie (ed.). *The Cambridge history of Latin America.* Cambridge: Cambridge University Press, Vol. 4.

Harris, Mark. 2010. *Rebellion on the Amazon: the Cabanagem, race, and popular culture in the north of Brazil, 1798–1840.* New York: Cambridge University Press.

Hurtado, José L. J. 2008. "Las ideas positivistas en la América Latina del siglo XIX." *Revista Via Iuris* 5: 91–102.

Love, Joseph L. 1995. Economic ideas and ideologies in Latin America since 1930. In: Bethell, Leslie (ed.). *The Cambridge history of Latin America.* Cambridge: Cambridge University Press, Vol. 6.

Love, Joseph L. 1996. *Crafting the Third World: theorizing underdevelopment in Rumania and Brazil.* Stanford, CA: Stanford University Press.

Lynch, John. 1973. *The Spanish American revolutions, 1808–1826*. New York: Norton.

Lynch, John. 1985. The origins of Spanish American Independence. In: Bethell, Leslie (ed.). *The Cambridge history of Latin America*. Cambridge: Cambridge University Press, Vol. 3.

Lynch, John. 2001. *Latin America between colony and nation: selected essays.* Houndmills, Basingstoke, Hampshire [England]: Palgrave.

Malta, Maria M.; Ganem, Angela. 2011. *Ecos do desenvolvimento: uma história do pensamento econômico brasileiro.* Rio de Janeiro: Ipea.

Maxwell, Kenneth. 1973a. *Conflicts and conspiracies: Brazil and Portugal, 1750–1808.* Cambridge: Cambridge University Press.

Maxwell, Kenneth. 1973b. The generation of the 1790's and the idea of the Luso-Brazilian Empire. In: Alden, Dauril (ed.). *Colonial roots of modern Brazil.* Los Angeles: University of California Press.

Meek, Ronald. 1967. *Economics and ideology and other essays.* Chapman & Hall: London.

Mello, Evaldo C. 2004. *A outra independência: o federalismo pernambucano de 1817 a 1824.* São Paulo: Ed. 34.

Molina, Rafael C. 2005. *Nacionalismo, nación y continentalismo en América Latina.* Xalapa (Mexico): Instituto de Investigaciones Histórico-Sociales/Universidad Veracruzana.

Novais, Fernando A. 1979. *Portugal e Brasil na crise do antigo sistema colonial (1777–1808).* São Paulo: Editora HUCITEC.

Paquette, Gabriel B. 2008. *Enlightenment, governance and reform in Spain and its empire 1759–1808.* Basingstoke [England]: Palgrave Macmillan.

Perez Caldentey, Esteban; Vernengo, Matias. 2012. "Retrato de un joven economista: la evolución de las opiniones de Raúl Prebisch sobre el ciclo económico y el dinero, 1919–1949." *Revista De La Cepal* (Santiago De Chile) 106: 7–22.

Romero, José L. 1977. Prologo. In: Romero, José L.; Romero, Luis A. (eds.). *Pensamiento político de la Emancipación.* Caracas, Venezuela: Biblioteca Ayacucho.

Safford, Frank. 1985. Politics, ideology and society in post-Independence Spanish America. In: Bethell, Leslie (ed.). *The Cambridge history of Latin America.* Cambridge: Cambridge University Press, Vol. 3.

Sember, Florencia. 2012. "El papel de Raúl Prebisch en la creación del Banco Central de la República Argentina." *Estudios críticos del desarrollo* 2(3): 133–57.

Sikkink, Kathryn. 1991. *Ideas and institutions: developmentalism in Brazil and Argentina.* Ithaca, NY: Cornell University Press.

Silva, Luiz G. 2006. *O avesso da independência: Pernambuco (1817–24).* In: Malerba, J. (ed.). *A Independência Brasileira: Novas Dimensões.* Rio de Janeiro: Editora FGV.

Sunkel, Osvaldo; Paz, Pedro. 1970. *El subdesarrollo latinoamericano y la teoría del desarrollo.* México: Siglo Veintiuno Editores.

Valdés, Eduardo. 1997. "O pensamento nacionalista na América Latina e a reivindicação da identidade econômica (1920-1940)." *Estudos Históricos*, Rio de Janeiro, 10(20): 321–43.

2 Circulating economic ideas

Adaptation, appropriation, translation

José Luís Cardoso

Introduction

The writing of this chapter was originally motivated by the general theme of the 4th ESHET Latin American Conference held in Belo Horizonte in November 2014, under the heading of *Originality, Adaptation and Critique: the Place of Latin America in the History of Economic Thought*. The conference featured a roundtable on the topic of the "International Dissemination of Economic Ideas." These notes correspond to the attempt that was made to promote the discussion of a few ontological and methodological issues related to the study of the spread and diffusion of economic ideas across countries and continents.

This research subject is of utmost relevance for countries and regions that are usually seen as net importers of original ideas created abroad. Notwithstanding the capacity to build up creative thinking in Latin American countries, especially as regards original contributions to the theories and policies of economic development, there is plenty of evidence of the richness of the procedures involved in the critical adaptation and appropriation of economic knowledge. The scholarly debates on the diffusion in many Latin American countries of Enlightenment ideas on economic reform, Adam Smith's political economy, List's system of national political economy, or Keynesian economic policies – to name just the obvious and well-studied cases – offer multiple reasons for claiming the relevance of studies of this kind in the dissemination of economic thought.[1]

The development of economic ideas and theoretical constructs in particular regional contexts is socially and politically determined, thus inviting historians to explain why, when, and how the spread and diffusion processes occurred. The aim of this contribution is to highlight a few points that help to understand this relevant issue in the historiography of economic thought. After a brief summary of canonical interpretations, I shall explore less cultivated territories of research, crossing borders within the universe of the social sciences.

Historiographical (and conventional) wisdom

The historiography of economic thought has accumulated enough evidence on the relevance of the theme of the international mobility and diffusion of economic ideas. The topic has been revisited many times and, to avoid redundancy, the reader should be invited to follow the main references suggested by a few bibliographic surveys.[2]

The theme suggests, first, a concern with the formation and production of economic ideas and with the conditions and obstacles that can accelerate or hinder the processes governing their transmission and diffusion. Second, if one adopts the position of the receiver country or institution, it is necessary to take into account the constraints dictated by different levels of economic development and by the greater or lesser degree of cultural and political cosmopolitanism, which determine both the opportunity for, and the depth of, the diffusion processes.

Another relevant issue explaining different levels of circulation is the capacity to deal with the technical content of economic theories that seem appropriate to justify the implementation of certain economic and social policies. The degree of development of the economics profession is indeed an important factor for explaining how economic ideas may develop and mature in a particular environment. The processes of communication and diffusion between professional economists, and between these and the public at large, as well as policymakers, are fundamental conditions that help to understand the spread of ideas and their impact in society. However, sometimes the flow to the public sphere is not particularly successful, as Robert Solow accurately points out: "The transmission of complicated ideas is imperfect. By the time an economic idea reaches its ultimate destination it has been changed, distorted in one way or another. This is surely the case when an idea diffuses outside the profession" (Solow 1989, 75).

Studying the processes of international transmission also allows for the formation of a critical view of the attempts to create rigid schemes – quite common within the conventional historiography of economic thought – tending to divide authors into distinct periods or to classify them according to schools or streams of thought. In fact, such attempts have always warned against the difficulty of establishing single definitive categories or typologies. If we look at the problem through the looking-glass of international transmission, it is quite common for authors who are rarely joined together in their country or countries of origin to be jointly and simultaneously imported or assimilated into a different country.

Finally, the study of the international transmission of ideas and theories offers an excellent pretext for furthering the analysis of the national histories and traditions of economic thought. The introduction of a national dimension does not seek to deny the universal character of economics, but rather to demonstrate the relevance of different adaptive processes in the spread of economic theories and ideas. The pertinence of a particular model for explaining reality does not depend only on the inner consistency of the theoretical and doctrinal discourse, but also, and indeed very particularly, upon the successful adaptation to this same reality of the political presuppositions and consequences that are inherent therein.

It is precisely this last issue, traditionally associated with methodological discussions on the international diffusion of economic ideas, that requires special attention, given its pertinence for explaining the specificity of national approaches, namely the "place of Latin America in the history of economic thought," this being the question that the title of the conference sought to address.

Innovative approaches: place and travel

The following remarks are intended to provide some useful paths of research to be followed in the process of dealing with issues relating to the dissemination of economic knowledge. These are topics that have received substantial attention from scholarly research in the fields of the history of science, the history of ideas, and other related subjects. They are not specifically addressed to the discussion of distinct problems in the economic sphere, though they have also certainly proved to be useful in this field.

History and social studies of science have given great prominence to the problem of place, which is equivalent to stressing the importance of the local context in the fabrication of knowledge. The idea of a universal science for which national and regional features are totally irrelevant has been gradually replaced by a new approach in the cultural and intellectual history of science that takes vigorous account of the "local manifestations of universal science" (Ophir and Shapin 1991, 5).

According to this viewpoint, science is generated and assessed as a response to the demands of specific geographic, historical, and institutional contexts. Science is locally shaped and its impact and domain of application also has a local dimension. This further means that knowledge creation is embedded in streams of practical life and occurs in spatial arrangements where social interaction takes place. The value assigned to place is a further element that emphasizes the role of social institutions in shaping cognition processes. In short: the importance granted to place in studies related to the history of science engenders renewed attention to the circulation and diffusion of knowledge, as well as to the process of the local, *in situ* development of science (cf. Livingstone 2003).[3]

By giving new focus to the points of reception and to the historical and institutional circumstances explaining the motives for both the adoption and the adaptation of economic ideas and practices, I wish to emphasize the relevance of the institutional milieu, in order to explain the conditions under which new forms of economic knowledge have emerged and developed, well suited to particular places and contexts of appropriation. It is therefore worth addressing the historical conditions that make the reading of certain authors or certain economic arguments useful and relevant in a given context.

We may take for granted that science is always marked by the local and spatial circumstances involved in its making. However, there are similar patterns of production in other places that make it possible for scientific discourse to travel from place to place. One of the main conditions for efficient travel is the degree of trust gained by unmodified scientific knowledge when it reaches similar contexts where it may be applied. As Shapin puts it: "The wide distribution of scientific knowledge flows from the success of certain cultures in creating and spreading standardized contexts for making and applying that knowledge" (Shapin 1998, 7). The travel of scientific knowledge has deserved close attention from scholars interested in studying the mastering of natural and economic resources in colonial empires, as a means both for improving agriculture and manufactures and for deepening the dependent relationship between peripheral colonial territories and the dominating metropolises.[4]

Nevertheless, this is not only an issue of efficiency, control, and power, but also an issue of trust and the appropriation of scientific knowledge in the public domain. An example that clearly illustrates this claim is given by the translation of scientific texts, which should be viewed as an instrument of the travel of knowledge that gains further meaning when it serves communities of different places.

The same considerations apply to the travel of ideas from place to place and to the study of the conditions that cause some ideas to flourish more vigorously in some places than in others. And they also explain why some ideas simply do not fit in with the intellectual context to which they have been imported. As far as economic science and thought are concerned, this issue has motivated previous studies, and the relevance of the subject, whenever methodological debates on national styles and traditions are under scrutiny, is broadly acknowledged.[5]

Adaptation, appropriation, and translation

The scholarly field of cultural studies has developed a concern with the uses of literary or scientific texts as part of an adaptation process that can be described as follows: "An acknowledged transposition of a recognizable other work or works; a creative and an interpretative act of appropriation/ salvaging; and an extended intertextual engagement with the adapted work" (Hutcheon 2006, 8).

Although the use of this type of approach is particularly important within the realm of literary and cultural studies, it is worth noting that an adaptation is not only a concrete product or outcome (e.g., the adaptation of a novel into a film, or a drama into a musical performance, or poetry into prose), but also a process of creation and reception that is applicable to other forms of communication. It is therefore interesting to apply this type of approach to the adaptation of ideas in different contexts of production and reception, in the sense that, "adaptation [is] an attempt to make texts relevant or easily comprehensible to new audiences and readerships via the processes of proximation and updating" (Sanders 2006, 19).

Running counter to the notion of homogeneity and cultural dominance, adaptations introduce elements of creative thinking, diversity, and variation that offer new insights for the study of the processes of transmission and diffusion, including those pertaining to the circulation of economic ideas. There is no longer a concern with remaining faithful to the original source, or studying influences within a static framework, but instead with the appropriation of words and arguments that gain a new meaning.

This notion of the appropriation of knowledge (or of scientific ideas, practices, and techniques) overcomes the less suitable notions of transmission, diffusion, and adaptation, because it underlines the active role, the strategy, and the planning of those directly engaged in the process of importing and assimilating ideas. It also obliges us to analyze the institutional conditions that enable us to legitimize the appropriated message or object, as well as to overcome the constraints and resistances that it may have experienced before becoming accepted. Briefly: "Thus our context is that of the active receiver, which entails a shift from the point of view of what has been transmitted to the view of how what was received has been appropriated" (Gavroglu et al. 2008, 154).

One of the instruments placed at the service of the strategies of appropriation is the translation into the national language of texts and books produced in a different national and linguistic setting. Translation thus reveals a heuristic capacity applied to the study of the processes of knowledge adaptation and appropriation.

The theme of circulation is closely associated with the history of book production and reading and therefore with the history of translation. This offers us the opportunity of thinking in terms of books as acts of communication with receivers (the audience), producers (authors and translators), modes and conventions of transmission (through rhetorical strategies), and feedback effects, thus allowing for the use of cybernetic models and concepts that were one of the basic tools of the conventional, canonical view on the spread and dissemination of ideas.

Another possible approach to the role of translation is based on the notions associated with knowledge or science in context, i.e., with the notion of "science as practical activity, located in the routines of everyday life" (Secord 2004, 657). According to this line of thought, it becomes apparent that a translation is an expression of knowledge in transit, an act of communicating science that allows for a better understanding of the generic regularities, as well as the local peculiarities, involved in the circulation of knowledge.

By following any of these paths of research we reach the same conclusion: circulation through translation helps to explain the processes of the spread and transmission of knowledge.[6]

It is also advisable to move forward to new directions and point out the importance of an interdisciplinary dialogue between historians of science and ideas and philologists, in order to gain a better understanding of the activity of translation as a means of tracing the transfer of scientific knowledge and the development of scientific vocabulary in each of the national and linguistic contexts considered (cf. Tymoczko 2002). This cooperation may bring new insights to the understanding of cultural contexts and language frameworks that are relevant for the analysis of the transmission and appropriation of scientific knowledge. In a nutshell:

> Renditions of scientific texts into other languages can serve the historian in more significant ways, however, than as an indicator of publishing success. With respect to translation studies, historians of science could profit by turning to philologists, who have long recognized that a translation is not merely a medium of transfer, but more importantly a mental meeting point where barriers of language and culture are crossed.
>
> (Rupke 2000, 209)

Translations of political economy texts: the Enlightenment context

In order to show the relevance of this topic for historians of economics, one may take as an example a specific period in the history of translation of economic texts, namely the period corresponding to the emergence and development of political economy as an autonomous field of scientific inquiry. Indeed, in the late eighteenth and early nineteenth century, there was an explosion of translations of economic literature which corresponded both to the euphoria of translation as a rewarding and useful endeavor, and to the growing relevance of political economy as a subject that had reached and captured the public domain.

In most European countries, by the mid-eighteenth century, translations into Latin were no longer needed for international readership, and Latin lost its role in scholarly writing, as well as in fiction and poetry. The Enlightenment had offered the opportunity for cosmopolitan conversation without a common or universal language, though French had gained the status of a *lingua franca*. However, being a *lingua franca* did not mean achieving exclusivity or uniqueness, and the common acceptance of French as a language of universal communication implied a wider process of translation from and into French of texts seeking widespread diffusion.

Translation was sometimes a process of creating new words and a new technical language. Thus, national cultures and national languages were somehow challenged and modified by means of translations:

> These [receiving] languages were, to various degrees, affected by the translated texts and influenced by new literary standards and ideas. They also transformed the texts themselves, both through active intervention and through the subtle mechanisms of linguistic shifts. Translation, the tool of a new Enlightenment cosmopolitanism, eventually became the medium (and target) of new linguistic self-awareness and cultural nationalism.
>
> (Oz-Salzberger 2006, 396)

In the late eighteenth and early nineteenth century, there was no legal control over the contents of translations. There were no assignments of copyright, and translators could take liberties with style and argument, without respecting the original message of the text (cf. Forget 2010, 655). Substantial differences could therefore be found whenever translators acknowledged the disclaimer of a "free translation," even when they claimed to have attempted to remain faithful to the author's central message.

Translators tended to serve their readers and show loyalty to them, addressing their interests in terms of comprehension, without caring too much about the authors that were being translated or quoted. In a certain way, one can describe this biased approach as a market-oriented strategy of publishing.

Traduttore becomes *traditore*. The purpose of being faithful notwithstanding, there are difficulties of expression in a different language that originate involuntary misunderstandings. But sometimes, the translators themselves express their disagreement with the ideas spelt out and thus delete full passages that sound inappropriate or insert footnotes explaining their opposition to the author's ideas.

Original texts are transformed in order either to attract readers or to create an audience better prepared to be aware of the contents of the message translated. However, by introducing notes and amendments to the texts, translators produce changes of meaning to the original, for the benefit of new audiences, for whom the transformed message seems to fit much better.

> Translation, however, does much more than substitute words of one language for those of another. Like popularization, translation allows us to see how a scientific work is received by a particular audience and how it may be adapted for other audiences.
>
> (Forget 2010, 674)

By the end of the eighteenth century, political economy was one of the main subjects contributing to the enlargement of the market for translations. The main purpose was to reach a broader audience interested in topics relating to public administration, the role of government, and the functioning of markets and economic life in general. This new science of the market and of the modern institutions that served the dynamics of the emerging industrial capitalism was also a science that was placed at the service of the legislator, with added responsibility in the design and implementation of the new functions granted to the state. It was therefore crucial to spread the good news concerning the interpretation and monitoring of economic life. Translations became an important vehicle for the diffusion and popularization of the new science of political economy and therefore a means for its appropriation in national contexts.

Translators of essays and tracts on political economy were also interested in maintaining a conversation and critically discussing the claims and arguments put forward by the authors translated. Thus, the process of translation was also a means of increasing public debate and revealing the role of the translator as someone who was entitled to the attributes of authorship.

Concluding remarks

The purpose of this chapter was to provide some motivation for an enlarged discussion of the relevance of the processes of diffusion, adaptation, and appropriation of economic ideas. Special emphasis was given to the function of translations, since they operate as an ideal demonstration of the route of economic ideas circulating in different historical and linguistic contexts.

It is undisputable that not all types of economic reasoning prove to be adequate for solving problems in any historical context. Therefore, the use and appropriation of economic discourse is, most of the time, a rhetorical device that serves as a means for claiming the appropriateness of certain economic policies aimed at achieving a predesigned set of political aims. The economists' voices are not echoed in the public sphere because they are right, but because they serve particular goals to foster innovative projects of economic and political reform.

The appropriation of ideas and the adaptation of analytical or political arguments are also associated with a process of emulation, according to which what has occurred in a country that has reached a certain degree of economic development may serve as both a stimulus and a model to be followed by countries seeking to catch up. In this sense, the circulation of ideas is a mimetic process that involves the tracking of basic steps previously experienced in other countries.

Throughout the process of their being appropriated and emulated, economic ideas are also subject to innovative adaptation and/or distortion. The way in which authors are quoted, the transcription of partial excerpts taken out of their textual context, the translation of widely influential books, are all selective processes of circulation and diffusion that may imply substantial changes to the original meaning of economic texts, as well as to the presentation of economic arguments.

Notes

1 For a global approach to recent examples of the study of the spread of economic ideas in Latin and South American countries, see Cardoso et al. 2014.
2 For a guide to further reading on this topic, see Colander and Coats 1989 and Cardoso 2003.
3 On this topic, see also Withers 2007.
4 On this topic, see Drayton 2000.
5 Many comparative studies have been developed, giving rise to relevant publications in the field, exploring the paths of convergence and divergence in different European countries, USA and Japan. Cf. Augello and Guidi 2001 and 2012.
6 This is the main concern of a recent research project on "*Economics translations into and from European Languages*" (EE-T project), coordinated by Marco Guidi at the University of Pisa, with the main goal of assessing the impact of translations of economic texts on the historical development of economic thought in Europe. Further information on the outcomes of this project is available at: http://eet.pixel-online.org/index.php.

References

Augello, Massimo and Guidi, Marco (eds.), 2001. *The Spread of Political Economy and the Professionalisation of Economists: Economic societies in Europe, America and Japan in the nineteenth century.* London and New York: Routledge.

Augello, Massimo and Guidi, Marco (eds.), 2012. *The Economic Reader: Textbooks and manuals and the dissemination of the economic sciences during the 19th and early 20th centuries.* London and New York: Routledge.

Cardoso, José Luís, 2003. The international diffusion of economic thought. In Samuels, Warren, Jeff Biddle, and John Davis (eds.), *A Companion to the History of Economic Thought.* Oxford and New York: Blackwell, 622–633.

Cardoso, José Luís, Marcuzzo, Maria Cristina, and Romero Sotelo, María Eugenia (eds.), 2014. *Economic Development and Global Crisis: The Latin American economy in historical perspective.* London and New York: Routledge.

Colander, David and Coats, A.W. (eds.), 1989. *The Spread of Economic Ideas.* Cambridge and New York: Cambridge University Press.

Drayton, Richard, 2000. *Nature's Government: Science, Imperial Britain, and the "improvement" of the world.* New Haven, CT and London: Yale University Press.

Forget, Evelyn L., 2010. "At best an echo": eighteenth- and nineteenth-century translation strategies in the history of economics. *History of Political Economy*, 42:4, 653–677.

Gavroglu, Kostas, Papanelopoulou, Faidra, Simões, Ana et al., 2008. Science and technology in the European periphery: some historiographical reflections. *History of Science*, xlvi, 153–175.

Hutcheon, Linda, 2006. *A Theory of Adaptation.* London and New York: Routledge.

Livingstone, David N., 2003. *Putting Science in its Place: Geographies of scientific knowledge.* Chicago and London: University of Chicago Press.

Montgomery, Scott, 2000. *Science in Translation: Movements of knowledge through cultures and time.* Chicago and London: University of Chicago Press.

Ophir, Adi and Shapin, Steven. 1991. The place of knowledge: a methodological survey. *Science in Context*, 4:1, 3–21.

Oz-Salzberger, Fania, 2006. The Enlightenment in translation: regional and European aspects. *European Review of History – Revue européenne d'histoire*, 13:3, 385–409.

Rupke, Nicolaas, 2000. Translation studies in the history of science: the example of "Vestiges." *The British Journal for the History of Science*, 33:2, 209–222.

Sanders, Julie, 2006. *Adaptation and Appropriation.* London and New York: Routledge.

Secord, James A., 2004. Knowledge in transit. *ISIS*, 95:4, 654–672.

Shapin, Steven, 1998. Placing the view from nowhere: historical and sociological problems in the location of science. *Transactions of the Institute of British Geographers*, N-S 23, 5–12.

Solow, Robert, 1989. How economic ideas turn to mush. In Colander, David and Coats, A.W. (eds.). *The Spread of Economic Ideas.* Cambridge and New York: Cambridge University Press, 75–83.

Tymoczko, Maria, 2002. Science in space and time: cultural refraction and linguistic impingement in the shaping of science. *ISIS*, 93:4, 655–657.

Withers, Charles W. J. 2007. *Placing the Enlightenment: thinking geographically about the age of reason.* Chicago: University of Chicago Press.

Part II

Protectionism and free trade in the nineteenth century

3 Latin America and the nineteenth-century British free trade project

Anthony Howe

Introduction

Latin America in many ways provides a microcosm of the rise and fall of the British free trade project in the nineteenth-century world. The beginnings of a shift towards policies of freer trade in Britain in the 1820s corresponded directly with the onset of independence in the former Ibero-Hispanic empires. As a result, Britain's relationship with those emerging postcolonial states was based largely on the model of a free market among commercial republics whose potential was held in greater esteem than reliance upon the "uncivilized" nations of the East. Later, when the East and Africa fell under the sway of competing (and largely protectionist) empires in the later nineteenth century, in Latin America, Britain continued to uphold a "fair field and no favor," although increasingly faced by the commercial power of the United States, often seeking exclusive advantages. At the same time, the Latin American states, building on progress in their primary sectors, sought increasingly to foster domestic manufacturing industries (Platt, 1968, 1972; Albert, 1983; Darwin, 2009, pp. 135–43). After World War I, with British economic paramountcy largely broken, the newly dominant United States herself turned towards the British-style freer trade, with Cordell Hull's "Good Neighbor" policies in many ways based on his understanding of the British model of the relationship between free trade, interdependence, and peace (Butler, 1998; see chapter by Meardon in this volume). Only after 1945 did this model become largely rejected in Latin America, with the emergence of the Prebisch-CEPAL inspired vision of autonomous, state-directed economic development, although the former's ideological content in terms of free markets and state intervention, unilateral or reciprocal free trade, dependence or interdependence, remained an ineluctable part of wider contemporary trade debates (Hirschman, 1961).

Nevertheless, conventional histories of free trade in the nineteenth century have unduly neglected Latin America (Schonhardt-Bailey, 1997; Duckenfield, 2008). Such an omission can be justified if we accept recent views that suggest its independent states always favored protectionism (Coatsworth and Williamson, 2004), or that free trade was in some ways a British-inspired aberration (Manchester, 1933, 1972). Yet this is clearly at variance with much evidence – many historians have detected traces of economic liberalism among the intellectuals, educated elites, and government officials, for whom liberalization of tariffs was an essential part of the optimum prescription for the development of postcolonial economies, justified by Ricardian comparative advantage, fiscal necessity, and the British example as well as in rejection of old imperial models (Love and Jacobsen, 1988; Gootenberg, 1993). Free trade was also a central part of the "Latin American utopia" envisaged by Jeremy Bentham, for whom open commerce was the route to prosperity and peace, as well as to the destruction of the "aristocratic abomination" of a monopolistic colonial trade (Cot, 2014). Even so, more usually free trade has been considered not so much as a voluntary political choice from within Latin American states but as a result of external coercion, imposed by Britain and designed to attach to it peripheral economic satellites. This dependency thesis and its obverse "free trade imperialism" have been extensively discussed and such inconclusive controversies need no repetition here (Mathew, 1968; Platt, 1968, 1972; Winn, 1976; Grosfuguel, 2000). However, within this literature there is an important but unquestioned assumption that "free trade" was a necessary purpose of the British state, a policy upon which all governments, civil servants, economic agents, and British public opinion were as a whole agreed. Nevertheless, such an approach fails to appreciate the degree to which "free trade" in the early years of Latin American independence was still a highly contested notion in Britain, and, as Furtado insightfully noted, by comparison with the advanced economic liberalism of the Brazilian writer Silva Lisboa, in British policy "some mercantilistic biases still prevailed whereas the Brazilian more clearly reflected ideas which were to prevail in England in later years" (Furtado, 1963, p. 101; see chapter by Countinho in this volume). Only therefore after the repeal of the Corn Laws in 1846 was mercantilism eradicated as Britain embarked upon what many considered an ill-fated "free trade experiment" (Howe, 1997). While many other factors contributed to Britain's adoption of free trade, especially the overriding debate on the domestic impact of the Corn Laws (Hilton, 2006), this chapter sets out to explore the degree to which the British free trade project was also in important ways inspired and defined by Britain's relationship with Latin America, notably Brazil, in the years before 1850. For this relationship engendered a vigorous debate which neatly paralleled that over the Corn Laws, for it embraced the central values of economic freedom, those of slavery, monopoly, and empire. The renegotiation of economic relations between Britain and Latin America in this period therefore had lasting implications for Britain as a "free trade nation" and for Latin America as an emerging region of the world economy. In particular, in the crucial decade of the 1840s, it was Britain's experience of Latin America which conditioned in important ways her adoption of "free trade" in its fullest unilateral form.

Before the Repeal of the Corn Laws in 1846, Britain's commitment to free trade was by no means full-blown; its system is far better conceived as one of "modified mercantilism" (Howe, 2002, pp. 193–213). Nowhere was this better demonstrated than in its relations with Latin America, based on reciprocity treaties, guaranteeing British shipping and British goods against discrimination, whilst in return Latin American states were guaranteed reciprocal treatment in Britain (Williams, 1972, pp. 252–91). Nor was Britain's yet a "free trade empire," rather imperial preference was deeply entrenched, favoring West Indian sugar in particular, but extended as late as 1843 to Canadian wheat; Brazilian sugar was in practice virtually excluded from the British market by high duties on "foreign" (i.e., not colonial) sugar while Brazilian coffee also faced duties almost double those on the colonial product (Brown, 1958, pp. 198–9). Britain in the 1840s was also engaged in an extensive search for new commercial relationships with the bulk of the world, not on a free trade basis but on the basis of reciprocity, a view which found important support from the economist Robert Torrens, whose ideas were well-known among the political elite, cited, for example, by the prime minister Sir Robert Peel when defending his commercial policy in what became known as the "political economy parliament" (*Hansard*, Apr. 25, 1843; Disraeli, 1880, chap. lxxi; Fetter, 1980, pp. 51–2). Nevertheless by 1846, this modified mercantilism had been blown apart; the repeal of the Corn Laws in 1846 signified the adoption of unilateral in place of reciprocal free trade; it determined equally the end of policies of preference within the British empire and of the Navigation Acts, which had since the seventeenth century sought to favor British shipping; it foreshadowed universal free trade. This was a huge new departure in Britain's economic relationship with the wider world. While many factors contributed to the political crisis which led to the repeal of the Corn Laws, Britain's relations with Latin America in the early 1840s played an important part both in shaping the arguments of radical free traders, and in shifting the government away from its favored path of reciprocity towards a unilateral model of free trade, which subsequently became the "British model." In this process, in the 1830s and early 1840s, before the Corn Laws became the all-consuming issue, Brazil was at the center of trade debate in Britain for its contested relationship with Britain involved three fundamental issues, reciprocal commercial treaties versus a unilateral tariff policy, free labor versus slave labor, and free trade versus imperial preference.

Latin America and British free trade in the 1840s

Reciprocity had dominated British trade policy before the 1840s. In the 1820s, the British model of freer trade set up by the so-called "father of free trade" William Huskisson was typically based on reciprocity treaties, although the most-favored nation clause had vastly extended their impact (Hilton, 1977; Cardoso, 2013). Notoriously but exceptionally in its 1827 treaty with Brazil, Britain had stipulated maximum customs duties of 15 percent on imports of its goods into Brazil. But the stipulation of 15 percent maximum duties in this treaty, the source of much controversy by the 1830s, was based on the high-handed action of the British diplomat on the spot Sir Charles Stuart, acting against the wishes of the liberal Tory ministers Canning and Huskisson whose commercial diplomacy had been based on the abandonment of the search for exclusive privileges (Manchester, 1933; 1972; Pryor, 1965). With great foresight, Huskisson wrote to Canning lamenting that the 15 percent maximum would create such "jealousy and ill-will" as to cancel out any commercial advantages, while for Canning the treaty was "foolish & mischievous." This treaty has been rightly considered as not only "a patent anachronism within the context of British commercial policy" but also ill-adapted to "the liberal spirit of economic thinking in Brazil" (Pryor, 1965, p. 47). Understandably therefore by the late 1830s many were calling into question this system, both in Latin America where the reality of reciprocity in the existing treaties was doubted and in Britain, where, as Lucy Brown (1958; "A member of the Brazilian Association," 1833) showed many years ago, the Board of Trade officials charged with their negotiation, had ceased to value such treaties. The growing complexity of trade negotiations, even in the 1840s, seemed increasingly to suggest the desirability of unilateral free trade. But this met little political favor; many, rather, as in the 1820s, continued to advocate the search for special privileges in return for British political support. This interventionist strategy was advocated in the much-cited "Murray memorandum" of December 1841 designed to guide the new Tory government of Sir Robert Peel (1841–6) in its Latin American policy (The National Archives [hereafter TNA], Foreign Office [hereafter FO] 97/284; Platt, 1968, pp. 321–2; Miller, 1993, p. 51; Knights, 1999). At the same time, William Gladstone, on taking up the commercial treaty reins at the Board of Trade, wrote a long memorandum for Peel emphasizing the importance of commercial negotiations in future policy (British Library [hereafter BL], Additional Manuscript [hereafter Add. MS] 40470, fos. 17–40, March 24, 1843; Hyde, 1934, pp. 54–80 and Appendix V). In the 1840s, Britain undertook a whole range of such negotiations, above all, with France, Portugal, and not least Brazil. Slavery complicated the latter negotiations (as we will see) but at this point Britain still retained a diplomatic belief in the value of such treaties, and sought, if possible, to retain the special privileges granted in 1827. This was therefore the background to the renegotiation of Britain's treaty with Brazil which had been attempted in the mid-1830s but which became a pressing issue in the early 1840s.

Brazil at this time was of major importance to British trade. Calculations as to how important varied but many suggested that it was Britain's third most important trading partner (Sturz, 1837). The Whig President of the Board of Trade, C. P. Thomson, in 1839 claimed that it was second only to the United States (*Hansard*, June 28, 1839); others placed it fourth after the United States, the German Zollverein, the East and West Indies (Ritchie, 1844, p. 39).[1] In particular it should be noted it was the largest single market for British cotton goods, and hence of great interest to the Manchester Chamber of Commerce (Redford, 1934, pp. 97–9, 101–3, 106, 146).[2] In fact,

Brazil remained until 1903 the most valuable single market for Lancashire's cotton goods; among those products, in printed goods, it replaced the United States as Britain's best customer in 1834 and retained that position until 1894 (Farnie, 1979, p. 94; "Our trade with Brazil," *The League*, Dec. 30, 1843). For Richard Sheil, Whig Vice-President of the Board of Trade (1839–41), here was "that splendid mart which is opened to us, in the young and prosperous empire of Brazil" (*Hansard*, May 18, 1841). This trade was largely an exchange of British manufactures for Brazilian agrarian produce, with coffee replacing cotton as the leading commodity, although Brazil remained Britain's third most important supplier of raw cotton until 1852 (Farnie, 1979, p. 94). Against this background, contemporaries debated the value of the Anglo-Brazilian treaty. In the light of Britain's strong anti-slavery predilections (which had led to the abolition of slavery in the British empire in 1834), some were now ready to argue that Britain should turn to the East for new markets. But in a British economy in deep crisis in the late 1830s, all markets were seen as vital; Brazil, given its European heritage, was esteemed by many as potentially far more valuable than "uncivilized" Eastern markets, and increasingly those most concerned with trade, the mercantile elites and radical free traders, argued not for the renewal of the Anglo-Brazilian treaty due to expire in 1842 (or 1844)[3] but for complete free trade with Brazil, abandoning any search for special or exclusive privileges and deploring attempts to interfere with Brazil's tariff policy. Among such advocates, the recently formed *Economist* (Feb. 24, 1845, p. 505), for example, argued that this was a vital matter of domestic legislation, not one for trade bargaining.

Brazil therefore now became a test case of the value of reciprocal free trade. For contemporary discussion over the renewal of its treaty with Britain provided the basis of the case for repudiating such treaties and for shaping a completely new trade policy in which commercial treaties as a whole would be abandoned; in effect Britain was urged to become a new type of "Great Power," relying on the force of its own free trade example to influence the world's economy, a linkage between free trade and British hegemony which has been much discussed (Clark, 2011). The case for the abandonment of all commercial negotiations in favor of unilateral tariff-making, had been strongly put forward, in part on the evidence of the protracted and fruitless negotiations with Brazil, in an important debate in the House of Commons in 1843, with support from Radical free traders such as Cobden, C. P. Villiers, and William Ewart as well as Whig leaders such as Lord John Russell (*Hansard*, Apr. 25, 1843; "Monopolist-Tariffs – Reciprocity," *The League*, Jan. 13, 1844). Such ideas did not lead to an immediate reversal of government policy but became an important part of the way in which trade policy was conceived; subsequently (after the repeal of the Corn Laws in 1846) a doctrine of unilateralism in trade policy encouraged Peelite Conservatives such as Gladstone not simply to acquiesce in a new course but enthusiastically to embrace it as did the Whig party which came to office in 1846 (Howe, 1997, pp. 38–69). Hence when the negotiations for the renewal of the treaty with Brazil "failed," such failure was in fact recast in the light of the positive adoption of a new trade strategy, one of free intercourse with all the nations of the world.

We should also note that it was against this background of debate that Robert Torrens produced his famous defense of reciprocity, not a work of abstract reasoning but a series of letters to politicians designed to warn them against moving towards unilateral free trade (Robbins, 1958; Irwin, 1996). Torrens in particular warned against the unconditional (unilateral) removal of duties as a "bounty upon the continuance of hostile tariffs," while supporting differential duties in favor of the British empire at the expense of Cuba and Brazil whose producers would be made "tributary to England and her tropical colonies" until they relaxed their own import duties. This use of retaliation, he believed, would promote long-term prosperity, "nothing could more powerfully conduce to the restoration of commercial prosperity than an extended trade under a scale of duties imposed, not for protection, but for revenue, with the flourishing island of Cuba and the extensive empire of Brazil" (Torrens, 1844, "Postscript to a letter to Sir Robert Peel," pp. 331–56). While Torrens feared that the influence of the radical Anti-Corn Law League ("an electioneering confederacy") would replace the reciprocity principles of Huskisson and Ricardo in the formulation of commercial policy, in advocating retaliation, he tended to ignore the extent to which cumulative disappointment with such trade bargaining, of which the interminable Brazilian negotiations were a good example, had become a vital pragmatic factor in encouraging the British government to move from reciprocity towards unilateralism.

Disillusionment with commercial bargaining cannot be put down solely to the negotiations with Brazil but they seemed to many to illustrate the travails of haggling and meddling in a way which it seemed increasingly desirable to avoid. Many too became aware of the damage done by Britain's own past protectionist commercial model which had misguided foreign nations, causing them to adopt a "most irrational, most pernicious view" (Gladstone, 1845, p. 61, cf. Gladstone, 1843). This at least was the conclusion of Gladstone, who completely reversed his position of 1843, coming by 1845 to argue that Britain, on this question of "immense moment," should rely on the example of her own prosperity under free trade to encourage others to move in this direction, to abandon any policy of retaliation as "suicidal." Here too was a distinct break with Peel's search for a wide range of reciprocal commercial treaties in 1842 (*Hansard*, Mar. 11, 1842).[4] Gladstone, as a minister in Sir Robert Peel's Conservative government, distanced himself at this stage from complete free trade but he was well aware that the radical free traders were ready to promote "the commercial intercourse of men on the footing of universal brotherhood" (Gladstone, 1845, p. 62).[5] It is true that some Whig politicians and diplomats later revived the notion of a reciprocity treaty with Brazil (Pryor, 1965, pp. 377–8; Bethell, 1970),[6] while Torrens, adhering to his reciprocity strategy, cultivated the support of the Protectionist leader Disraeli. But after 1846 the tide had turned towards completely sweeping away all protection in Britain, incidentally removing in its wake any need for the retaliation Brazil had contemplated in its 1844 tariff after the failure of the treaty negotiations (Hamilton to Aberdeen, Jan. 21, 1845, BL Add. MS 43160, fos. 74–82; "Brazilian Tariff – Retaliation," *Economist* (Oct. 26, 1844); "The Brazilians and our Duties on their Sugars," ibid. (May 3, 1845); Bethell, 1970, pp. 239–40). Torrens' ideas, as Irwin has argued, remained the "most widely acknowledged and generally accepted restriction to free trade admitted by economic theory" but they lost political relevance after the Protectionist party abandoned its opposition to free trade in the early 1850s (Irwin, 1996, p. 115; Brown, 1943).[7]

Sugar and slavery

In the Anglo-Brazilian negotiations, the main stumbling block to the renewal of the 1827 treaty was in fact slavery, not reciprocity. The 1827 treaty had been preceded by one in 1826 in which Brazil agreed to move towards slave abolition but abolition had made little progress (Bethell, 1970). Indeed, the lack of progress now encouraged the British government to re-entwine commerce and politics in a very un-*laissez-faire* manner in its negotiations for the renewal of the treaty. For the position of the government was quite clearly one which sought political gains from economic instruments, quite contrary to any theories of the invisible hand. Thus, the Foreign Secretary, Aberdeen, wrote bluntly: "This [abolition of slavery] is the condition upon which the British market will be opened to Brazilian sugar" (Aberdeen to Ellis, Sept. 28, 1842, TNA, FO131/12). However, this in turn precipitated a volte-face in attitudes, for the Brazilian refusal to compromise on this issue prompted economic radicals to disavow diplomatic (and indeed physical) means towards abolition of the slave trade in favor of the free market. Brazilian tenacity over slavery proved a crucial turning-point in British free trade and slavery debates.[8] For the leading advocates of radical free trade such as Richard Cobden argued strongly that free labor must prove more productive than slave labor and that free trade was the only solution to the slavery question; that only the free market, and neither treaties nor the British Navy's African squadron would lead to its abolition; rather such sanctions would make Brazil more reluctant to abandon slavery. For the radicals this strengthened the case for non-intervention in foreign policy as the complement of free trade, although the British government itself was still ready to exchange political support for moral rewards by offering to intervene, on Brazil's behalf, in the River Plate in return for a commercial treaty and a slave trade agreement (Aberdeen to Howden, Dec. 4, 1844, BL Add. MS 43160, fos. 74–82; Bethell, 1970, pp. 240–1; McLean, 1995).

Against this background, Brazil played a central part in the British debate over the sugar duties, for, despite supposed reciprocity, in practice Britain excluded Brazil's main potential commodity for the British market, slave-grown sugar (Williams, 1964). This debate over sugar led in many interesting directions, however, for it paralleled and coincided with the vibrant contemporary debates over the deleterious effects of the Corn Laws in Britain. For example, it was argued that British working-class consumers were denied not only "cheap bread" but also cheap sugar (namely that of Brazil and Cuba) by the abolitionist exclusion of slave-grown sugar from the British market (Porter, 1841, p. 28).[9] The asymmetrical trade pattern was also criticized, for while Brazil had become a leading importer of British goods, she had in effect been denied a market for her leading return good, so reducing Brazilian demand for British goods in the long run; British shipping also suffered from a lack of direct return cargoes, although many were employed in indirect trade to third markets, for example, employed in transporting coffee to the Cape of Good Hope, which was then transhipped to England as a colonial product (Brown, 1958, p. 150).[10] At the same time, it was widely pointed out that Britain was beginning to face competition in Latin American markets, from Germany and the United States, raising the possibility of further trade losses (Pryor, 1965, p. 268). Interestingly in this context, the advocate of protectionism in the German states Friedrich List was a particularly strong proponent of a commercial agreement between Brazil and the Zollverein (Boianovsky, 2013). Nor were moral arguments lacking with radical free traders pointing to the hypocrisy involved in the use of slave-grown raw material by Britain's leading industrialized sector, cotton, as well as in transporting Brazilian sugar in British ships to third markets.[11] Above all, Britain's discriminatory duties against slave-grown sugar were condemned by Cobden, leader of the Anti-Corn Law League, ready to prove, in the context of "putting discriminating duties upon the produce of our colonies & Brazil," "the unsoundness of any & every measure which is incompatible with the most perfect freedom of trade" (Cobden to Joseph Sturge, Feb. 26, 1841; Howe, 2007, p. 216). As Morgan has shown, Cobden's influence proved crucial in moving the anti-slavery cause away from its support for trade discrimination, but, as Huzzey too has argued, free trade contained its own moral economy of abolition; this was a change of means, not of goals (Morgan, 2009; Huzzey, 2010). The debate on Brazil therefore in the early 1840s played an influential part in reorienting the anti-slavery movement and in highlighting the wider moral implications of free trade, for the radical British free trade model become one in which the free market itself would achieve the moral goal of abolition, dispensing with the costly suppression activities of the Royal Navy (Howe, 2010, pp. 128, 233, 234–5, 268, 270; Huzzey, 2012, pp. 113–24). Only free trade, such abolitionists believed, "can destroy slavery," for "Free labour must drive out of the market the labour of the slave" (Ritchie, 1844, pp. 8, 20). Leading free traders, including Bright, Cobden, and Gibson, became persistent critics of the activities of the Navy off the coast of Brazil.[12] The growth of trade with Brazil, they believed, would provide greater leverage against slavery and encourage Brazilian opinion to turn against it, so that slave-holding would peaceably disappear.[13] But "for this country to attempt to control the social state of other countries by our fiscal arrangements was a complete mistake" (James Oswald, cited in Huzzey, 2012, p. 103). Here was an important step towards free trade becoming not simply a commercial strategy but an all-enveloping *Weltanschauung*. Once again this was not a position the Conservative Government of Sir Robert Peel was yet ready to adopt – his government retained (while lowering) the differential duties on both sugar and coffee (Bethell, 1970, p. 240) – but the case for the equalization of slave- and free-grown sugar duties had been powerfully made. Brazilian sugar thus proved a battering-ram against abolitionist-inspired trade discrimination but at the same time spawned a new abolitionism centered on free trade.

Empire and emancipation: ending the "corn, sugar, coffee and timber oligarchy"

The British sugar duty debates concerned not only the question of slavery, but also had far-reaching implications for the economic organization of the British empire, the third great issue which arose from the Anglo-Brazilian commercial connection. For in effect the existence of differential duties on free- and slave-grown sugar was vital to a system of imperial preference which had existed since the seventeenth century. At the same time any progress on slavery in Brazil was, as Gladstone noted, not only a question of humanity but would also affect "the colonial interests who would have less claim to protection" (Gladstone to Aberdeen, Oct. 16, 1841, BL Add. MS 44088, fos. 29–32).[14] According to the radical *Liverpool Mercury* (Jan. 5, 1844; Mar. 14, 1845), the breaking-off of negotiations with Brazil in 1844 was in fact a deliberate attempt by the Tory government to give a lifeline to the West Indian interest, while the continuing preference for the British empire indicated that "we are throwing away a lucrative and most extensive trade with Cuba and Brazil" "to benefit the West Indies." Hence Brazil and Cuba were intimately part of a debate on the reshaping of the British empire in the 1840s, with the radical free traders ready to abandon, not British rule, but its reliance on market distortions, urging that the West Indies would thrive best under free trade, accepting the greater productivity of free labor and the potential benefits of competition even with slave-grown products.

The growing opposition to imperial preference was perfectly well-grounded in economic theory (Schulyer, 1945; Winch, 1965), although disputed by Torrens, as we have seen, but the political cutting edge came from the 1840s debate over the slave-grown sugar of Latin America. Once support for the exclusion of slave-grown sugar was abandoned, the whole edifice of surviving mercantilism in Britain would be threatened. Hence the radical free traders sought to use the issue of Brazilian sugar to undermine the wider case for monopoly and empire. Thus, Cobden cited a Brazilian senator who had reputedly denounced the British as "the slaves of a corn, sugar, coffee, and timber oligarchy" (*Hansard*, Apr. 25, 1843). The free trade case against the Corn Laws protecting the landed interest was seen as identical to that against the protected sugar interests of the West Indies. This protected vested interest (the "preference interest," "M.T.B." [John Macgregor], 1841a; Macgregor, 1841b) was seen as providing a shield for the landed interest under the Corn Laws; thus, for Henry Labouchere, the erstwhile Whig President of the Board of Trade (1839–41), in a debate on "Relations with Brazil," the sugar duties were "the buttress and bulwark of the Corn Laws" (*Hansard*, Mar. 7, 1844). Existing commercial policy was identified with "class legislation" to the detriment of the "industrious classes" and so linked to the disaffection of the laboring classes, the source of many a contemporary fear of revolution at a time of widespread working-class unrest in the form of the Chartist movement (*Economist*, Feb. 24, 1844; Hilton, 2006). Here too the argument was powerfully made by the radical free traders that once the West Indian monopoly was abolished, the Corn Laws would follow. Or rather that it was only in order to defend the Corn Laws that a Tory government continued to retain preference for the West Indies. For most arguments in favor of admitting slave-grown sugar, especially those of consumer welfare and export growth were equally, if not more, applicable to corn. But it also followed that once the Corn Laws were repealed, imperial preference would also disappear – which it swiftly did. For, following the collapse of the Tory government after Repeal, the new Whig Prime Minister Lord John Russell moved immediately to equalize (albeit gradually) the foreign and colonial sugar duties in July 1846 (Howe, 1997, pp. 40–56). The older school of abolitionists proved impotent, lamenting, "the slave masters and the slave traffickers of Brazil have won a triumph which will fill their hearts with joy" (Temperley, 1972, p. 161).[15] As a result, after 1846, Protectionist critics of the Whig government, such as Bentinck and Disraeli, continued to believe that the interests of Brazil had been put before those of the British empire (*Hansard*, July 27 and 28, 1846, respectively).

Conclusion: did Latin America "impose" free trade on Britain?

Britain's adoption of free trade, cemented by the repeal of the Corn Laws in 1846, was influenced by a wide range of factors (Schonhardt-Bailey, 2006). Nevertheless, in the crisis of 1846, occasioned by the growing famine in Ireland, the attractiveness of unilateral free trade rather than the Protectionist remedy of suspending temporarily the Corn Laws, was in part conditioned by the earlier debates through which Latin America was vitally connected with the future of free trade in Britain, and in turn the world economic order. Those debates had highlighted the issues of reciprocity, slave labor, and imperial preference, and had fully acknowledged the importance of Latin America and its connections with the British economy. To a large extent the problem of Brazil in particular had provided a battering ram against surviving mercantilist ideas which remained an important influence on the "protectionist" government of Sir Robert Peel (1841–6). In this way many of the defenses of the ideological structure of protectionism had been weakened before the Repeal of the Corn Laws in 1846, and it was her Latin American experience in the early 1840s that in important and neglected ways pushed

Britain towards unilateral free trade, towards ending imperial preference, and to rethinking the anti-slavery cause. For the failure of the Anglo-Brazilian negotiations marked the end of the old commercial order in which nations sought commercial advantage at the expense of others. John Stuart Mill would later spell out the lesson that "a nation adopting this policy is a novelty in the world; so much so, it would appear that many are unable to believe it when they see it" (Mill, 1859, p. 111). As Mill rightly foresaw, the British free trade experiment in 1846 would engender as much suspicion and Anglophobia as its long practice of mercantilism had done.

Latin America had therefore played a significant part in the evolution of a new global economic order in the 1840s, although at this stage she remained only partly integrated into it, for example, with Brazil only abolishing slavery in 1888; nor was there lacking a strong strain of native hostility to the new economic order, with, for example, one Brazilian politician reported to reject "that European civilization which makes us the slaves of the axioms of certain economists at the expense of the internal prosperity of the Country."[16] However, what is clear is that Britain had no power to impose its favored economic regime in Latin America; rather it was the failure of Britain's Latin American commercial diplomacy which constrained Britain's policy choices and encouraged her to adopt the more radical principles of free trade which would define both her position in the world order but also the political character of the "free trade nation."[17] Many of those who upheld such values also believed they would benefit Latin America, that, as radicals since Adam Smith had argued, free commerce would not only free slaves but also reduce the power of postcolonial landed elites and encourage political liberalization. As a modernizing ideology, the advance of free trade ideas in Europe met a positive response in diverse but not necessarily atypical circles, including Colombia tobacco merchants, Brazilian bureaucrats, and Argentinian land-owners, for whom liberal political economy continued to promise agricultural specialization, rising revenues, and diversification of manufactures while finally undermining the hold of the "financial prejudices" inherited from former colonial rule (Graham, 1970, pp. 105–10; Love and Jacobsen, 1988, *passim*). This was confirmed in Brazil by its governmental inquiry in 1853 into the working of the tariff it had unilaterally adopted in 1844. This concluded that the best development strategy for Brazil lay, not in protective duties, but technical education, a revenue tariff, and capital investment in industry (not slavery), so reaping "the benefits of a produce-exporting economy in a world of economic interdependence" (Pryor, 1965, pp. 399–400; Graham, 1970, p. 107). Here was in embryo a national strategy for growth and emancipation, for, as the leading Brazilian essayist, Aureliano Bastos (1839–75), proclaimed, "factories in Brazil are an accident; agriculture is the true national industry" (1862, cited in Love, 1996, p. 143; Graham, 1970, pp. 108–10). Nevertheless, a growing number of critics of free trade would later discern in such policies the subordination of a peripheral nation to the imperatives of a dominant Western economy.

Notes

1 "... the fourth foreign market we have, we are about to lose." Significantly, Ritchie had resigned from the British & Foreign Anti-Slavery Society over this issue, Huzzey, 2012, pp. 104–5.
2 In giving evidence to the 1840 Select Committee on Import Duties, the President of the Chamber, J. B. Smith, stated "Brazil is now become the best customer we have in the world for cotton goods" (qu. 2042), *Parliamentary Papers* 1840 (601).
3 The actual date of expiry was a matter of dispute between Britain and Brazil.
4 Gladstone noted "Nor can I deem it wise to diminish the hope of satisfactorily arranging these relaxations with foreign nations by rashly reducing the amount of duties on articles which must form the bases of negotiation," March 11, 1842, *Hansard*, vol. 61 cc. 452–3.
5 See too Gladstone, 1845, pp. 53–4 for his justification of gradual liberalisation, cf. those who saw "it [commercial restriction] as an evil necessarily greater than that of a sharp and violent transition to freedom; as a source of all our economical difficulties; and even as a violation of the law of God."
6 Howden upheld reciprocity as a "great maxim of political economy" as the Whigs toyed with the idea of further negotiations with Brazil, Pryor, 1965, pp. 377–8; Bethell, 1970, pp. 278–82.
7 Ideas of reciprocity later revived in a "fair trade" context, Brown, 1943.
8 Brazil refused to negotiate unless its sugar was admitted to the British market and declined "to connect the subject of the abolition of slavery with a Commercial Treaty," Aberdeen to Gladstone, Oct. 1, 1843, BL Add MS 43670, fos. 56–7.
9 "... we plead for the over-taxed and under-fed hard-working men and women of Great Britain" (p. 28). See too Ritchie, 1844, p. 38, "we would not damp the sympathy which is felt for the enslaved *producer* of sugar in Brazil; but we would claim the same portion of sympathy on behalf of the toil-worn *consumer* at home"; "The Burthen of the Sugar Monopoly," *The League* (Nov. 11, 1843).
10 In addition, much Brazilian sugar was carried in British ships, to the extent of 23,889 tons in 1845, Huzzey, 2012, pp. 103–4.
11 For the "sheer impossibility of imagining a British economy without any slave-grown imports" as "perhaps the greatest single impediment to excluding slave grown sugar on anti-slavery grounds," Huzzey, 2012, p. 102.
12 See for example the debate on the Aberdeen (Brazilian) treaty, Apr. 24, 1849, *Hansard*, vol. 104, cc. 757–806. They argued that not only did the Royal Navy fail to achieve suppression of the slave trade but such activities gave rise to greater expenditure and fostered resort to warfare.
13 By contrast, *The Economist* warned, the British policy of discrimination against slave-grown produce not only damaged Britain materially but destroyed "our moral influence over the Brazilian empire," May 17, 1845, p. 454.
14 At this point Gladstone had been advised by Porter at the Board of Trade that Brazil "would negotiate upon the basis of the 'gradual' extinction of slavery."
15 Lord Brougham decried the Sugar Duties Bill as " 'A Bill for encouraging by a high Premium the Brazilian and Cuban Planter to bring over from Africa 40,000 Africans' – freemen as yourselves at this moment – for the purpose of making them slaves in the plantations of the New World," July 27, 1846, *Hansard*, vol. 88, c. 9.
16 Cited in Ellis to Aberdeen, from *O Brazil* (Apr. 30, 1844), BL Add. MS 43160, fos. 21 ff.
17 Torrens (1844, p. 63), for example, believed the fate of the Whig aristocracy was at stake in Britain's rejecting reciprocity in favor of unilateral free trade, Letter X (Dec. 17, 1843).

References

Albert, B. 1983. *South America and the World Economy from Independence to 1930*, London, Macmillan.
Bethell, L. 1970. *The Abolition of the Brazilian Slave Trade: Britain, Brazil and the Slave Trade Question, 1807–1869*, Cambridge, Cambridge University Press.
Boianovsky, M. 2013. Friedrich List and the economic fate of tropical countries, *History of Political Economy*, vol. 45, no. 4, 647–91.
British Library [BL], Additional Manuscript [Add. MS].
Brown, B. H. 1943. *The Tariff Reform Movement in Great Britain, 1881–1895*, New York, Columbia University Press.
Brown, L. 1958. *The Board of Trade and the Free-Trade Movement, 1830–1842*, Oxford, Clarendon Press.
Butler, M. A. 1998. *Cautious Visionary: Cordell Hull and Trade Reform, 1933–1937*, Kent, OH, The Kent State University Press.
Cardoso, J. L. 2013. Lifting the continental blockade: Britain, Portugal and Brazilian trade in the global context of the Napoleonic Wars, in Coppolaro, L. and McKenzie, F. (eds.), *A Global History of Trade and Conflict since 1500*, Basingstoke, Palgrave, pp. 87–104.
Clark, I. 2011. *Hegemony in International Society*, Oxford, Oxford University Press.
Coatsworth, J. H. and Williamson, J. G. 2004. Always protectionist? Latin American tariffs from independence to the Great Depression, *Journal of Latin American Studies*, vol. 36, no. 2, 205–32.
Cot, A. L. 2014, Jeremy Bentham's Spanish American Utopia, in Cardozo, J. L., Marcuzzo, M. C., and Romero Sotelo, M. A. (eds.), *Economic Development and Global Crisis: The Latin American Economy in Historical Perspective*, London, Routledge, pp. 34–52.
Darwin, J. 2009, *The Empire Project: The Rise and Fall of the British World System*, Cambridge, Cambridge University Press.
Disraeli, B. 1880. *Endymion*, London, Longmans, Green.
Duckenfield, M. ed. 2008. *Battles over Free Trade* (4 vols), London, Pickering & Chatto.
Economist, 1843–6.
Farnie, D. A. 1979. *The English Cotton Industry and the World Market, 1815–1896*, Oxford, Clarendon Press.
Fetter, F. W. 1980. *The Economist in Parliament: 1780–1868*, Durham, NC, Duke University Press.
Furtado, C. 1963. *The Economic Growth of Brazil: A Survey from Colonial to Modern Times*, Berkeley, CA, University of California Press.
Gladstone, W. E. 1843. The course of commercial policy at home and abroad, *Foreign and Colonial Quarterly*, vol. 3.
Gladstone, W. E. 1845. *Remarks upon recent commercial legislation, suggested by the expository statement of revenue from customs and other papers lately submitted to Parliament*, London, John Murray.
Gootenberg, P. 1993. *Imagining Development: Economic Ideas in Peru's 'Fictitious Prosperity' of Guano, 1840–1880*, Berkeley, CA, University of California Press.
Graham, R. 1970. *Britain and the Onset of Modernization in Brazil, 1850–1914*, Cambridge, Cambridge University Press.

Grosfoguel, R. 2000. Developmentalism, modernity, and dependency theory in Latin America, *Nepantia: Views from the South*, vol. 1, no. 2, 347–74.

Hansard's Parliamentary Debates, third series.

Hilton, A. J. B. 1977. *Corn, Cash, Commerce: The Economic Policies of the Tory Governments, 1815–1830*, Oxford, Oxford University Press.

Hilton, B. 2006. *A Mad, Bad, and Dangerous People? England, 1783–1846*, Oxford, Clarendon Press.

Hirschman, A. O. 1961. Ideologies of economic development in Latin America, in Hirschman, A. O. (ed.), *Latin American Issues: Essays and Comments*, New York, Twentieth Century Fund, pp. 205–32.

Howe, A. 1997. *Free Trade and Liberal England, 1846–1946*, Oxford, Clarendon Press.

Howe, A. 2002. Restoring free trade: the British experience, 1776–1873, in Winch, D. and O'Brien, P. K. (eds.), *The Political Economy of British Economic Experience, 1688–1914*, Oxford, The British Academy, pp. 193–213.

Howe, A. ed. 2007. *The Letters of Richard Cobden. Vol. 1. 1815–1847*, Oxford, Oxford University Press.

Howe, A. ed. 2010. *The Letters of Richard Cobden. Vol. 2. 1848–1853*, Oxford, Oxford University Press.

Huzzey, R. 2010. Free trade, free labour, and slave sugar in Victorian Britain, *Historical Journal*, vol. 53, no. 2, 359–79.

Huzzey, R.2012. *Freedom Burning: Anti-Slavery and Empire in Victorian Britain*, Ithaca, NY and London, Cornell University Press.

Hyde, F. E. 1934. *Mr Gladstone at the Board of Trade*, London, Cobden-Sanderson.

Irwin, D. 1996. *Against the Tide: An Intellectual History of Free Trade*, Princeton, NY, Princeton University Press.

Knights, A. 1999. Britain and Latin America, in Porter, A. (ed.), *The Oxford History of the British Empire: The Nineteenth Century*, Oxford, Oxford University Press.

The League, 1843–6.

Liverpool Mercury 1844–5.

Love, J. L. 1996. *Crafting the Third World: Theorizing Underdevelopment in Rumania and Brazil*, Stanford, CA, Stanford University Press.

Love, J. L. and Jacobsen, N. eds. 1988. *Guiding the Invisible Hand: Economic Liberalism and the State in Latin America History*, New York, Praeger.

'M.T.B.' [Macgregor, J.] 1841a. *The Preference Interests or the Miscalled Protective Duties, Shown to be Public Oppression. Addressed to All Classes and Parties*, London, Henry Hooper.

Macgregor, J. 1841b. *The Common Sense View of the Sugar Question, Addressed to All Classes and Parties*, London, Henry Hooper.

McLean, D. 1995. *War, Diplomacy, and Informal Empire: Britain and the Republics of La Plata, 1836–1853*, London, British Academy Press.

Manchester, A. K. 1933; 1972. *British Preeminence in Brazil: Its Rise and Decline*, Chapel Hill, University of North Carolina Press; reprinted, New York, Octagon Books.

Mathew, W. M. 1968. The imperialism of free trade: Peru, 1820–70, *Economic History Review*, N.S. vol. 21, 562–79.

"A member of the Brazilian Association of Liverpool," 1833. *Some Remarks and Explanatory Observations on a petition to Parliament from the merchants and ship owners of Liverpool praying for the admission to consumption of the productions of Brazil*, Liverpool, G. and J. Robinson.

Mill, J. S. 1859. A few words on non-intervention, in *The Collected Works of John Stuart Mill* ed. F. E. I. Priestley et al. (33 vols), vol. XXI, Toronto, University of Toronto Press.

Miller, R. 1993. *Britain and Latin America in the Nineteenth and Twentieth Centuries*, London, Longman.

Morgan, S. J. 2009. The Anti-Corn Law League and British anti-slavery in transatlantic perspective, *Historical Journal*, vol. 52, no. 1, 87–107.

Platt, D. C. M. 1968. *Finance, Trade and Politics: British Foreign Policy, 1815–1914*, Oxford, Oxford University Press.

Platt, D. C. M. 1972. *Latin America and British Trade, 1806–1914*, London, Adam and Charles Black.

Porter, G. R. 1841. *The Many Sacrificed to the Few, Proved by the Effects of the Sugar Monopoly*, London, Henry Hooper.

Pryor, A. J. 1965. "Anglo-Brazilian Commercial Relations and the Evolution of Brazilian Tariff Policy, 1822–1850," unpublished University of Cambridge PhD thesis.

Redford, A. 1934. *Manchester Merchants and Foreign Trade, 1794–1858*, Manchester, Manchester University Press.

Ritchie, J. E. 1844. *Thoughts on Slavery and Cheap Sugar*, London, Aylott and Jones.

Robbins, L. 1958. *Robert Torrens and the Evolution of Classical Economics*, London, Macmillan & Co.

Schonhardt-Bailey, C. ed. 1997. *The Rise of Free Trade* (4 vols), London, Routledge.

Schonhardt-Bailey, C. 2006. *From the Corn Laws to Free Trade: Interests, Ideas, and Institutions in Historical Perspective*, Cambridge, MA, MIT Press.

Schuyler, R. L. 1945. *The Fall of the Old Colonial System*, New York, Oxford University Press.

Sturz, J. J. 1837. *A Review, Financial, Statistical, and Commercial of the Empire of Brazil and its Resources, together with a suggestion of the expediency and mode of admitting Brazilian and other foreign sugars into Great Britain for refining and exportation*, London: Effingham Wilson.

Temperley, H. 1972. *British Anti-Slavery, 1833–1870*, London, University of South Carolina Press, Columbia S.C. and London, Longman.

The National Archives [TNA], London.

Torrens, R. 1844. *The Budget: On Commercial and Colonial Policy*, London, Smith, Elder.

Williams, E. 1964 (first ed. 1944). *Capitalism and Slavery*, London, André Deutsch.

Williams, J. B. 1972. *British Commercial Policy and Trade Expansion, 1750–1850*, Oxford, Clarendon Press.

Winch, D. 1965. *Classical Political Economy and Colonies*. London, G. Bell & Sons.

Winn, P. 1976. British informal empire in Uruguay in the nineteenth century, *Past & Present*, no. 73, 100–26.

4 Silva Lisboa on free trade and slave labor

The fate of liberalism in a colonial country

Maurício C. Coutinho

1 Introduction

José da Silva Lisboa (1756–1835), a Brazilian-Portuguese political economy writer and a controversial figure in the Brazilian political scene, is taken as a prototypical liberal both in Portugal and in Brazil. Since the edition of his first political economy book, *Princípios de Economia Política* (1804, *Princípios* hereafter),[1] he defended liberal economic principles and emphasized his strong allegiance to Adam Smith's liberalism. His many books on political economy represented not only a defense of free trade and free industry: they were also conceived as instruments for the diffusion of the emerging science of political economy among Portuguese speaking audiences.

Specifically in Brazil, Silva Lisboa became a controversial figure. Liberal in the realm of economy and economic principles, he was a political conservative both in principles and in the Brazilian political scene. A staunch supporter of the Braganças, the ruling Portuguese and Brazilian royal dynasty, his name was to become somehow stained in history, exactly because of the support given to the anti-liberal and autocratic attitudes of Brazil's first emperor, Dom Pedro I. Throughout his life, he was a declared enemy of the French Revolution, as well as of any of its political and intellectual offsprings. His distaste for Napoleon is quite understandable, considering the invasion of Portugal by French troops in 1807 and Napoleon's purpose of extinguishing Bragança rule over Portugal. But, more than being anti-France, Silva Lisboa felt at home with the English malaise over the French revolutionary ideas – thus, his admiration for Burke, an author whose works he published in Brazil, does not come as a surprise. Suggestively, Silva Lisboa did not miss an opportunity to express his distaste for Rousseau.

It must be said that his defense of liberal economic principles and, most of all, of the commercial agreements between Portugal and England, signed after the transfer of the royal court to Brazil in 1808, were met with opposition during his lifetime. These agreements were taken, mostly by Portuguese merchants, as harmful to Portugal's (and Brazil's) manufacturing and commercial interests. Indeed, after his death, the defense of these agreements contributed to inscribe Silva Lisboa's name on the index of historical enemies of the national industry. In the end, his economic liberalism and political conservatism, as well as his subservient attitude before the Braganças, contributed to transform him into one of the most controversial names in the Brazilian historiography.[2]

Although a source of controversies among Brazilian historians, Silva Lisboa's name has been favorably reevaluated by historians of economic ideas, mostly in Portugal, but also in Brazil.[3] *Princípios* is admitted as the first book to display the name of the novel science in its title and as the first overview of the liberal economic principles in Portugal. His many texts on free trade, particularly the series of *Observações...*, written between 1808 and 1810 in defense of the royal acts and commercial agreements between Portugal and England, following the arrival of the Portuguese court in Brazil, are taken not only as an exclusive defense of free trade, but as a suggestive instance of his rejection of the colonial system.[4] On the other hand, *Estudos do Bem-comum e Economia Política* (1819–1820, Estudos hereafter),[5] Silva Lisboa's rather ambitious treatise of political economy, evidences a broad and updated knowledge of political economy treatises and writers.[6] In relation to the diffusion of political economy, it should be added that Silva Lisboa's son, Bento Lisboa, under the auspices of the father, was the translator of the first Portuguese edition of *The Wealth of Nations* (Smith, 1776, *Wealth of Nations* hereafter), in 1810/1811.

But the fact is that Silva Lisboa's economic liberalism was, as any, embedded into a precise historical context.[7] First of all, his intellectual formation was quite Portuguese: he studied from 1775 to 1778 at the recently reformed University of Coimbra, Canons, Law and Greek being his major study fields. In a sense, he was a typical representative of the Portuguese Enlightenment and of the reforms imposed by the Marquis of Pombal upon the country and the university, well portrayed by Maxwell (1995). Silva Lisboa was to become one of the many Coimbra graduates to achieve high positions in the public administration – in his case, in the colonial administration. Most of all, for our purposes, *Princípios* may be seen as quite representative of the debates among the Coimbra graduates of his generation.

Silva Lisboa was also marked by his birthplace, the city of Salvador, in the captaincy of Bahia, Brazil, the main gate of the Portuguese colonial trade until the end of the eighteenth century, part of an important sugar and tobacco production region, as well as a decisive slave trade center. Later professional assignments, in Salvador and Rio de Janeiro, made him highly acquainted with the specificities of the colonial economy, including the slave trade. From this standpoint, and in face of the *de facto* transformation of Rio de Janeiro in the seat of the Portuguese empire in 1808, it seems understandable that Silva Lisboa felt comfortable opposing the formerly prevalent colonial rule and endorsing free trade. In his view, the colonial rule had blocked commerce, harming Brazil's economic freedom and progress.

On the other hand, his theoretical standpoint in defense of free industry and free labor, of the advantages of manufactures, as well as of the primacy of intellectual activities over pure physical activities, collided with the colonial reality. In Brazil, slave labor was dominant, agriculture and mining representing the main economic activities. How to reconcile Silva Lisboa's principles with a colonial economy based on slave labor, agriculture and mining? How to defend the post-1808 free trade economic agreements between Portugal and England, when it was clear they were a barrier to the development of Brazil's manufacturing activities, not to mention the constraints imposed upon Portugal's manufactures? Most of all, how to reconcile Silva Lisboa's liberal system of political economy with the crude reality of slave labor? As we shall see, Silva Lisboa considered slave labor an impediment to the development of free labor in Brazil.

Finally, we cannot let aside the fact that the beginnings of the 1800s were unusual times. The transfer of the court to Rio de Janeiro – an episode that took place in 1808 and lasted until 1821 – subverted the colonial logic, gave way to a sense of loss of political centrality in metropolitan Portugal and reinforced the political and economic role of Brazil.

Besides, it was a period marked by a dramatic expansion of Brazilian slave trade and by a continuous growth of the slave population. The reality of Brazilian agriculture reinforced Silva Lisboa's dilemma: how to reconcile the dominance of the slave labor regime with the defense of the superiority of free labor? We will see that, in debating slave labor versus free labor, as in any other economic issues, Silva Lisboa appealed to the authority of the political economy masters.

Our purpose is to examine Silva Lisboa's texts on political economy, in order to discuss how he managed to sustain a strict defense of liberal principles and the eulogy of manufactures, in the context of a thorny reality that implied the dominance of slave labor and the absence of any important manufacture in Brazil, apart from sugar production. Following this Introduction, Section 2 provides a sketch on relevant facts about Silva Lisboa's activities and about the Brazilian economy of his time. Section 3 will present some general traces of Silva Lisboa's approach to labor and trade, distinguishing his 'theoretical' books and the books devised as comments on the Brazilian ongoing economic debates. Section 4 will concentrate on the divide between slave labor and free labor. Finally, Section 5 presents the main conclusions of this chapter.

2   Silva Lisboa's life and the Brazilian economy of his time: a few benchmarks

As mentioned, Silva Lisboa was born in the city of Salvador, in the captaincy of Bahia, the colonial capital until 1763. The city surroundings were the site of a diversified agriculture, comprising sugar cane, tobacco, some cattle, and some manioc, the main Brazilian foodstuff. Salvador's port was a very important trade connection in the eighteenth century, absorbing the local trade with surrounding villages and fields (the *Recôncavo* region), as well as the open ocean trade with Rio de Janeiro, the Brazilian southern territories and the La Plata River, and the Atlantic trade with Portugal and Africa.[8] The local elite was formed by sugar cane planters and sugar producers (*'senhores de engenho'*), but also by powerful Portugal-born traders, especially slave traders that kept strong connections with Africa. These traders acted as money lenders, particularly to sugar producers, which meant their business was complex, comprising lending activities, slave trade, metropolitan trade, navigation, acquisition of local stuff, mainly tobacco and *cachaça* (sugar-cane brandy), used as means of exchange for slaves in Africa.[9]

Although born into a humble family, Silva Lisboa was sent to Coimbra in order to complement his education. Having graduated in Law and Canons in 1778, he became qualified to act as a lawyer or to enroll in the public administration, but after some failed attempts to conquer a position in Lisbon, he returned to Salvador, where he acted for several years as a Greek and Philosophy teacher (Kirschner, 2009). Much later, in 1797, he was given a strategic position in the colonial administration: Chief (Secretary) of the Board of Inspection of Agriculture and Commerce in the city of Salvador.

In 1798, Silva Lisboa began publishing in Lisbon a multi-volume collection on maritime and commercial law, *Princípios de Direito Mercantil e Leis da Marinha*.[10] He intended to conclude this collection with a volume aimed at political economy in general, but at last decided to publish this text as an independent work in 1804, the already referred *Princípios*.

Kirschner (2009) brings to our attention some important facts, which were not clear in previous biographies. First of all, prior to 1798 Silva Lisboa stayed a long period in Lisbon, where he revived his connections with his fellow graduates from Coimbra, now in strategic positions in the Portuguese administration. It was through these connections that he got his high position in the colonial administration. Behind Silva Lisboa's nomination was Rodrigo de Souza Coutinho, a Coimbra graduate who, after a long career in the Portuguese diplomacy, achieved a ministerial position in 1795. Later on, in 1807, D. Rodrigo became the leader of the Portuguese strategy of transferring the royal court to Rio de Janeiro. It is worth mentioning that D. Rodrigo belonged to the 'English party,' the Portuguese political group that favored the alignment with England, and not with France, and that he was also an attentive reader of Smith's *Wealth of Nations*: two points that contributed to the affinities between Silva Lisboa and Souza Coutinho.

It was during this stay in Lisbon that Silva Lisboa started writing his commercial law treatise – and, again, sufficiently strong ties allowed him to have the work published. In Lisbon, but also in Salvador, he kept attuned to the intellectual and political debates in Portugal, which explains the fact that his *Princípios* would emerge as an instance of these debates, being an entirely 'Portuguese' book, in spite of having been written and published in the moment the author was immersed in colonial problems.

It is important to highlight Silva Lisboa's experience in the Board of Inspection, in Salvador, because his activities implied an extensive and first-hand knowledge of the colonial economy. In fact, some documents, such as the letter he wrote in 1781 to Domingos Vandelli, an intellectual connected to Coimbra and to Lisbon's Royal Academy of Science, are evidence that Silva Lisboa was well informed about Bahia's natural resources, trade and agriculture, even before becoming Secretary of the Board of Inspection. But this position required a strict control of the data on agriculture, exports, imports, slave trade, navigation and taxes. That is, Silva Lisboa was entirely knowledgeable about the colonial economic life, when Dom João and his retinue arrived in Salvador, in the beginning of 1808, fleeing from Napoleon's invasion of Portugal. His involvement with the Prince Regent's entourage must have been natural and instrumental, given the scarcity of high-grade officials in Brazil. Needless to say, Silva Lisboa's political inclinations facilitated the engagement: a religious (Catholic) man, monarchist, faithful to the Braganças, biased toward England and against France. Most of all, a defendant of free trade, in a moment when circumstances obliged the Prince Regent, Dom João, to open the Brazilian ports to all friendly nations, thus disrupting the axis of the colonial system, that is, the dependence to metropolitan Portugal.

The move of the Portuguese court to Rio de Janeiro meant the end of the Brazil–Portugal colonial system. Indeed, a fast succession of official acts eliminated the dependent status of Brazil. The already referred opening of the Brazilian ports to all friendly nations directly connected Brazil to England, benefitting English shippers and traders and disrupting the metropolitan privileges in the Brazil–Europe trade. Another act, of April 1st, 1808, extinguished the prohibition to install manufacturing facilities in Brazil, a barrier that had been erected in 1785 in order to protect Portugal's manufactures. An act of April 28th, 1809 assured tax exemption to manufacture inputs, and promised incentives to the acquisition of new machinery. The last stroke was the momentous 1810 Portugal–England Treaty of amity, commerce and navigation (commonly referred to as the 'Strangford Treaty'), which assured a special treatment, and the lowest import duties, to English merchandises. The treaty was complemented by legislation that eliminated obstacles within the internal commerce.[11] In the political sphere, the dissolution of the colonial status was formalized in 1815, by the establishment of a new political entity, the United Kingdom of Portugal, Brazil and the Algarves. In principle, Brazil was raised to Portugal's level.

In the beginning of 1808, Silva Lisboa was invited to join the royal court, envisaging the establishment of a political economy course (*cathedra*) in Rio de Janeiro. Although the teaching activities of the *cathedra* were never realized, the offer illustrates the importance Portuguese high officials, and especially Souza Coutinho, attributed to political economy as an instrument in building a fair and wise public administration. Another position attributed to Silva Lisboa was instrumental in the development of his intellectual activities: censor and member of the supervising committee of the Royal Press, the first press to be admitted in Brazilian territory. As censor, he was in contact with the many titles that demanded licenses for translation, edition and circulation in Brazil. As manager of the Royal Press, he was in a special condition to print his own books. Symbolically, the first book to be published by Rio de Janeiro's Royal Press was his *Observações sobre o comércio franco no Brasil* (1808, hereafter *Observações 1*).

Silva Lisboa's transfer to Rio de Janeiro was instrumental not only in keeping him in the list of high advisors to the court. The city was blooming: many thousand Portuguese courtiers were suddenly transferred to and lodged in Rio; English traders opened their offices or shops and flooded the city with their merchandises; diplomatic representatives circulated in the city. Most of all, the axis of Brazilian trade was dislocated from Salvador to Rio and the city consolidated itself as the center of the Brazilian slave trade.

This change on the central position in Brazilian slave trade, from Salvador to Rio, was associated to two geographical moves. The first one was related to the origins of the slaves: Salvador slave trade had West Africa (Mina Coast) as its main source, while Rio de Janeiro slave traders exploited sources in Central Atlantic Africa, mainly Luanda and Benguela, which became progressively dominant. The second move was related to the destination of the slaves: while Recife, Salvador and their environments, and even the mining regions in Minas Gerais, lost their relative importance as slave absorbers, the Brazilian Southeast sugar-cane and coffee plantations around Rio de Janeiro became an increasingly important attractor. From 1780 on, Rio de Janeiro became an enormous slave port and the city itself, when Dom João arrived, was heavily populated by slaves.[12] In moving from Salvador to Rio, Silva Lisboa moved from a traditional slave region to a rising, and yet consolidated, slave center. Additionally, being part of the royal entourage under Dom João from 1808 to 1821, and under Dom Pedro from 1821 to 1831, Silva Lisboa had access to the intricacies of the international slave trade politics, a permanently pressing issue, because of English attempts to extinguish slave trade from 1808 on.[13] In a symbolic way, the 1810 Treaty of amity, navigation and commerce contained an innocuous compromise, by Portugal, of furthering the extinction of slave trade.

The slave question was to be an important piece of the Portugal–Brazil controversies that led to the return of Dom João to Portugal, and, in sequence, to the Independence of Brazil.[14] Not coincidently, independence and the building of the new nation implied, among other issues, a pact among the Brazilian elites to uphold slavery. As a participant in the Brazilian Constitutional Assembly, and, later on, in the legislative body, Silva Lisboa was surely aware of the maneuvers by planters elite to maintain the slave system and its fundamentals: robust and bustling, constantly replenished by the Atlantic trade. On the other hand, and although slave labor spread throughout urban areas, its persistence was related to agricultural and mining activities, the country's economic core. As an Adam Smith enthusiast, Silva Lisboa was aware of the advantages of manufacturing activities, but had to adapt his liberal creed to a

situation that opened few opportunities for the development of simple manufactures, let alone modern industry. In principle, free trade and slave labor
implied resigning to the modern industry. What were the lessons and advices
one could gather from political economy books in an agricultural, slave labor-
dominated country? In the following section we discuss how Silva Lisboa rec-
onciled free trade with the possibilities of economic diversification. In Section
4 we shall focus on slave labor.

3   Silva Lisboa on industry and trade

Sections 3 and 4 will gather textual evidences from Silva Lisboa's political
economy books. It is important to begin by distinguishing *Princípios*, published
in 1804, from post-1808 works, because his first political economy treatise
is not inspired by the Brazilian intellectual scene, whereas the subsequent
works are aimed at the emerging commercial problems brought about by
the transfer of the Portuguese court to Brazil. Such a distinction does not
imply any difference in principle among Silva Lisboa's economic texts, since
he thought of himself as a disciple of Adam Smith from the beginning to the
end of his intellectual life.

The most characteristic trace of *Princípios* is the objection to physiocracy;
more precisely, Silva Lisboa's objections to the Portuguese followers of physiocracy, particularly Joaquim Rodrigues de Brito. In the end of the eighteenth
century, there was a particular revival of physiocracy in Portugal, less focused
on the theoretical intricacies of Quesnay's political economy than on the
defense of the primacy of agricultural activities.[15] The priority attributed to
agriculture served as theoretical support for the defense of policies favorable
to this sector, as well as an instrument to attack the residues of Portuguese
Colbertism, that is, the remains of Pombal's policies envisaging the protection
of Portuguese manufactures.

Silva Lisboa appealed to the authority of Smith in his attack on physiocracy, insisting that the physiocrats had not perceived the virtues of labor in
general, so well established in the *Wealth of Nations*.[16] The liberal (Smithian)
system not only extoled human activity, but also the virtues of free trade
among individuals and among nations. That is, Silva Lisboa jumped from
labor into trade and division of labor, connecting his attack to the principles
of physiocracy to his defense of the creative capability of labor in general and
to trade, internal and international. His conclusion was that the advantages
brought about by the division of labor recommend keeping trade open.

Silva Lisboa's stress on the division of labor is key to understanding his
equivocal insistence in putting physiocracy apart from liberalism. In his view,
there is a connection between division of labor, free trade and free industry.
Free industry and free trade further the division of labor – which implies the
non-exclusiveness of agriculture. On the other hand, the general advantages
brought about by the division of labor and by free trade outweigh any possible advantage brought about by protecting individual branches of business. It

is interesting to note that this anti-protectionist reasoning stems from Smith, but it also entails a perspective on state and society surely alien to Smithian liberalism. In fact, Silva Lisboa shares a typically Catholic and Portuguese conception, which conceives society as an organism commanded, or somehow patronized, by the sovereign. To use a frequently repeated image, the sovereign is "the chief of a vast family" (*Princípios*, p. 34),[17] a vision that suggests a type of Aristotelian understanding of the economic activity as part of the *domus*, and also a conception that takes society and state as an organic body, commanded by the king.

This sort of organicism, or paternalism, leads to a rejection of any type of protection devised at favoring a specific corpus of the society, to the detriment of others. As in a family, the father (sovereign) must protect everyone, avoiding distinctions. Of course, Silva Lisboa is referring to Pombalian-like measures of protection, especially applied to manufactures. But he is also thinking of impediments to the free exercise of craftsmanship, as well as of the restrictions imposed upon the free choice of crops and activities within agriculture. All three types of impediments, the remains of ancient Portugal, were for many reasons not fit for the reality of Brazil, in which slave labor prevailed, residues of corporations and guilds were inexistent, and impediments to specific types of agricultural activities according to regions or to individuals were scarcely, or not at all, observed.

Furthermore, the rejection of all sorts of favors and/or protections in internal activities was immediately extended to the international trade. The free choice of activities would produce a type of specialization, in which each country would be driven to the production of the commodities it exceled in, or each country would achieve "natural monopolies" (*Princípios*, pp. 36–7), fit to its particular soil and human propensities. Most of all, Silva Lisboa insists, professional activities should be spontaneously chosen by individuals. In adherence to Smithian self-interest, quite surprising given the above mentioned organicist conception of society, he concludes that all individuals aim at the betterment of their conditions. In short, he resorts to some sort of Smithian self-love, exercised under the protection of the sovereign, a combination that would lead to common wealth through competition.

It must be noted that even Smith's passages on the division of labor are brought to the fore in defense of the free choice of professional activities. Silva Lisboa derives policy guidance suggestions from these passages, concluding that the state should not envisage the internalization of all branches of industry, since any protection implies diversion of capital from its most profitable applications. Not to divert capital from its most profitable applications was a general maxim, later applied to Brazil in order to show that the protection of manufactures would represent the diversion of capital from the most lucrative local branch of business, i.e., agriculture.

As mentioned in Sections 1 and 2, the invasion of Portugal by Napoleon implied the dismantlement of the Portugal–Brazil colonial pact. Immediately after his arrival in Brazil, Dom João had to circumvent the blockage produced by the occupation of Portugal's territory, opening the Brazilian ports to all friendly nations. In context, this meant opening the ports to English ships, thus disrupting the until then mandatory Brazil–Portugal trade route. Silva Lisboa's *Observações 1*, edited in June 1808, is entirely referred to the Royal Charter responsible for the opening of Brazilian ports on January 28th, 1808. As we will see, the new circumstances implied an adaptation of Silva Lisboa's liberal creed.

Silva Lisboa was adamant, although pragmatic, in acknowledging that opening the ports was a mandatory consequence produced by a new and atypical situation. Portugal had no other alternative, since the sovereign had lost control over its European territory. As expected, the opening of trade to all countries was followed by a flood of English manufactures; to no harm, according to Silva Lisboa, since Brazil had few, or no manufactures, because of the prevalent prohibition to install them. The colonial system had led to a concentration in agriculture and mining, concluded Silva Lisboa – and, after all, Portuguese ships and capitals were on this occasion prevented from leaving Portugal.

Silva Lisboa's arguments were not entirely on the defensive side. In his view, the opening to world trade would intensify competition among suppliers and facilitate the exports of Brazilian colonial products, sugar especially. Competition among suppliers would become a recurrent argument, in this as in other texts. According to Silva Lisboa, England's trade was hugely competitive, competitiveness implying low prices. In fact, it might be argued that in this issue he had second thoughts: while insisting that English manufacturers and traders did not act as monopolies (*Observações 1*, p. 232), in some passages he admitted the existence of remaining monopolies, "the dark side of British government" (*Observações 1*, p. 293). He also referred to the Navigation Acts, just to conclude that they were part of England's defensive strategy, always threatened by jealous enemies... It must be recalled that, apart from his overt pro-British stand, Silva Lisboa was tolerant of some strategic monopolies – and we should not forget that the Portuguese crown still kept some monopolies.[18]

Silva Lisboa considered that the impact of Napoleon's aggressive politics, in the end, had turned the international scene in favor of Brazilian interests. In his view, Brazil was in a position to expand its exports, since in that precise moment the threats to England and the curtailing of this country's international trade area had brought British and Portuguese interests into convergence. England wanted to export to Brazil and Portugal was offered a chance to raise Brazilian exports to England and, indirectly, to the rest of the world. Besides, Portugal and Brazil were short of funds, while English tradesmen had plenty of funds to transfer or lend to Brazil directly. Finally, Silva Lisboa fancied the English would facilitate Portuguese operations in India, as long as Portugal opened the *La Plata* trade to England.

All in all, the new situation was considered a blessing, despite the fact it resulted from a violent political accident. Brazil would be able to stage an unheard of liberalism. As Silva Lisboa said in *Observações sobre a prosperidade do estado pelos liberais princípios da nova legislação do Brasil* (Lisboa, 1810c, *Observações 3* hereafter), Napoleon's follies had led to the establishment "of an economic policy which any government neither permitted, nor considered prudent" (*Observações 3*, pp. 4–5). Silva Lisboa remarks that, while even Adam Smith stuck to the sober conclusion that the old mercantile system would only gradually be extinguished, the Brazilian situation allowed boldness:

> since the Pseudo-Alexander suddenly cut the Gordian knot, harming all system of civilization, and of regular government; it was necessary to anticipate the stroke with another and more effective counterstroke, opening new channels to the blocked industry and to the restrained, spoiled, and injured, wealth.
>
> (*Observações 3*, p. 430)

In this as in other points, Silva Lisboa expected Brazil to follow the example of the United States, and he credited to international trade the prosperity of North America. In many passages of *Observações 1* and in other texts, he took North America as a positive example, and believed Brazil should try to follow their policies, which in his view consisted of emphasizing exports, opening internal markets and admitting foreign labor and capital. We will come later to other aspects of Silva Lisboa's mirroring of North America.[19]

It is worth noting that Silva Lisboa was attentive to the already existent criticisms to the 28/01 Charter.[20] Part III of *Observações 1* is entirely dedicated to the main points of these criticisms, which were: 1) the opening of ports would contribute to increase the scarcity of money, draining away Brazilian bullion and coins; 2) English competition would threaten national traders; 3) navigation and industry would be annihilated; 4) Portuguese manufacturers would lose Brazilian markets; 5) admission of commodities from abroad, without reciprocity, was an error; 6) even England was not a practicer of free commerce, preserving its colonial system.

It is not possible to review the entirety of Silva Lisboa's responses to these objections, that encompass a wide range of points, from the criticism to old fashioned mercantilist approaches to money and bullion, to the admission that the modest Portuguese traders in Rio would not be able to uphold the immense challenges and opportunities created by majestic events. Concentrating in the main points, Silva Lisboa considered that the massive arrival of courtiers in Rio, and the non-negligible interest of English tradesmen in the Brazilian markets, opened new and large alleys to the Portuguese-Brazilian trade. Possibly, Brazilian and Portuguese traders would not be able to face the challenge, but it was not wise to ask for protection, since the interests of individual traders were not synonymous to the 'interests of trade' in general. In the end, concluded Silva Lisboa, Rio de Janeiro's traders were just trying to get extra profits from the sudden widening of the Brazilian markets. Although one can infer from his response that Brazilian traders were in reality preoccupied with the literal invasion of their markets by British traders (Pantaleão, 1962), Silva Lisboa followed his general criterion, equating liberalism with general advantages to society and combatting all protection to specific categories.

It is interesting to note that Silva Lisboa extended the use of the word 'industry,' which was mostly taken as 'labor exertion' in *Princípios*. Now he distinguishes "industry in the vulgar sense" (*Observações 1*, p. 263) from mechanical arts, establishing a gradient, or priorities, since in his view Brazil could not house complex mechanical factories. In the end, this sort of gradualist view was associated with the necessary prevalence of agriculture:

> It is only convenient to establish in Brazil such industries *[factories]* slow and gradually, beginning by the rudest to those of higher order, beginning by those next to agriculture, that, by now and for a long time, should ... represent our main manufacture.
>
> (*Observações 1*, p. 263)

Industry could never exceed the available capital, and the building of mechanical factories in Brazil would represent a *'diversion of the nation's capital.'*

Behind Silva Lisboa's position there is a blind faith in gradualism: everything at its due time. He sustained that industries in Brazil would spontaneously emerge, because of the availability of primary inputs. What the territory lacked, he said, were "masters, capitals, arms, models, instruments and machinery from abroad" (*Observações 1*, p. 264). Brazil should – as North America did – try to attract European capitalists and skilled laborers.

But Silva Lisboa had to respond to another, and more objective, concern. Portuguese traders considered that the direct admission of English ships and commodities in Brazil, without their intermediation, would harm Portugal's mercantile interests. It was admitted that, at the beginning of 1808, Brazil and Portugal faced exceptional conditions; however, once Europe regained normality, what would happen to the metropolitan privileges? Silva Lisboa's response was direct: the Portuguese crown sacrificed its most profitable colonial asset for securing its own survival. Now, a Union was needed, one beneficial to all components of the monarchy, in Europe and America. He deployed some soothing arguments, in order to show that the new conditions would not harm Portuguese trade, given the old and special connection between Brazil and Portugal (*Observações 1*, p. 270). All in all, these were unconvincing arguments and his further conclusion was that Portuguese factories were "proportional to the country's circumstances..." The factories which had already achieved "perfection and cheapness..." (*Observações 1*, p. 272) were able to compete with the foreigners. To less efficient factories, he proposed some tax compensations and preference in governmental acquisitions. In the end, 'premature' factories would disappear, their funds becoming available for more profitable application.

If the undeniable loss suffered by metropolitan industries was not enough, Silva Lisboa still had to respond to the questioning that England kept its colonial system – that is, England continued buying sugar preferentially in its colonies. Silva Lisboa conceded it would be difficult to sell sugar to England and suggested, in this case, that Portugal should consider not the equivalence between pairs of commodities, taken individually, but the whole balance of trade. A detour on the author's line of thought, ending up in a platitude: buying and selling always implies reciprocity, since exchange means equivalence (*Observações 1*, pp. 282–3).

Observações sobre a franqueza da indústria e estabelecimento de fábricas no Brazil (1810a, *Observações 2* hereafter), published in 1810, extensively refers to the 04/01/1808 and 04/28/1808 Royal Charters.[21] The first charter abolished the prohibition on building manufactories in Brazil, while the second complemented it by establishing tax exemptions to raw materials, as well as incentives to innovative machinery. Both charters complemented the dismantlement of the Portugal–Brazil colonial system. In my opinion, *Observações 2* is the most consistent of Silva Lisboa's works and, at the same time, the one where the limits of a liberal order in backward regions are best evidenced.

Observações 2 has some additional appeal in its frequent references to North America. Yet, Silva Lisboa begins by remarking Benjamin Franklin's observation about the difficulties in attracting artisans to North America, in order to establish manufactures. According to Franklin (*apud* Lisboa), labor was so expensive in North America that only labor-sparing manufactures, or those protected by high costs of freight, could possibly prosper. That is, in North America labor was scarce and expensive, and that was the reason why only simple manufactures and ship building had spread in its Northeastern coast, in spite of the lack of protection. Despite all obstacles the region thrived, concluded Silva Lisboa, suggesting that Brazil would also benefit from adopting a liberal legislation. Silva Lisboa was especially enthusiastic about North America's openness to European workers.[22] In fact, in all his works, he remarked on North American free trade policies. In *Estudos*, his most ambitious book from the theoretical point of view, he insists that free trade had been essential to the development of North America.

A good reason to follow the spirit of North American policies, according to Silva Lisboa, was the scarcity of the white population in Brazil. The Brazilian working population was mostly composed of slaves, more fit to agricultural activities. How to provide for manufactures, without capital and without free labor? These conjectures led Silva Lisboa to peruse the meanings of the term 'industry' again, pondering that, besides representing active labor, industry also meant carefully and artfully exerted labor. Finally, industry meant labor inserted in big mechanical factories. In Silva Lisboa's view, this last definition had unfortunately implied a negative side effect, many persons taking it as an evidence that simple work in agriculture did not require industry – now understood as analogous to intelligence – which was an error. To sum up, in his view, industry – in the sense of intelligent and diligent labor exertion – included personal activities of any sort, in agriculture, navigation, commerce, mining, etc. This is the reason why Brazil:

> may have a high level of industry and wealth, even if the country does not shelter superior arts and manufactures, that are natural in Europe; and to the extent there is availability of extensive and fertile soil, no activity can be as lucrative as agriculture, mining, internal and external commerce...
>
> (*Observações 2*, p. 335)

In parallel, Silva Lisboa disputed privileges demanded by the Brazilian manufacturers, who argued they were introducing machines that up to the moment were not available in the territory. As we have seen, the 04/28/1808 charter considered protection to new equipment. Contrary to the demanders, Silva Lisboa argued that the charter meant to protect inventors and introducers of new – in the sense of innovative – equipment. In a loose sense, all machinery was new in Brazil, since the colony was devoid of manufactures due to the 1785 Act. Silva Lisboa took new equipment in its strictest sense, and he was quite consistent in this interpretation, as proved by his attitudes as chief of staff of the board that examined the demands for incentives: he denied almost all petitions for privileges, arguing that the implied manufactures lacked innovation.[23] The demands referred to several types of manufactures and businesses: paper, bricks, spinning, weaving, shipyard, navigation, etc. Many proprietors were Portuguese – they were possibly transferring their businesses from Portugal – and, as such, were accustomed to the privileges still prevalent in Portugal.

Most of all, in *Observações 2*, Silva Lisboa stressed his point on the priority that should be given to agriculture. Recalling Smith's example of the English wool industry, which had naturally followed sheep breeding, Silva Lisboa concluded that Brazil's priority was definitely agriculture and interconnected economic activities: "By now, our great and immediate necessity is … to build roads and navigable channels; house building, and rural and urban construction; manufactures associated to agriculture and navigation, …" (*Observações 2*, p. 380). After all, Silva Lisboa concluded, the Brazilian industry was already protected by a tax imposed upon imports. If 16 percent, the effective rate, was not enough, this was a sign that the business was not naturally viable.

4   Slave labor

In spite of Silva Lisboa's firsthand knowledge of all the dimensions of slave labor in Brazil, his political economy writings offer only glimpses and scattered passages on slave labor. These passages evidence his discomfort with slave labor, in face of the assumed superiority of free labor.

The full extent of Silva Lisboa's discomfort is best displayed in a short text, written at a later age and published only posthumously, in 1851, *Da Liberdade do trabalho* (1851, *Da Liberdade* hereafter). In this text, Silva Lisboa frankly distills his judgment about the drawbacks of slave labor. According to him, all the 'beneficial effects' of industry are associated with free labor only, which was generally considered superior to slave labor, in all occupations: agriculture, mining, manufactures. Furthermore, slave labor creates a duality. On the one hand, slaves are mistreated and poorly fed by their owners; on the other, slaves dissimulate and always try to evade continuous effort. Slavery creates a mischievous proprietor class and a non-industrious labor force.

On the minimum application by slaves, and on the negative effects produced by slavery upon the proprietor class, Silva Lisboa echoes the warnings of Smith and Hume.[24] Silva Lisboa goes further, saying that black slaves arouse in their owners the worst behaviors, such as gratuitous violence and despising manual labor. In this particular, he once more follows Smith's (or Hume's) comments on the violence upon slaves in ancient Rome or in the modern West Indies, but his life experience was at hand, showing that in Brazil the simplest and most trivial manual activities were avoided by slave proprietors and the white population in general, since that was 'up to the slaves.'

In face of so many negative aspects, how to justify the permanence of slave labor, not to mention the massive dominance of slave labor in sugar-cane plantations? Silva Lisboa recalls Montesquieu's proposition, echoed by Smith in the *Wealth of Nations*, that modern colonial slave labor was a necessary byproduct of the harshness of sugar-cane production under tropical climates.[25]

For Silva Lisboa, however, the crux was the impossibility of combining slave labor with free labor: under the dominance of the former, free men simply refuse to work. To the extent progress depends on inventive labor, economical ways of living and frugality, it seems that Brazil was condemned not to prosper, or at least not to achieve Silva Lisboa's dream of prosperity under free labor, inspired in North America. Immigration of free white men was a frustrating experience in Brazil, because either potential white immigrants did not consider coming to the country, or accommodated themselves to the local habits of exploiting slave labor, after arriving.

Yet, in *Da Liberdade* we find a rare distinction, considering the bulk of Silva Lisboa's works, between northern and southern North America. The text blatantly proposes that, while in northern English colonies progress was evident, in the South, under slave labor and tobacco and sugar production, misery, mischief and villainy were the rule. Considering Silva Lisboa's passages on slave labor, this is a unique fragment in two senses: first, for admitting the reality of slave labor in North America; and second, for assuming that the English mainland colonies (as the United States) were not a uniform white immigrants' paradise. Of course, as in many other of Silva Lisboa's illustrations, this one exhibits some historical inaccuracy, because southern cotton production became a thriving reality, in the early 1800s. Here, Silva Lisboa echoes Adam Smith's comments on the divide between northern and southern colonies, or the dominance of free labor versus the dominance of slave labor, blurring the fact that Smith's horizon was mid-eighteenth century America.

In the rest of Silva Lisboa's works, the observations on slave labor and slave trade are effectively scattered and not woven into a general explanation of slavery in his country. In *Observações 1*, he briefly mentions the abolition of the slave trade in England, seeing it as a sign of philanthropy and wisdom (*Observações 1*, p. 294). For a number of reasons, the slave trade was a very sensitive issue in Brazil. First of all, when the three *Observações* were written (1808–1810), Brazil was regaining its leadership in the slave trade, after England's 1807 abolition, and after France became engulfed in the ups and downs of its post-Revolution colonial trade and slave regime. Besides, English pressure towards the abolition of the Portuguese and Brazilian slave trade escalated after 1810. Finally, in the top rank of Brazilian mercantile bourgeoisie were Salvador's and Rio's big merchants, chief agents of the slave trade.[26] Silva Lisboa was silent in this respect, being surely aware of the strategic position occupied by slave traders. Curiously, in this context he affirms that the slave trade was not a very profitable branch of business – a doubtful assertion. His pro-free trade conclusion, however, was that foreigners should be welcomed to the slave trade, as far as slaves were indispensible and the slave trade still represented a useful activity. Here we have another lapse, because Silva Lisboa was quite aware of the strategic position occupied by Brazilian traders in the slave business. The slave trade was an activity dominated by Brazilian traders, who would hardly be outdone by foreigners. By the way, in the same passage Silva Lisboa reminds us that Bahia's tobacco was used as a means of exchange for slaves in Africa, acknowledging the benefits the slave trade brought to tobacco plantations (*Observações 1*, p. 241). It is interesting to note that, although sugar-cane brandy (*cachaça*) was one of the main Brazilian exportable products, being intensively exchanged for slaves in Africa, Silva Lisboa was silent about this branch of trade.[27]

Even conceding that it was out of question to eliminate slave labor in Brazil, Silva Lisboa circled around his mainline subject: the necessity of originating a free labor alternative in the territory. This endeavor was hampered by slave labor. Silva Lisboa recurrently insisted on his double face dilemma, the superiority of free white labor in face of the difficulties in combining free and slave labor.

Besides resorting to a Montesquieu-like explanation to the spread of slave labor in sugar-cane plantations, based on the harshness of tropical conditions, Silva Lisboa appealed to an elementary economic motive, viz. scarcity of white free labor, which implies free labor costliness. And he also resorted to uncommon causation. For instance, in *Estudos* he put forward a curious interpretation of the spread of the African slave labor in South America. According to his account, the Spanish conquerors disseminated the idea that the indigenous American population was brutal and should be extinguished; when this erroneous idea finally went out of fashion, the Spanish started diffusing the view that America was not a good place for Europeans, thus requiring African and local native arms – an initiative that ended up in slavery. Silva Lisboa concludes that it was this (questionable) Spanish chain of reasoning that blocked the "good transmigration of Europeans," operating the "meta-morphosis of America into a negroland" (*Estudos*, p. 252).

Irrespective of the accuracy of Lisboa's tale of the Spanish rationale, his conclusion illustrates the permanent concern with opening the country to European immigrants, the only way to transform Brazilian labor into indus-trious labor. It seems that he was convinced that both the Portuguese and the Brazilian would have to come to terms with the inevitability of extinguishing slavery and the slave trade; at least this interpretation clearly surfaces in *Da Liberdade*. The same position also emerges in a historical writing, a Memory in praise of Dom João (Lisboa, 1818). It is arguable that he supposed that, under English pressure, Brazil would end up extinguishing the slave trade. In this situation, the impending scarcity of labor would soften the control upon slaves, once the lengthening of their lives became imperative.[28] Lisboa's opinion was not original, since it was a sort of common sense among the abolitionist movements that the extinction of the African slave trade was expected to contribute to the relief of the dire conditions endured by slaves in America.[29]

It is arguable that Lisboa was wrong, as proven by history. In spite of England's pressure, the slave trade was prohibited in Brazil only in 1850. As already mentioned, in Lisboa's lifetime, the abolition of the slave trade was simply not considered by the planters elite, not to mention the power-ful group of slave traders. Even liberal politicians kept the problem of aboli-tion out of their horizons. The end of the slave trade and the abolition of slavery were almost a non-issue in the constitutional debates that followed the independence of the country, in 1822, and Lisboa was a representative in the Constitutional Assembly. Slave labor was a non-questionable reality, and Silva Lisboa, as a pragmatic conservative, was cautious. The following sentence, part of one of the several passages attributing North America's pro-gress to free labor, well describes Lisboa's cautious attitude towards the slave trade: "I will not insist on this delicate subject, which touches the territory of politics: I just protest against the preached absurdity that in Brazil the slave regime is a necessary evil" (*Estudos*, p. 242).

As in other economic issues, questions concerning the advantages and profitability of slave labor were submitted to the authority of the political economy masters. According to a view exposed in *Estudos*, this question was beyond the scope of what Lisboa classified as 'general political economy,' whose objective was to study "the true social system, based on the fundamen-tal laws of the moral order" (*Estudos*, p. 96). The dilemma pertained to the realm of 'particular political economy,' a discipline related to the 'national' wealth and industry. Silva Lisboa had no doubts: "It is obvious that a nation inhabited by uneducated persons cannot have the same political economy as a nation formed by a civilized population, advanced in arts and sciences" (*Estudos*, p. 97). He added that the same political economy applicable to nations where civil liberty was the rule could not be applied to nations where slave labor, or serfdom, was the norm.

A quotation from Dugald Stewart's *Elements of the Philosophy of the Human Mind*, a few pages before the above-mentioned distinction between 'general' and 'particular' political economy, strengthens Silva Lisboa's point. According to Silva Lisboa, in criticizing political arithmetic, Stewart wrote that the American colonists' experience of slave labor differed from the views of the discipline: while political economists extolled the virtues of free labor, American colonists assured that slave labor was more productive than free labor (*Estudos*, p. 91). Silva Lisboa does not elaborate on this difference of opinions, supposedly because it pertains to the distinction between 'general' and 'particular' political economy. However, he continuously upholds the superiority of free labor. In *Da Liberdade* he insists that the returns from free labor are bigger in all economic activities: agriculture, mining, manufactures. In this passage, he appeals to the authority of Adam Smith, in order to confirm the lack of inventiveness of slaves and to remind us that, irrespective of high salaries, free labor had already proven itself more advantageous in England's mainland American colonies. The diffused motto '*no slaves, no colonies*' seemed absurd to Silva Lisboa. In fact, in *Estudos* he concludes that this misleading motto had been diffused by 'selfish economists,' omitting a longstanding colonial popular motto in Brazil, that goes '*without Angola, no Brazil,*' meaning that Angola's slaves were indispensable to the Brazilian economy.

In his observations on slave labor, Silva Lisboa referred not only to Adam Smith and to Dugald Stewart, as seen, but also to James Steuart, Say and Sismondi. His mentions of these three economists are less specific, in the sense of not making reference to specific topics, but to their general stand on slave labor. The way these authors are quoted is nonetheless equivocal, in the sense of not being faithful to the contexts, meaning and chronology of their approaches to slave labor. For instance, Steuart admits in his *Principles of Political Economy* (Book II) that slavery and industry are incompatible,[30] but not by the same reasons considered by Silva Lisboa. According to Steuart, the owners must keep their slaves in simplicity, which means a level of consumption possibly not acceptable by free men. The high level of frugality, and low level of consumption, collides with the perspectives of free laborers. Again, sugar-cane plantation comes to the surface as a typical and extreme situation of adversity to free labor.[31]

Say and Sismondi are even more embarrassing authorities to appeal to, because both were frankly hostile to slave labor. Sismondi, while insisting on the lack of intelligence and zeal associated with slave labor, reminds us the frequently forgotten fact that slave labor was a synonym of the depletion of the slave population. In the Gulf of Mexico, where the 'pernicious system' prevailed, the slave population had to be permanently replenished, he writes. Sismondi attributes the economic survival of slavery to monopolist practices and lack of competition in the sugar market. However, the more important element is his moral stand on the subject. In his *Nouveaux Principes* (Sismondi, 1819), slavery is simply admitted as a variety of robbery not punished by law, a criminal act contrary to natural law, even when supported by positive law. Both arguments, the insistence on monopolist practices and the moral aversion to slavery, collide with Silva Lisboa's understanding and were, of course, kept hidden by him.

Say is a special case, because Silva Lisboa did not disguise his admiration for the French author. Say was clearly opposed to slave labor in moral terms, and insisted that, among the reasons that explained the possibility of operating slave sugar-cane plantations profitably was the possibility of putting slaves to work to death, given the existence of an open source for fresh substitutes. And Say, in his *Traité* (Say, 1803) insisted that, at least in France, the sugar price was a 'colonial' price, that is, a monopolist price, far from competitive standards. That is, Say's passages on slave labor are thoughtful and non-trivial, and stand completely apart from Silva Lisboa's overall position.

It is difficult not to conclude that, in his treatment of slave labor, Silva Lisboa ended bowing to his pragmatism and kept faithful to simple principles and dogmas: scarcity of labor, harshness of working conditions in tropical plantations, simplicity of tasks... However, he did not lose sight of his main line of questioning: given the superiority of free labor, how to implement it in Brazil? Since the abolition of slavery was out of question, Silva Lisboa reached for a possible, but difficult, compromise: the slow penetration of white immigrants into a slave labor economy. He did not give details on how to achieve this combination. A simple formula to circumvent the same barrier did occur to Steuart, including government management and strict division of tasks and fields of activity between free and slave labor. Contrarily to Steuart, Silva Lisboa simply had no formula to propose.

5 Conclusion

Throughout the previous sections, our aim was to show José da Silva Lisboa's economic liberalism as a peculiar, not to say problematic, liberalism. His model was the teachings of Adam Smith, basically the advocacy of free trade, free industry and the acceptance of labor as a constitutive principle of value. Additionally, he assumed Smith's (and many other economists') defense of the superiority of free labor, in contrast to slave labor, following a norm deep ingrained in late eighteenth and early nineteenth century political economy.

It was not difficult for Silva Lisboa to defend, in his first political book, the superiority of free labor, free circulation of labor among offices, free choice of crops within agriculture, not to mention the convenience of free trade. However, the transposition of Silva Lisboa's liberal positions to Brazil implied hard choices and the necessity to adapt his creeds to an economy based on slave labor, with its predominant activities being agriculture and mining. Manufactures (apart from sugar production) were out of the question, be it because the colonial statutes prohibited them, be it because, from 1808 on, the transformation of Rio de Janeiro in the seat of the Portuguese empire changed the terms of trade between Brazil and Europe. The adoption of free trade implied that British products entirely outcompeted Portuguese and Brazilian manufactures. The dominance of slave labor meant that the envisaged immigration of free white laborers was scarce. Moreover, the available contingent of free workers scarcely penetrated into the core economic activities.

Irrespective of the fact that British imports outcompeted Brazilian and Portuguese manufactures, free trade continued to be Silva Lisboa's motto. Free industry, in the ancient Portuguese sense of mobility among professions and trades, was a nonsensical claim in Brazil, be it because the impediments to the free practice of activities were hardly enforced in the territory, be it because slave labor was the dominant form of labor in Brazil. Likewise, contrarily to Silva Lisboa's (and many economists') opinions on the inadaptability of slaves to skilled tasks, a good number of artisanal activities were practiced by slaves in Brazil, some of them quite qualified. For instance, the key technical figure in a sugar producing plant, the master ('*mestre de açúcar*'), was in some cases a slave, in others, a free worker of African descent.

In spite of the circumstances, Silva Lisboa's adherence to free trade was irremovable. Against the demands of Brazilian and Portuguese traders, he consistently continued to object any protection to incoming manufacturers, as special tariffs and monopolies. Silva Lisboa's free trade stand was at the same time consistent and non-negotiable. It might be argued that it was also suicidal, in the sense that the possibility of erecting manufactures in Brazil was brushed aside by British competition. Silva Lisboa suggested that artisanal and manufacturing activities connected to agriculture would naturally prosper, propelling Brazilian industry, an alternative that was of course untenable. That is, coherence in this case meant renouncing the possibility of developing a type of industry – manufacturing industry – that, as a Smithian, he considered superior.

Additionally, and despite being a defender of free labor, Silva Lisboa silently observed the rising tide of slave trade to Brazil, at the beginning of the 1800s, which definitely tied the country to slave labor and reinforced the central role of the already existent moguls of the Brazilian trade, the slave merchants.

Silva Lisboa's defensive strategy aimed at conciliating the reality of slave labor and the envisaged immigration of white free workers. In Silva Lisboa's imagery, Brazil should mirror the example of England's North American mainland colonies, and later of the United States, regions that were opened to immigrants and foreign capital.

It must be considered that Silva Lisboa, due to his intellectual formation, his professional activities in Salvador and his access to ample literature and to privileged information in Rio de Janeiro, was entirely knowledgeable about agriculture, trade in general and the slave trade in particular. His omissions in establishing a real portrait of the Brazilian and Portuguese trade and traders, as well as the lack of a deeper discussion about the extension and particularities of the Brazilian slave regime, are disconcerting, considering his extensive and first-hand knowledge of the real trade and of slave labor. He remained attached to principles. 'José da Silva Lisboa, a pragmatist attached to principles,' would have been a good epitaph for him.

Notes

1 Principles of Political Economy.
2 On the controversies on Silva Lisboa among Brazilian historians, see Rocha (2001) and Kirschner (2009).
3 Among others, Cardoso (1989), Rocha (1996), Almodovar and Cardoso (1998).
4 Balanced opinions on these texts can be seen in Novais and Arruda (1999) and Rocha (2001).
5 Studies of Common Good and Political Economy.
6 Rocha (1996) suggests that Silva Lisboa had not really read the panoply of political economy writers mentioned in this book. A skeptical view on Silva Lisboa's fluency on the economic theory of his time is in Coutinho (2011).
7 On Silva Lisboa's liberalism, see Paim (1968), Almodovar (1993), Cardoso (2002).
8 A description of Salvador's economic activities during the colonial period can be found in Schwartz (1985). A synthesis of the Brazilian economy in the late colonial period is in Alden (1987).
9 On Brazilian trade, economic activities in general and social structure, Alden (1987) and Schwartz (1987).
10 Principles of Mercantile Law and Maritime Legislation.
11 A good description of these commercial measures is in Silva Lisboa (1818).
12 For slave trade statistics, according to regions, see Florentino et al. (2004) and Soares (2012).
13 On English, Portuguese and Brazilian interests regarding slave trade, see Bethell (1970).
14 D. João returned to Portugal shortly after the outburst of a constitutional movement in the country. On the Constitutional Assembly activities, including the debates on slave labor in Brazil, see Alexandre (1993).
15 On the characteristics and meaning of physiocracy in Portugal, see Cardoso (1989) and Pereira (1992).
16 Coherently, Silva Lisboa criticizes some *Wealth of Nations* passages conducive to the admission of the superiority of agricultural labor (*Princípios*, appendix 3, p. 149).
17 All citations were translated from Portuguese into English by the author (MCC).
18 The monopoly of gunpowder production was defended by Silva Lisboa. Apart from this, the crown kept public monopolies (*estancos*) in the commercialization of diamonds, *pau-brasil* (brazilwood), tobacco to be sent to India, gold dust.
19 Novais and Arruda (1999) called attention to the fact that Silva Lisboa took the United States as the model to be followed, not a very typical position in Brazil.
20 *Observações 1* includes short notes on the 11/03/1808 Charter, enacted by England, which leveled the charges paid by the commodities exported to England by Portugal or by its Southern colony, whenever transported in Portuguese ships. According to Silva Lisboa, this meant reciprocity to the opening of the Brazilian ports.
21 And so does *Observações 3*, also edited in 1810, but much less substantive than *Observações 2*. The Treaty of amity, commerce, and navigation was discussed in other texts, particularly Lisboa (1818).
22 Silva Lisboa never makes it clear whether he is speaking of colonial North America or of post-independence United States. And insofar as his hero – Franklin – was active in both situations, the picture is still confusing. The lapse of time is important: what manufactures did Silva Lisboa refer to: Franklin's 1750–1780 manufactures or the much more complex 1810 industries?

23 Faria Junior (2008) presents an extensive list of solicitations to the Royal Board of Commerce, Agriculture, Factories and Navigation, and the responses to them (in general, negative).
24 For instance, in Smith, *Wealth of Nations*, Book I, chapter IV; Book III, chapter II; Hume (1777), *Essays*, XI (Of the Populousness of Ancient Nations).
25 According to Montesquieu, *De L'Esprit des Lois*, Livre XV.
26 On slave traders in Salvador and Rio, see Florentino (2002) and Soares (2012).
27 On the importance of tobacco and sugar-cane in African trade, see Alencastro (2000).
28 In Brazil, contrarily to North America, the slave population never achieved a self-reproducing stage. See Luna and Klein (2010).
29 On the expectations of the abolitionist movements, see Blackburn (1988).
30 "It is a very hard matter to introduce industry into a country where slavery is established..." (Steuart, 1767, p. 168).
31 Steuart gives a negative answer to his question: "Could the sugar islands be cultivated to any advantage by hired labour?" (Steuart, 1767, p. 168).

References

Alden, D. 1987. Late Colonial Brazil, 1750–1808. In: Bethell, L., *Colonial Brazil*. Cambridge, Cambridge University Press.
Alencastro, L.F. 2000. *O Trato dos Viventes – Formação do Brasil no Atlântico Sul*. S. Paulo, Companhia das Letras.
Alexandre, V. 1993. *Os Sentidos do Império. Questão nacional e questão colonial na crise do antigo regime português*. Porto, Afrontamento.
Almodovar, A. 1993. *Introdução*. In: Lisboa, J.S. *Escritos Económicos Escolhidos* (1804–1821), 2 vols. Coleção de Obras Clássicas do Pensamento Econômico Português 5, Lisboa, Banco de Portugal.
Almodovar, A. and Cardoso, J.L. 1998. *A History of Portuguese Economic Thought*. London, Routledge.
Bethell, L. 1970. *The Abolition of the Brazilian Slave Trade*. Cambridge, Cambridge University Press.
Blackburn, R. 1988. *The Overthrow of Colonial Slavery – 1776–1848*. London, Verso.
Cardoso, J.L. 1989. *O Pensamento Económico em Portugal nos Finais do Século XVIII – 1780–1808*. Lisboa, Editorial Estampa.
2002. *O liberalismo económico na obra de José da Silva Lisboa*. In: História Econômica e História de Empresas, ABPHE, v.5, n. 1.
Coutinho, M.C. 2011. *José da Silva Lisboa: to what extent a Brazilian liberal?* In: ANPEC, Congresso Brasileiro de Economia. Foz do Iguaçu.
Faria Junior, C. 2008. O Pensamento Econômico de José da Silva Lisboa, Visconde de Cairu. PhD thesis, USP, S. Paulo.
Florentino, M. 2002. *Em Costas Negras. Uma história do tráfico de escravos entre a África e o Rio de Janeiro*. S. Paulo, Companhia das Letras.
Florentino, M., Ribeiro, A.L., Silva, D.D. 2004. *Aspectos Comparativos do Tráfico de Africanos para o Brasil (Séculos XVIII e XIX)*. In: Afro-Ásia, 31.
Hume, D. Essays I–XXI. In: Hume, D. (1777). *Essays Moral, Political and Literary* (edited by E. Miller). Indianapolis, Liberty Fund, 1985.
—Of the Populousness of Ancient Nations, Essay II–XI. In: Hume, D. (1777). *Essays Moral, Political and Literary* (edited by E. Miller). Indianapolis, Liberty Fund, 1985.

Kirschner, T.C. 2009. *José da Silva Lisboa, Visconde de Cairu – Itinerários de um Ilustrado Luso-Brasileiro.* S. Paulo, Alameda.

Lisboa, J.S. 1804–1821. *Princípios de Economia Política* (1804). In: Lisboa, J.S. *Escritos Económicos Escolhidos*, vol. 1. Coleção de Obras Clássicas do Pensamento Econômico Português 5, Lisboa, Banco de Portugal, 1993.

—1810a. *Observações sobre a Franqueza da Indústria e Estabelecimento de Fábricas no Brasil.* In: Lisboa, J.S. *Escritos Económicos Escolhidos* (1804–1821), vol. 1. Coleção de Obras Clássicas do Pensamento Econômico Português 5, Lisboa, Banco de Portugal, 1993.

—1810b. *Observações sobre a Prosperidade do Estado pelos Liberais Princípios da Nova Legislação do Brasil.* In: Lisboa, J.S. *Escritos Económicos Escolhidos* (1804–1821), vol. 1. Coleção de Obras Clássicas do Pensamento Econômico Português 5, Lisboa, Banco de Portugal, 1993.

—1810c. *Observações sobre a prosperidade do Estado pelos liberaes princípios da Nova Legislação do Brasil.* Rio de Janeiro, Impressão Regia. In: www.brasiliana.usp.br/bbd/handle/1918/03878600.

—(1808–1809). *Observações sobre o Comércio Franco do Brasil.* In: Lisboa, J.S. *Escritos Económicos Escolhidos* (1804–1821), vol. 1. Coleção de Obras Clássicas do Pensamento Econômico Português 5, Lisboa, Banco de Portugal, 1993.

—1818. *Memoria dos Benefícios Políticos do Governo de El-Rey Nosso Senhor D. João VI.* Rio de Janeiro, Impressão Regia. In: www.brasiliana.usp.br/bbd/handle /1918/00859000.

—(1819–1820). *Estudos do Bem-Comum e Economia Política.* In: Lisboa, J.S. *Escritos Económicos Escolhidos* (1804–1821), vol. 2. Coleção de Obras Clássicas do Pensamento Econômico Português 5, Lisboa, Banco de Portugal, 1993.

—2001. *Da Liberdade do Trabalho.* In: Rocha, A.P., *José da Silva Lisboa, Visconde de Cairu.* S. Paulo, Ed. 34.

Luna, F.V. and Klein, H.S. 2010. *Escravismo no Brasil.* S. Paulo, Edusp.

Maxwell, K. 1995. *Pombal – Paradox of the Enlightenment.* Cambridge, Cambridge University Press.

Montesquieu, C.S. 1748. *De L'Esprit des Lois.* www.uqac.quebec.ca /zone30.

Novais, F.A. and Arruda, J.J.A. 1999. *Prometeus e Atlantes na Forja da Nação.* In: Lisboa, J.S. (1810) *Observações sobre a Franqueza da Indústria, e Estabelecimento de Fábricas no Brasil.* Brasília, Senado Federal, Coleção Biblioteca Básica Brasileira.

Paim, A. 1968. *Cairu e o Liberalismo Econômico.* R. Janeiro, Tempo Brasileiro.

Pantaleão, O. 1962. *A presença inglesa.* In: Holanda, S.B. (ed.) *História Geral da Civilização Brasileira.* São Paulo, Difusão Européia do Livro.

Pereira, J.E. 1992. *Introdução.* In: Brito, J.J.R. *Memórias Políticas sobre as Verdadeiras Bases da Grandeza das Nações, e Principalmente de Portugal (1803–1805).* Coleção de Obras Clássicas do Pensamento Econômico Português, Lisboa, Banco de Portugal.

Rocha, A.P. 1996. *A Economia Política na Sociedade Escravista.* S. Paulo, Hucitec.

2001. *José da Silva Lisboa, Visconde de Cairu.* S. Paulo, Editora 34.

Say, J.B. 1803. *Traité d'Économie Politique.* Paris, Calmann-Lévy, 1972.

Schwartz, S.B. 1985. *Sugar Plantations in the Formation of Brazilian Society, Bahia 1550–1835.* Cambridge, Cambridge University Press.

1987. Plantations and Peripheries, c. 1580–c. 1750. In: Bethell, L. *Colonial Brazil.* Cambridge, Cambridge University Press.

Sismondi, S. 1819. *Nouveaux Principes d'Économie Politique*. Paris, Calmann-Lévy, 1971.

Smith, A. 1776. *The Wealth of Nations*. Oxford, Oxford University Press, 1976.

Soares, C.F.L. 2012. *Bahia e Angola: Redes Comerciais e o Tráfico de Escravos – 1750–1808*. Tese de doutoramento. Niterói, UFF.

Steuart, J. 1767. *An Inquiry into the Principles of Political Economy*. Ecco Print Editions.

5   The (far) backstory of the US–Colombia Free Trade Agreement

Stephen Meardon

1   Introduction

The US–Colombia Trade Promotion Agreement, also known as the US–Colombia Free Trade Agreement, was signed in November 2006. The United States Congress passed legislation implementing it in October 2011. The five years from the agreement's signing to its passage is a long time for any particular trade deal, but it is a brief moment in the longer history of US trade policy concerning Latin America, and even of US trade deals with Colombia. That history – call it the far backstory of the agreement – goes back to 1824, when the first US commercial treaty with a Latin American partner was signed in Bogotá. It includes three other momentous episodes in the interim.

The backstory adds nuance to a longstanding discussion about the political economy of bilateral trade agreements. Bilateralism could serve free traders by working as "a strategic device to manipulate the political economy environment and to harness it in a war against protectionist forces" (Bhagwati and Irwin 1987: 125). Or it could work as a device for the diversion of trade and thus aid protectionists. So holds the discussion's consensus. The devil, one supposes, is in the agreements' details, which may be construed to include not only their texts but also their supporting institutions. The nuance added by this chapter is that the supposition may be wrong. The devil may lie in details outside the agreements' texts and institutional superstructures.

Put differently, although the history of US–Colombia trade deals supports the consensus view that bilateralism may promote the interests of either free traders or protectionists, that is not why it matters. The history matters because it points up the ambiguity of bilateralism even while holding constant the trade partners, and, what is more, holding more or less constant the deals' textual provisions and institutional superstructure. In two pairs of episodes, first in 1824 and 1846 and then in 1892 and 1935, similar US–Colombia trade deals or their enabling laws were embraced first by protectionists and then by free traders. The upshot is that in order to understand which doctrinal position a given deal promotes and why, identifying the partners, reading the text, and being mindful of the supporting institutions (e.g., Irwin 2002) may not suffice. The intentions and ideological affinities of the players carry a good deal of weight regardless of the rules of the game.

We are left with a twist on Daron Acemoglu and James Robinson's (2008: 285) argument that, although political institutions generally curb *de facto* political power, "some specific dimensions of political institutions can be undone by the greater exercise of *de facto* political power." Acemoglu and Robinson refer to the effective undoing of *changes* in institutions of democratic decision-making. But their argument applies as well to the effective undoing of *persistence* in institutions of trade policy-making, including trade deal-making. The far backstory of the US–Colombia FTA shows how. It also sheds light on the agreement's five-year delay in coming to fruition.

No similar history has been published, although several bodies of literature inform this chapter and a few works overlap it in part. The first category includes important contributions to the general tariff history of United States (Taussig 1892; Stanwood 1903), the diplomatic history of US territorial expansion and trade with Latin America (Bemis 1943; Pletcher 1962, 1973, 1998), the economic and tariff history of Colombia (Ospina Vasquez 1955; McGreevey 1971; Ocampo 1984; Ocampo and Montenegro 2007), and the general history of diplomatic relations between the two countries (Parks 1935; Randall 1977, 1992). The second includes an excellent but brief survey of the history US reciprocity policy (Irwin 2002), and longer studies that are more limited in the kinds of reciprocity admitted (Laughlin and Willis 1903) or the time period canvassed (Setser 1937; Terrill 1973; Steward 1975; Butler 1998). It includes also three other works that occupy nearly the same place as this chapter in all the foregoing historical literature, albeit for briefer periods of US reciprocity with Colombia (Huck 1991; Delpar 1999) or for reciprocity with a different partner, namely Mexico (Riguzzi 2003). This chapter draws from them but tells a different story.

Sections 2 and 3 of the chapter concern two treaties signed in 1824 and 1846 with similar contents but different proponents and purposes. Section 4 centers on a proposed executive agreement of 1892 that yielded only acrimony; Section 5, on an agreement of 1935 with related institutional foundations but different motives and consequences. Section 6 concludes.

2   The Treaty of 1824

The first US commercial treaty with an independent American republic was signed in Bogotá on October 3, 1824, near the end of John Quincy Adams's tenure as Secretary of State to President Monroe. The date of ratification, six months later, came in the first days of Adams's own presidency and Henry Clay's leadership of the State Department. Adams and especially Clay advocated tariff protection for US import-competing goods. How their protectionism related to the treaty is the question to be considered here.

Although Clay was newly installed in his position, his advocacy of a closer commercial relationship between the United States and Spanish America was longstanding. No sooner had peace been restored to Europe with Napoleon's final defeat in 1815 than the victors began a "scramble for the spoils of Bonaparte's empire," as Clay had put it (*Annals of Congress* 1818: 1494). Collectively, the kingdoms of Great Britain and Europe maneuvered to stifle the republican aspirations of Spanish America. Individually, they sought to win control for themselves – or, failing that, to block transfer of the provinces' sovereignty to anyone else.

From the beginning of the Spanish American struggle for independence its leaders looked to the United States as the exemplar of New-World republicanism and resistance. From the US they received popular sympathy in return (Rivas 1915: 7–8, 14–15). Clay, then Speaker of the House, had proposed that the US government should grant the new republics not only sympathy but also recognition. Political recognition would be given practical effect by stronger commercial ties (Clay and Swain [1818] 1843: 90–93).

Promoting a republican hemisphere by moral suasion and commercial ties was a central pillar of Clay's "American system" (Campbell 1967). It was consistent with President Monroe's famous message of 1823, which held the circumstances of US relations within the hemisphere to be "eminently and conspicuously different" from those outside of it.[1] In Clay's view, and likewise in John Quincy Adams's, the pillar of US hemispheric stewardship and the better-remembered one of tariff protection were mutually reinforcing.[2] The US–Colombia treaty of 1824 was the outgrowth of that view.

To be sure, in promoting hemispheric solidarity Clay had begun with moral not commercial arguments. Spanish America, he declaimed to Congress in March, 1818, was subject to a "stupendous system of colonial despotism" (*Annals of Congress* 1818: 1477) entailing both violent repression and commercial restriction. Not even the United States had suffered such tyranny before breaking from its master. Spanish America was an abused and neglected relation who asked merely for recognition from her republican kin, and the US was obliged to offer it.

But soon he came to practical considerations. Great Britain and Spain had barred access to the ports of the West Indies and Spanish America to all but the ships of the mother countries, and had governed their agriculture so as to serve imperial rather than colonial interests. Such was the system of the Old World. In contradistinction, the system of the New was identified not only with republican forms of government but also with breaking the fetters on international navigation and establishing laws to serve the needs of each country. The benefits for the United States of the Spanish-American provinces' adoption of such a system – which, two years later, he would call explicitly the "American system" (*Annals of Congress* 1820: 2228) – were manifest. Although for the moment the US produced few products of importance to them, nevertheless, once Spanish-American ports were opened without discrimination, the advantage in shipping would lie with the burgeoning US merchant marine. "Our navigation will be benefitted by the transportation," said Clay, "and our country will realize the mercantile profits" (*Annals of Congress* 1818: 1486). Besides, US manufacturers, however few they presently were, would find a ready market in the Americas – while the more numerous tillers and miners of the land would be unthreatened by imports of precious metals, cocoa, coffee, sugar, and assorted other articles, of which, by Clay's calculations, less than 2 percent, consisting mainly of cotton, competed with their products (ibid.: 1484–1486).

The treaty of 1824 with Colombia (then "Gran" Colombia, encompassing Venezuela and Ecuador as well as New Granada) was supposed to provide the legal framework to promote those results. The treaty's centerpiece was Article II, which stipulated the most-favored-nation (MFN) principle in its conditional form. The US and Colombia promised reciprocally not to grant any favor in commerce and navigation to third parties without its being made extensive to the other treaty partner, "who shall enjoy the same freely if the concession was freely made, or on allowing the same compensation if the concession was conditional" (Malloy 1910, vol. 1: 293).

Yet providing the legal framework to promote the results Clay foresaw was not the same as actually promoting them. That would require more than MFN guarantees. After all, although MFN implied nondiscrimination in the com-mercial relations of the US and Colombia, it was only in the limited sense of each country's eschewal of discrimination against its treaty partner vis-à-vis all other countries. Each country reserved the right to discriminate against its treaty partner in favor of itself. That is to say, MFN did not imply national treatment of the partner's commercial agents or ships, nor of the partner's goods as free trade would require.

Indeed, MFN as inscribed in Article II of the US–Colombia treaty did not really even demand that each country's future commercial favors to third par-ties be extended to the other treaty partner. The conditional clause appears to make room for such extensions; in practice it made them unlikely. With con-ditional MFN, favors granted afterward to another country by a subsequent treaty could always be construed as having been made only on condition of all other articles in the treaty. The favors would have to be made extensive to the original partner, therefore, only on condition of the partner's assent to a complete set of identical articles. A country's treaties with its several partners differed in a sufficient number of articles, and in sufficient detail, that such an event could scarcely ever happen. In short, the extent to which the MFN treaty really promoted US navigation and exports of US goods was bound to depend mainly on circumstances outside of the treaty's text.

The circumstances for promoting exports were not wholly favorable so long as US manufacturers required protection in order to prosper, and so long as their protection remained a political priority. So it remained during Adams's presidency. Adams did *not* aim to make reciprocal commitments that might result in general reductions of tariffs on US imports and thus expand simul-taneously the field for the principal US exports (which comprised mainly agri-cultural goods, provisions, and lumber).[3] Protection for manufactures entailed keeping US merchandise tariffs high – even increasing them, as Congress did with the protectionist tariff of 1824, which Adams was understood to favor (Stanwood 1903, v.1: 241; see also Table 5.1).

Table 5.1 US tariffs on imports from colombia under major tariff acts, 1816–1930

	Bananas	Cinchonal Peruvian bark (for quinine)	Cochineal	Cocoa	Coffee	Dye-Wood	Gold & silver coins, Bullion	Hats	Hides raw/salted	India rubber	Indigo	Petroleum Crude	Platinum	Silk,raw	Suger, Brown	Tabacco, Unmanuf.
1816	n/a	n/a	n/a	2c./lb	5c./lb	Free	Free	30%	Free	n/a	15c./lb	n/a	n/a	n/a	3c./lb	15%
1824	"	"	"	"	"	"	"	50%	"	"	"	"	"	"	"	"
1828	"	"	"	"	"	"	"	"	"	"	20–50c./lb	"	"	"	"	"
1832	"	Free	Free	Free	Free	"	"	30%	"	"	15%	"	Free	12.50%	25c./lb	"
1842	Free	"	"	1c./lb	"	"	"	35%	5%	30%	5c./lb	"	"	50c./lb	"	20%
1846	20%	15%	10%	10%	Free	5%	"	30%	"	10%	10%	"	"	15%	30%	30%
1857	8%	Free	4%	4%	"	Free	"	24%	4%	4%	4%	"	"	Free	24%	24%
1861	Free	10%	Free	Free	"	"	"	30%	5%	Free	Free	"	"	"	0.75c./lb	25%
1864	25%	20%	3c./lb	3c./lb	5c./lb	"	"	40%	10%	10%	"	10c./lb	"	"	3c./lb	35c./lb
1870	10%	Free	2c./lb	3c./lb	"	"	"	"	"	Free	"	20c./lb	"	"	1.75c./lb	"
1872	10%	"	Free	Free	Free	"	"	"	Free	"	"	20c./lb	"	"	1.75c./lb	"
1874	10%	"	"	"	"	"	"	"	"	"	"	"	"	"	2.1875c./lb	"
1883	Free	"	"	"	"	"	"	30%	"	"	"	10%	"	"	1.4c./lb	"
1890	"	"	"	"	"	"	"	Free	"	"	"	Free	"	"	0.95c./lb	"
1894	"	"	"	"	"	"	"	"	"	"	"	"	"	"	40%	"
1897	"	"	"	"	"	"	"	35%	15%	"	"	"	"	"	0.95c./lb	"
1909	"	"	"	"	"	"	"	Free	Free	"	"	"	"	"	"	"
1913	"	"	"	"	"	"	"	25%	"	"	"	Free	"	"	0.71c./lb	"
1922	"	"	15%	"	"	"	"	35%	"	"	7 c./lb+45%	"	"	"	1.24c./lb	"
1930	"	"	Free	"	"	"	"	25%	10%	"	"	"	"	"	1.7125c./lb	15%

Sources: For the tariff act of 1816 up to that of 1846, US House Doc. No. 227, 29th Cong., 1st Sess. (1846): for 1842 to 1864, US Senate Ex. Doc. No. 2, 39th Cong., 2nd Sess. (1867), Appendix C; for 1816 to 1890, US Senate Report No. 2130, 51st Cong., 2nd Sess. (1891); for 1890 to 1897, US Senate Doc. No. 329, 55th Cong., 2nd Sess. (1898); for 1897 to 1909, US House Doc. No. 948, 61st Cong., 2nd Sess. (1910); for 1913 to 1930, US Senate Doc. No. 119, 71st Cong., 2nd Sess. (1930); and for all years, the texts of the tariff acts as reprinted by Northrup and Turney (2003).

Notes: Rows with boldfaced entries and borders highlight tariff laws in force during all or part of a period of US–Colombia commercial negotiations: 1824, 1846–1848, 1891–1894, and 1932–1933. Cells shaded in gray show when certain Colombian goods were imported to the US duty-free.

Promoting navigation was more promising. The benefits of a treaty, Adams told Richard C. Anderson, his chargé d'affaires in Bogotá, lay in Americans' prospects as "*carriers* to and for [Colombia] of numerous Articles of Manufactures, and of foreign produce" (Adams to Anderson, May 27, 1823: 298).[4] In order to improve the prospects he sought, first, an end to Colombia's rebate of between 5 percent and 7.5 percent on the *ad valorem* duties levied on goods imported directly from Europe (including Great Britain) – a rebate that was not applied to goods imported from the United States whether indirectly or directly. According to the Colombian Minister of Foreign Relations, it was intended to promote direct trade between Europe and Colombia and thereby European recognition (ibid: 286). Adams appreciated the ultimate aim but not the instrument. The MFN provision of Article II would prohibit it, thus guaranteeing US navigation at least nominally a more level footing.

The other twenty-nine articles of the treaty worked mainly to the same effect. They left both parties entirely free to pursue a protectionist policy; they allowed the United States to promote selected industries, especially manufactures, while eliminating the most explicit acts of discrimination against US ships in Colombian ports.

Samuel Flagg Bemis ([1949] 1973: 468) characterized the policy of Adams's secretaryship and presidency as "reciprocal freedom of commerce with all nations and colonies." The characterization is accurate only by narrow definitions of "freedom" and "commerce." The US–Colombia treaty stipulated, albeit conditionally, nondiscrimination in importation of goods and in shipping between the other party and all other partners. In that sense the treaty provided for greater liberalism in shipping – but not exchange of the goods to be shipped. It fostered more equal treatment of intermediaries, irrespective of nationality – but not greater freedom for consumers or producers. Even allowing for those concessions to expediency that are inevitable in a political system of checks and balances, Adams's program did not resemble remotely what then or now would be called "free trade." "A level footing for commercial services" would be more apt.

The treaty of 1824 was an imperfect instrument for promoting some of Adams's and Clay's designs. It hastened European recognition of Colombian independence (Parks 1935: 103–105), and, notwithstanding growing doubts in the United States about General Simón Bolívar's commitment to republicanism (Rivas 1915: 69–71; Parks 1935: 151–158), it helped to maintain Colombia's attachment to that form of government by lending moral support to its advocates. The treaty also proved to be perfectly compatible with the protective tariff of 1824, and even the "Tariff of Abominations" of 1828, which raised the average US tariff to approximately 60 percent by 1830.[5]

On the other hand, the treaty did not, as Adams and Clay had hoped, put the US on a footing that was truly level with that of any other Colombian trade partner. We shall see why not. The upshot was that it was not long before US–Colombia commercial negotiations commenced again.

3   The treaty of 1846

The reason for the 1824 treaty's failure to fulfill completely the hopes of its US authors was the same as that of its considerable success. It was the leeway for both parties to adopt policies that were neither expressly entertained nor plainly proscribed by the treaty's text but were surely at odds with its spirit. Colombia's government happened to be adept at using that leeway.

Colombian trade policy at the time discriminated among foreign suppliers of goods and services, as well as between foreign and domestic suppliers, in multiple dimensions. Take for example a US vessel's shipment of US soap and tallow candles – manufactures baser than Adams and Clay envisioned but among the few that were actually exported to Colombia. Under the tariff law of 1821, Colombia subjected the shipment to a net 25 percent import duty, a significant but not extraordinary degree of protection. But Colombian soap and candle producers were not the only ones protected. If the merchandise came in a Colombian rather than a US vessel, the duty was 20 percent. If similar merchandise came from Europe rather than the United States, and if it was transported to Colombia directly (without passing through any other port) in a foreign vessel, then too the duty was 20 percent. If it came from Europe directly in a Colombian vessel, the duty was 12.5 percent. Thus the discrimination of which Adams complained was part of a larger tangle. Colombian duties discriminated in favor of domestic as opposed to foreign producers, domestic as opposed to foreign shipping, and direct commercial intercourse with Europe as opposed to the United States.

In 1823, in anticipation of the treaty negotiations, the Colombian government brought the tariff law into conformance with the treaty's expected MFN stipulation.[6] This was accomplished simply by rewording the law to afford the same treatment to shipments arriving from the United States as from Europe, all else equal. Thus *de jure* discrimination against the United States ended.

Yet *de facto* discrimination continued, as Colombian customs officials collected an additional 5 percent *ad valorem* duty on goods imported in US vessels when the goods were not produced in the United States. William Henry Harrison, who was briefly US Minister to Colombia for President Andrew Jackson, saw the impediment that the duty entailed for the US carrying trade as "almost constituting a complete prohibition" (quoted by Rivas 1915: 76). The legal basis was a matter of perplexity. Thomas P. Moore, who succeeded Harrison from 1829 to 1833, professed his inability "to ascertain whether this practice is founded on law, on arbitrary usage, or on the caprice or cupidity of the collectors" (Moore to Minister of Foreign Relations, Nov. 4, 1831); the Colombian ministers of whom he inquired could do no better (ibid.; also Minister of Foreign Affairs to Moore, Nov. 9 and 14, 1831).[7] The likeliest basis was the interpretation by Colombian officials of their country's tariff law, which levied *ad valorem* duties 5 percent lower upon "goods, imported in foreign vessels that proceed … from Europe or the United States" (Ley de 13 de Marzo, 1826), to mean that the lower duties applied only when the goods as well as the vessels "proceeded" from Europe or the United States, *and* that they did so in the sense of the goods having been produced in the particular place whence the vessel arrived.[8]

Of all the more-or-less reasonable ways of construing the law, this would arguably have been on the less reasonable end of the spectrum. It would surely have been the least obvious; the most advantageous to Great Britain, whose vessels could be laden wholly with British exports; and the most injurious to the United States, whose vessels, for lack of variety in US manufactures, were laden with mixed cargoes of US flour and manufactures together with re-exported British, French, and other goods (Moore to Secretary of State Edward Livingston, Nov. 21, 1831).[9]

During the political turmoil of the early 1830s, as Ecuador and Venezuela separated from New Granada (here to be called Colombia, the name readopted by the diminished country in 1863), Minister Moore's diplomacy was successful in eliminating temporarily the discriminatory 5 percent duty. To the dismay of US officials, the elimination lasted only a year before the Ministry of Finance effectively reimposed it. Secretary of State John Forsyth smelled the influence of "the importunities of the Representative of His Britannic Majesty" (Forsyth to Chargé d'Affaires Robert B. McAfee, May 1, 1835: 15).[10] Several years later, a new chargé, William M. Blackford, identified the deeper reasons for the discriminating duty's tenaciousness. On the one hand, many Colombians had a deep-seated fear that abolishing it "would throw the whole of the commerce of the country into our [US] hands" (Blackford to Secretary of State Daniel Webster, June 3, 1843).[11] On the other, many more held the "delusive idea" that preserving it would foster a Colombian merchant marine (Blackford to Webster, March 18, 1843).[12]

During the remainder of President Jackson's administration and the succeeding ones of Van Buren, Harrison, Tyler, and Polk, the State Department sought a new treaty abolishing the discriminating duty once and for all. This was to be done not by trying to state or enforce more adequately the United States' MFN standing, but by securing a firmer standing altogether. As Secretary Forsyth explained, MFN as provided by Article 2 of the treaty of 1824 proved "in practice to be uncertain and illusory": so it could be "with the best intentions on both sides," and so it surely would be "with a desire to disregard the spirit of the article by either" (Forsyth to John G. A. Williamson, chargé d'affaires to Venezuela, Apr. 15, 1835: 9). The aim was full national treatment in navigation. The model was the United States' treaty of 1828 with Brazil, guaranteeing that each country's duties would apply equally to imports brought by vessels of either country, regardless of the origin of their cargoes (Forsyth to McAfee, May 1, 1835).[13]

At the same time, another US aim in the region was coming clearly into view. The Isthmus of Panama had long been the site of interest from Europe, the United States, and Colombia in a permanent route uniting the oceans, whether by macadamized road, railroad, or canal. In the 1830s, interest intensified. Panama's stirrings of independence from Colombia was a reminder of the contingency of the Isthmus's political attachment to Bogotá. An important faction of influential Panamanians favored independence, which they proposed to secure by way of a protectorate under Great Britain, France, or the United States (Martínez Delgado 1972: 60). Each of those powers endeavored anxiously to stop the others from winning control of the Isthmus, and with it trans-Oceanic commerce. No less anxious was the government and political class of Colombia, for whom sovereignty over the Isthmus implied the collection of whatever rents might be garnered from an Isthmian passageway.

The combination of the US aims regarding navigation and the Isthmus, Colombian worries about Isthmian sovereignty, and changed political circumstances in both the US and Colombia beginning in 1845 finally broke the treaty logjam. In the United States, the Democratic Party took control of both the Senate and the executive office. President Polk's program was the acquisition of all of the southwest of the present-day United States, including California. His anticipation of acquiring California made the construction of an Isthmian passageway, and the rights of US citizens to use it, matters of special urgency. In Colombia, a new president assuming office simultaneously with Polk, Tomás Cipriano de Mosquera, drew his breath from the same ideological winds that would soon produce Great Britain's abolition of the Corn Laws and the United States' liberal Walker Tariff (Mejía Arango 2007: 35). The consequences were a significant reduction in Colombian tariffs and a fraying attachment to the discriminatory 5 percent duty (Mejía Arango2007: 35–36; Ocampo 2007: 299).

The second consequence, however, had an additional cause. Colombian resentment toward Great Britain had been mounting since British naval actions earlier in the decade challenged Bogotá's sovereignty north of the Isthmus on the Mosquito coast.[14] While the Colombian government protested the moves, it also gave authority in 1843 for its chargé d'affaires in London to negotiate with one or more of the governments of Great Britain, France, the United States, Holland, and Spain, either to construct a canal, ceding such tolls as would be necessary to reimburse the expenses of construction, or to guarantee the neutrality of the canal while construction and operation of was undertaken by a private company. In either case the proposed treaty would recognize Colombian sovereignty over the canal territory.[15] When the British government rebuffed both the treaty and Colombia's claims concerning the Mosquito coast, Colombian opinion took a turn. Discrimination for Great Britain and against the United States lost official favor (Parks 1935: 198–200). The United States had not even to ask for the abolition of the discriminating duty. In return for a guarantee of sovereignty over the Isthmus, President Mosquera's Minister of Foreign Affairs, Manuel María Mallarino, offered it upfront (enclosure, Chargé Benjamin A. Bidlack to Secretary of State James Buchanan, Dec. 10, 1846).[16]

The official interests of the United States and Colombia at last coming into alignment, the treaty proposed by Mallarino was signed on December 12, 1846 (Malloy 1910: 302–314). The United States obtained the abolition of discrimination by way of national treatment in navigation (Article

IV). National treatment for re-exportation from each country in vessels of the other was also explicitly allowed. But these provisions were no longer ends in themselves: now they amounted to an assurance that no other power would win exclusive privileges in trans-Isthmian commerce. The assurance was elaborated in Article XXXV, which also contained the crucial US guarantee of "the perfect neutrality" of the Isthmus. The guarantee required the United States to use its power "positively and efficaciously" to prevent any interruption of the free passage of goods and people over the territory – and, "in consequence," to maintain Colombia's sovereignty over it. In later years Colombians would see the guarantee as having precisely the opposite consequence (Díaz-Callejas 1997). For the moment, however, the guarantee met resistance not mainly in Colombia but rather in the United States, where it awakened old apprehensions of "entangling alliances" (Parks 1935: 208–209).

Yet there were even greater apprehensions about the treaty than those stirred up by Article XXXV. When at last the treaty was ratified by the US Senate on June 3, 1848, a full year and a half after its signing, only four of the twenty-nine senators voting in favor were from the Whig Party, which counted Adams and Clay among its elder statesman. Of those four, none was from farther north than Pennsylvania. Of the seven voting against, six were Whigs and one a Free Soiler, none from farther south than New Jersey.[17] All of them, for and against, saw the treaty rightly as part and parcel of the program for territorial expansion pressed by President Polk and the Democratic Party – a program intended to extend the potential domain of slavery. By their lights the text of the treaty mattered less than the intentions of the administration that negotiated it.

4   The spurned proposal of 1892

Before the US Civil War, the doctrinal pendulum swung between free trade and protection without much consequence to US–Colombia reciprocity. Administrations in both countries and of both doctrinal inclinations pursued commercial treaties of basically the same form, centered on the MFN principle in goods trade and MFN or national treatment in navigation. After the Civil War, despite some challenges, protectionism prevailed for nearly half a century. Its prevalence entailed changes to US–Colombia commercial relations. And yet the changes did not go in the direction of restricting trade.

The Morrill Tariff of 1861, together with three more acts through 1865, raised duties steeply. In 1848, total customs duties were 23 percent of the value of merchandise imports and 26 percent of dutiable merchandise imports. By 1866 the figures were 42 percent and 48 percent.[18] The duties garnered revenue for prosecuting the war; they also stimulated the United States' nascent and import-competing manufacturing industry. The protective doctrine of the time articulated rationales and sought legislation for cementing the gains to manufacturing and promoting their growth. Doing so involved, in two distinct senses, a diversion.

First, duties on food staples and raw materials could be reduced so as to divert the political will for comprehensive tariff reductions. As the moderate protectionist (and then Congressman) James A. Garfield put it in 1870, without a "reasonable reduction" of tariffs the backlash against them would "soon seriously shatter our whole protective system" (*Cong. Globe*, 41st Cong., 2nd sess., appendix: 272). So the Tariff Act of 1870 added unmanufactured lumber, "india" rubber, rags for paper-making, and cinchona bark for quinine-making to the free list, and reduced substantially the tariffs on other items. Free rubber and cinchona were a boon to Colombia, but it was the other reductions that mattered more, especially coffee. Then coffee was added to the free list two years later, and likewise cocoa, so as to "take the taxes from the breakfast table" (Stanwood 1903, v.2: 173). Hides were added as well, as were bananas in 1883 (see Table 5.1). Thus was established by the end of the 1880s a seemingly paradoxical state of affairs. By assent of protectionist legislators, and without the Colombian government having to offer a single concession, every single one of the top five US imports from Colombia entered duty-free.

Second, protectionists embraced the use of reciprocal-trade deals to divert Latin American imports of manufactures from Great Britain and Europe to the United States. For most protectionists the embrace entailed an awkward shift of policy and doctrine. The reciprocity deals that were needed were not the old MFN kind. They were a new kind that garnered positive discrimination in favor of the United States, and granted it reciprocally to the partner, by stipulating preferential duties that each party would levy on the other's products. A treaty to that effect had been tried with Canada in 1854 and protectionists had widely condemned it. In the 1870s protectionists began to see things differently, at least where tropical countries were concerned. Such countries, according to protectionist apostle Henry C. Carey (1876: 8), offered "commodities for which [US] soils, or climates, are not well fitted," so arrangements fostering their purchase in exchange for US manufactures could be mutually beneficial.[19]

The new view was inscribed in several treaties, first during the administration of President Grant and later that of President Arthur. But lingering skepticism among some protectionists and gathering opposition from free traders stalled most of the treaties in Congress. Their stalling somewhere on the way to enactment was hard to circumvent because their stipulation of particular tariffs qualified them as revenue acts. As with any revenue act, and unlike other treaties, the approval of not only the Senate but also the House was needed – a high hurdle. Only the controversial treaty of 1875 with Hawaii, allowing that country's sugar to enter the US duty-free in exchange for reciprocal preferences for a host of US goods, while expressly prohibiting Hawaii to make the preferences extensive to any other country, overcame all the obstacles and became law. Treaty projects with Mexico, Spain (for Cuba and Puerto Rico), Santo Domingo, Great Britain (for the West Indies), El Salvador, and Colombia all failed at one stage or another.[20]

Opponents of the treaties had two main reasons for voting against them. The reason of liberal traders was given in the adverse report of the House Ways and Means Committee on the failed Mexican treaty of 1883. The Committee, then dominated by Democrats, urged Congress to "reform and reduce the tariff and neither offer nor ask special treaties or provisions from any nation, but openly, fairly, and honestly … compete for the trade of all nations" (House Rept. No. 2615, 49th Cong., 1st sess.: 5).[21] The other main reason for voting No, although incongruent with the first, was given in the same report. Mexico offered no concessions with respect to cotton textiles, a manufacture that US *protectionists* hoped to promote. And why *should* anyone expect Mexico to concede anything? As with Colombia, most of what the United States imported from Mexico already entered duty-free. So it could hardly have been surprising that Mexico "refuses the only concession which would in a measure compensate for what she receives" (ibid.: 5).

The obstacles to reciprocity in the 1870s and 1880s were pregnant with lessons. Protectionists had already seen the futility of using commercial treaties to divert goods trade unless the treaties stipulated preferential tariffs, not just MFN treatment. Now they saw the difficulty of getting such treaties through the US House of Representatives as well as the Senate. And they saw the unlikelihood of negotiating significant concessions, even from relatively weak partners, when the reciprocal concessions wanted by the partners were inscribed from the get-go in the US tariff schedule. If reciprocity was to be undertaken for protectionist ends, then it had to be undertaken differently.

By the turn of the 1890s, Secretary of State James G. Blaine's plan to achieve those ends was to forgo treaties altogether. Better to avoid their "delay and uncertainty" and vest power in *the President* to declare US ports free to the entry of goods from partner countries that did the same for US foodstuffs, lumber, metals, machinery, and other products (Sen. Ex. Doc. No. 158, 51st Cong., 1st sess.: 6). Thus was conceived Section 3, the "reciprocal trade provisions," of the Tariff Act of 1890. Although coffee, tea, and hides would remain on the free list (and sugar and molasses added to it), the President was authorized to levy an alternative schedule of higher duties on those products, so long as they originated from any country whose treatment of US products was, in his judgment, "reciprocally unjust and unreasonable" (26 *US Stat*: 612).

The authorization was effective January 1, 1892. Some countries hastened to head off an adverse judgment before that date: by the end of 1891, Blaine had extracted agreements for the modification of the tariff laws of Santo Domingo, Cuba, Puerto Rico, El Salvador, and Guatemala (ibid.: 472). Colombia took a different tack, and waited. A week after the deadline, Blaine informed the Colombian minister to the United States, José Marcelino Hurtado, that waiting would do no good. The President deemed Colombia's treatment of US goods unequal and unreasonable. Section 3 of the new tariff act would be invoked if "some satisfactory commercial arrangement" were not reached by mid-March (Blaine to Hurtado, Jan. 7, 1892, in US Dept. of State 1894: 2–3).

On behalf of his government Hurtado offered several responses. He led with his weaker ones – which, nevertheless, were not easily dismissed. Colombia's tariff law, for instance, was no more burdensome to the United States than it was to Great Britain, France, and Spain (Hurtado to Blaine, Feb. 25, 1892, ibid.: 5). For some goods of interest to the US, like manufactures of wood, iron, and steel, it was no burden at all. They entered duty-free. Admittedly, for goods not on the free list, tariffs were high, but the purpose of high tariffs was to raise revenue. Tariff discrimination against the United States would be valid grounds for complaint, but the height of nondiscriminatory tariffs was not (ibid.: 10). Thus by Hurtado's lights the United States' complaint was really an unjust interference in Colombian governance.

Then came his stronger argument. Even if Colombia's tariffs were too high, US retaliation with discriminatory tariffs on Colombian goods would violate US treaty obligations. For under the treaty of 1846, Hurtado reminded Blaine, his country was guaranteed MFN treatment.

Until the United States followed through with the threatened retaliation, Hurtado did not emphasize the last argument. Then President Harrison issued the proclamation of higher duties on Colombian goods effective March 15, 1892. Thereafter Hurtado wrote repeatedly, indeed relentlessly, that the United States was in violation of Article II of the treaty of 1846. He did so, it is interesting to note, *not* mainly in reference to the more favorable treatment afforded to Santo Domingo, Cuba, Puerto Rico, El Salvador, and Guatemala, from whom the United States had extracted agreements. Instead he took a position more difficult to assail. He referred to the favorable treatment afforded to Argentina, Uruguay, Mexico, the Dutch Caribbean colonies, Chile, and Peru, from whom the United States had not extracted agreements, and yet against whom the United States did not retaliate. "Under these circumstances," he insisted, "the favor which is gratuitously and freely granted to other nations, as above set forth, should immediately become common to Colombia, who can not be deprived the enjoyment thereof without the violation of express treaty stipulations" (Hurtado to Blaine, March 25, 1892, ibid.: 18).

Blaine and his successor as Secretary of State, John W. Foster, brushed off the argument. Blaine rejected the allegation that the United States was discriminating against Colombia, for "the law cited applies the same treatment to countries whose tariffs are found by the President to be unequal and unreasonable" (Blaine to Hurtado, May 31, 1892, ibid.: 25). As for Hurtado's reference to Argentina, Uruguay, et al.: notwithstanding the United States' inability as yet to reach an agreement with them, "it may be stated that the negotiations so far conducted with them have not been attended with the same unsatisfactory results which have marked our efforts to reach an agreement with Colombia" (ibid.: 25). In short, the theory that the US remained faithful to its MFN commitment hinged on Colombia's singular unreasonableness – as evidenced by Blaine's opinion that Colombia was unlikelier than other countries to offer a deal to his liking. No special Colombian sympathies are required to say the theory was pretty tenuous.

To Hurtado it was worse than tenuous. He protested at length against the "unwarranted and unjustifiable violations" of the treaty of 1846; he demanded not just a remedy but reparations (Hurtado to Foster, July 28, 1892, ibid.: 34). But the protest only set Secretary Foster more solidly against him. To Foster, hearing the United States so "arraigned" confirmed Colombia's unreasonableness: "You must ... readily comprehend, Mr. Minister, how great an obstruction exists in your note of July 28 to any friendly settlement of the reciprocity question" (Foster to Hurtado, Sept. 8, 1892, ibid.: 38).

Relief for Colombia came after the fall election and the substitution of Grover Cleveland for Benjamin Harrison in the White House. The Democratic platform of 1892 denounced the "sham reciprocity" of the 1890 Tariff Act, which, it claimed, pretended to foster trade while really suppressing or diverting it. But undoing the Harrison administration's reciprocity diplomacy was more complicated than opposing it. Rather than accepting publicly the validity of the Colombian case, the Cleveland administration found it expedient to simply push for a new tariff act repealing Section 3 of the previous one. Congress acquiesced. With the Wilson Tariff Act of 1894 the United States returned to a nondiscriminatory tariff, rendering moot the demand for a remedy. That was good enough for Colombia's government, which dropped the demand for reparations.

The post-Wilson Act improvement in US–Colombia trade relations was tempered by two other consequences of the trade-policy maneuvers of 1890–1894. One was the example set by United States' extraction of concessions from its partners not mainly by offering concessions in exchange, but by leveraging the favorable tariff treatment already afforded. It had been done threateningly by the Harrison administration. In Colombia's case, it had been done ineffectively and in violation of treaty obligations. But in no fewer than nine cases, it had worked. Even free traders took note.

The other consequence was a lingering suspicion among the United States' hemispheric partners, especially Colombia, that Uncle Sam negotiated in bad faith. What did a trade deal with the US imply, when its government could construe the text contrary to the plainest (and traditionally American) understanding? When a settled bargain could be effectively renegotiated at the United States' will?

5 The agreement of 1935

Such suspicion abroad was the backdrop of the first major report of the permanent United States Tariff Commission, established under President Woodrow Wilson in 1917. The commission determined that the country's admixture of conditional and unconditional MFN treaties, preferential treaties, and executive tariff bargains was a recipe for discord. "Concessions are asked; they are sometimes refused; counter concessions are proposed; reprisal and retaliation are suggested; unpleasant controversies and sometimes international friction result" (US Tariff Commission 1919: 10). At a moment when the United States' general foreign-policy objective was to build a post-war order that would reduce international friction, a new model for US commercial relations was required.

Reciprocity along the lines of the McKinley Act, which was "in reality simply a penalizing measure" (ibid.: 193), did not seem to fit the bill. In 1923, President Harding and Secretary of State Charles Evans Hughes reckoned they found a congenial substitute in a program of commercial treaties centered on the unconditional MFN clause. But meanwhile the ebb and flow of the general tariff law left most US imports from Colombia, as from other countries of the hemisphere, duty-free.[22] So the problem of getting hemispheric partners to lower barriers on US exports was pretty much the same as President Harrison and Secretary Blaine faced thirty years before. And so was the solution: a penalizing measure. Section 317 of the Fordney–McCumber Act of 1922 authorized the President to levy additional duties of up to 50 percent *ad valorem*, or even to issue an outright ban, on goods imported from countries discriminating against the United States. The Harding administration and subsequent ones wielded the stick of Section 317 together with the carrot of unconditional MFN treaties. In order to wield the stick effectively they sometimes did it menacingly (Meardon 2011a).

Enactment of the Hawley–Smoot Tariff of 1930 hardly made the US stance less menacing, but other foreign-policy initiatives of the late 1920s and early 1930s were at least intended to do so. The United States' repudiation of the Roosevelt corollary of the Monroe Doctrine during the tenure of President Hoover and Secretary Stimson laid the foundation of the Good Neighbor policy. The policy was embraced early and vigorously by President Franklin D. Roosevelt upon his inauguration in 1933, but what it implied concretely for trade policy was unclear. Good-neigborliness in that domain might have seemed more likely if US tariff law and negotiations were guided by some fixed principle: say, nondiscrimination. But a fixed principle was not enough – certainly that one was not. The reciprocity negotiations under the McKinley Act had been guided by the principle of non-discrimination against the United States. Those under the initiative of Secretary Hughes had been guided by the principle of reciprocal nondiscrimination, as inscribed in mutual grants of unconditional-MFN status. As the Tariff Commission had foreseen in its report of 1919, the effect of adopting any particular principle really depended "upon the honesty, consistency, and rigidity or liberality with which the application is made to conform to the principle" (US Tariff Commission 1919: 42). To Latin Americans, the United States' good-neighborliness in respect to trade policy would be seen not in the text of any new agreements but in their context.

In the first year of FDR's presidency the context was an abundance of uncertainty about even the general direction of US trade policy, let alone its application. Hull was a committed free trader whose thinking on the subject hearkened back to the Democratic party of his youth in the 1880s and 1890s

(Allen 1953). The President's closest advisers – the "Brains Trust" centered originally around Columbia University law professor Raymond Moley – were more inclined toward "putting first things first," subordinating international trade to domestic recovery. Roosevelt fingered Moley to be Assistant Secretary of State even as he promised Hull, as Secretary, a free hand (Steward 1975: 13–16; Butler 1998: 15–22).

Hull envisioned a diplomatic initiative for worldwide tariff cuts. What he got from President Roosevelt was consent to negotiate several reciprocity treaties that would be submitted to Congress by the usual process. Hull acquiesced and started with Colombia.

The "great interest" that Colombian President Enrique Olaya Herrera was reported to have in the project cooled when the United States' aims were clarified. State Department cables to the US chargé in Bogotá inquired about "reductions which Colombia is prepared to accord to American products in return for leading Colombian products remaining on the free list" (US Dept. of State, *Foreign Relations* 1933: 219). By this time, "leading Colombian products" meant coffee, which constituted no less than three-quarters of US imports from that country.[23] But coffee had now entered duty-free for half a century (Table 5.1). Once again, the United States was playing for tariff concessions in return for a guarantee of the status quo. What had changed was mainly that the stakes were higher than ever for Colombia, whose exports had come to be remarkably concentrated in a single commodity.

To President Olaya it seemed a hard bargain (US Dept. of State, *Foreign Relations* 1933: 227). Likewise to the Colombian press, including editorialists at the leading bogotano newspaper, *El Tiempo*.[24] Nevertheless they accepted their lot. As one editorialist put it, "Colombia could hardly feel disinclined to negotiate with the nation that, among other things, buys four-fifths of her coffee" (*El Tiempo*, Dec. 9, 1933: 4). The Colombian mission in Washington went so far as to issue a joint statement with the State Department upholding the resulting treaty, signed but not yet ratified, as "a practical example of the policy of 'neighborliness' in the American continents" (US Dept. of State 1934: 6). In fact, the question of the United States' neighborliness was unsettled and the treaty was never ratified.

Even while Secretary Hull was negotiating the Colombia treaty, President Roosevelt was backing legislation that would require its renegotiation. The legislation authorized foreign trade agreements in advance without any subsequent congressional action. Specifically, it allowed agreements for the reduction of US duties (or, it bears noting, their *increase*) by up to 50 percent of existing rates. It also provided that the duty changes would "apply ... to all foreign countries," which was consistent with the agreements' inclusion of an unconditional MFN clause. With minor amendments, the Reciprocal Trade Agreements Act (RTAA) became law on June 12 (48 *US Stat.*: 943–945).

The conventional historical view of the RTAA sees it as "a new institutional foundation" for trade policy-making that eventually cleared a path for the US and the world toward postwar trade liberalization (Schnietz

2000: 417).[25] This chapter will argue that the conventional view of the RTAA overstates its importance. In any case, though, its enactment threw up a barrier to the unratified Colombia treaty. The easier way to enact the treaty's provisions would be to reframe them as an agreement under the RTAA. To do so would occasion some degree of renegotiation, which, depending on the degree, could cause consternation in Colombia. But that seemed a small bump in the road for State Department officials, who figured on the whole the new way was better.

While the RTAA itself cheered Hull and his deputies, at least one element of its institutional architecture worried them. In response to Hull's own urging for "an adequate and coordinated method of dealing with commercial policy questions," the President had already established in November 1933 an interdepartmental Executive Committee on Commercial Policy. In March 1934 he added a new member: George N. Peek, Roosevelt's Special Adviser in Foreign Trade.[26] Peek was the worrisome element. His view of the problem of US and world trade was completely different from Cordell Hull's.

As Hull surveyed the international scene, he saw "skyscraping trade obstructions that bristle on every economic frontier," evidence of economic illiberalism that had "almost become a disease" (US Senate 1934: 5). While Hull's remedy for the disease was to quit exposure to the toxin, Peek's was more in the way of an antibody. To him, inspection of the nation's balance sheets for international transactions revealed export surpluses that happened to be unpromising for the promotion of exports. The surpluses were financed by net US capital outflows that were "compelled" by widespread exchange controls. Exporters faced political impediments to receiving hard currency payments in foreign markets; the volume of exports that could be supported without such payments was small. Some "positive action" by the government was required, for otherwise, foreign governments would continue to channel their countries' hard currency earnings toward priorities other than the purchase of US exports. What was needed was "constructive stimulation and direction for the current movement of goods and services": to wit, countervailing exchange controls, and thereby "a program of selective imports and exports with particular countries" ("Report No. 1 on Foreign Trade," Exhibit No. 2, May 1934, FDR Papers, OF 971, Box 1).

Come June, Peek found a more appealing pitch for his program, now more apple pie than antibody. "Yankee trading," he called it in another radio address. The sensible way "through the maze of restrictions and barriers which now impede our trade" was simply to practice "the old Yankee method of bartering – goods for goods, equal value given and received, a fair bargain on both sides" (Peek 1934: 2).

In order to understand Hull's eventual triumph and how it affected US–Colombia trade relations, it is essential to note that President Roosevelt's signing of the RTAA on June 12 still did not secure that triumph. Nor did it destroy Peek's program. Although the State Department construed the act to authorize trade agreements based on the unconditional MFN clause, there was quite another way to construe it. The act's stipulation that any changes in US duties inscribed in trade agreements would "apply ... to all foreign countries" has already been noted. But there was a qualification. The act also stipulated that the President could suspend any such changes as they applied to countries undertaking "discriminatory treatment of American commerce" or "other acts or policies" which he perceived as working against the act's purposes (48 *US Stat.*: 944). As Peek would write to the President later that fall, the act was designed in the first place for "expanding foreign markets for the United States" (ibid.: 943). Numerous practices of other countries worked against that purpose, including exchange restrictions, debt defaults, violations of MFN commitments to the United States through negotiation of barter agreements with third parties, and failures to reciprocate any favors received in consequence of US trade agreements with third parties (Peek to Roosevelt, Nov. 12, 1934, in FDR Papers, OF 971, Box 1). In this manner Peek showed that the RTAA could be construed reasonably to authorize trade agreements based on the conditional rather than the unconditional MFN clause. Conditional MFN agreements would not have been sufficient to implement his program of countervailing exchange controls and international barter, but they could easily have been deemed consistent with it. In short, even after the signing of the RTAA, the course of US trade policy was up for grabs between policy-makers with sharply contrasting visions. And so were trade relations with Colombia.

The State Department gave formal notice of its intent to negotiate a trade agreement with Colombia under the RTAA on September 5, 1934 (Gellman 1966: 69). The debate about the contents of that particular agreement, as well as implementation of the trade-agreements program in general, intensified. Peek continued to argue vigorously against unconditional MFN and for making trade agreements contingent on satisfactory settlement of "blocked exchanges" (Peek to Hull, Sept. 22, 1934, FDR Papers, OF 971, Box 1).[27] Such a contingency would entail new obligations for Colombia, which practiced exchange control. The responsible subcommittee of the Executive Committee on Commercial Policy thus amended the draft agreement with a new article – which was then excised at the request of the State Department (Peek to Assistant Secretary of State Francis B. Sayre, Dec. 7, 1934, enclosure, FDR Papers, OF 313). In effect, State had taken the position that the agreement should be drafted with as little renegotiation as was legally possible. One reason was anxiety about the risks of delay or failure of ratification by Colombia. But there was a bigger reason. While Hull, too, was troubled by exchange controls, he determined that "the wisest policy" sought gradual liberalization of exchange by other means. He avowed his extreme reluctance "to see any arrangements adopted that make any such outcome more difficult or more tardy" (Hull to Peek, Oct. 5 1934, as quoted in letter of Peek to Sayre, Dec. 7, 1934, ibid.).

Peek protested, pointing out the labyrinth of "exclusive bilateral agreements" and controls that US trade partners had erected and that would continue to distort trade under Hull's proposed program ("Foreign Restrictions and Agreements Affecting American Commerce," June 30, 1935, FDR

Papers, OF 971). The implication was that Hull was bound to fail even on his own terms. But Roosevelt decided against him and for Hull. Regretting the difference of opinion and requesting the continued benefit of his services, the President advised his Special Adviser to "get a vacation" (copy, Roosevelt to Peek, July 25, 1935, FDR Papers, OF 971, Box 2).

Hull's formal reply to Peek's protest justified the President's decision by trumpeting first principles. Although Peek was right to worry about the proliferation of exclusive agreements, "the remedy lies not in withdrawing into a conditional policy, but in increasing the number and widening the scope of our reciprocal unconditional obligations." The United States should not respond with exclusive agreements of its own, for, "being generally discriminatory, they provoke retaliation, and, in the end, diminish rather than increase the sum total of world trade." The Roosevelt administration's economic program, "instead of pursuing this narrow and destructive trade policy, points in the opposite direction." As it must do, for "if some country does not thus take the lead another economic collapse … will be almost certain" (Hull to Roosevelt, Aug. 18, 1935, FDR Papers, OF 971, Box 2).

The foregoing blasts signaled Cordell Hull's triumph. He had engineered a significant redirection of US trade policy, against firm opposition, toward an end he had sought for most of his political career. The argument here is that the RTAA was utterly insufficient for the triumph. The triumph was owing mainly to Hull himself and the free-trade doctrine animating the RTAA under his leadership. The institution could very well have been, and nearly was, animated by a doctrine of protection and retaliation. After all, its main provisions, which comprised executive authority, a carrot of dubious appeal, and a stick of possible menace, resembled the reciprocity provisions of the protectionist McKinley Act. In both instances the gist was congressional pre-approval of tariff reductions that were neither far reaching nor far below the existing US tariff schedule for the goods mainly at issue, and possible penalties for partners who declined to deal. And the same carrot and stick, albeit without the same executive authority, were held out in the decade before FDR's administration by the Republican ones of Harding, Coolidge, and Hoover.

To be sure, the result of Hull's triumph was not free trade. It was the modest expansion of US trade for a short while during the interwar years, without much resort to threats of retaliation and without validating the worst apprehensions of bad faith. The US–Colombia trade agreement was signed on September 13, 1935 in nearly the same form that was agreed to two years before (US Dept. of State, EAS 89). That was progress in light of the record of the preceding half century.

6 Conclusion

In one contribution to the growing literature on institutions and economic development, Ha-Joon Chang (2010) suggests that institutions are neither as determinative nor as constraining as they are imagined in theory. In order to understand how they do function, "our [institutional] theories need to be more richly informed by real-world experiences – both history and modern-day events" (Chang 2010: 23). This chapter follows the suggestion into the domain of trade policy, particularly bilateral trade deals. The history of US–Colombia trade agreements from the 1820s to the 1930s gives insight into how the institutions of trade agreements affect their orientation toward free trade, protectionism, or something else.

The insight is that the influence of political institutions on the actual orientation of trade policy is less decisive than is commonly imagined. In the history told here, economic doctrines and the interests they promote have been more decisive, bending institutions to one end or another depending on which doctrine or interests hold sway. The conditional MFN treaty between the US and Colombia of 1824 was consistent with protectionism, by John Quincy Adams's lights, and by Henry Clay's it fostered that end. But by 1846 a similar US–Colombia treaty was opposed by Adams's and Clay's Whig Party, and even by Adams and Clay themselves. The problem was not that protectionist Whigs came around to disapprove of the form of the treaty but that predominantly free-trade Democrats took it up and invested it with a new purpose. The purpose happened not to be free trade but the expansion of US territory, which most free traders saw as a kindred cause, and thereby the domain of slavery.

Similarly, the McKinley Tariff Act of 1890 included "reciprocity" provisions that gave President Harrison and his Secretary of State, James G. Blaine, the authority to negotiate agreements with countries exporting certain primary goods for the reduction of those countries' tariffs on US goods. The authority included a retaliatory measure that the President could apply if the other countries did not negotiate to his satisfaction. The act's advocates and opponents alike saw the reciprocity provisions as protectionist, and with good reason. They sparked indignation abroad, especially in Colombia, which declined to meet US terms and met retaliation instead. Several decades later, however, a new act with a similar grant of executive authority for trade agreements caused noticeably less indignation abroad. There was still some, to be sure, including in Colombia, which signed a new agreement with the US in 1935. But it was muted by comparison to 1892. The difference lay not mainly in the act but in the interpretation of it by Secretary Hull, whose doctrinal allegiance was to liberal trade.

The historical account thus corroborates Acemoglu and Robinson's (2008) argument that although political institutions exist to curb *de facto* political power, sometimes the reality is different: *de facto* power is wielded to undo political institutions. Where the institutions of trade agreements are concerned, "sometimes" are oftentimes.

For further corroboration one may look to the current US–Colombia Free Trade Agreement. Most of the five years from its signing to its passage are attributable to a three-year detour from the three-month timeline that the US

Congress had stipulated for its consideration under "fast track." In the longer history of US trade agreements (and disagreements) with Colombia, such flexible interpretation of the trade-agreement rules is more in keeping with the norm than in violation of it.[28] So is the flexibility manifest in the FTA's effective amendment, despite fast track's no-amendment principle, to include a labor side-agreement that was anathema to its original proponents.[29] Policy-makers have always been able to bend the institutions of trade agreements in the direction of their political and doctrinal predilections, even when the required contortions have been great.

Acknowledgments

I thank the Fulbright Commission of Colombia and the Facultad de Economía of the Universidad de los Andes for material assistance in support of this project, and Jon Goldstein, Fabio Sánchez, and Miguel Urrutia for helpful comments. Any errors are mine.

Notes

1 *American State Papers: Foreign Relations*, vol. 5, no. 360, 18th Cong., 1st Sess. (Dec. 2, 1823): 250.
2 Bemis ([1949] 1973: 362) describes how Adams's view of the United States' role in the hemisphere, which had long been more limited, had by 1823 come to resemble Clay's broader vision.
3 For the year ending 30 Sept., 1825 (the first in which data for US exports to Colombia were reported separately from those to other former Spanish South American colonies), approximately $54 million of the $67 million of total exports of US products to all destinations were agricultural. Exports of US products to Colombia were but 2 percent of the total. Of that, $217,000 consisted of flour, $140,000 soap and tallow candles, $97,000 of pork, hams and bacon, lard, and hogs, $57,000 of tallow, hides, horned cattle, $42,000 of furniture, and $40,000 of boots and leather shoes. Exports of foreign products from the US to Colombia were approximately the same value as exports of US products to that country, but the products were largely cotton and linen fabrics. See Senate Doc. 76, 19th Cong., 1st Sess. (March 31, 1826).
4 In US Department of State (1801–1906), v. 9, emphasis in the original. The letter is reproduced in US Senate Doc. 68, 19th Cong., 1st Sess. (March 22, 1826): 127–149.
5 The average tariff is defined here as the ratio of total customs duties to the value of either dutiable imports or total imports. The data are taken from US Bureau of the Census (1975), series U207, U208, U210.
6 See *Codificación Nacional* (op. cit.: 58, 262–264) regarding decree no. 93 of June 23 and law no. 132 of August 5, 1823, respectively.
7 The correspondence from and to Moore may be found in House Doc. No. 46, 22d Cong., 1st Sess. (Jan. 10, 1832): 4, 5, 9.
8 In Colombia's *Codificación Nacional* (op. cit.), Tomo II: 204–206. Article 8 of the law, for example, reads in Spanish, "Los mismos efectos [including the aforementioned soap and candles], importados en buques extranjeros procedentes de colonias, pagarán un 25 por 100, y de Europa o de los Estados Unidos, un 20 por 100."
9 In House Doc. No. 173, 22d, Cong., 1st Sess. (March 16, 1832): 11.
10 In US Dept. of State (1801–1906), v. 15.

11 In Senate Ex. Doc 5 (Confidential), 28th Cong., 2nd Sess., Feb. 26, 1845: 15; which document may be found in US Senate, Committee on Foreign Relations (1816–), 29B–B8.
12 In US Dept. of State (1820–1906).
13 In US Dept. of State (1801–1906), v. 15.
14 See Blackford's dispatch to Secretary of State John C. Calhoun, July 26, 1844, and the enclosed statement of the Colombian Minister of Foreign Affairs on British incursions on the Mosquito coast, in Manning (1935: 608–618).
15 The instructions may be found in Manning (1935: 601).
16 In Manning (1935: 630–631).
17 Roll call and US *Senate Exec. Journal* 1848, June 3; *Biographical Directory of the United States Congress*).
18 See Carter et al. (2006: Ee429–430).
19 As quoted in Meardon (2011b: 329).
20 Pletcher (1962: 179) and Crapol (1973: 126) alike refer to negotiations with Great Britain, El Salvador, and Colombia, as well as the other countries named.
21 Quoted in Spanish from another source by Márquez Colin (2012: 15).
22 Under the Underwood Tariff the ratio of total duties to the value of total imports, and of duties to dutiable imports, had fallen considerably, to 9 percent and 29 percent. The protectionist Fordney–McCumber Act of 1922 raised them to 15 percent and 36 percent (Carter et al. 2006: Ee429–Ee430). Imported straw hats, which had become Colombia's fourth largest export to the US, saw a 10 percentage-point increase in their *ad valorem* duty, to 35 percent (Table 5.1). But tariff increase for straw hats was the exception.
23 The other Colombian products enumerated in the treaty were: bananas, balata, platinum, emeralds, ipecac root, raw reptile skins, tagua nuts, and tamarinds (Unsigned State Dept. memo, "Memorandum: Colombia," June 28, 1934: 6. FDR Papers, OF 313, Box 1).
24 See issues of *El Tiempo* dated Nov. 28, Nov. 30, Dec. 1, Dec. 3, Dec. 5, and Dec. 7, 1933.
25 See also Butler (1998) and Irwin et al. (2008). Hiscox's (1999) view, which complicates the conventional one, is more consistent with the account in this chapter.
26 Correspondence between the Secretary of State and the President establishing the functions and membership of the Executive Committee of Commercial Policy is recorded under the date October 27, 1933, in the FDR Papers, OF 971, Box 1.
27 See also Peek to Roosevelt, Nov. 12 and 14, 1934, FDR Papers, OF 971, Box 1.
28 The details of the 2002 Trade Promotion Authority Act, under which the US–Colombia FTA was negotiated, are laid out by Hornbeck and Cooper (2011). Villareal (2011) discusses briefly the House resolution suspending the expedited procedures of TPA in the US–Colombia case. The suspension was in force from April 2008 to June 2011.
29 The labor agreement may be found in "Colombian Action Plan Related to Labor Rights" (April 7, 2011), published by the Office of the United States Trade Representative (www.ustr.gov/uscolombiatpa/labor, accessed July 24, 2013). For an opinion of the labor agreement held by longstanding proponents of the FTA, see "Trumping Trumka," editorial, *The Wall Street Journal*, April 19, 2011.

References

Acemoglu, D. and J. A. Robinson. (2008) The Persistence and Change of Institutions in the Americas, *Southern Economic Journal* 75 (2), pp. 281–299.
Allen, W. R. (1953) The International Trade Philosophy of Cordell Hull, 1907–1933, *The American Economic Review* 43 (1), pp. 101–116.
Annals of Congress. (1789–1824) Washington, DC.

Bemis, S. F. (1943) *The Latin American Policy of the United States: An Historical Interpretation* (New York: Harcourt, Brace and Company).

Bemis, S. F. ([1949] 1973) *John Quincy Adams and the Foundations of American Foreign Policy* (New York: W. W. Norton & Co).

Bhagwati, J. and D. A. Irwin. (1987) The Return of the Reciprocitarians – U.S. Trade Policy Today, *World Economy* 10 (2), pp. 109–130.

Biographical Directory of the United States Congress. (1774–2005) House Document No. 108–222 (Washington, DC: Government Printing Office).

Butler, M. A. (1998) *Cautious Visionary: Cordell Hull and Trade Reform, 1933–1937* (Kent, Ohio: Kent State University Press).

Campbell, R. B. (1967) The Spanish American Aspect of Henry Clay's American System, *The Americas* 24 (1), pp. 3–17.

Carey, H. C. (1876) To the Friends of the Union Throughout the Union, in: William Elder, ed., *Miscellaneous Works of Henry C. Carey*, vol. 2. (Philadelphia: Henry Carey Baird & Co., 1883).

Carter, S. B., S. S. Gartner, M. R. Haines, A. L. Olmstead, R. Sutch, and G. Wright, eds. (2006) *Historical Statistics of the United States, Earliest Times to the Present: Millennial Edition* (New York: Cambridge University Press).

Chang, H.-J. (2010) Institutions and Economic Development: Theory, Policy and History, *Journal of Institutional Economics* 7 (4), pp. 473–498.

Clay, Henry and James B. Swain. ([1818] 1843) *The Life and Speeches of Henry Clay* (New York: Greeley & McElrath).

Crapol, Edward P. (1973) America for Americans: Economic Nationalism and Anglophobia in the Late Nineteenth Century (Westport, Conn.: Greenwood Press).

Delpar, H. (1999) Colombia: Troubled Friendship, in: Thomas M. Leonard, ed., *United States-Latin American Relations, 1850–1903: Establishing a Relationship* (Tuscaloosa: The University of Alabama Press), pp. 58–80.

Díaz-Callejas, A. (1997) *Colombia-Estados Unidos: Entre la Autonomía y la Subordinación, de la Independencia a Panamá* (Bogotá: Planeta Colombiana Editorial S.A.).

Gellman, I. F. (1966) *The Abortive Treaty that Failed: United States-Colombian Reciprocal Trade Policies, 1933–1936*, MA Thesis, Department of History, University of Maryland.

Hiscox, M. J. (1999) The Magic Bullet? The RTAA, Institutional Reform, and Trade Liberalization, *International Organization* 53 (4), pp. 669–698.

Hornbeck, J. F. and W. H. Cooper. (2011) Trade Promotion Authority and the Role of Congress in Trade Policy, CRS Report RL33743 (Washington, DC: Congressional Research Service).

Huck, E. R. (1991) Early United States Recognition of Colombian Independence and Subsequent Relations to 1830, in: T. Ray Shurbutt, ed., *United States-Latin American Relations, 1800–1850: The Formative Generations* (Tuscaloosa: The University of Alabama Press), pp. 197–227.

Irwin, D. A. (2002) Reciprocity and the Origins of U.S. Trade Liberalization, in: Jagdish Bhagwati, ed., *Going Alone: The Case for Relaxed Reciprocity in Freeing Trade* (Cambridge, Mass.: The MIT Press), pp. 61–84.

Irwin, D. A., P. C. Mavroidis, and A. O. Sykes. (2008) *The Genesis of the GATT* (New York: Cambridge University Press).

Laughlin, J. L. and H. P. Willis. (1903) *Reciprocity* (New York: The Baker & Taylor Co.).

McGreevey, W. P. (1971) *An Economic History of Colombia, 1845–1930* (New York: Cambridge University Press).

Malloy, W. M. (1910) *Treaties, Conventions, International Acts, Protocols and Agreements Between the United States and Other Powers, 1776–1909*, Senate doc. 357, 61st Cong., 2nd sess. 2 vols. (Washington, DC: Government Printing Office).

Manning, W. R., ed. (1935) *Diplomatic Correspondence of the United States: Inter-American Affairs, 1831–1860*, vol. 5: *Chile and Colombia* (Washington: Carnegie Endowment for International Peace).

Márquez Colín, G. (2012) El Tratado de Reciprocidad de 1883: ¿una oportunidad perdida?, *Historia Mexicana* 61 (3).

Martínez Delgado, L. (1972) *Panamá: su Independencia de España – su Incorporación a la Gran Colombia – su Separación de Colombia – el Canal Interoceanico* (Bogotá: Ediciones Lerner).

Meardon, S. (2011a) On the Evolution of U.S. Trade Agreements: Evidence from Taussig's Tariff Commission, *Journal of Economic Issues* 45 (2), pp. 475–484.

Meardon, S. (2011b) Reciprocity and Henry C. Carey's Traverses on "the Road to Perfect Freedom of Trade," *Journal of the History of Economic Thought* 33 (3), pp. 307–333.

Mejía Arango, L. (2007) *Los Radicales: Historia Política del Radicalismo del Siglo XIX* (Bogotá: Universidad Externado de Colombia).

Ocampo, J. A. (1984) *Colombia y la Economía Mundial, 1830–1910* (Bogotá: Siglo Veintiuno Editores).

Ocampo, J. A. (2007) Librecambio y Proteccionismo en el Siglo XIX, in: J. A. Ocampo and S. Montenegro, *Crisis Mundial, Protección e Industrialización* (Bogotá: Grupo Editorial Norma), pp. 279–336.

Ocampo, J. A. and S. Montenegro. (2007) *Crisis Mundial, Protección e Industrialización* (Bogotá: Grupo Editorial Norma).

Ospina Vasquez, L. (1955) *Industría y Protección en Colombia, 1810–1930* (Medellín: E.S.F.).

Parks, E. T. (1935) *Colombia and the United States, 1765–1934* (Durham, North Carolina: Duke University Press).

Peek, G. N. (1934) Foreign Trade and Yankee Trading, Press Release No. 2, Special Adviser to the President on Foreign Trade, in: FDR Papers as President, OF 971, Box 1, June 9.

Pletcher, D. M. (1962) *The Awkward Years: American Foreign Policy Under Garfield and Arthur* (Columbia: University of Missouri Press).

Pletcher, D. M. (1973) *The Diplomacy of Annexation: Texas, Oregon, and the Mexican War* (Columbia: University of Missouri Press).

Pletcher, D. M. (1998) *The Diplomacy of Trade and Investment: American Economic Expansion in the Hemisphere, 1865–1900* (Columbia: University of Missouri Press).

Randall, S. J. (1977) *The Diplomacy of Modernization: Colombian-American Relations, 1920–1940* (Toronto: University of Toronto Press).

Randall, S. J. (1992) *Colombia and the United States: Hegemony and Interdependence* (Athens, Georgia: The University of Georgia Press).

Riguzzi, P. (2003) *Reciprocidad Imposible?: La Política del Comercio entre México y Estados Unidos, 1857–1938* (Toluca, México: Instituto Mora).

Rivas, R. (1915) *Relaciones Internacionales entre Colombia y los Estados Unidos* (Bogotá: Imprenta Nacional).

Roosevelt, F. D. Papers as President (FDR Presidential Library, Hyde Park, New York).

Schnietz, K. E. (2000) The Institutional Foundations of U.S. Trade Policy: Revisiting Explanations for the 1934 Reciprocal Trade Agreements Act, *Journal of Policy History* 12 (4), pp. 417–444.

Setser, V. G. (1937) *The Commercial Reciprocity Policy of the United States, 1774–1829* (Philadelphia: University of Pennsylvania Press).

Stanwood, E. (1903) *American Tariff Controversies in the Nineteenth Century*, 2 vols. (Boston: Houghton, Mifflin).

Steward, D. (1975) *Trade and Hemisphere: the Good Neighbor Policy and Reciprocal Trade* (Columbia: University of Missouri Press).

Taussig, F. W. (1892) *The Tariff History of the United States*, 2nd ed. (New York: G.P. Putnam's Sons).

Terrill, T. E. (1973) *The Tariff, Politics, and American Foreign Policy, 1874–1901* (Westport, Conn.: Greenwood Press).

US Bureau of the Census. (1975) *Historical Statistics of the United States, Colonial Times to 1970*, Bicentennial ed., part 2 (Washington, DC: US Government Printing Office).

US Department of State. (1801–1906) *Diplomatic Instructions of the Department of State, 1801–1906*, Series M77, US Department of State Papers (United States National Archives, College Park, Maryland).

US Department of State. (1820–1906) *Despatches from U.S. Ministers to Colombia, 1820–1906*, Series T33, US Department of State Papers (United States National Archives, College Park, Maryland).

US Department of State. (1870–1946) *Papers Relating to the Foreign Relations of the United States*, Washington, DC: US Government Printing Office.

US Department of State. (1894) Import Duties on Certain Products. ("Report submitted by the Secretary of State inclosing correspondence between the governments of the United States and Colombia, Venezuela, and Haiti ...") Senate Ex. Doc. No. 56, 53rd Cong., 2nd Sess.

US Department of State. (1930–1946) Executive Agreement Series [EAS] (Washington, DC: US Government Printing Office).

US Senate, Committee on Finance. (1934) Reciprocal Trade Agreements: Hearings. 73rd Cong., 2nd Sess., Thursday, April 26.

US Senate, Committee on Foreign Relations. (1816–) Committee Papers (ARC ID 559842). Center for Legislative Archives (National Archives, Washington, DC).

US *Senate Executive Journal*. (1789–) (Washington, DC).

US *Statutes at Large*. (1789 -) (Washington, DC).

US Tariff Commission. (1919) *Reciprocity and Commercial Treaties* (Washington, DC Government Printing Office).

Villareal, M. A. (2011) The Proposed U.S.-Colombia Free Trade Agreement, CRS Report RL34470 (Washington, DC: Congressional Research Service).

6 The Treaties of 1810 and the crisis of the Luso-Brazilian Empire

Milena Fernandes de Oliveira and Nelson Mendes Cantarino

The purpose of this article is to analyze the Treaties of Commerce and Navigation signed between Britain and Portugal in 1810, and the debates they gave rise to in the nineteenth century. Signed in the context of the Old Regime crisis[1] the Treaties represented an important turning point in Brazilian history, having contributed to the rapprochement between Brazilian and British merchants, the independence movement of Portuguese America, and the rise of the Brazilian Empire.

Some of the liberal reforms that were tried in the Portuguese Empire in the beginning of nineteenth century failed. Given they were not accompanied by structural transformations, their enforcement resulted in a deeper reliance by the Portuguese Empire on slavery and colonial exclusiveness. The 1810 Treaties were one of the expressions of such attempts at liberal reformism by the Luso-Brazilian Empire. As conceived by the so-called Generation of the 1790s, they intended to reinforce the Portuguese Empire making use of the principles of English political economy and liberalism. One of the most representative exponents of this position was D. Rodrigo de Souza Coutinho, who, as the Secretary of War and Foreign Affairs in Brazil, negotiated the clauses of the treaty with Lord Strangford, the British representative. Some of the economic ideas espoused by D. Rodrigo de Souza Coutinho, and which, therefore, informed his position in the proceedings, are discussed in the first part of this chapter.

The Treaties of Commerce and Navigation were also the object of a broad debate among Luso-Brazilian intellectuals at the time. Some of them, such as Hipólito da Costa, had a very peculiar opinion about the outcomes of the agreements signed in 1810. Influenced by a visit to the US, Hipólito da Costa took issue with the liberal tone embodied in the Treaties. His ideas, published in *Correio Braziliense* since 1808, together with the interpretation conferred upon them by Portuguese, Brazilian, and British historiographies, constitute the object of our exposition in the second part of this chapter. At this point, we also analyze the text of the Treaties in more depth, using the Portuguese version published in the Bank of Portugal's collection, and the English version published in Hertslet's collection of treaties and conventions.

Finally, in the third and last part of the work, we place the Treaties of 1810 alongside similar agreements struck between Portugal and Great Britain at different moments, as well as treaties signed by the latter with other countries since 1807, in an attempt to contextualize them within the Old Regime crisis and discuss their significance for the decay of the Luso-Brazilian Empire.

The Generation of the 1790s and D. Rodrigo de Souza Coutinho

Kenneth Maxwell described the Generation of the 1790s as the educated Luso-Brazilians who took the pressing issues of the Portuguese Empire into account, and aimed to redress them. Coming from educational institutions that were reformed during the Marquis of Pombal's administration (1750–1777), these men went on scientific expeditions to other countries of Europe, like England, France, and Italy. Under Government sponsorship, they published memoirs relating their findings and experiences – all this as part of a plan to improve agriculture and the production of raw materials (Dias 1968, pp. 105–170; Maxwell 1973; Lyra 1994).

In this context, marked by both the French Revolution and the rise of British industrial power, the Portuguese Crown made concerted efforts to implement a reform of imperial administration. In 1792, Prince Regent John replaced Queen Maria I in the administration of Government Affairs. In 1796, government officers appointed Souza Coutinho as the Secretary of Navy and Overseas Dominions, at a time when he was serving as the Portuguese representative at the Court of Turin.[2] The Piemontese Court was a focal point for the European Enlightenment (Venturi 1984; Israel 2006), where Souza Coutinho could become acquainted with recent advances in the fields of philosophy and science. Additionally, he also had the opportunity to travel to pre-revolutionary France, where he witnessed *in loco* the monumental failure of Jacques Necker's reformist program (1732–1804).[3]

Born in 1755 into a noble family, Souza Coutinho received a sophisticated education, spending a season at the College of Nobles, and also attending a course at the reformed University of Coimbra. To the Marquis of Pombal and his colleagues, this constituted the ideal education for a future administrator of Crown business. Souza Coutinho subsequently traveled to Switzerland and France in order to complete his training for the Royal service.

Upon his return to Lisbon in 1796, Souza Coutinho had already visited several courts in Europe, and became aware of new ideas and practices in colonial administration. Cognizant of the conditions that permeated Portuguese overseas administration, Souza Coutinho came to embody the great dilemma of the '*estrangeirado*'[4]: how to reorganize the imperial economy according to liberal economic principles, as an alternative for the old mercantile system.[5]

Valentim Alexandre argues that, since the time of Pombal's tenure as Prime Minister, Souza Coutinho provided a new ideological makeup for the defense of the Colonial Pact (1993, pp. 84–85). Aspects such as military defense, the organization of courts, and the administration of justice, which aimed at a more refined control by the Crown, were the major concerns in Lisbon. In a report, Souza Coutinho defended the colony's functional organization in two "power hubs, one in the North and another in the South" (Coutinho 1993 [1797–1798], p. 50), an administrative division that was suggested during the Iberian Union.

According to Kenneth Maxwell (1973), such reformism was an "accommodation" of Portuguese Crown policies. For the Generation of the 1790s, the old colonial order should be reformed to safeguard the revenues of the Crown. An example was the tax reform suggested by Souza Coutinho when he was Secretary of Overseas Territories (Cardoso 2001, pp. 79–83), which related the Portuguese Empire's financial problems to Adam Smith's ideas:

> the nature of taxation, in a way that it can be very productive with little weight to those who contribute …, depends on the origins of society's wealth, and one can hardly address any point that concerns the first object without first examining the second one.
>
> (Coutinho 1993 [1797–1798], p. 55)

Taxation should also be organized in order to promote commercial activity and production, limiting monopolistic practices. The reform should be established based on four principles:

> a more productive and less burdensome taxation to those who contribute, the use of modern accounting methods, the improvement of the credit system and monetary circulation and, finally, the organization of tax collection so as not to encourage the development of "a useless and unproductive class of men," with damage to the useful and industrious classes dedicated to agriculture, arts and commerce.
>
> (Coutinho 1993 [1797–1798], p. 55)

Another expression of this "accommodation" was the signing of the Treaties of 1810. As Minister of War between 1810 and 1812, Souza Coutinho conducted the negotiations on the Portuguese side, trying to incorporate some liberal principles into the trade relations between Brazil and Great Britain. Souza Coutinho believed that "Brazilian products were to be admitted in England under the same conditions enjoyed by the products of the British West Indies" (*Correio Braziliense*, February 8, 1809). According to the liberal principles overseeing the international division of labor, as proposed by Adam Smith and followed by Souza Coutinho, the advancement of commerce should be the foundation for the development of nations – in this case, the entire Luso-Brazilian Empire (Cardoso 2001).

The Treaties of 1810: Commerce and Navigation, Alliance and Friendship

London, February 8th, 1809. In the first page of *Correio Braziliense*'s "Commerce and Arts" section, Hipólito José da Costa announced:

> Here, the minister abolished the rights paid for Portuguese products stored in export warehouses. In Brazil, a new tax was agreed upon, which will considerably reduce the valuation of English goods on which customs duties are charged in Brazilian ports; it was understood that this regulation would have a backward effect.
>
> (*Correio Braziliense*, "Commerce and Arts," February 8, 1809, p. 194)[6]

In 1809, Hipólito da Costa reported some of the free trade clauses that had been accorded between the Portuguese plenipotentiary in London, D. Domingos de Souza Coutinho, and George Canning. At the time, Hipólito da Costa was a journalist in London, where he had established *Correio Braziliense* and used it as a means to report on the problems of the Portuguese Empire. The clauses discussed in the article anticipated some of the elements incorporated in the Treaties of 1810, of which Costa was soon to become one of the major critics.

Before he was arrested by the Portuguese Inquisition in 1804, Hipólito da Costa had visited the United States in 1798 at the behest of Rodrigo de Souza Coutinho. As a diplomat, his mission in the US was to study the regional species of plants and minerals. He went to London in 1802, again at the command of D. Rodrigo de Souza Coutinho, in order to acquire books, machines, and papers for the Royal Portuguese Press. In both these missions, he became closely acquainted with one of Prince Regent John's ministers, the future Count of Linhares.[7]

Part of the scholarly discussion on the Treaties of 1810, both from the nineteenth and twentieth centuries, dedicates attention to the role played by Hipólito José da Costa. Within this literature, one can identify different positions regarding the motivations underlying the agreement. Some of the authors see it as a diplomatic game between Percy Smythe, the Viscount of Strangford, and D. Rodrigo de Souza Coutinho, Minister of War in Rio de Janeiro since 1808. According to this view, Strangford was the main culprit behind the loss of the most important Portuguese colony. As an ambassador of Great Britain in Portugal since 1806, he arranged for the transfer of the Portuguese royal family to Brazil in 1808 and, following in the footsteps of George Canning, took the lead in the negotiations for a free trade treaty.

Another historiographical current pictures the Treaties of Commerce and Navigation as expressions of diplomatic tensions and balances between Portugal and England. Some Portuguese authors, such as Eduardo Brazão, see the signing of the treaties as harmful to the economic interests of Portugal: "Portugal made a commitment not to take any actions that could harm the economic interests of the British, and Great Britain, in its turn, was obliged to treat us as the most favored nation" (Brazão *apud* Ramos 1988, p. 332). Other authors, such as Joaquim Verissimo Serrao, Francisco Antonio Correa, Jaime Cortesão, Oliveira Marques, and Jorge Borges de Macedo, follow this same path, claiming that Great Britain replaced a series of treaties that had been previously signed with Portugal since at least 1640, with a treaty that clearly caused damages to the Portuguese nation. The Treaties of 1810 imposed a heavy burden on Portuguese industry, sentencing Portugal to occupy a second-tier position among the international powers. One can clearly see that diplomatic analyses of this sort incorporate a very strong nationalistic discourse, making Great Britain and its expansionist policies responsible for Portuguese backwardness.

While Portuguese authors, from the 1930s to the 1980s, associate the signing of the 1810 Treaties with Portuguese decline, some Brazilian studies see in them the moment when Brazil was finally released from Portugal, thus marking, along with the events of 1808, the beginning of Brazilian history. Among the authors subscribing to this interpretation are Rocha Pombo, Varnhagen, Pandiá Calógeras, and Oliveira Lima, the latter of whom stated that "Linhares' political work was, therefore, beneficial to Brazil, even in its least defensible aspects" (Lima 1945, v. 2, p. 434).

Brazilian authors recognize that Hipólito da Costa was the first to imply that the Treaties of 1810 were responsible for the end of the Portuguese Empire and the birth of the Brazilian nation, even though this may have occurred under British domination:

> A trade agreement between Brazil and England is one of the most sensitive situations in which Brazil could find itself, for the *"braziliense"* negotiator does not have any precedents to guide him. The treaties that existed between England and Portugal were established on mutual export interests of Portuguese mass consumption goods in England, such as wine, olive oil, etc., … the main products in Brazil are far from being largely consumed in England, so they are forbidden because of the competition they offer to the British colonies.
>
> (*Correio Braziliense*, "Commerce and Arts,"
> February 8, 1809, p. 195)

Despite the importance of the Treaties to Brazilian political independence, some interpreters see this moment as marking the beginning of the country's dependence on England, as notably observed in the works of Alan K. Manchester, Caio Prado Jr., and Nelson Werneck Sodré. In this respect, Manchester states, in his *Preeminência inglesa no Brasil*: "In 1808, the colony was economically emancipated from the decaying metropolis; in 1810, it got a rich stepmother" (1973, p. 54).[8] Caio Prado Jr. and Nelson Werneck Sodré, two Brazilian Marxist scholars, admit that English influence extended both to Portugal, by virtue of the 1703 Methuen Treaty, and to Brazil, through the Treaties of 1810 – which complicated the overall situation faced by the Portuguese Empire. Both Prado Jr. and Sodré mention the signing of the Treaties among the facts that mark the beginning of the nineteenth century, alongside Portugal's invasion by Napoleonic troops, the Portuguese Crown's transfer to Rio de Janeiro, and the opening of Brazilian ports in 1808 (Sodré 1978; Prado Jr. 2006).

Yet other authors, such as Fernando Antonio Novais, Emilia Viotti da Costa, Valentim Alexandre, and José Jobson de Andrade Arruda, see the Treaties within the context of the Old Regime crisis. From this broader perspective, structured around the absolutist state and mercantile accumulation (Novais 1979), one can see how the signing of the Treaties related, at the same time, to the end of the Portuguese Empire (Alexandre 1998, pp. 215–227), the origins of the Brazilian nation, and the consolidation of the British Empire.

In addition to the different meanings commonly assigned to the Treaties of Commerce and Navigation between Portugal and Great Britain, it is also worth considering the controversy surrounding some of its specific articles. Of these, the most controversial was undoubtedly Article 15:

> All goods, merchandises, and articles whatsoever of the produce, manufacture, industry, or invention of the Dominions and subjects of His Britannic Majesty, shall be admitted into all and singular the Ports and Dominions of His Royal Highness the Prince Regent of Portugal, as well in Europe as in America, Africa and Asia, whether consigned to British or Portuguese subjects, on paying generally and solely, duties to the amount of fifteen percent.
>
> ("Treaty of commerce and navigation" 1820 [1810]; p. 47)

There is a slight difference between the drafts of the Treaties, written in 1809, and the Treaties as actually signed in 1810. In the drafts, the agreement about a 15 percent *ad valorem* tax corresponds to Article 19, while in the Treaties they are the subject of Article 15. However, the phrasing in both of them is identical.[9]

Criticism directed towards the 15 percent tax on British goods emphasized that England did not conform to its part of the agreement (Coutinho, "Esboço de um Tratado" 1993 [1809], p. 380).[10] According to Oliveira Lima, the reciprocity "of this regime of real favor, for being exclusive, was just an illusion," since Brazilian goods similar to the British colonial products "were excluded from the United Kingdom market" (1986, p. 176). In theory, Brazilian and Portuguese products would enjoy the condition of most favored nation. However, articles that competed with English colonial products, such as sugar and coffee, were not included in the most-favored-nation clause.

According to Hipólito da Costa, Francisco Correa, Oliveira Marques, and Oliveira Lima, the most-favored-nation clause imposed a heavy burden on Portuguese industry and, consequently, on Brazilian industry as well. According to Francisco Correa:

After the signing of the Treaty, monopoly trade with Brazil passed into the hands of the British. Because of the crisis we had gone through during the French invasion, our industry was declining, and it was not possible to reconstruct it, since we could not compete in the metropolis against the English industry, much less in Brazil; a market that was completely closed to us.

(Correa *apud* Ramos 1988, p. 333)

It was impossible for Brazilian producers to compete against English cotton fabrics, and soon, as stated by Valentim Alexandre, the 15 percent tax on cotton fabrics would be extended to wool fabrics as well, an article that had until this moment enjoyed the protection of a 30 percent rate. Brazilian industry would also suffer in the long run:

Another setback that would be experienced by the *"braziliense"* negotiator was the impossibility to predict the path taken by different branches of agriculture or manufacturing in Brazil, particularly if the treaty persisted for many years.

(*Correio Braziliense*, February 3, 1809, p. 195)

The principle of reciprocity concerning shipping would be inapplicable as well. England had the world's strongest and largest fleet of merchant warships. Even with his experience in the Department of Navigation and Overseas, the Count of Linhares did not have any control over the British Navy. The article on navigation outlined by Souza Coutinho in the drafts of the Treaties was different from the article that appeared in the signed version of 1810. While articles relating to navigation appeared, in the drafts, towards the end of the text (articles 33 to 37), in the Treaties of 1810, the clauses that establish free navigation and reciprocity were the very first ones (articles 2 to 7). Francisco de S. Luís Saraiva, a nineteenth-century historian, thus discusses the effects of the 1810 Treaties:

It was not valid to call "reciprocal" the freedom that was given to Portuguese ships to carry our goods to England and to British ships to bring theirs directly to Portugal, when, as mentioned, "everyone knows that while two or three Portuguese ships sail to England, two or three hundred come from there to the national ports."

(Saraiva *apud* Ramos 1988, p. 337)

According to Valentim Alexandre, the enforcement of free trade principles was stricter in the Luso-Brazilian system than in its British counterpart. Whereas Portugal and Brazil received the status of most favored nations, Great Britain enjoyed the privilege of a 15 percent customs duty in Brazil, while preserving the protection of its colonial production (1993, p. 217).

A second controversial point in the Treaties of 1810 refers to Portuguese trade monopolies. After the transfer of the court from Portugal to Brazil, escorted by Britain, what would be the shape of a free trade agreement with the latter? Which monopolies would be maintained, and which eliminated? Two articles tried to redefine what constituted an object of free trade, and what remained within the rules of the Portuguese regime of exclusive trading. Article 8 discussed free trade in the Portuguese dominions, identifying products that remained under exclusive rights:

> the subjects of Great Britain shall have free and unrestricted permission to buy and sell from and to whomsoever, and in whatever form or manner they may please, whether by wholesale, or by retail, without being obliged to give any preference or favour in consequence of the said monopolies, contracts, or exclusive privileges of sale or purchase.
>
> ... the present Article is not to be interpreted as invalidating or affecting, the exclusive right possessed by the Crown of Portugal within its own Dominions to the farm for the sale of ivory, brazil-wood, urzela, diamonds, gold dust, gunpowder, and tobacco in the form of snuff: provided however, that should the above-mentioned articles, generally or separately, ever become articles of free Commerce within the Dominions of His Royal Highness the Prince Regent of Portugal, the subjects of His Britannic Majesty shall be permitted to traffic in them as freely and on the same footing as those of the most favoured nation.
>
> ("Treaty of commerce and navigation"
> 1820 (1810), pp. 37 and 39)

Hipólito da Costa stated that the translation of this article into Portuguese was itself a problem. 'Snuff' was translated into Portuguese as 'manufactured tobacco.' This apparently small mistake limited even further the scope of Portuguese trade, not only restraining the movement of powder tobacco, but also preventing the circulation of "cigarettes and, in general, most any way in which tobacco plant can be manufactured" (*Correio Braziliense*, s.d., facsimile, vol. V, n. 27, pp. 189–191).

Article 20, on the other hand, established that "there are some articles of Brazilian growth and produce, which are excluded from the market and home consumption of the British Dominions, such as sugar, coffee, and other articles similar to the produce of the British Colonies." The Brazilian products that could offer competition to similar items produced in the British colonies were only allowed to stay in English warehouses "for the purpose of re-exportation" ("Treaty of Commerce and Navigation" 1820 [1810], p. 55).

For Manuel de Oliveira Lima, the perfect freedom of trade between Portugal and England, with the sole exception of royal monopolies, would cause a deep shock to the Portuguese economy. Take, for instance, the case of the "Alto Douro Wine Company, a creation of Pombal through which the culture of the vine was revived in the kingdom" (Lima 1908, pp. 388–389). With the Treaties of Commerce and Navigation, the old problems that had led to the establishment of the Company in 1756 resurfaced: the wine produced or re-exported by Great Britain now competed with similar Portuguese articles.[11]

The signing of a series of free trade agreements orchestrated by England disrupted the Portuguese and Spanish empires. As a consequence, a new kind of relationship, structured around free trade, emerged between centers and peripheries. The old colonial mercantile networks were increasingly absorbed by the British Empire. Due to the Napoleonic occupation of Europe – the most important market for British exports – Great Britain started to regard the Atlantic as a strategic channel for its economic survival (Cain and Hopkins 1980). As a pioneer of the industrial revolution, Great Britain could "produce more goods at a smaller cost to sell them at lower prices than those of any competitor"(Manchester 1973, p. 75).[12] This competitive advantage notwithstanding, in order to gain access to the markets it would be necessary to destroy Iberian mercantile monopolies.

The production of cotton fabrics at lower prices would not have been possible without the free trade relations established between England and Brazil. During the convention of 1807, when the transfer of the Portuguese Court to Brazil was decided, the Brazilian market was Britain's foremost goal, not only as a supplier of raw materials such as cotton, but also as a consumer of industrial products. Since 1776, the United States had curtailed the supply of cotton to Great Britain and fostered its own textile production, thus becoming a competitor in international markets. At this point, Brazilian cotton became a valuable commodity. Relations developed between Brazilian cotton producers and traders, on one hand, and British industrialists on the other. In return, Britain would look the other way regarding the slave traffic in the Atlantic, which supported the entire Brazilian economy. The opening of the Brazilian ports and the Treaties of 1810 contributed to consolidate these ties between Brazilian and English traders.

The third polemical point raised during the debates on the Treaties of 1810 was the maintenance of slave trade and slave labor. The Treaties did not specifically mention anything on this topic, but slave traffic was the most delicate and essential point to the survival of the Luso-Brazilian Empire. Since 1715, Britain already detained the right of Asiento, by virtue of which she enjoyed the monopoly in the introduction of slaves in Spanish America. With the signing of The Slave Trade Act in 1807, Great Britain committed itself to bringing slave trade to an end in all the Atlantic, thus starting a war against slave traffic.

Article 28 of the drafts of the Treaties of Commerce and Navigation stated that "Portugal ... decided to cooperate with H. British M. in the cause of humanity and justice, adopting the most effective means of achieving a *gradual abolition* of slave trade in the full extent of its domains" (Coutinho, "Esboço de um Tratado" 1993 [1809], p. 392). This clause completely disappeared in the signed version of the Treaties, being replaced by the right accorded to Britain to appoint British Judges Conservator in Portuguese dominions.[13]

The same article in the drafts also delimited the places where traffic should cease, and those where it could be continued – provisions that appeared later on in the Additional Convention of the Vienna Treaty, signed in 1817. It also discussed compensations to slave dealers more extensively. In the signed version, this point was also completely omitted.

The suppression of any clause concerning slave traffic and slave labor from the final version of the 1810 Treaties is remarkable. A mention to the subject of traffic in the Atlantic would only be included in a treaty signed between Britain and Portugal on February 22, 1815.[14] Commerce, exchange rates, mining and industry, and the division of labor were all subjects of interest to Enlightened Luso-Brazilian intellectuals, but a deafening silence hung over the theme of slave traffic, as pointed by another intellectual, Antonio Ribeiro dos Santos (Neves 2001, pp. 13–62). This silence speaks powerfully to the crucial importance of slavery in the Portuguese Empire.

The meaning of the Treaties within the crisis of the Old Regime

The traditional basis of Portuguese wealth during the Old Regime consisted in its overseas trade. According to Jorge Pedreira (1994, p. 270), the colonial system had four main functions in the imperial economy: the supply of provender and raw materials; the creation of markets for products such as manufactured goods and wines; the strengthening of exchange among colonies, especially through the slave trade; and the re-exportation of colonial products on a large scale to Europe, and of European products to the colonies at high prices.

The crisis of the Old Regime, in which context the Treaties of 1810 should be understood, changed this situation. Despite the liberal reforms conducted by the Generation of the 1790s, the Empire was doomed. Liberalism could rationalize the way in which the Portuguese Empire worked, but it could not and did not change its most profound structures, such as colonial exclusiveness and the Atlantic slave traffic (Novais 1979).

Iberian empires, the first of their kind in the Modern Age, were undermined by the two most important events underlying the crisis of the Old Regime. The English Industrial Revolution, which made it possible that cotton fabrics were sold at unrivalled prices, allowed Great Britain to conquer new markets; the French Revolution, on the other hand, determined the end of traditional monopolies, turning slavery and slave traffic into international issues that required a firm commitment from Britain.

France competed against England for world hegemony. During the Napoleonic Wars and the imposition of the Continental System, Britain could not export its manufactured goods to Europe, the most sizeable market for British production at the time. Simultaneously, the United States restrained even further the supply of cotton available to Great Britain. North

American cotton was of great importance to the fledgling English industry, but since its independence, as stated above, the US had turned into a competitor to England in international cotton textile markets.

The solution found by distinguished British strategists and diplomats, such as Strangford, was to turn to the peripheries of mercantile capitalism, especially the Spanish and Portuguese colonies. To London, controlling the Brazilian trade would correct several imbalances at once. For instance, it would reduce, and perhaps even eliminate, the trade deficit with Portugal, while also curtailing the Brazilian supply of cotton to France and Portugal, thus guaranteeing the raw materials necessary for British industry. The relevance of the Brazilian market, which accounted at the time for two thirds of British exports to Latin America, was yet another factor underlying this strategic move (Arruda 2008, p. 54).

Another consequence of Napoleonic expansion was forcing Portugal to succumb to British pressure: in exchange for the escort provided by the British Navy in the tranfer of the royal family agreed to Brazil, Portugal conceded to signing a free trade agreement with England. The opening of the Brazilian ports in 1808 strengthened the relations between Brazilian and British traders, and the acts that followed this critical event, such as the Secret Convention of 1809 and the Treaties of 1810, were part of the same process, inherently inscribed in the crisis of the Old Regime – although they held altogether different meanings for each of the parties involved.

Luso-Brazilian scholarship has never reached a consensus regarding the effects of the 1810 Treaties for the Portuguese economy. While some argue that the metropolitan industry was not affected given the eminently regional nature of its market, to which English production did not offer competition, others advocate that a widespread crisis did occur, affecting not only Portugal but also most of Europe (Pedreira 1994, pp. 343–350). According to Valentim Alexandre, this was a crucial historical moment because it determined the establishment of a new economic order. One of the direct consequences of the Treaties of 1810 was highlighting the importance of Portuguese colonies in Africa. The economic survival of Brazil depended on the Portuguese enclaves on the African coast, the source of slave labor for the large-scale Brazilian crop production. Furthermore, the prosperity of the Portuguese economy, in particular its incipient industry, may have been doomed with the loss of the Brazilian market (Alexandre 1998, pp. 215–227).

A new imperial structure emerged from the crisis of the Old Regime, and the Treaties of 1810 pointed to three different fates within this new order. The first was the rise of a new hegemonic power – Great Britain – who was forced by the pressures occasioned by the Napoleonic Wars to invent a new imperial order, based on industrial capitalism and liberal principles. The second encapsulated the case of the Iberian nations, the first empires in the modern world, which eventually became part of the European periphery. And finally, the old American colonies, such as Brazil, which managed to obtain their political independence.

The absorption of the old colonies into the new world economic order, and their transformation into peripheries specialized in the production of raw materials signified a real revolution in the Atlantic world. According to Gabriel Paquette (2013), economic liberalism reached America prior to political liberalism. At first, colonial traders were integrated in the international market, and only later the idea of political independence was built. However, by preserving the main pillars of colonial exploitation – monoculture, latifundium, and slavery – the former colonies were prevented from experiencing a radical transformation, perpetuating instead the social *status quo* they had inherited from the colonial period.

The Treaties of 1810 offer a privileged perspective, since they simultaneously captured the three movements that marked the decline of the Old Regime: the destruction of an old imperial order, centered around Portugal; the establishment of a new British empire, built on a radically different basis; and the hesitant rise of a new nation, Brazil.

Concluding remarks

The signature of the Treaties of Commerce and Navigation between Britain and Portugal in 1810 provoked intense debate. One position was supported by the Generation of the 1790s, to which belonged D. Rodrigo de Souza Coutinho, the negotiator of the clauses from the Luso-Brazilian side. To these intellectuals, the reform of the Portuguese Empire should respect the principles of English political economy, in particular the social division of labor. In this sense, the Treaties of Commerce and Navigation would represent a watershed between the old organization of the Portuguese empire and a new one, consistent with liberalism and a new international order.

Another position was held by Hipólito José da Costa. Observing the negotiations between Portugal and Britain since 1808, he claimed it would not be possible to apply the principles of free trade between Portugal, a nonindustrialized country, and Great Britain, an industrialized one. Influenced by a visit to the United States in the late eighteenth century, Costa defended industrialization as the only possible path to sovereignty.

This apparent ambiguity in Luso-Brazilian liberal thought reflected the different consequences of the Old Regime crisis for the Portuguese and British Empires. While Portugal witnessed the loss of its former colonies, Great Britain, by contrast, asserted its world hegemony through the use of free trade agreements, such as the Treaties of 1810.

Notes

1 Old Regime or *Ancien Régime* are the terms used to express the political, economic, and social order that prevailed in Europe between the sixteenth and eighteenth centuries. In this chapter, we opted for the first term, following Paquette (2013).
2 During the period from 1778 to 1796, Souza Coutinho served as a diplomat at the Court of Turin (Diniz Silva 2002, vol. I, pp. 39–63).

3 The Swiss Jacques Necker (1732–1804) was in charge of formulating French economic policy in the throes of Louis XVI reign (Diniz Silva 2002–2004, pp. 27–53).

4 We call '*estrangeirado*' the group of Portuguese intellectuals who, after a journey of studies in England, returned to Portugal and contributed to the reform of the Portuguese Kingdom, especially during Pombal's administration (Martins 1965, pp. 122–129; Macedo 1974).

5 "… the result was a mercantilism inspired by the Enlightenment; the Enlightened Mercantilism … The mercantilist vision of colonization remains, therefore, at the base of the educated Luso-Brazilian reflections" (Novais 1979, pp. 230–231).

6 We have consulted an online version of *Correio Braziliense*: http://bndigital.bn.br/ hemeroteca-digital/. All excerpts from Portuguese references were translated by us, unless otherwise stated.

7 About Hipólito José da Costa, see Dourado (1957); Rizzini (1957).

8 In this work, we have used and translated excerpts from the Portuguese version (Manchester 1973, p. 54). The English version is *British Preeminence in Brazil: Its Rise and Decline: A Study in European Expansion*. Chapel Hill, NC: University of North Carolina Press, 1933.

9 There was only one treaty in discussion during the 1809 negotiations. In 1810, however, they became two: one of Alliance and Friendship, regarding liberty of religion, and another of Commerce and Navigation, regarding free trade. In the collection published by the Bank of Portugal there is a "Draft of a unique Treaty of Alliance and Commerce with Britain," written in French and consisting of 22 articles (pp. 371–379). There is also a "Draft of a unique Treaty of Alliance and Commerce," written in Portuguese, with 39 articles and two additional and secret articles (pp. 380–397). In this work, we use both the "Drafts of the Treaties" and the "Treaties" published in Hertslet's collection in English and Portuguese ("*Tratado de comércio e navegação entre Grã-Bretanha e Portugal, assinado em Rio de Janeiro dos 19 de fevereiro de 1810*"; "Treaty of Commerce and Navigation between Great Britain and Portugal, signed at Rio de Janeiro, 19th February, 1810," pp. 26–65). There is also a version published in *Correio Braziliense* with the title "Friendship, commerce and navigation between His Britannic Majesty and His Royal Highness the Prince of Portugal" (*Correio Braziliense*, s.d., agosto de 1810). For the Secret Convention, we have consulted the document "Secret Convention of London of 1807," which can be found in the attachments to Arruda (2008). There is an extensive documentation on the Treaties, including the debates raised during the nineteenth century. For this, we have consulted Alexandre (1993, pp. 209–232). After the signing of the Treaties on August 27th, 1811, D. Rodrigo de Souza Coutinho wrote some notes, entitled "*Apontamentos em defesa do tratado de comércio de 1810*," also found in the collection organized by the Bank of Portugal (pp. 398–400).

10 The reciprocity clause appears in the first article of the drafts and in the fourth article of the Treaties:

> there shall be a perfect reciprocity on the subject of the duties and imposts to be paid by the ships and vessels of the high Contracting Parties, within the several ports, harbours, roads, and anchoring places belonging to each of them; to wit, that the ships and vessels of the subjects of His Britannic Majesty shall not pay any higher duties or imposts (under whatsoever name they be designated or implied) within the Dominions of His Royal Highness the Prince Regent of Portugal, than the ships and vessels belonging to the subjects of His Royal Highness the Prince Regent of Portugal shall be bound to pay within the Dominions of His Britannic Majesty, and vice versa.
>
> ("Treaty of Commerce and Navigation"
> 1820 [1810], p. 31)

11 A few years after the agreement became effective, dealer Tollenare noticed that the franchise of ports – or the 1810 agreement – greatly affected the Company, making its administration impossible. Importers saw benefits in bringing wines from Spain and elsewhere, preferably from Porto, so that the warehouses runiously accumulated the harvests. In 1816, Tollenare saw over 80,000 unsold barrels in the warehouses (Lima 1945, p. 389).

12 The excerpt was taken from the Portuguese edition (Manchester 1973, p. 75), and translated by ourselves.

13 A *Conservator* is a person appointed by the Court to handle the financial matters and property of a minor or disabled adult person. In the eighteenth century, a *judge conservator* (the Latin term) "was to enforce the execution of the Treaties signed between ... two Crowns" (King et al. 1713).

14 His Royal Highness, the Prince Regent of Portugal, having, by the 10th Article of the Treaty of Alliance, concluded at Rio de Janeiro, on the 19th February 1810, declared His determination to co-operate with His Britannic Majesty in the cause of humanity and justice, by adopting the most efficacious means for bringing about a gradual Abolition of the Slave Trade; and His Royal Highness, in pursuance of His said Declaration, and desiring to effectuate, in concert with His Britannic Majesty and the other Powers of Europe, who have been induced to assist in this benevolent object, an immediate Abolition of the said Traffic upon the parts of the coast of Africa which are situated to the northward of the Line.

(Treaty between Great Britain and Portugal. Signed at Vienna, 1820 [1815], vol. 2, pp. 73 and 75)

Sources and bibliography

Sources

"Agreement on four points connected with the execution of the Treaty of 1810, signed at London, 18th December 1812" (1820). In: *A complete collection of treaties and conventions at present subsisting Great Britain and foreign powers*. Compiled from authentic documents by Lewis Hertslet's, London, printed for T. Egerton, vol. II.

Costa, Hipólito José da. "Exame do Tratado de Comércio entre as cortes do Brasil e da Inglaterra," in *Correio Braziliense*, s.d., vol. V, n. 27, 189–191. Available on the National Library website: http://bndigital.bn.br/hemeroteca-digital/.

Coutinho, Rodrigo de Souza. (1993). "Apontamentos em defesa do Tratado de comércio." In: *Textos políticos, econômicos e financeiros (1783–1811)*, Lisboa, Banco de Portugal, Coleção de Obras Clássicas do Pensamento Econômico Português, Tomo II, pp. 398–400.

Coutinho, Rodrigo de Souza. (1993). "Esboço de um Tratado único de aliança e comércio" (in Portuguese, consisting of 39 articles and 2 additional and secret articles, no date available, 1809). In: *Textos políticos, econômicos e financeiros (1783–1811)*, Lisboa, Banco de Portugal, Coleção de Obras Clássicas do Pensamento Econômico Português, Tomo II, pp. 380–398.

Coutinho, Rodrigo de Souza. (1993). "Esboço de um Tratado único de aliança e comércio" (in French, consisting of 22 articles, no date available). In: *Textos políticos, econômicos e financeiros (1783–1811)*, Lisboa, Banco de Portugal, Coleção de Obras Clássicas do Pensamento Econômico Português, Tomo II, pp. 371–379.

Coutinho, Rodrigo de Souza. (1993). "Memória sobre o melhoramento dos domínios de Sua Majestade na América (1797–1798)." In: *Textos políticos, econômicos e financeiros (1783–1811)*, Lisboa: Banco de Portugal, Coleção de Obras Clássicas do Pensamento Econômico Português, Tomo II, pp. 47–69.

Couto, José Vieira. (1994). *Memória sobre a Capitania das Minas Gerais: seu território, clima e produções metálicas*, Estudo crítico, transcrição e pesquisa histórica de Júnia Ferreira Furtado. Belo Horizonte, Sistema Estadual de Planejamento/ Fundação João Pinheiro/ Centro de Estudos Históricos e Culturais.

King, Charles, Martin, Henry, Gee, Joshua. 1713. *The British Merchant; Or, Commerce Preserv'd: In Answer to The Mercator, Or Commerce Retriev'd. To be Publish'd Every Tuesday and Friday*. A[nn]. Baldwin near the Oxford-Arms in Warwick-Lane.

"Tratado de comércio e navegação entre Grã-Bretanha e Portugal, assinado no Rio de Janeiro dos 19 de fevereiro de 1810" (1820). In: *A complete collection of treaties and conventions at present subsisting Great Britain and foreign powers*. Compiled from authentic documents by Lewis Hertslet's, London, printed for T. Egerton, vol. II, 27–65.

"Treaty of commerce and navigation, signed at Rio de Janeiro, 19th February 1810" (1820). In: *A complete collection of treaties and conventions at present subsisting Great Britain and foreign powers*. Compiled from authentic documents by Lewis Hertslet's, London, printed for T. Egerton, vol. II.

"Treaty between Great Britain and Portugal. Signed at Vienna, the 22nd January 1815" (1820). In: *A complete collection of treaties and conventions at present subsisting Great Britain and foreign powers*. Compiled from authentic documents by Lewis Hertslet's, London, printed for T. Egerton, vol. II.

Bibliography

Alexandre, Valentim. 1993. *Os sentidos do Império: questão nacional e questão colonial na crise do Antigo Regime Português*. Porto: Edições Afrontamento. Coleção Biblioteca das Ciências do Homem.

Alexandre, Valentim. 1998. "O fim do Império luso-brasileiro." In: Bethencourt, Francisco and Chaudhuri, Kirti (Eds.) *História da Expansão Portuguesa: do Brasil para África (1808–1930)*. Lisboa: Círculo de Leitores, Vol. IV, pp. 215–227.

Arruda, José Jobson de Andrade. 2008. *Uma Colônia entre dois impérios: a abertura dos portos brasileiros (1800–1808)*. Bauru/SP: EDUSC.

Cain, Peter, Hopkins, A. G. 1980. "The political economy of British expansion overseas, 1750–1914." *Economic History Review*, second series, v. 33, no. 4, Nov., pp. 463–490.

Cardoso, José Luís. 2001. "Nas malhas do Império: a economia política e a política colonial de D. Rodrigo de Souza Coutinho." In: Cardoso, José Luís (Ed.) *A economia política e os dilemas do império luso-brasileiro (1790–1822)*. Lisboa: Comissão Nacional para as Comemorações dos Descobrimentos Portugueses.

Cardoso, José Luís. 2009. "Free trade, political economy and the birth of a new economic nation: Brazil, 1808–1810." *Revista de Historia Económica. Journal of Iberian and Latin American Economic History*, v. 27, iss. 2, pp. 183–204.

Carvalho, Daniel Elias de. 2008. "A Historiografia luso-brasileira e as Manifestações dos Tratados de 1810: um balanço historiográfico." In: Mata, Sérgio Ricardo, Mollo, Helena Miranda, and Varella, Flávia Florentino (Eds.) *Caderno de resumos & Anais do 2º. Seminário Nacional de História da Historiografia. A dinâmica do historicismo: tradições historiográficas modernas*. Ouro Preto: EdUFOP.

Dias, Maria Odila da Silva. 1968. "Aspectos da Ilustração no Brasil." In: *Revista do IHGB*, Rio de Janeiro, Jan/Mar., v. 278, pp. 105–170; and Maria de Lourdes Viana Lyra, *A Utopia do poderoso império*, Rio de Janeiro, Sette Letras, 1994.

Diniz Silva, Andrée Mansuy. 2002–2004. *Portrait d'un homme d'Etat: D. Rodrigo de Souza Coutinho, Comte de Linhares 1755–1796*. Lisbon; Paris: Fundação Calouste Gulbenkian, 2 vols.

Dourado, Mecenas, 1957. *Hipólito da Costa e o Correio Brasiliense*. Rio de Janeiro: Biblioteca do Exército Editora.

Freitas, Caio de. 1958. *George Canning e o Brasil*. São Paulo: Cia Editora Nacional, 2 vols. www.brasiliana.com.br/obras/george-canning-e-o-brasil.

Israel, Jonathan. 2006. *Enlightenment Contested: Philosophy, Modernity and the Emancipation of Man*. Oxford: Oxford University Press.

Lima, Manuel de Oliveira. 1908. *D. João VI e o Brasil*. RJ, Tipografia do Jornal do Comércio, 1ª edição.

Lima, Manuel de Oliveira. 1945. *Dom João VI no Brasil*. Rio de Janeiro: Livraria José Olympio Editora.

Lima, Manuel de Oliveira. 1986. *O Império Brasileiro, 1822–1889*, new ed.; Brasília: Editora Universidade de Brasília.

Lyra, Maria de Lourdes Viana. 1994. *A Utopia do Poderoso Império*. Rio de Janeiro: Sette Letras.

Macedo, Joaquim Borges de. 1974. *Estrangeirados-um conceito a rever*. Braga: Edições do Templo.

Manchester, Alan K. 1973. *Preeminência inglesa no Brasil*. São Paulo: Ed. Brasiliense.

Martins, Antonio Coimbra. 1965. "Estrangeirados." In: Serrão, Joel (Ed.) *Dicionário da História de Portugal*, vol. II. Lisboa: Iniciativas Editoriais.

Maxwell, Kenneth. 1973. "The Generation of 1790's and the idea of Luso-Brazilian Empire." In: Alden , Dauril (Ed.) *Colonial Roots of Modern Brazil*. Berkeley: University of California Press.

Neves, Guilherme Pereira das. 1995. "Do Império luso-brasileiro ao império do Brasil (1789–1822)." In: *Ler História*, Lisboa: v. 27–28, pp. 75–102.

Neves, Guilherme Pereira das. 2001. "Guardar mais silêncio do que falar: Azeredo Coutinho, Ribeiro dos Santos e a escravidão." In: Cardoso, José Luís (Ed.) *A economia política e os dilemas do império luso-brasileiro (1790–1822)*. Lisboa: Comissão Nacional para as Comemorações dos Descobrimentos Portugueses.

Novais, Fernando. 1979. *Portugal e Brasil na crise do antigo sistema colonial (1777–1808)*. São Paulo: Hucitec.

Novais, Fernando. 2005. *Aproximações: estudos de história e historiografia*. São Paulo: Cosac Naify.

Paquette, Gabriel. 2013. *Imperial Portugal in the Age of Atlantic Revolutions: The Luso-Brazilian World, c. 1770–1850*. Cambridge: Cambridge University Press.

Pedreira, Jorge Miguel. 1994. *Estrutura industrial e mercado colonial: Portugal e Brasil (1780–1830)*. Lisboa: Difusão Européia do Livro.

Prado Jr., Caio. 2006. *História Econômica do Brasil*. São Paulo: Brasiliense.

Ramos, Luís A. de Oliveira. 1988. "Em torno dos tratados de 1810." In: Atas do Colóquio Comemorativo do VI centenário do Tratado de Windsor, Porto.

Rizzini, Carlos. 1957. *Hipólito da Costa e o Correio Brasiliense*. São Paulo: Cia. Editora Nacional, Brasiliana Grande Formato nº 13.

Schultz, Kirsten. 2013. *Tropical Versailles: Empire, Monarchy, and the Portuguese Royal Court in Rio de Janeiro, 1808–1821 (New World in the Atlantic World)*. New York; London: Routledge.

Sodré, Nelson Werneck. 1978. *As razões da Independência*. 3rd edn. Rio de Janeiro: Civilização Brasileira.

Venturi, Franco. 1984. *Settecento Rifomatore: la caduta dell'Antico Regime (1776–1789)*. Torino: Giulio Einaudi, v. 4, t. 1.

Part III
Ideas from abroad

7   Julio Menadier

A Listian economist in the economic policy debate in Chile (1860–1880)

Claudio Robles Ortiz

In Chile, the danger of blindly following the European practices is not inferior to the one of following their economists' fine theories.

(Julio Menadier, 1869)

The economic policy debate that took place along with the transition to capitalism in Latin America in the nineteenth century offers a relevant perspective to examine the assimilation, discussion, and reformulation of economic paradigms and ideas (Mallon, 1988; Coatsworth and Williamson, 2004; Jacobsen, 2007). In particular, conflicts regarding customs tariffs can illustrate how economists and policymakers not only adopted, but also adapted economic doctrines to support different business sectors and social classes' often contradictory interests. Such was the case of Julio Menadier, a Prussian lawyer born in 1823, who arrived in Chile in 1849, and soon revealed himself as an erudite analyst of agriculture and rural society. In addition to his theoretical knowledge, Menadier acquired first-hand familiarity with Chile's economic issues and institutions. In the 1860s, Menadier served as head of the Customs House in Valparaíso, then a major commercial center in the South Pacific coast; shortly after, in 1869, the National Agricultural Society (SNA) hired him as its secretary and chief editor of its agricultural magazine, which he created and directed until 1883.[1] In that capacity, Menadier became the most important agrarian ideologue in nineteenth-century Chile. He published nearly a hundred articles in the *Bulletin of the National Agricultural Society* (BSNA), thus producing a work that dealt with an impressive variety of topics, ranging from agronomic and technical matters to social and economic issues. As such a knowledgeable expert, he also actively participated in Chile's oligarchic public sphere, representing the landed elite's interests, and becoming the SNA's authoritative spokesperson. Menadier was also a Listian economist, whose ideas added unexpected complexity to the ongoing confrontation between protectionism and liberalism. Thus, he played a significant role in the economic policy debate in the late 1860s and the 1870s, a critical period in Chile, characterized by several controversial tariff reforms and, in response, a growing questioning of free trade as theoretical base for economic policy.

At the same time, Julio Menadier's adherence to Listian political economy seems relevant, and even puzzling, from the perspective of the theoretical models employed to explain the transmission of economic ideas. The very fact that Menadier was a Listian economist is difficult to document, since he made no references to List's work in any of his numerous articles in the SNA's bulletin. In addition, there is no information about Menadier's early contacts with Listian political economy. Yet, since he came to Chile in 1849, eight years after the publication of List's "The System of National Political Economy," it is very likely that Menadier had contact with List's ideas, which, in fact, were rather popular if not dominant in Germany in the 1840s. Thus, following Mäki's (1996) "information theory model," the "port of exportation" of Listian ideas remains unclear, but Menadier certainly was the "port of entry" for those ideas to reach a peripheral nation like Chile. Moreover, in this regard Menadier seems to have created in the SNA's bulletin a venue of his own for the dissemination, or at least the debate, of Listian political economy. Indeed, a recent study of the political economy textbooks written by the leading Chilean economists in the nineteenth century, Miguel Cruchaga, Zorobabel Rodríguez, and Guillermo Subercaseaux, shows that what we may call "academic economists" did not include List as one of their sources (Couyoumdjian, 2015). Menadier's ideas, therefore, were a particular adaptation of Listian political economy, and, given his role as SNA's spokeperson, such adaptation was primarily geared for those involved in the more practical and urgent realm of economic policy debate.

Focusing on his role as the SNA's leading expert, this chapter studies the arguments that Menadier employed to substantiate that organization's demands in the debate concerning the tariff reforms instituted from the middle of the 1860s, particularly on taxes levied on agricultural machinery imports. By examining Menadier's ideas and role in the economic policy debate, we argue that, contrary to conventional interpretations, which depicted large landowners as a backward group uninterested in technological innovation, the SNA lobbied for, and Menadier argued in favor of, a policy of full exemption on customs duties for the importation of agricultural equipment. Based on his understanding of agriculture as the "mother industry," that is, the most important of all economic activities in a country, Menadier contended that such policy would significantly facilitate the introduction of "modern machinery," and thus further stimulate the process of agricultural mechanization initiated in the early 1850s, when Chile began to export wheat to California, Australia, and then England. Closely related to Menadier's thought on customs tariffs and taxes on imports, the chapter also discusses his use of List's ideas to demand protectionist economic policies for encouraging the development of Chile's foundries and metal-mechanic sector. In his view, this incipient industrial sector was an "infant industry" that, if assisted, could make an important contribution to the technological modernization of agriculture. The metal sector consisted of a small number of foundries that emerged as part of Chile's "early industrialization," a process that developed along with the cycle of export-led economic growth that the country experienced in the second half of the nineteenth century. For Menadier, the metal industries had been "victims" of a wrong "rent-seeking" economic policy, which government had introduced in the custom tariffs reforms passed in the 1860s. Instead, he argued that economic policy should protect foundries and metal industries because they supplied agricultural machines and implements that, although produced at a very small scale, were nonetheless technically more suitable for Chilean farming practices, and, in some cases, less expensive than imports. Thus, until the economic crisis of 1878, and using Friedrich List's national economics doctrine, the SNA's spokesman would also play an active role in the "defense of national industry."

The analysis of Julio Menadier's thought provides new insights on the circulation of economic ideas in nineteenth-century Latin America and Chile. As it has been pointed out for other countries, like Mexico, for instance, Latin American economic thought during the nineteenth century was not only influenced by free-trade doctrines but also by positivism, that is, the philosophical and, then, practical movement which demanded scientific intervention in the social realm by the government. According to Charles Hale (1995), after 1870, amidst a new political consensus, "the classic liberal doctrines based on the autonomous individual gave way to theories constructing the individual as an integral part of the social organism." Thus, Hale noted, a "theoretical conflict existed between classic or doctrinaire liberalism and the new concepts (often referred to loosely as 'positivism'), but it was a conflict that could be submerged in an era of consensus" (Hale, 1995, pp. 135–136). Thus, Julio Menadier's critique of Chilean economic policy can be interpreted as an early manifestation of the end of free trade's hegemony as an economic paradigm. This shift marked the end of what Jacobsen (2007, p. 136) called the era of the "triumphant liberalism" in Latin America, a change that took place in the 1880s for some countries, or in the 1890s for others. The period ranging from the 1880s to the 1920s was, according to Jacobsen, a transition period throughout which some elite circles advocated and accepted state intervention. Since Menadier's Listian ideas preceded the movements referred above, it could be argued he was one of the precursors of a movement that would gain terrain in Latin America a little later.

From a local, that is, Chilean perspective, studying Menadier's ideas allows for a reconsideration of conventional wisdom regarding nineteenth-century economic thought. First, it can be demonstrated that Friedrich List's national economics was known and discussed by Chilean economists, and that it had influential followers among agrarian analysts and ideologues. Second, Menadier's participation in the economic policy debate reveals that the supposedly hegemonic free trade paradigm was challenged with protectionist arguments, even to lend support to Chile's powerful agrarian interests, which contradicts the idea that large landowners unreservedly adhered to free trade (Véliz, 1963). Furthermore, the "protectionist" discourse that Menadier formulated in support of the metal-mechanic industries demonstrates that the business sectors that competed against each other in the public sphere employed economic doctrines as legitimating discourses. As was the case with the SNA, they selectively adapted economic ideas to their political agendas, in order to address the specific issues that arose in concrete situations. Thus, contrary to what prior studies suggested (Will, 1960, 1964), the supposed "doctrinaire" adherence to economic free trade among state policymakers, such as, for example, financial authorities, seems less relevant in order to understand the content and the impact of economic policies. On the other hand, this study allows us to revise one of the most influential notions regarding the export-led agrarian expansion, that is, the assertion contending that large landowners had no interest in technological modernization of the agricultural sector (Bauer, 1975).

Menadier and the debate on tariff reforms

As the SNA demanded that the state adopted measures to facilitate technological modernization in the agricultural sector, especially the diffusion of mechanization, its analysts, primarily Julio Menadier, actively participated in the public debate regarding the function and effects of economic policy, and of customs tariffs in particular. The main venue for exposing their economic ideas was the SNA's *Bulletin*, a modern, comprehensive agricultural magazine that published a number of "economic studies" and articles of an apparently technical character, but which were actually formal expressions of the SNA's institutional interests. Menadier strongly criticized the tariff reforms instituted in the early 1860s, arguing that they had negative effects on the capital goods market, increasing the price of machinery imports and, therefore, making it more difficult for landowners to further mechanization. His critique of the "economic effects" of the Customs Ordinance of 1864 was the starting point for the elaboration of an economic discourse that was based on List's thinking. The tariff reform of 1864 had eliminated the *ad valorem* taxes of 30 percent, 6 percent, and 2 percent on all imports, replacing them with a general rate of 25 percent; however, at the same time, it introduced a 15 percent *ad valorem* tax on imported machinery. This reform was a response to the increasing fiscal deficit that, starting in 1848, became one of the main issues influencing the debate and subsequent revisions of the Customs Ordinance (Ortega, 1985). In 1869, the board of the SNA commissioned Menadier a study on the matter, the results of which would constitute its official position. The report questioned both the "practical results" of the reform, as well as the ideological basis of the economic policy. Thus, along with stating that "no tax" was so "precise," "determinant," and "equitable" as the "customs tariffs," as long as it were always established "according to the economic necessities of each nation," Menadier criticized the authorities for resorting to the "most comfortable and secure expedient in order to get out of the difficult fiscal situation," namely, that of "burdening imports with higher duties." Thus, he questioned the reform for being a mere resource to increase fiscal income, since its "cardinal principle" was to obtain higher amounts of revenue (Menadier, 1869, pp. 34, 43).

Moreover, Menadier held that, in formulating the tariff reform, the authorities did not consider "the economic implications of the new tax on productive goods," that is to say, the capital goods and raw materials that the economic sectors, not only agriculture, required for their development. Therefore, along with recognizing that "a great step into free trade" had been taken with the reform that eliminated the general tax rate of 30 percent levied on a number of imported goods, he criticized that, "accompanied with, as it were, with a tax from 15 to 25 percent on raw materials," in the reform of 1864 "the fair proportion of duties between objects of necessity and luxury goods" had been "destroyed." By this, Menadier referred to the fact the new tariff levied taxes on "productive goods," including products that due to their low price "could not easily bear" a surcharge, in the same manner as a variety of expensive goods that "only satisfied the caprice of fashion and luxury" (Menadier, 1869, p. 36).

For Menadier, the provisions included in the new customs tariff were errors derived from the application of a "rent-seeking" criterion and, in opposition to it, he demanded the adoption of an "economic principle" that considered the utility and nature of the goods on which the taxes were levied. Even more so, he considered that, when taking into consideration the "economic nature of the goods," not only could there be an increase in fiscal income, but also a possibility to eliminate the "obstacles that burden the national industry and production." To this effect, he proposed that any future reform should be made according to the "cardinal principle" of "lowering taxes on productive goods and of first necessity, and to increase them on luxury items." Furthermore, Menadier maintained that long distances from production centers made freight on "productive goods," especially those of large volume and weight, such as machinery, rise to "a value much superior than the cost price," which was a sufficient "motive for not making them even more expensive, holding them to strong importation rights." Thus, against the opinion of those who justified higher taxes by contending that freight rates were considerable in France and Germany, Menadier argued that this was possible in Europe only because freight rates added an "insignificant surcharge" to the final price. At the same time, he criticized local adherents of free trade who claimed that they supported changes recently introduced in Chilean economic policy because they were in line with trends in the European nations, which they considered models. Adopting a more pragmatic approach, instead, Menadier categorically warned local "free traders" that "in Chile, the danger of blindly following the European practices is not inferior to the one of following the fine theories of their economists." In his view, the assimilation and implementation of economic doctrines, like free trade, should take into account the particularity of the economic situation of the country. Consequently, he argued that it was indispensable that the customs system were organized in a manner that it would fulfill the double task of "securing revenue for the state and educating national industries" (Menadier, 1869, p. 37).

Seeking that purpose, in his "Studies on the customs legislation of Chile" Menadier exposed considerations for elaborating a new customs reform project. The project reflected his interest in the "protectionist" function that, in his concept, the tariffs should fulfill, but also, the objective of conjugating the fiscal interest and that of the "national industries." Menadier's proposal considered increasing the tax on imported consumer goods similar to those produced in the country, and reducing the customs duties to only 5 percent *ad valorem* for a series of goods of a "productive" character; those were capital goods and raw materials on which the customs ordinance levied duties of 15 percent or 25 percent, but that had been previously exempted. According to Menadier, this measure was necessary in order to stimulate economic growth, because "the bigger the increase on foreign 'productive goods,' the less the national industry is served." The proposal reflected Menadier's concern for the current situation of Chilean agriculture, in particular for the fall of wheat exports, which was a consequence of falling international prices. For Menadier, it was necessary to remove the obstacles government had placed by levying taxes on the importation of indispensable means of production for agriculture. Thus, he proposed the reduction of taxes on imports of a number of "productive goods," including, naturally, agricultural equipment and machinery. Finally, he concluded by formulating a demand that, given the contradictory interests it involved, resulted in an almost utopian request: "When will the day come in which Chile will obtain a customs code that conciliates the fiscal interest, those of commerce, and of industry?" (Menadier, 1869, pp. 25, 42).

The authorities did not ignore that the taxes introduced had had a negative impact in the economic sectors, and admitted the convenience of reducing them or, even, suppressing some, but only in a gradual manner, and once having fulfilled the purpose of increasing fiscal income.[2] However, the economic crisis that began in 1874, in which the export sector collapsed, imposed once again the necessity of increasing customs duties. In October of 1876, the government presented, and Congress approved, a bill that introduced, for a period of 18 months, a general surcharge of 10 percent on the import duties set in the Customs Ordinance of 1872. As the Lower House's Finance Committee projected a deficit of $3 million for the fiscal year of 1877, the so-called "surcharge bill" was certainly a new resource to deal with the reduction in fiscal income resulting from the crisis in international commerce.[3]

The "surcharge bill" exempted a few goods, but agricultural machinery was not amongst them, for which, if the bill was approved, the *ad valorem* tax levied on it would be of 16.5 percent. Facing that prospect, the SNA opposed the project in Congress as well as through its intervention in the public debate. By then, Julio Menadier's participation in the debate concerning customs tariffs had led him to the formulation of a true program for agricultural promotion, in which the demand of full exemption for imported machinery was now integrated. In this program, published in the SNA's bulletin while the surcharge bill was being debated in Congress, Menadier called not only for the simple reduction of import duties levied on certain "productive goods," but a rather drastic reform. Its main elements included the "duty-free importation of all raw materials and capital goods that contribute to increase national production," the introduction of "additional taxes on all manufactures already produced by national industries," and, finally, to impose "the highest tariff rates" on all "luxury products," "regardless if they are produced in Chile or not" (Menadier, 1876, pp. 404–405).

From this point onwards, Menadier's arguments became the basis for the SNA's official position in the matter. According to it, the first "economic" function that customs duties should perform was the protection of "national industries," above agriculture. The "protectionist" demand that Menadier formulated was determined not only by his opinion about the effects of the economic crisis of 1874–1878 in the agricultural sector, but, fundamentally, by his analysis of the character of the Chilean economy. In doing so, he revealed the influence of Friedrich List's thinking, particularly with respect to the necessity of protecting the incipient manufacturing sector (Sporzluk, 1988; Levi-Faur, 1997). Menadier argued that Chile was a backward country that should "educate" all "national industries," among which agriculture was certainly the most important one. To that end, he regarded the "protectionist" intervention of the state as indispensable. In fact, according to the SNA's expert, "in a country that for centuries has received all manufactures from abroad," it was not sufficient to have "duty free importation of raw materials, implements, tools, and other 'productive' goods." Thus, he requested the adoption of a new customs ordinance that established "a system of additional rights," the purpose of which would be, precisely, "to introduce and educate the incipient industries which from their inception cannot stand foreign competition" (Menadier, 1876, p. 407).

Based on this line of thought, the SNA intensified its criticism of the economic policy in view of the "emergency measures" that the government adopted in order to deal with the economic crisis of 1874–1878. Thus, the SNA's board of directors sent to the Chamber of Deputies a long study prepared by a special committee presided by Julio Menadier, the purpose of which was to directly influence the legislative debate. In this report, Menadier argued that the economic crisis was caused not only by changes in the international market, but was also due to, precisely, the harmful effects of the previous tariff reforms. Therefore, he insisted that the importation of capital goods be fully exempted of any taxes, stating that:

> From the year 1865, all the national industries have urged government for a revision of the Customs Ordinance requesting, if not a complete abolition, at least a reduction of the rights imposed on raw materials and on productive goods that are needed to supply the domestic market in competition with imported goods, or to secure or regain our foreign markets.[4]

In sum, for Menadier it was indispensable that the government rectified the economic policy, introducing changes in the customs tariffs in order to stimulate growth of the Chilean economy. As he argued, "the increase of fiscal income must not be sought after in that of taxes but in that of production, facilitating it, improving it and lowering its costs" (Menadier, 1876, p. 556). Furthermore, Menadier denounced that the authorities had excluded national businessmen from the economic policy debate, since the committee charged with studying customs reform was to a large extent composed of foreigners, most of whom belonged to the international commercial firms based in Valparaíso. As he indicated in the report sent to the Chamber of Deputies, under those circumstances it was "almost impossible that politicians in Santiago could form themselves a thorough opinion on the changes that the committee in Valparaiso had proposed." Moreover, he asserted that "a detailed and conscientious study on the commercial, industrial, social and rentistic importance of each imported good" was needed; without which neither government nor Congress could "proceed with the right decisions that are required by the principal source of public revenue, the progress of the industries and the prosperity of all of Chilean society" (Menadier, 1876, p. 560). Although a month later the government appointed him in the committee created for the discussion of the customs reform, Menadier continued to criticize the economic policy, holding the government responsible for the severity of the economic crisis, and sentencing with pessimism that "Chile under the current customs legislation has been thrown into a chronic crisis that is undermining all its productive forces."[5]

Defending the national metal-mechanic industry

There probably were no other "productive forces" for which such criticism was so pertinent than the foundries and metal industries of the small, but modern Chilean industrial sector (Kirsch, 1977; García, 1989). According to the first industrial census, which the Society for Promoting Manufacturing (SFF) carried out in 1895, there existed 2449 "industrial establishments," half of which were located in Santiago and Valparaíso. Nevertheless, by contemporary international standards, only 124 of those firms were modern industries, properly speaking, as their processes of production rested on the use of energy supplied by steam engines, each firm employed a workforce of at least ten workers, and all of them were fully wage-earners (Ortega, 1981).

Owned by Chilean and especially foreign industrialists, some of whom were also referred to as "engineers," by 1870 the foundries and metal industries produced capital goods of a certain complexity at a small scale, as was precisely the case with agricultural machinery. Considering the industrial sector's structure, these metal-mechanic industries were one of the two most important sub-sectors in terms of employment and the number of firms, and were located not only in Santiago and Valparaiso, but also in provincial capitals located throughout the agricultural region of Central Chile, in addition to the mining districts in the north. As can be seen in commercial advertisements in newspapers and agricultural magazines, both foundries and metal industries played an important role in the introduction and diffusion of imported agricultural equipment. From the simple repairing of imported machinery, these industries went on to adapt and, later on, to manufacture modified versions of some of the more demanded models among Chilean landowners. In this manner, at least the larger foundries, like "Klein Brothers," of Santiago, developed a modest, but promising line of machines, like wheat reapers, especially, which was more appropriate for the usually irregular cultivation fields of many Chilean large estates.

Yet, in the late 1870s, the Chilean metal industries were confronted with a profound crisis. After decades of competing with the international firms that controlled the capital goods market, they had been facing an ever-increasing influx of manufactured consumer goods and machinery, which were imported from England, principally. For this reason, some of the most important industrialists in the metal industrial sector began a movement in order to demand "protection to the national industry." Although certainly acting upon its own interests, the SNA became part of the so-called "protectionist industrialist movement," to which it added its selective and quite moderate "protectionist" stance. Even so, the convergence of interests between these two sectors that challenged the handling of the economic policy, SNA's landowners and metal industry owners, brought more tensions to the already conflict-ridden oligarchic public sphere in Chile.

Indeed, in the political and economic debate, there was an escalating confrontation between two positions concerning the role of the foundries and metal industries. On the one hand, that of those who considered that the foundries had all the necessary conditions and potential to consolidate themselves and, therefore, they should be treated as a kind of "infant industry," for which the application of protectionist policies was perfectly rational and justified. On the other hand, that of their critics, who argued that, due to foundries' "scarce development," any protectionist measures to attempt to foster their growth lacked ground, and, consequently, if enacted, would only serve certain business interests but not the national interest. Representing the SNA, for his part, Julio Menadier argued that, even if modest in quantity, foundries' production was an alternative supply of agricultural machinery and, in some cases, a more affordable option. At the same time, he considered that metal industries contributed to the growth of a "mechanical culture," even within rural society, because they were real workplace environments that allowed for the practical training of the skilled workers needed not only in the manufacturing sector itself, but also in other activities in which the introduction and diffusion of modern tecnology required qualified personnel. In fact, that was the case in agriculture, where the ongoing mechanization in large haciendas made it necessary for a pool of mechanics, machinists, and workers familiarized with the operation of modern agricultural machinery.[6]

Due to those reasons, from his position in the SNA, at least until the economic crisis of 1874–1878, Julio Menadier kept demanding economic policy measures that would promote the development of the foundries. Like a few entrepreneurs in the industrial sector, Menadier and other economic analysts considered that the foundries were victims of the rent-seeking economic policy, particularly the recent custom tariff reforms. Thus, in his capacity as chief editor of the SNA's *Bulletin*, not only did Menadier give ample coverage to foundries and enthusiastically publicize their products, but, above all, he allowed industrialists themselves to contribute notes and articles, and thus to participate in the public debate in order to defend their interests. It was in the *Bulletin*, precisely, that in 1874 the engineer Víctor Carvallo expressed the metal industrial sector's rejection of the economic policy. The Chilean industrialist strongly denounced national foundries' crisis, establishing that it was the foreseeable consequence of exposing them, without any protection, to competition with imports and the "grand foreign commerce." Thus, he added, in practice, Chilean foundries had, no less, to face the power of European industry, the intermediaries of which in the domestic market were the "commission houses" based in Valparaíso. According to Carvallo, given the incipient level of development of the metal-mechanic industry, by levying new taxes and increasing the existing ones on the raw materials required for producing machinery in Chile, the government had done nothing more than to add more obstacles to the country's economic development. In his view, this was, of course, absolutely unjustified, because:

> For those who are aware of the resources that the large European manufacturers have in terms of markets, capital, raw materials, and the workforce's skills, and can compare these elements with those our nascent, feeble, and neglected industry has, it will become evident that it would be madness to pretend that our products to do better than the foreign ones.[7]

Nevertheless, the convergence of interests between the National Agricultural Society and foundries' owners was far from being absolute. In reality, there existed discrepant opinions within that organization, just like among the industrialist entrepreneurship. It was relevant, therefore, that once again Julio Menadier allowed Víctor Carvallo to write in the SNA's *Bulletin*, this time in 1876, to reply to Enrique Ariztía, a prominent landowner and SNA member, who, in a letter sent to Menadier himself, indicated that, since the production of agricultural machines in the country was insignificant and scarcely competitive, the demands of protectionist measures for the metal-mechanic sector were totally unjustified. The controversy between Carvallo and Ariztía, moreover, reflected the so-called "unjustified preference" for imported machinery among Chilean landowners, an attitude that some metal-mechanic industrials considered a "disdain" for "national production." In addition to its expression in certain individuals' opinions and behavior, such "disdain" had institutional and bussiness dimensions. As Víctor Carvallo observed, by promoting the acquisition and diffusion of agricultural machinery, the policies the SNA advanced had also negatively affected the foundries, especially when pressing for a reduction or the elimination of taxes levied on imported equipment. Specifically, Carvallo directed his criticism at, in his opinion, the disastrous consequences of the National Agricultural Exhibition, which the SNA had organized in 1869, and which was no less than its most important effort to promote agricultural mechanization in Chile. Thus, if foreign manufacturers had saluted the exhibition as a "great feast" for industry, in 1876 Carvallo stated in the very same SNA's *Bulletin* that:

> If the exposition of 1869, stimulating a considerable importation of these machines, put an end to the nascent national industry, we should blame the public's unjust preference for everything that is foreign, and also the customs legislation, which burdens the importation of raw materials with considerable taxes, while permitting the duty-free entrance of manufactures. The death of this industry, which could provide employment for a good number of hands, has not been caused, then, by the natural decomposition of what does not have vitality in itself. It has been brought violently about by foreign commerce, the innate enemy of all national industry; and it has been helped, which is very regrettable, by our landowners' disdain. But let's go at once to the essence of the issue at hand: Is it fair and rational to support and sustain a nation's industry? Perhaps such is in good terms the issue under consideration. Let us be permitted to condole ourselves that such be the times so that we have to persist in proving what is clearly an axiom of economic sciences. Will we ever understand that foreign commerce has been relentlessly exploiting our ignorance and disdain for factory work, and like a vampire, it ends up leaving us without blood? What a strange thing! The United States practices the most exaggerated protectionism. Chile, instead, has enthroned in its altars the golden calf of free trade in its most implacable form. Can we, then, be surprised that the whip be necessary to keep at bay the deaf discontent of the lower classes?
>
> (Carvallo, 1876, p. 376)

In spite of certain differences, the discourse that the SNA formulated in its *Bulletin* coincided with that of the metal-mechanic industrialists, like Víctor Carvallo. Among other initiatives to promote the mechanization of Chilean agriculture, for almost a decade, from the foundation of the SNA, the analysts who edited its agricultural magazine had systematically publicized and praised foundries' activitity, in order to inform and persuade landowners to acquire tools, implements, and even machines that those industries produced. At the end of the 1870s, however, the SNA was making a more resolved defense of the national foundries through its participation in the debate regarding customs reforms. Thus, facing the measures that the government was adopting to increase fiscal income, such as the surcharge on import duties added in 1877, Julio Menadier published in the *Bulletin*, in April of 1878, an article, merely informative in its appearance, about the Kleins' foundry, in which he actually leveled strong criticism at the authorities. Menadier's stance was based on his view that, among all kind of factories relevant to agriculture, "none excercises greater influence on its development and prosperity than the establishments dedicated to manufacturing machines," as was the case of Chilean foundries. Those industries, Menadier went on, had managed to subsist despite having to face "customs legislations which had adopted all the [means] to disrupt or destroy industrial establishments that were of absolute necessity for the development of the manufacturing, mining and agricultural industries." Particularly, he denounced the fact that the growth of those industries had been severely limited by the lack of state support, and the rising prices of its raw materials, the latter being direct consequence of recent changes in customs tariffs. Hence, in contrast with the "great influence that the Klein factory had long excercised upon the agricultural and industrial development of the Republic," Menadier also denounced that, in the present situation, even this establishment, one of the most important of the metal-mechanic sector, was seeing itself "often obligated to do repairs and maintenance works in order to employ its numerous workers, who would not be easily replaced if they were laid off."[8]

In light of those considerations, once again Julio Menadier would write in the *Bulletin* to voice the SNA's principal economic policy demands. At a time when the economic crisis was in full swing, Menadier did not restrict himself to asking for the implementation of measures that would promote the productive capacity of the foundries, but a complete reformulation of the economic policy. Moreover, he pointed out that this was not a new pursuit of his, but one he had campaigned for long before the present ecomomic downturn. Thus, he concluded the article on the Klein Foundry, by stating that:

> For almost ten years, the *Bulletin, vox clamantis in deserto*, has been asking for a radical reform of our current customs legislation, to dictate it in accordance with relevant information provided by distinguished economists, merchants, and industrialists, so as to elevate to the ranks of true Chilean autonomy tariff regulations that emanated from actually rather international committees, to which it is not possible to reasonably demand the sacrifice of their personal interests for the sake of the common good.[9]

However, Menadier was certain that, amidst the severe economic crisis that Chile was facing, the materialization of such aspiration was quite difficult. Yet, he would insist in the necessity of discussing economic policy beyond the present short-term situation, and the government's pressing need for revenue. Thus, Menadier focused on criticizing the very structure of the tax system as a whole and the rent-seeking rationale behind the economic policy. Thus, he indicated that:

> As long as customs tariffs provide more than half of state revenue, there will always be a tendency to increase customs duties in order to balance the budget, [since] there is no easier way to get out of, at least apparently, distressing situations, than indiscriminately levying more taxes on imports, and halting not only production but national industry as well.[10]

In fact, the customs reforms of July of 1878, which the government had announced in 1877, did not modify the "rent-seeking" orientation of the economic policy. Even so, it introduced certain changes that responded to "protectionist" pressures from different business groups, chiefly the increasingly concerted industrial entrepreneurship.[11] The new law mantained the general tax of 25 percent on imports, but elevated it to 35 percent for more than 150 consumer goods, and established an exemption for the raw materials required to produce those goods in the country. At the same time, with the new law (no. 397, July 18, 1878), the government levied a tax of 15 percent on all types of vehicles, machinery, and engines (Anguita and Quesney, 1902, pp. 443–447). The latter tax was of great relevance for the SNA, which, due to the crisis of the export sector and its impact on public finances, failed to obtain the full exemption regime for agricultural equipment it had demanded since its foundation in 1869. Even worse, although the 1878 reform was promulgated for only 18 months, the authorities extended its validity several times, so it remained in place until 1884. The SNA resumed its lobbying in favor of duty-free importation of agricultural machinery only in the second half of the 1880s, when the economic crisis was way over, and the Chilean state enjoyed an unprecedented prosperity thanks to huge revenue from nitrate exports (Wright, 1982, pp. 16–19). By then, however, the SNA's most qualified analyst and spokesperson, the Listian economist Julio Menadier, had deceased.

Conclusion

Due to its commitment to promoting the modernization of the agricultural sector, the National Agricultural Society, large landowners' main organization, became an influential pressure group in the public sphere and, as such, actively participated in the debate concerning economic policy in Chile. In this realm, one of its main strategies in order to further the mechanization of estate agriculture was to request a full exemption regime for the importation of agricultural machinery, a demand that the SNA posed in the debate regarding the successive customs reforms of the 1860s and 1870s. In ideological terms, this demand reflected the growing influence that economic liberalism had among upper-class politicians, policymakers, and intellectuals interested in economics. However, the SNA's participation in the debate on customs tariffs reform also shows that, contrary to the conventional vision according to which the elites adhered in a dogmatic manner to "free trade," there prevailed a rather pragmatic approach towards economic doctrines and, consequently, with respect to economic policy. The principles of free trade were accepted as a valid paradigm, but at the same time, they were judged in terms of their impact in the economy and, above all, discussed and applied in consideration of concrete business interests. It is not surprising, then, that in this context, the SNA's most important analyst, Julio Menadier, could find a place in the debate, establishing himself as an authoritative "practical," instead of purely theoretical, "economist." Thus, Julio Menadier added complexity to the economic policy debate, owing to his

Listian approach to economics. He argued that customs tariffs should fulfill an "economic" function instead of a merely "rent-seeking" one; and that, therefore, it was necessary to levy taxes on imported consumer goods, particularly luxury products, while at the same time to abolish duties on imports of "productive goods," such as capital goods and raw materials that were not produced in the country. Menadier's pragmatic approach also illustrates that, as was the case of other analysts, Chilean economists tended to situate themselves in a variety of concrete positions between the two "theoretical" poles constituted by protectionism and free trade.

The debate concerning customs tariffs and their impact on the incipient Chilean metal-mechanic industry shows important aspects of the public sphere in which the economic policy was formulated, implemented, and contested. In Chile, in the period between 1860 and 1880, the supposed hegemony of "free trade" in the leading circles and in public opinion was far from absolute, since its validity and pertinency were questioned by a socially heterogeneous "protectionist movement." It included not only artisans displaced by the capitalist modernization, but properly capitalist businessmen, like the industrialists in the metal-mechanic sectors, who were negatively affected by foreign competition. Through the SNA, for their part, a sector of self-described "progressive landowners," that belonged to the core of the agrarian oligarchy, also circumstantially joined this movement. They did so in order to advance their own "agricultural protectionism" program, which, revealing Friedrich List's influence, Julio Menadier gradually formulated as he was becoming a relevant actor in the economic policy debate. Yet, the SNA's economic discourse was not a mere reflection of its analysts' ideological preferences. As in the notable case of Julio Menadier, agrarian ideologues acting as economic thinkers employed liberal, protectionist, or even Listian arguments, when it suited their interests. Thus, as was the case during the crisis of 1874–1878, their adherence to free trade was not an obstacle to adopt, and modify, the protectionist discourse that other social actors employed to challenge the economic policy. In addition, the arguments that Menadier elaborated for the SNA also demonstrate that the protectionist discourse was not homogeneous, and that protectionist challenges to free trade began quite earlier than the crisis of the export sector, which was traditionally regarded as the critical event that would have given momentum to the "protectionist thought" that, in the conventional view, rose in the last third of the nineteenth century (Carmagnani, 1971).

Notes

1 The National Agricultural Society (SNA) was founded in 1869 to promote the development of agriculture, and still today is the principal association of large landowners in Chile (Carriére, 1981; Wright, 1982).
2 *Memoria del Ministro de Hacienda* (1870), p. 25; *Memoria del Ministro de Hacienda* (1871), p. 26.

3 "Informe de la Comisión de Hacienda," Cámara de Diputados, Sesiones Extraordinarias, session 7, October 30, 1876, p. 104.
4 "Reforma de la Ordenanza de Aduanas. Informe presentado por el Directorio de la Sociedad Nacional de Agricultura a la Comisión de Hacienda de la Cámara de Diputados," *BSNA*, VII: 23 (1876), p. 555.
5 "Ley de Aduana de la República Argentina," *BSNA*, VI: 4 (1877), pp. 73–76.
6 "Las grandes fábricas de Santiago. La fundición de don Carlos Klein," *BSNA*, vol. IX, no. 12 (1878), p. 230.
7 *BSNA*, vol. V, no. 17 (1874), p. 376.
8 "La Fundición de Klein Hermanos," *BSNA*, IX: 12 (1878), p. 230–231.
9 "La Fundición de Klein Hermanos," *BSNA*, IX: 12 (1878), p. 231.
10 "La Fundición de Klein Hermanos," *BSNA*, IX: 12 (1878), p. 231.
11 "Solicitud presentada por una Junta de Industriales," Cámara de Diputados. Sesiones Ordinarias, session 5, June 11, 1878, pp. 68–69.

References

Boletín de las Sesiones de la Cámara de Diputados, Sesiones Ordinarias y Extraordinarias, 1876–1878.
Boletín de las Sesiones de la Cámara de Senadores, Sesiones Ordinarias y Extraordinarias, 1876–1878.
Boletín de la Sociedad Nacional de Agricultura, 1869–1880.
Memoria del Ministro de Hacienda, 1870–1871.
Memoria del Superintendente de Aduanas, 1875.
Anguita, R. and Quesney, V. 1902. *Leyes promulgadas en Chile desde 1810 hasta 1901 inclusive*, Santiago de Chile, Imprenta Barcelona.
Bauer, A. 1975. *Chilean Rural Society from the Spanish Conquest to 1930*, Cambridge, Cambridge University Press.
Carmagnani, M. 1971. *Sviluppo Industriale e Sottosviluppo Economico. Il Caso Cileno (1860–1920)*, Torino, Fondazione Luigi Einaudi.
Carrière, J. 1981. *Landowners and Politics in Chile. A Study of the 'Sociedad Nacional de Agricultura,' 1932–1970*, Amsterdam, CEDLA.
Carvallo, V. 1876. Trilladoras chilenas. Contestación al Sr. Enrique Ariztía, *BSNA*, vol. VII, no. 18, 376–377.
Coatsworth, J. and Williamson, J. 2004. Always Protectionist? Latin American Tariffs from Independence to Great Depression, *Journal of Latin American Studies*, vol. 36, no. 2, 205–232.
Couyoumdjian, J. 2015. Importando modernidad: la evolución del pensamiento económico en Chile en el siglo XIX, *Historia*, no. 48, 44–75.
García, R. 1989. *Incipient Industrialization in an "Underdeveloped" Country. The Case of Chile, 1845–1879*, Stockholm, Institute of Latin American Studies.
Hale, C. 1995. Political Ideas and Ideologies in Latin America, 1870–1930, in Bethell, L. (Ed.) *Ideas and Ideologies in Twentieth Century Latin America*, Cambridge, Cambridge University Press.
Jacobsen, N. 2007. Liberalismo tropical: cómo explicar el auge de una doctrina económica europea en América Latina, 1780–1885, *Historia Crítica*, no. 34, 118–147.
Kirsch, H. 1977. *Industrial Development in a Traditional Society. The Conflict of Entrepreneurship and Modernization in Chile*, Gainsville, University Press of Florida.

Levi-Faur, D. 1997. Friedrich List and the Political Economy of the Nation-State, *Review of International Political Economy*, vol. I, no. 4, 154–178.

Mäki, U. 1996. Economic Thought on the Outskirts: Toward a Historiographical Framework for Studying Intellectual Peripheries, *Research in the History of Economic Thought and Methodology*, vol. 14, 307–323.

Mallon, F. 1988. Economic Liberalism: Where We Are and Where We Need to Go, in Love, J. and Jacobsen, N. (Eds.) *Guiding the Invisible Hand: Economic Liberalism and the State in Latin American History*, New York, Praeger, 177–186.

Menadier, J. 1869. Estudios sobre la lejislacion aduanera de Chile, *BSNA*, vol. I, no. 3, 34–43.

——1876. La crisis actual. El modo de combatirla, *BSNA*, vol. VII, no. 20, 404–405.

Ortega, L. 1981. Acerca de los orígenes de la industrialización chilena, 1860–1879, *Nueva Historia*, no. 2, 3–54.

——1985. Economic Policy and Growth in Chile from Independence to the War of the Pacific, in Abel, Ch. and Lewis. C. (Eds.) *Latin America: Economic Imperialism and the State*, London, The Atholone Press, 147–171.

Sporzluk, R. 1988. *Comunism and Nationalism: Friedrich List and Karl Marx*, Oxford, Oxford University Press.

Véliz, C. 1963. La mesa de tres patas, *Desarrollo Económico*, no. 3, 231–248.

Will, R. 1960. La política económica de Chile, 1810–1860, *El Trimestre Económico*, vol. XXVII, no. 2, 238–257.

——1964. The Introduction of Classical Economics into Chile, *HAHR*, vol. 44, no. 1, 1–21.

Wright, T. 1982. *Landowners and Reform in Chile: the Sociedad Nacional de Agricultura, 1919–1940*, Urbana, University of Illinois Press.

8 Jean-Baptiste Say's social economics and the construction of the nineteenth-century liberal republic in Colombia

Jimena Hurtado

Introduction

The history of Colombian thought has received little attention in national and international scholarship. As a peripheral country, Colombia has been considered a net importer of ideas with little to raise scholarly interest. Until the last decades of the twentieth century, historians of economic thought had centered their attention on ideas considered general and universal in their scope and reach, focusing mostly on traditions of thought associated with what could be considered as net exporter of ideas as Great Britain, France, Germany, Italy and the United States. This has started to change since the beginning of the twenty-first century, when Spanish and Portuguese scholars have led the recovery and reconstruction of national traditions in their countries.[1]

This chapter intends to contribute to this growing literature focusing on the adoption of Jean-Baptiste Say as one of the references for economic education during most of the nineteenth century, exploring his influence in Colombia. Beginning almost at the time of Independence in 1810 up to the 1880s Say was considered as the major economic author, and one of the most influential in the formation of the new citizens of the Republic. Those who adopted Say's ideas saw them as the expression of the scientific spirit of modern times, and an important guide in the way to the modernization of the country and its integration in the international division of labor. More than just an economist, Say was part of a group of authors united under the banner of sensationism, representing modern scientific knowledge. The adoption of his ideas in Colombia was part of the strategy of making a new people, away from the Spanish tradition marked by the influence of Scholasticism and the Catholic Church.

But this is not how the story has traditionally been told. Colombian historiography has rather interpreted this process as a failed attempt to lay solid foundations for the new Republic. Not only did Colombian thinkers adopt the wrong economic ideas, so traditional analysis suggests, but they also failed to understand the ideas they adopted, trying to import ill-adjusted theories to the Colombian context (cf. Jaramillo Uribe 1974; Ramírez Gómez 2004).

Such a view supposes, on the one hand, there are correct economic ideas,[2] and on the other, that Colombian thinkers were unable to understand the ideas they imported, and the context they lived in.

This chapter will take another approach; one closer to Cardoso's (2003) argument for the history of national traditions:

> the ease or difficulty with which economic doctrines, theories, and policies are accepted is always constrained by the particularities of the economic reality, social and political institutions, and scientific environment in the receiver country. It is precisely the way in which a country uses and adapts the influences received that makes the study of the history of economic thought worthwhile from a national point of view.
>
> (Cardoso 2003: 625, cf. Cardoso 2009: 254)

The aim of this chapter then is not to reconstruct or discuss a certain aspect, concept or idea of Say's thought. Rather, I intend to present how his ideas were adapted to the Colombian context, and used to legitimate and advance a certain liberal social project compatible with the religious tradition of the nascent Republic. This will allow discussing the beginnings of Colombian economic thought not as a minor isolated phenomenon in a peripheral country, but as a part of the construction of a new Republic.

Actually, those Colombian thinkers who imported ideas were not mere scholars. They were active in the Republic's political destiny, occupied high places in government when in power, and represented a strong opposition, even military at times, when out of power. Those who imported the ideas of this sensationist school, upheld a liberal project that went beyond eliminating colonial protectionism, defending free markets, industrialization, social mobility and entrepreneurship. Their project implied building a new nation based on what they considered a rational and illustrated citizenry.

They did not intend, however, to build from scratch and eradicate all tradition. They adapted those ideas, and did their best to make them compatible with Christian values. Their intention was to zap the authority of the Catholic Church, and all possible remains of Spanish nostalgia. In what became a battle for the minds, Liberals aimed at forming an individual capable of relying on reason rather than faith, familiar with the scientific method based on observation and experience, and able to participate in the growing market economy. They believed all these were characteristics of citizens prepared and educated for freedom. Within this context, Say's economic ideas were part of a much larger project, which seems to have been overlooked not only because its advocates utterly lost power and influence in the mid-1880s but also because the nineteenth century was far from peaceful and the constant war effort, added to the inherited debts from the Independence, made the fiscal situation rather precarious. Political instability and almost permanent bankruptcy made the construction of a new institutional framework an almost impossible task.

Moreover, the beginnings of the history of economic ideas in Colombia might have been obscured because of the authors the first citizens read. Colombian historiography rarely considers Jeremy Bentham and Antoine-Louis-Claude Destutt de Tracy as economists, or Jean-Baptiste Say as a major economic reference, as he has generally been presented as nothing more than a disciple of Adam Smith. These three authors became the backbone of economic education for all those in higher education, who more likely than not would occupy influential positions in society. The alleged absence of David Ricardo's books in public education or the minor discussion around John Stuart Mill's *Principles* have been presented as proof of the lack of interest, knowledge and understanding of the first generations of Colombians of economic theory (cf. Jaramillo Uribe 1974).

However, this lack of interest, especially in Ricardo, might have an alternative explanation. The three major authors that were incorporated in public education, discussed and debated over in the main national newspapers, and whose works played a major role in the building of the new Republic were Bentham, Destutt de Tracy and Say.[3] The three of them were presented as representatives of liberal ideas built on, what was believed to be, the illustrated and modernizing approach of utilitarianism, or sensationism.[4]

Liberal Colombian thinkers, who came to power during the period known as the *Olimpo Radical* (1863–1886), were convinced that breaking with the Colonial past begun with renewing ideas regarding, not only public policy, but especially those about the human condition. This meant eliminating Scholasticism from public education, and weakening the Catholic Church's influence on the formation of young minds. The Liberal project was associated with a modern citizenship, which was believed to be accomplished with a modern education based on utilitarianism and positivism. But this did not necessarily mean breaking with traditional values, and Liberal thinkers strived hard at rendering Catholic values compatible with their modernizing project. This led to an interpretation and adaptation of utilitarian ideas, and particularly of the ideas of Bentham, Tracy and Say that eliminated most of their discrepancies and contradictions,[5] and presented them as representatives of one and the same view on the possibility of a prosperous social organization made of free and pious individuals.

It was not a particular economic theory they were embracing, it was a whole conception on human behavior and social organization. Ricardo appeared insufficient for this purpose. Instead Bentham, Tracy and Say were presented as having built a whole social theory, far more reaching and promising than Ricardo's defense of free markets based on the economic laws of distribution, and with no apparent relation with a clear idea of human nature.[6] These three authors offered what the Colombian liberals understood as a complete plan for reformation based on a profound understanding of human nature, and its potentialities. For a Revolution made in the name of freedom this seemed a much more appealing approach.

In this chapter I will concentrate on their reading of Say within this context. In particular I will focus on how Ezequiel Rojas (1803–1873) incorporated Say's teachings into his own thought. Rojas is a particularly interesting figure because he was considered as the main professor of the *Radical* generation, he was a prominent political figure, and he was considered as the representative of utilitarianism in the Nueva Granada being the most important advocate and defender of making compulsory Bentham's, Tracy's and Say's reference texts for higher public education.

In order to do this, the text is divided into four sections besides this introduction. The first section sets the reception of Say's ideas in the context of an ambitious national education project. Becoming an independent republic implied training its citizens with the appropriate tools and skills for the modern world. The debate around this project focused on the right balance between new modernity and tradition, which would assure national prosperity. The second part deals with the features the Radicals, and, in particular, Ezequiel Rojas found particularly attractive in Say's thought. Economics as the foundation of a moral education, based on a scientific approach appeared as one of the main elements in their attempt to achieve modern citizenship. Say's own educational project, in line with the pedagogical aims of *idéologie*, preparing individuals to participate in the free market, understanding their own enlightened interest, and its direct relation with the common good, appeared particularly close to the Radicals' own social project. However, as shown in the third section, a balance with tradition had to be kept, and an explicit attempt to makes Say's ideas, in particular, and sensationism, in general, compatible with Christianity also occupied an important part in the overall educational project. The last section draws some conclusions.

Higher education in the second half of the nineteenth century

The organization of higher education was a priority during the period. After having set the institutional framework for primary and secondary education, and having created the first normal schools in 1822, even with very scarce resources, legislators produced an extremely detailed regulatory frame for higher education.

On March 18, 1826, under the administration of Vice-president Francisco de Paula Santander, a General Law of Education was issued. The Law organized the education system of the new Republic to its minor details. It created the public universities of Quito, Bogotá and Caracas, with faculties of philosophy, jurisprudence, medicine, theology and natural sciences (Jaramillo Uribe 1982: 299). In 33 chapters and more than 300 articles, the law left little leeway. However, it did not represent a complete break with the past. It followed in the steps of a prior reform proposed by Francisco Antonio Moreno y Escandón in 1774. In the spirit of the Bourbon reforms, Moreno y Escandón's Plan of Studies proposed the creation of a public university[7] and delineated the program of general studies around the teaching of physics, mathematics and trigonometry. The Plan, intended as a modernization scheme for education, never received the approval of the Crown even though the Viceroy Guirrior had commended it in 1776. It was completely abandoned in 1779, and although it resurfaced several times before the Independence, and some professors put in practice its recommendations, its intended break with Scholasticism was not accomplished.

The major difference between Moreno y Escandón's 1774 plan, and the 1826 law was that the latter introduced the teaching of political economy,[8] and changed the texts and references used for teaching law and philosophy. The law determined that political economy would be taught using Jean-Baptiste Say's *Treatise*, and that other authors, including Montesquieu and Mably, would be used in the other courses (Jaramillo Uribe 1982: 300).

In particular, searching to introduce experimental methods associated with the latest trends in scientific enquiry, liberal legislators considered the sensationist tradition as the source of progress and civilization. With this tradition they included utilitarianism, and particularly Jeremy Bentham's works.[9] Alongside Bentham, for the course in philosophy and natural sciences, the Law decreed the teaching of Ideology or metaphysics using Antoine-Louis Claude Destutt de Tracy's *Ideology*, accompanied, if needed, by Condillac in courses of logics, and the origin of human knowledge and sensations. Tracy and Condillac were viewed as the direct heirs to Locke, whom the conservatives considered as the founder of materialism, of which sensationism was a strict equivalent, the most complete and absolute opposite of Catholic values.[10]

Strong opposition coming from the Conservatives and the Catholic Church met these reforms because of their alleged pernicious effects on the morality of the youth. The debate on the texts, and, in particular, on the syllabus of the economics' courses, became a debate on moral education. Sensationism and its direct consequence, materialism, were accused of promoting greed and self-interest, leading the young generations to lives of material pleasures, abandoning charity, simple manners and austerity, which were considered as the core values of the Catholic faith. Such lessons would lead to selfish, self-indulgent and libertine citizens, certainly resulting in the ruin of the new republic.

Against these claims, the Radicals, led by their Professor Ezequiel Rojas, argued in favor of sensationism as the theory that correctly explained how individuals acquire knowledge, and thus become enlightened. This approach, when correctly understood, in no way contradicted the precepts of the Catholic faith. So it seemed essential to begin guaranteeing such correct understanding.

Rojas (1881–1882, 230–231) defended sensationism, and distinguished between sensationist philosophy and sensationist morality. The first corresponded to a "doctrine that recognizes that the *faculty of feeling with which the soul is endowed, constitutes the faculty of knowing*, and that without this faculty man would know nothing" (Rojas 1881–1882: 230, italics in the original, my translation). The second was a

> doctrine that recognizes that *happiness and disgrace consist in the way the soul feels*: that pains make men miserable, and the satisfaction of his needs, through good means, makes his happiness, and that if men did not feel, they would not be miserable or happy.
>
> (Rojas 1881–1882: 230, italics in the original, my translation)[11]

There was no contradiction with the lessons of religion because

> Jesus Christ's morals aim at directing men so that those who practice it faithfully will find the salvation of their souls: when souls are saved they avoid eternal pains, and relish in eternal joys: thus the aim of Jesus Christ's morals is to avoid pains and provide joys to men: HENCE THIS MORALITY IS SENSATIONIST.
>
> (Rojas 1881–1882: 230)

It is clear then that Rojas not only saw no contradiction between sensationism and Christianity but he actually considered them equivalents. The sensationist texts, therefore, could not be considered detrimental to public morality or public prosperity. On the contrary, they would allow these citizens-to-be to understand the true lessons of religion beyond mere faith and dogma. Enlightened citizens would understand their true interest not only as directly related to those of their fellows and of the nation as a whole, but also as a part of the Divine plan for humanity.[12]

Hence, education was a priority for the Radical generation. In spite of the difficult situation of public finance, when in government, they issued several laws and decrees on public instruction. They were convinced that free public education for children was the first, and most important service government should provide (Camacho Roldán 1868). Education was the way to civilization and progress; it differentiated human beings from other animals, and gave sense to rights (Camacho Roldán 1868). It should be considered the supreme interest of modern peoples, and the guarantee of morality, security, wealth, fraternity and even religion (Camacho Roldán 1868).

When the generation of the Radicals came to power they established a new Constitution[13] for the Republic built upon a federal system and the protection of individual freedom. Their political project relied heavily on an education reform because they were convinced that democracy required educated citizens, who had the right to receive free education, which the government had the duty to provide. In Article 15 of the Second part on the "Guarantee of individual rights" the 1863 Constitution consecrates the freedom of "giving and receiving the instruction they wish, in establishments not financed with public funds" (Constitución 1871: 9). Article 18 decrees that promoting public instruction is a function the central government will share with the states (Constitución 1871: 11). Even if in the Constitution they had included academic freedom, legislation on public instruction was very strict. Through the Law of 1868 and the Organic Decree of 1870 they regulated the content, texts, teaching methods and evaluations for all levels of education.

These were political weapons Radicals used against the influence of the Catholic Church. Article 36 of the Organic Decree states that Government will not take part in religious instruction but schools would ensure children had the time to pursue the religious instruction their parents saw fit. Even if this was what the law said, their intentions were clear. As Camacho Roldán (1868) put it, public education "is religion, because if God reveals himself through his works, it is the eyes of the soul rather than those of the body that show him to us in all the prodigies that science teaches men."

Compulsory public primary education and religious neutrality were the main pillars in what these men conceived as the liberation of the Colombian spirit from the retarding effect of religion. Opposition to such reforms did not wait. The Constitution and, especially, the 1870 Organic Decree of Primary Education was presented as contrary to freedom of instruction and to the Catholic beliefs of the majority. Before this Decree, the Santos Gutiérrez Administration had issued a law in 1868 on public instruction where higher education was also regulated.

The same year, the public university *Universidad Nacional* was finally founded. The purpose and plan of studies of the University was clearly set from the beginning. In the words of one of the protagonists:

> If we have founded a university, if we have a university, it is to teach liberal doctrines, to form liberals. Not eclecticism. Balmes and Bentham cannot shake hands within the university. As long as the Liberal Party remains in power, it must teach liberalism. Political honesty demands it. If, in good faith, we believe that liberalism is what the country needs, liberalism is what we must teach our youth. When the Catholic Party comes to power it will command, following Philip II, the teaching of Catholicism, and it will have the right to do so.
>
> (Galindo quoted in Jaramillo Uribe 1982: 317, my translation)

Public debate then was not limited to the compulsory character of primary education or religious neutrality; it extended to the Government's prerogative of determining the texts to be used in each course. As had happened with the *Benthamite Dispute*, from 1870 to 1880 a new confrontation raised dealing, particularly, with the use of Destutt de Tracy's *Idéologie* in philosophy courses. The clash was known as the *Question on Texts* (*Cuestión de textos*) and was synthesized in three reports written by top intellectual liberal and conservative figures of the time: Manuel Ancízar, Francisco E. Álvarez and Miguel Antonio Caro (Universidad Nacional 1870). Ancízar's and Caro's reports were unfavorable to Tracy's text qualifying it as unscientific for Ancízar, and contrary to the truth as revealed in the Gospel for Caro. Civil war brought an end to the debate that finally revolved around individual rights, and the right of families to choose the education they considered fit for their children.

However, Say's *Treatise* was never the object of much debate or public confrontation. His ideas did not seem to contradict Catholic values, and most everyone was in favor of free markets. But there was something more to Say's thought that could have appeared especially attractive. May a quote from Forget (1999: 178) illustrate the point:

> Although he argued ... that economic liberalism was desirable, Say maintained, ..., the notion that *laissez-faire* is only appropriate within the context of a well-defined institutional structure imposed from without. Moreover, individuals must be made aware of their own "true" interests if the benefits of the market and industrialism are to be realised. ... Say argued that the administration must take an active role in both moral and intellectual education and in designing and imposing institutions consistent with the welfare of the people. Say's economic liberalism, that is, required the firm intervention of an enlightened élite, not in the markets themselves but in society within which the markets unfold.

Therefore, Say gave the new rulers the approach they needed to build a liberal republic. Just as Bentham in matters of legislation, Say gave them the necessary tools to justify an active rule of the legislator in establishing, and guaranteeing a new liberal social order. Reflecting the ideas of *idéologie*, Say believed "that social order is the consequence of good legislation and, even more importantly, good education designed to subordinate individual self-seeking behaviour to the social good by teaching people their true interests, which are in more cases than not harmonious" (Forget 1999: 107). Following this argument, in the next section we will see how Rojas understood and adapted Say's ideas for the official syllabus of the courses of political economy in Colombian universities.

Social economics and the moral education of the people

Science was considered as the maximum expression of modernization and progress, and was associated with discovery and systematization through observation and experience. The scientific method was only one, and led to the truth of all things, human and natural, physical and metaphysical. Through observation and experience, facts and laws could be deduced from casual relations, unraveling the "nature and consequences of human actions and institutions on happiness" (Dávila Dávila 2007: 78, my translation). Human beings were deemed capable of discovering these laws, and finding explanations without having recourse to divine revelation, but making use of God's greatest gifts: reason and sensibility. Facts were beyond religious discussions, dogmas or interpretations. The truth was to be found in Nature, and could only be one; individuals, making use of their divine gifts, would come to understand God's work (Rojas 1881–1882).

The proper use of reason and sensibility required a certain education. Rojas was convinced that what he called a liberal education would teach individuals how to observe and interpret facts. Reason would order and organize observed sensations and the impressions humans perceive through their senses. So, reason rather than revelation, would allow all and any individual to discover the truth:

> Truth can only be discovered, known and taught through a true logic: sensationist logic is this true logic; thus sensationist logic is the one that leads to discovery, knowledge, and teaches the truth. ... Hence it is the sensationist logic the one that those who need to know and teach the truth need, and are complied to teach, as well as those who govern and direct human conduct.
>
> (Rojas 1882: 231, my translation)

It was the same logic Rojas used in his own teachings. He was in charge of the political economy courses for a long time. His syllabus was adopted as the official one in 1844, and followed closely the structure of Say's *Treatise* (1816). The syllabus begun, as Say's and Tracy's work also do, with an explanation of the scope and method of political economy. In 1866 there was another official publication of Rojas' syllabus entitled *Syllabus for the Teaching of Social Economics, formed by the Professor Doctor Ezequiel Rojas*. There were little differences between the two, except for the name of the course (cf. Hurtado 2016). It changed from political economy to social economy, in line with Say's discussion about dropping the adjective of the name of the discipline, as it had nothing political to it; its subject matter was not the balance of power but the way in which nations provide for their own subsistence, making not a science for men of State but for all members of society (Say 1821[1966]: 309). This change of names must have been very appealing to Colombian liberals, as it allowed them to dissociate at least this part of their project from any political discussion, making it a matter for everyone, and underlining the need for educated citizens to advance national prosperity. Social economy then dealt with the proper functioning of society as a living body that needed the prosperity and happiness of each of its members to subsist.

Moreover, economic phenomena were seen as the result of the aggregate transactions and decisions of individuals searching for prosperity; thus, the economy corresponded to the unintended consequences of human actions tending to maximize individual utility within a particular institutional framework. Such individual actions were spontaneous and, in general, were of no concern to the government because each agent was the best judge of her own interest, and of the best way to advance it (Hurtado 2016). Therefore, regardless of the existing government, individuals would try to increase their material well-being; meaning that the economy was not the business of politicians, even if economic education was a government matter.

In the *Preliminary Discourse* to his *Treatise*, Say points at the confusion between the science of government and political economy, which he strives to straighten out. Wealth is independent from the existing type of government as long as it is well administered (Say 1816: LXVII). This means, very much as the Radicals believed, that political freedom is only indirectly favorable to the growth of wealth, depending on instruction (Say 1816: LXVII). Therefore, learning that commerce and the arts are the true sources of wealth was much more important than any law that could only touch them accidentally and indirectly (Say 1816: LXIX). This was why all citizens must receive instruction in political economy (Say 1816: LXX).

In the line of *Idéologues*, Say's main concern has to do with the education of citizens in order to stabilize the institutions of the Republic. The *Treatise* is the handbook for the moral instruction needed to achieve this goal (Tiran 1995). Most of his writings are aimed at illustrating citizens so that they will come to understand their place within the functioning of the social organization, so that all sinister interests can be transformed and controlled into enlightened interests.

> What he seeks is a greater lucidity in his fellow citizens .... Interest, feeling and reason are enough to make us comply with our duties. This religion of duty is related to the modern confidence in education and its effect on the perfectibility of humankind.
>
> (Tiran 1995: 115)

Such instruction, as Say stated in *Olbie*, is the foundation of moral education; that which will assure individuals as much happiness as their nature might allow them (Say 1800: 2). This could be accomplished because Say believed that it was the enlightenment about their own interests that made instruction to favor morals (Say 1800: 5), and thus happiness. Say believed individuals are moved by their vanity, making the interactions between them crucial to satisfy such vanity (Tiran 1995: 105). Thus, others' opinion is crucial, and their esteem is a major influence on human behavior, and the source of sociability, which opens the way to introduce "moral obligation as mutually beneficial" (Tiran 1995: 107) precisely because acting morally, respecting and caring for others, improves the individuals image among her fellow citizens hence flattering her vanity.

As subsistence is a major element of such happiness, and subsistence depends upon the correct administration of wealth, economics should be part of any citizen's education. Say clearly stated that "Good education, instruction, of which comfort will be the source and good morals the consequence, will never germinate except with the comfort of the people" (Say 1800: 11; translation Forget 1999: 200).

Economic education should be based on the *"legitimate consequences that arise from the perfect observation of facts"* (Say 1816: LXXI, italics in the original, my translation). The observation of facts required knowing that they are divided in two groups: those the laws of Nature produce in similar cases, which are general and constant; and those also due to the laws of Nature but that depend on causes that change according to circumstances, making them variable and particular (Say 1816: LXXI). Political economy was concerned only with the former, describing general facts regarding

> the way in which wealth is formed, how it is distributed and consumed; what are the causes of its increase or decrease, and what its necessary relations with population, with the power of the states, and with the fate of the people.
>
> (Say 1816: LXXII, my translation)

Dealing with general facts, political economy was made of "a small number of fundamental principles, and a multitude of corollaries and consequences of these principles" (Say 1816: LXXXV). As with other exact sciences, the principles were derived from observation, making any proof useless because they were known to all (Say 1816: LXXXV). The scientific method implied then that these observations were ordered and systematized so that the relations between them were easily perceived (Say 1816: LXXXV). These relations could not be expressed in mathematical terms even if, in general, they dealt with orders of magnitude, because such orders were subordinated "to the action of the faculties, needs and the will of men ... for the causes that determine those values are partly moral, and are not subject to any kind of calculation" (Say 1816: LXXXVI, my translation).

Rojas took this kind of statement to heart. He saw no separation between the administration of wealth and that of human beings. Only a true understanding of human nature could guarantee a prosperous nation, because as wealth was the result of the action of certain natural laws, the same happened with human behavior.

This knowledge could only be attained through the scientific method:

> the new method of studying and dealing with sciences, not as is usually done, that is, not by examining its principles in a vague and abstract way, but going up from the best and most constant observed facts to their causes, which can only be discovered through rigorous reasoning.
>
> (Say 1816: CVI, my translation)

Say called it the spirit of analysis.

Say's preliminary discourse in the *Treatise* actually deals with little more than method. Forget (1999: 122–129) shows Say's method corresponds with that of the *idéologues*. Indeed, Say, as part of this tradition, claims to follow closely their method, which Forget (1999: 122–123) identifies with six common features:

> First, Bacon and Newton, and very often Locke, are icons displayed for admiration. Second, they always attack "system" … Third, these methodological introductions advocate the careful observation of the "nature of things" and trust in the evidence of our senses, so that first principles may be derived inductively. Fourth, argument is said to proceed from "particular" to "general" truths. Fifth, the author invariably makes clear a desire to use simple and unadorned language, free of the excesses of rhetoric and obfuscation. Sixth, the author spends a good deal of effort on matters of organisation and presentation of the "truths" in the work, so that pedagogy … is enhanced.

We have already seen several of these features in Say and in Rojas: likening morals and economics with natural sciences; the attack on systems or dogma with no scientific foundation; the distinction between general and particular facts; the relation between particular facts and general principles; and, finally their concern with language and order of presentation for pedagogical reasons (cf. Forget 1999: 123–127).

This is precisely the method Rojas applies explicitly in his *Moral Philosophy* (Rojas 1881–1882). This text was published in Bogotá in 1868 and in Paris in 1870, as a compilation of several of his articles published in the *Revista Colombia* as a reply to Ricardo de la Parra who had dared him to compose a single piece exposing the compatibility between Christian values and Utilitarianism by answering to the question about the foundations of universal morality. Rojas sent his response to several European academies, including the *Institut de sciences morales et politiques*.

In it he argued he had followed a strict scientific analysis proving beyond any doubt the truth of his conclusions. He stated that observation establishes that the purpose of life is to be happy and avoid pain, hence when answering what happiness and disgrace consist in, it is possible to know what good and evil are (Rojas 1881–18822: 45, 67):

> Adjectives represent qualities, or circumstances, or ways of being. These two, *happy* and *miserable*, represent the *condition, circumstance or way of being* in which men live: they represent then real facts existing in man: these facts considered from an abstract point of view are called *good or evil*, and when they are considered as residing in men, they are called *happiness and disgrace*.

(Rojas 1881-1882: 82, original italics)

Observing human conduct it was possible to establish that humans seek happiness and avoid disgrace, pain makes them miserable and joy makes them happy, meaning that happiness and pains, and therefore good and evil, consist in "the way the soul feels" (Rojas 1882: 46). Observation and reason then were the key to the exercise of the spirit of analysis. In Rojas' words: "To my understanding, sciences are the exposition of the facts as they exist or as they happen, in other words, sciences are the description of the beings and the exposition of the laws of nature" (Rojas 1882: 62, 80).

Social economics and Christianity

For those who would come to power under the Radical banner, Say clearly belonged to Bentham's school. He, as well as Destutt de Tracy, was perceived as a Benthamite Utilitarian, or rather they were all seen as part of the sensationist school, and representatives of the analytical method. Not much difference was made between Utilitarianism and *Idéologie* (cf. Hurtado 2015), as they were seen as sharing not only their sensationist foundations but also the importance given to active legislation in the social order, and to public education.

Following Schoorl (2002), Say meets Bonner's seven criteria for economic utilitarianism:

> 1. A single overriding objective [utility]; 2. Consequentialism [the maximization of utility is the criteria for good and bad]; 3. Welfarism [all social and individual actions should aim at maximizing utility]; 4. Individualism [the explanation of social phenomena derives from the understanding of individual actions]; 5. Equality [no person's utility is worth more than anyone else's]; 6. Aggregation [the highest sum of personal utilities is the most desirable state of affairs of society]; 7. Measurement [dislike of mathematical reasoning. But he advocates the measurement or at least comparison of utilities].
>
> (Schoorl 2002: 34, 46–47)

As Forget (1999) has shown, *Idéologie* marked Say's economics but it is "not all clear ... that *idéologie* is necessary to our understanding of Say's economics" (Forget 1999: 178–179). In particular, his theory of value and distribution or the law of the markets "stand alone in the sense that we can understand them quite adequately without the baggage of *idéologie*" (Forget 1999: 179). What is clear, and so appeared to the Radicals, is Say's opposition to Ricardo, and it was these ideas they were importing as representatives of modernization and progress, and those that generated so much controversy during the first century of Republican life.

However, as already noted, Say's texts were never the object of such high-toned public debates as were Bentham's, and much less those of Destutt de Tracy. Whereas Bentham and Destutt de Tracy were accused of materialism and anti-Catholic ideas, contrary to Colombian culture and values, Say was mostly spared of these accusations because his ideas were seen as favorable to free market with little consequence for public morals. His relation with

Bentham or with the *Idéologues* (cf. Schoorl 1982, 2002; Tiran 1995; Forget 1999) was rarely held against him, as if his economic ideas could be completely separated from his intellectual background and associations.

Opening the market and participating in the international division of labor were projects supported, to different degrees, by liberals as well as conservatives. Economic freedom then was not questioned; public debate focused on how individual freedom should be understood, and which were the general rules of conduct the new citizens should embrace. All sides were defending public morals from different perspectives. A modern Republic made of free, responsible and illustrated citizens required a strong public education, which explains that this topic occupied much of public debate during the nineteenth century.

This general context also allows seeing how some separated Say's economic ideas from a more general context of philosophical economics Conservatives considered that promoting economic freedom, understood as free markets, was not related to a specific economic anthropology or conception of human behavior. Human beings need not be guided by pleasure and pain, or by utility calculations, to appreciate the benefits of economic freedom. Free markets could be seen as promoting interdependence, cooperation, and improving living conditions for those who most needed it, all valuable aims from a Catholic perspective. Say's law of the markets could even be interpreted as a divine algorithm, so to speak, promoting the importance of giving in order to receive. But its main point is showing the impossibility of long term disequilibrium and the equilibrating role of market forces.

Few seem to have noticed Say's harsh attack on religion, in general, and on Catholicism, in particular, in *Olbie*. In Note (C), he strives at proving "that they [religions] rarely make human morals better" (Say 1800: 83; translation Forget 1999: 221). Say is convinced that "The times of the greatest devotion have always been the times of the greatest ferocity, of the most profound barbarism" (Say 1800: 83; translation Forget 1999: 22). Even worse, Say continues, "religions do not eliminate those vices and crimes to which they appear most opposed" (Say 1800: 84; translation Forget 1999: 221).

Christianity is not free of blame. Say remarks the dire contradiction between Christian principles of humility and forgiveness, and

> The time when that religion burned with the greatest brightness ... was a more fertile period for crimes than any other, and the discovery of a new world served only to extend further human horrors and the barbarism of the disciples of sweet Jesus.
>
> (Say 1800: 84; translation Forget 1999: 221)

In fact, Say asserts that it is rather the lack of reason and institutions "undoubtedly the principal cause of that great deterioration of morals; the evidence shows rather that religion did nothing to hinder it" (Say 1800: 85; translation Forget 1999: 222). This last argument sounds closer to what Rojas argued. Through sensationism, true Christianity, free from the manipulation of the Catholic Church, would recover its true principles, and the hearts of the people. Cultivating reason, just as Say advanced, was the best remedy against fanaticism, which hindered any chance of civilized dialogue.

Moreover, Radicals would also echo Say's condemnation of the impact of religious practices on the economy (Say 1800: 89). Not only can such practices be contrary to civic duties, they also occupy large portions of people's time in unproductive tasks; not to mention the national wealth used in supporting religious orders. So the Radicals shared Say's criticisms to institutionalized religion that only led to weaken moral principles because people identified morality with dogma, an incomprehensible and unreachable doctrine that alienated them from what Rojas, for example, considered as the true lessons of Christianity. His pedagogical project strived precisely at redressing this situation, and Say provided more than just economic concepts and tools to do it.

Say's oeuvre beyond his economic texts seemed fit for this larger aim of building an economic doctrine from a certain conception of human behavior, thus closer to a general science of society, blurring the frontiers of economic science no longer limited to the study of the production, consumption and distribution of wealth. Following in Say's steps, Rojas was convinced that only the knowledge of this science, as the science of freedom, could guarantee national prosperity. So he shared with Say the major role given to education, and the possibility of influencing individual calculations of pleasure and pain through the law (Schoorl 2002: 35); social economics "teaches how to distinguish good from bad means, and lends its power to legislators as well as moralists, so that they will put in practice the former and ban the latter" (Rojas 1881–1882: 201). Social economics corresponds to the

> knowledge of all those needs; of the good means to obtain the proper objects to satisfy them; of the mediate and immediate causes that produce those means and those needs, or what is the same, the knowledge of the essential and accidental organs that compose the social body, of the functions each one performs
>
> (Rojas 1881–1882: 202)

Instruction in social economics would make individuals see the direct connection between happiness and material well-being, putting economics as a fundamental part of moral philosophy (Rojas 1862: 46). Just as Say states in *Olbie*, Rojas believed that social economics was the most important science "if morality and the happiness of human beings deserve to be regarded as the most worthy object of research" (Say 1800: 10; translation Forget 1999: 200). This is why in *Olbie* "the first book of morality was ... a good treatise of political economy" (Say 1800: 25; translation Forget 1999: 204). And this was how God intended it to be. The divine laws of nature were the expression of God's will, and in searching happiness and avoiding pain, or what is the same, in striving for material well-being, humans follow the divine tendency God had instilled them with (Rojas 1862: 46–47). Indeed, according to Rojas, God made human beings sensible creatures so they would be able to discover the truth about their nature, and hence about the world they lived in.

The fulfillment of this same tendency explained the production of wealth. Humans produced useful things, valuable things, in order to satisfy their needs; as each individual has her own needs, each one tries to have the goods she needs, and, Rojas (1862: 49) continued, this explains the existence of private property, in line with the seventh commandment[14] (i.e., "Thou shalt not steal").

According to Rojas, humans were a compound of body and mind, whose organization and the use of their faculties, beginning with sensibility, explained their needs, passions, tendencies and desires (Rojas 1862: 79). Fulfilling their desires was the same as following their nature, and hence complying with the good (Rojas 1862: 86). Physical and moral suffering was evil, as enjoying good health and "possessing in a secure manner the means needed to satisfy all the needs of body and soul" was good (Rojas 1862: 86). Therefore desirable, useful things, for short wealth, were one of the causes of happiness, and, in this sense could be considered good.

Once again the importance of economic education is apparent because learning to administrate wealth correctly would multiply sources of comfort and reduce necessities. In the absence of such education, human beings would indulge in vice for

> Man aspires without cessation after happiness, and principally after the closest and most obvious happiness: if there is no path before him to attain happiness except that of crime he will pursue it. If the path of virtue can lead him to wellbeing, he prefers it.
>
> (Say 1800: 16; translation Forget 1999: 202)

Misery, asserted Say, exposes individuals to continuous temptations and imperious needs (Say 1800: 23–24) making a very unequal distribution of wealth undesirable, and leveling it a prerequisite to promote the morality of the people.

In his syllabus Rojas, as Say in the first two chapters of the *Treatise*, dealt with wants, utility and value, and stated that utility was the foundation of value; just as he would in his *Moral Philosophy*, where he advanced: "When this fact was recognized: that utility is what constitutes wealth, many systems invented to explain economic phenomena plummeted" (Rojas 1881–1882: 88). With this statement, Rojas was clearly ascribing to the theory according to which value is a function of usage, and utility is equivalent to price. Using Schoorl's (2002: 34) classification, Rojas, as Say, is a subjectivist economist with regard to value theory.

Tiran (1995) classifies Say as a transition author, which is particularly visible, in his theory of value. This is an interesting point for our story. Value theory was a point of debate between Ricardo and Say. They exchanged several letters on the matter, and even if Ricardo stated Say's theory was mistaken, the latter seems to think their differences are less stark. In December 1814 and August 1815 Say and Ricardo correspond on the subject, and it is clear Ricardo believes Say's mistake lies in making utility the measure of value when it is the difficulty of production which constitutes the true measure of value. Say answers by saying he could not enter into much detail on value in a book intended for the great public, which might explain an apparent disagreement with Ricardo's theory. However, he continues stating that even if utility is not the first cause of value it is its main cause. If commodities were not useful they would not be demanded even if he concedes that the price paid must be enough to cover the commodity's production costs. From this exchange it seems Say does not see such a distance between the two theories. Following Béraud and Faccarello (2014), value theory was still being discussed and its terms were not yet fixed, making the dialogue between Ricardo and Say difficult and hesitant.

This situation started changing in the following years as French liberals in general, and Say in particular, stated more clearly that the cost of production acted only as a floor for the price of a commodity but that it was its utility that determined its value. Such a theory was also more in line with a vision of social organization, and economic phenomena as the product of human interactions and individual behavior rather than the abstract forces of the market. In this sense, and contrary to Cousin's criticisms of Chevalier's definition of economics in 1853, political or social economics dealt with every aspect of human life precisely because it dealt with the production of wealth or the production of useful things through productive labor, which, as Say had shown, could be physical, intellectual, entrepreneurial or artistic. This definition meant, political economy dealt with every aspect of human life as it had to do with the production of wealth, necessary for the well-being and happiness of individuals.

The questions in Rojas' syllabus showed a direct relation between wealth and desires, leaving aside considerations of the productive capacity of capital goods or labor. However, further on, the questions dealt with productive and unproductive labor, and he gave a large space to a topic Say had introduced in his *Treatise*, material and immaterial production. He gave special attention to the importance of services in the creation of national wealth, in particular, to entrepreneurship. Within this analysis, the organization and direction of production, as well as intellectual labor, appeared as major sources of the innovation and the design needed to advance industry. Rojas included several questions on the relation between the sciences and industry. As Say, Rojas considered the importance of intellectual property for the promotion of industry. He extended these questions to include how private property should always be preserved, and the inconveniencies associated with threats to or expropriation of private property.

All these points build upon the central concern for both, Say and Rojas, of understanding the nature of wealth. Social economics, as the science that deals with the laws and principles that govern wealth, and therefore, individual action related to wealth, presents the natural laws explaining its sources. Commerce, one of those sources, appears in his syllabus as a major mechanism to coordinate individual actions. This is a topical subject in the 1840s in Colombia. More specifically, participating in the world market is a priority for liberal governments, and so Rojas dedicates several points of his syllabus to discussing how international commerce, in particular, and commerce, in general, increases wealth.

As Say, Rojas defended a simple and dependable economic legislation, with ample room for an active role of government. Neither government nor legislation could create wealth but they could promote the mechanisms that produced it. In particular, government could foster industry, so it was important to correct the erroneous perception governors might have of being able to guide industry. The most they could do was to create proper conditions for private initiative, and educate children in practical and applied sciences, so they would become productive members of society, as well as informed citizens capable of checking public economic policies. Education appeared, once again, as the major concern for this professor, politician, congressman, ambassador and promoter of sensationism in Colombia.

Concluding remarks

Rojas met Say in Paris in 1829 after having been banned from Colombia for his alleged participation in the assassination attempt against Bolívar in 1828. In his biography, he remembers this encounter vividly and reproduces Say's farewell:

> Given that you are so enthusiastic about freedom and that you have been condemned for this cause, I recommend that when you go back to your country you dedicate yourself to the propagation of the science of Political Economy. When the people are illustrated in the knowledge of their true interests, their liberty cannot perish, nor can tyrannical governments or those that through privileges transform society in their own patrimony or that of some other class last long time. Among sciences it is this one, which most usefully instructs them and which undermines through its foundations bad institutions and bad governments. ... The advice is interesting; hopefully many will follow it: for my part I have followed it every time I have been able to, the generation educated from 1833 onwards in this city as my witness. I constantly strived to raise their interest for the study of the sciences that teach to know the

causes of well-being, progress, greatness and power of nations .... In this I believe to have served my country usefully, in this I have served.

(Rojas 1862: 32–33, my translation)

He dedicated most of his life precisely to the education of the younger generations because it was virtue rather than wealth that would guarantee national prosperity and independence. Following Say's ideas, Rojas and the Radical generation gave a central place to economic education, so that citizens would become enlightened regarding their own interests, and would profit from the benefits of free trade without facing the threat of being dominated by the pure desire of gain.

In *Olbie*, Say warned against extreme inequalities in the distribution of wealth, as well as against the consequences of free trade when embraced only for greed. He gives direct warning to the United States of America, telling that nation to "beware [of] the general tendency of mind in your beautiful republic. If what is said of you is correct, you will become wealthy, but you will not remain virtuous, and you will not long remain independent and free" (Say 1800: 31; translation Forget 1999: 206). It was these consequences that the Radicals tried to avoid through their ambitious economic education program based precisely on Say's *Treatise*.

Notes

1 For a detailed account of this historiography and its origins see Cardoso (2003).
2 A similar position, but defending precisely those ideas considered to be wrong, can be found in one of the founding texts of contemporary economic theory:

> Firstly, I am convinced that the doctrine of wages, which I adopted in 1871, under the impression that it was somewhat novel, is not really novel at all, except to those whose view is bounded by the maze of the Ricardian Economics. The true doctrine may be more or less clearly traced through the writings of a succession of great French Economists, from Condillac, Boudeau, and Le Trosne, through J.-B. Say, Destutt de Tracy, Storch, and others, down to Bastiat and Courcelle-Seneuil. ... The truth is with the French School...
>
> (Jevons 1871: 37)

3 Part of the explanation might also be that the influence of the French liberals, especially through Destutt de Tracy and Say as representatives of *Idéologie*, came with the rather unfavorable reception of Ricardo's work in France (Béraud and Faccarello 2014).
4 Both terms were used almost interchangeably, with positive or negative connotations depending on who used them.
5 For an exploration of certain tensions between Utilitarianism and Ideology, in particular regarding individual rights, and Ezequiel Rojas' attempted reconciliation see Hurtado (2015).
6 This is precisely one of the points behind the mitigated reception of Ricardo's work in France. Béraud and Faccarello (2014) show how Ricardo's deductive method was considered a step back from Smith because his focus on general principles made economics complex and almost irrelevant precisely because it did not take into account human behavior or motivations as building blocks of the social organization.

7 It was not until 1868 that the Congress approved an Organic Law creating the *Universidad Nacional*. Ezequiel Rojas was appointed as its first President. The Radicals meant this designation as an honor to their professor, who due to health problems did not accept. Manuel Ancízar was then appointed as the University's first President.

8 The first courses in political economy date from 1824 for Law students, and they used Say's *Treatise*. For a description of the teaching of political economy in Colombia see Pico (2016), and for a description of Ezequiel Rojas' course syllabus see Hurtado (2016).

9 After the attempt on his life in 1828, Bolívar banished Bentham's texts, ensuring the allegiance of the Catholic Church to his administration, as a way of marking his rejection and complete separation from the young liberals close to Santander, whom he considered responsible for the attempt. In 1835, once Santander came back to power, Bentham's texts were reinstated.

10 All these accusations, debates and discussions were part of what has come to be known as the *Benthamite Dispute* (*Querella benthamista*) that lasted from the first years of the Republic up to 1832 (López Domínguez 1993). Ezequiel Rojas, still a young professor of Political Economy, was one of the most active participants in this *Dispute*.

11 The proximity to the premises of French Sensationism is clear. Knowledge comes through the senses, and sentient beings act in response to sensations of pleasure and pain are the core principles of the school that has been traced from Locke to Turgot, Condillac, d'Holbach, Helvétius and the *idéologues* (cf. Faccarello 1991 and Faccarello and Steiner 2008).

12 This contrasts sharply with Say's and his colleagues at the *Décade* position on religion. They were very critical of the revival of the Catholic religion in France especially in 1793. Say in *Olbie* affirms that this religion makes people sad, gloomy and dazed (Tiran 1995). Say was brought up in the Calvinist doctrine but he was not a religious man:

> It is remarkable that even if he is an atheist until the end of his days, he does not challenge his protestant education. His atheism is one which opposes the secular institution, the Church as a social force of oppression and any kind of transcendence.
>
> (Tiran 1995: 100, my translation)

This contrast shows precisely how ideas are adapted to a particular context, and in particular how Rojas adapts sensationist ideas to the Colombian context marked by a strong influence of Catholicism in public and private life.

13 The Constitution was signed after the civil war (1859–1862) won by the Liberal coalition known as the *Gólgotas*, formed under Ezequiel Rojas.

14 In fact, according to Rojas, the ten commandments are the expression of those divine natural laws that guarantee reaching happiness and avoiding pain, following God-given human nature.

References

Béraud, A., Faccarello, G. (2014). "'Nous marchons sur un autre terrain.' The reception of Ricardo in the French language: episodes from a complex history," in G. Faccarello, M. Izumo (eds.), *The Reception of David Ricardo in Continental Europe and Japan*. London: Routledge, pp. 10–75.

Camacho Roldán, S. (1868). "La educación popular," in *La Paz*, Bogotá.

Cardoso, J.L. (2003). "The international diffusion of economic thought," in W.J. Samuels, J.E. Biddle, J.B. Davis (eds.), *A Companion to The History of Economic Thought*. United Kingdom: Blackwell Publishing, pp. 622–633.

Cardoso, J.L. (2009). "Reflexões periféricas sobre a difusão internacional do pensamento econômico," *Nova Economia*, 19:2, pp. 251–265.

Constitución política de los Estados Unidos de Colombia sancionada el 8 de mayo de 1863 (1871). Edición oficial revisada por una commission de la Camara de Representantes, compuesta por un miembro de cada Estado. Bogotá: Imprenta i estereotipia de Medardo Rívas.

Dávila Dávila, J.M. (2007). "La sensación es el principio del pensamiento. La introducción de la filosofía experimental en Colombia en el siglo XIX," *Memoria y sociedad*, 11:23, pp. 73–92.

"Decreto orgánico de la instrucción pública primaria" (1871). In *La Escuela Normal, Periódico oficial de la Instrucción Pública*, 1, 2 y 3, Bogotá, January 1871.

Faccarello, G. (1991). "Le legs de Turgot. Aspects de l'économie politique sensualiste de Condorcet à Roederer," in G. Faccarello, Ph. Steiner (sous la direction de), *La pensée économique pendant la Révolution Francaise*. Grenoble: Presses Universitaires de Grenoble, pp. 67–107.

Faccarello, G., Steiner, Ph. (2008). "Interest, sensationism and the science of the legislator: French 'philosophie économique,' 1695–1830," *European Journal of the History of Economic Thought*, 15:1, pp. 1–23.

Forget, E.L. (1999). *The Social Economics of Jean-Baptiste Say: Markets and Virtue*. London and New York: Routledge.

Hurtado, J. (2015). "Ezequiel Rojas: entre utilitarismo e ideología," *Economía*, 38:75, pp. 151–174.

Hurtado, J. (2016). "La economía política en los estudios superiores en la segunda mitad del siglo XIX en Colombia. Ezequiel Rojas, sus influencias y programas," in A. Álvarez, J.S. Correa (eds.), *Ideas y políticas económica en Colombia durante el primer siglo republicano*, Bogotá, D.C.: Ediciones Uniandes y Editorial CESA.

Jaramillo Uribe, J. (1974). *El pensamiento colombiano en el siglo XIX*. 2nd edition. Bogotá: Editorial Temis.

Jaramillo Uribe, J. (1982). "El proceso de la educación del Virreinato a la época contemporánea," in *Manual de Historia de Colombia*. Tomo III. 2nd edition. Bogotá: Instituto Colombiano de Cultura, pp. 249–339.

Jevons, W.S. (1871). *The Theory of Political Economy*. 3rd edition, 1888. London: MacMillan. http://oll.libertyfund.org/titles/jevons-the-theory-of-political-economy.

López Domínguez, L.H. (ed.) (1993). *La querella benthamista*. Bogotá: Biblioteca de la Presidencia de la República.

Pico, C. (2016). "The teaching of political economy, circulation of ideas and economic performance. A review of the Colombian experience in the nineteenth century," in M. García-Molina, H.-M. Trautwein (eds.), *Peripheral Visions of Economic Development: New Frontiers in Development Economics and the History of Economic Thought*. Oxon and New York: Routledge, pp. 286–305.

Ramírez Gómez, M.A. (2004). "Pensadores económicos de la segunda mitad del siglo XIX," *Ecos de Economía*, 19, pp. 121–146.

Rojas, E. (1862). *El doctor Ezequiel Rojas ante el tribunal de la opinión*. Bogotá: Imprenta de Echavarría Hnos.

Rojas, E. (1881–1882). *Obras del doctor Ezequiel Rojas coleccionadas y publicadas con una biografía del autor por Ángel M. Galán*. 2 vols. Bogotá: Imprenta Especial.

Say, J.-B. (1800). *Olbie, ou essai sur les moyens de réformer les moeurs d'une nation*. Paris: Deterville, Treuttel et Wurtz.

Say, J.-B. (1816). *Tratado de economía política ó simple exposición del modo en que se forman, distribuyen y consumen las riquezas. Refundido por el mismo y aumentado con un epítome que comprende los principios fundamentales de la economía política y una tabla analítica de materias.* Traducido al castellano por Don Manuel María Gutierrez y Don Manuel Antonio Rodriguez. Tomo Primero. Madrid: Imprenta de Collado.

Say, J.-B. (1821 [1996]. *Cours d'économie politique et autres essais.* Paris: Flammarion.

Schoorl, E. (1982). "Bentham, Say and Continental Utilitarianism," *Bentham Newsletter,* 6, pp. 8–18.

Say, J.-B. (2002). "Jean-Baptiste Say as a Benthamite Utilitarian," *History of Economic Ideas,* X:1, pp. 33–47.

Tiran, A. (1995). "Jean-Baptiste Say (1767–1832). Essai biographique," in *Jean-Baptiste Say. Manuscrits sur la monnaie, la banque et la finance (1767–1832).* Cahiers Monnaie et Financement,* No. Hors Série, pp. 46–129.

Universidad Nacional (1870). "Texto de Ideolojía. Informes," *Anales de la Universidad,* IV:22, pp. 293–407.

9 From "social economy" to "national political economy"

German economic ideas in Brazil

Luiz Felipe Bruzzi Curi

Introduction

German economic thought, particularly the German Historical School of economics in the nineteenth century, is notorious for the influences it exerted on national contexts external to Germany, especially the United States and Japan.[1] However, not much is known about its dissemination to other non-European countries, such as Brazil. Apart from the contribution by Mauro Boianovksy (2013) on the spread of Friedrich List's ideas in "tropical countries," studies on the history of Brazilian economic thought in the twentieth century have not included a specific analysis of German influences. Dealing with another temporal scope, Alexandre Cunha and José Luís Cardoso (2012) have convincingly argued that there was an appropriation of Cameralism into Luso-Brazilian economic thought through ideas related to public administration and economic policymaking in the late eighteenth and early nineteenth centuries.

About one century later, there was continuity and change in what concerns both the German world and the Brazilian recipient context. In the course of the nineteenth century, Germany went through a complex process of political unification under the Prussian aegis, while simultaneously ascending from a backward economic position to a stance of industrial leadership in Europe. In spite of changes to the original Cameralist approach to economic matters, particularly due to the absorption of Smithian ideas, the connections between economics and public administration lingered on in Germany. Brazil, in turn, became an independent country ruled by a centralized Monarchy, which was dethroned at the end of the nineteenth century and replaced by a Federal Republic. An important continuity is that Brazilian elites, now ruling an autonomous political entity, persisted in their search – a politically conflictive search – for economic strategies to construct their nation. The German world was one of their sources of inspiration throughout this process.

From the end of the nineteenth century through the first decades of the twentieth, it is certainly possible to find indications of the diffusion of German economic ideas in Brazil. In this chapter I highlight two key moments in which it is possible to identify the spread of such ideas. The first one is part of the discussions on economic policy that took place when the Republic was implemented in Brazil. Rui Barbosa was the first republican Finance Minister of Brazil, and he was in office between late 1889 and early 1891. Originally a lawyer, he was a polymath, whose training in economics and finance had been primarily a self-taught endeavor. In his reports and speeches, there were references to Adolph Wagner, Roscher, Schäffle, Gustav Cohn, among others. In one of the parliamentary speeches delivered by Rui Barbosa, in which he attempted to defend the economic policy he had carried out as Minister, he quoted excerpts from Wagner's texts, translating the idea of *Volkswirtschaft* as "social economy." I argue that this translation was embedded in a context that lent itself to a specific sort of appropriation of Wagner's ideas: Barbosa's involvement with the federalist spirit that was associated with the framing of republican institutions in Brazil, as well as his intellectual background, conditioned the way he read German authors and integrated their ideas into his own texts.

The second moment refers to Roberto Simonsen, a businessman, economist, and economic historian. Originally the owner of a building company, Simonsen became an important spokesman for the movement in favor of industrialization in Brazil after being elected a federal deputy representing the industrialists from São Paulo state. The aspect of his work relevant to this analysis refers to a parliamentary debate, which took place in 1935, about the ratification of a Free Trade Agreement between Brazil and the United States. Adolph Wagner and Karl Rodbertus were mentioned in this context as intellectual authorities whose economic ideas were considered very appropriate to tackle Brazilian economic problems. Especially Wagner's concept of *Volkswirtschaft*, translated as "national economy," was praised by Simonsen as the best approach to economics available at the time. The overtly protectionist tone of Simonsen's parliamentary speech in 1935 certainly determined why and how Rodbertus and particularly Wagner were cited in his discourse.

This is a singular situation in which the very same concept traveled the same intercontinental journey twice, with a gap of about three decades separating the two occasions – and very different outcomes. A common trait of these two moments of appropriation was that a political debate was then in course: the economic policy of the first republican administration was under scrutiny in the first case, and a Free Trade Agreement was supposed to be ratified in the second. The idea of *Volkswirtschaft* was mobilized for specific purposes and in two distinct contexts – the different translations it was given are an important indication of the peculiarities of each appropriation.

The scenario presented here can be approached from many methodological perspectives, two of which are central to the construction of the argument. The first one focuses on the international diffusion of economic thought, as a process whose study may provide relevant insight on the source as well as on the recipients of the ideas concerned. José Luís Cardoso (2009) argues that the study of the reception, selection, and re-creation of economic ideas can be useful in questioning the aura enjoyed by some thinkers as pioneers and in measuring the impact of foreign schools within a certain context, thus making more flexible the usual schemes used to classify authors.

The second important approach is the history of concepts (*Begriffsgeschichte*), which shows how these are intertwined with the social reality in which they are produced and used. Reinhart Koselleck (1979, pp. 112–113) advocates that by means of textual exegesis, the study of sociopolitical concepts and their meanings takes on a socio-historical status. This happens because the semantic struggle to define social positions and, through definitions, to keep or occupy these positions belongs to every critical moment in history, particularly in late modernity. Melvin Richter (1990) correctly argues that the history-of-concepts method assumes that concepts both register and affect the transformations of governmental, social, and economic structures.

In order to address the aforementioned topics, this chapter is divided into three sections that follow this introduction. The second section briefly traces the historical origins of the concept of *Volkswirtschaft*, situating it within the German intellectual environment. In the third, I focus on Finance Minister Rui Barbosa and his appropriation of German ideas, in the context of the republican transition in Brazil (1889 and the early 1890s). The fourth part deals with the role played by the German lineage of thought in Roberto Simonsen's critique of the US–Brazil Free Trade Treaty of 1935. Lastly, in the final remarks, I sketch a comparison between the two pictures drawn, closing the argument.

The concept of *Volkswirtschaft* and Adolph Wagner

In order to trace the historical origins of the concept of *Volkswirtschaft* in Germany, it is crucial to analyze the Cameralist idea of *Staatswirtschaft* (state economics). Johannes Burkhardt (1991, pp. 567–569) contends that eighteenth-century Cameralism performed the theoretical shift that led to a modern conception of the economy in Germany. His general argument is that state administration was the "medium" through which a connection could be established between the original "economic" terminology (in the Greek sense) and its commercial counterpart. It is worth noting that, in the ancient and medieval traditions, the dimension of life qualified as "economic" used to be related to household matters, preserving its connection with the original meaning of "*oikos*," the Greek domestic unity. Commercial ideas that emanated from the world of merchants and artisans, particularly the ones pertaining to interest, were regarded with suspicion until early modern times by the literature dealing with the affairs of the "house" (the house could also be a princely one). The fluidity of the terminology, under the shelter of the State, made the borders between economic language and mercantile thought more tenuous. This process started with the creation of cameralistic chairs in Germany, which were meant to provide adequate technical instruction for Prussian civil servants.

The first chairs of *Staatswirtschaft* at German universities were created by king Frederick William I of Prussia, whose government was characterized by an expansion of the Army, unification of the private and public financial agencies of his kingdom, and support to economic development – textiles and other exports were fostered by means of what was termed "royal mercantilism" by Perry Anderson ([1974] 2013, pp. 245–246). The development of Cameralism was thus closely intertwined with the growth and centralization of the Prussian state. Intellectually, the cameral science (*Kameralwissenchaft*) was a system of knowledge in which public administration and the general organization of the state were essential parts of economic thinking. According to Johann Heinrich Gottlob von Justi (1717–1771), perhaps the most prominent representative of eighteenth-century Cameralism, the ultimate goal of this system of thought was the general satisfaction or general happiness of a nation: this general welfare involved the reconciliation of the interests of the individual with those of the state. In other words, the interests of the individual were not seen as autonomous, but rather as part of a totality whose order was provided by the state (Cunha, 2013, p. 7).

The works of Justi were essential for establishing and disseminating Cameralism and its correlated, integrative way of understanding the economy. By means of Justi's work – particularly his 1755 book *Staatswirthschaft* – this perspective was conceptualized. Burkhardt (1991, pp. 572–573) argues that the image of a large public household, producing economically and invigilating its subjects, contributed to the abstraction efforts that led to a general, all-encompassing concept of economy and to the formation of a system of economic thought. In a detailed analysis of Justi's *Staatswirthschaft*, Alexandre Cunha (2013, pp. 10–12) observes that it was drafted as a course plan for officials, integrating the dimensions of political theory, internal policy, and public finance into one complete teaching program for cameral matters. Cunha also recognizes the editorial fortune of the 1755 edition of *Staatswirthschaft*, which sold out quickly.[2] Until the turn of the century, the term *Staatswirtschaft* was disseminated and commonly used in Germany: even the reception of Smith's ideas, around 1800, took place mainly under the prevalence of this terminology. This designation would start to wane in the course of the nineteenth century, which saw an increasing preference for the terms *Nationalökonomie* and *Volkswirtschaft*.

Keith Tribe (1988, pp. 149–182) sees the emergence of *Nationalökonomie* from the 1790s as an important modification in the discursive structure of German economics. He argues that Cameralism presupposed a human subject whose welfare could be identified with the needs of the state and whose needs could thus be prescribed by the government. Alternatively, for *Nationalökonomie* the striving of individual subjects for the satisfaction of material needs was the mainspring of economic activity. This major shift in German economic discourse is associated with the separation of the spheres of state and of civil society that paved the way for a redefinition of social life and for multiple conceptual changes. According to Tribe, this appearance of a new way of conceiving the economy in the German language area did not mean a move towards theorization. On the contrary, the new German approach to economics as a system of needs was descriptive rather than theoretical and it followed the pedagogic tradition of university teaching established by Cameralism; this ambiguity became clear when thinkers such as Müller and List dismissed Smithian economics as "cosmopolitan." The philosophical move operated by Kant, relocating reason from the planful activities of government to the human person, as well as the dissemination of Physiocracy and of Adam Smith's *Wealth of Nations*, were interrelated events associated to the constitution of *Nationalökonomie*.[3]

The "national" aspect of this way of referring to economics, initially not very important, would gain political significance in the Vormärz time, which roughly corresponds to the years between the fall of Napoleon in 1815 and the 1848 revolutions in the German Confederation. In 1830, Alexander Lips dealt specifically with national economic matters in his *Deutschlands National-Oekonomie*. In a tone that would later be associated with him and his followers, Friedrich List emphasized in his *National System of Political Economy* (1841) that *Nationalökonomie* was in charge of the economic education of the nation. Marking the consolidation and dissemination of the concept are the foundation of the journal *Jahrbücher für Nationalökonomie und Statistik* in 1863 and the publication of Roscher's *Geschichte der National-Oekonomie in Deutschland* (1874), which employed this terminology to refer to a doctrinal history of economics encompassing the early modern times. Upon the foundation of the German *Reich* in 1871, which overcame the tension between the state and the nation, the expression *Nationalökonomie* became a common term: in the turn of the century, it designated economic approaches to large political unities, as well as any other economic approach in a more technical sense. The concept, nevertheless, fell into disuse after World War II, due to a crisis in the German concept of nationality and its general loss of prestige.

The concept of *Volkswirtschaft* fared similarly. The term gained significance due to the importance of Karl H. Rau's *oeuvre*, who translated Storch's *Cours d'économie politique* as *Handbuch der National-Wirthschaftslehre* (1819) and, in his own *Lehrbuch der politischen Ökonomie* (1826, vol. I), was the first to use the heading *Volkswirtschaftslehre*, even though he apologized for the neologism. In a tripartite division that would be long-lasting in the German textbook tradition, Rau separated *Volkswirtschaftslehre* from economic policy (*Volkswirtschaftspflege*) and the science of public finance (*Finanzwissenschaft*): each of these fields received its own volume. Initially, the concept of *Volkswirtschaft* was only a synonym for *Nationalökonomie* in textbooks and lexicons. Meyer's lexicon, however, indicated in 1878, under the entry *Nationalökonomie*, that *Volkswirtschaft* was the most common concept, referring the reader to the latter entry, where an explanation was provided. As the twentieth century approached, preferences tended to shift to *Volkswirtschaft*, as this word accommodated the historical-holistic interpretive necessities of the German Historical School.

Disseminated in nineteenth-century Western Europe, the development of the concept of "political economy" shows the flipside of the history behind the conceptual pair *Nationalökonomie-Volkswirtschaft*. Given that the original idea of economy related to the household was almost absent in a Western-European context dominated by the conceptual framework provided by Physiocracy and the classics, the concept could be reduced to "*économie*" or economics. In Germany, this nomenclature saw its popularity gradually dwindle during the nineteenth century, having survived until the turn of the century and almost disappearing by the time of World War I. In the aftermath of World War II, it experienced a frantic revival: publishing houses would reprint recently published books in order to change their titles if they were using the traditional "national" terminology (Burkhardt, 1991, pp. 581–583).[4]

It was during the prevalence of the conceptual pair *Nationalökonomie-Volkswirtschaft*, particularly in its Germanized form, that Adolph Wagner (1835–1917) wrote some of his most relevant works, including the ones that eventually reached South America. Adolph Wagner received his doctorate degree in *Staatswissenschaft* from Göttingen University and started his career at the University of Dorpat (Livonia), a former Prussian city that is now called Tartu and part of Estonia. In the 1860s, faced with the prospect of German unification, Wagner returned to what is nowadays recognized as the German territory. After a brief period as director of the Chair of Cameralistic Science at the University of Freiburg im Breisgau, in Baden, he moved away in 1870, securing a professorship for *Staatswissenschaft* at the prestigious University of Berlin (Meyer, 1968).   ·

Wagner was a self-declared member of the Historical School; however, as he stated in his review of Marshall's *Principles*, he was more inclined towards theorization than, for example, Gustav Schmoller. In this review of Marshall, Wagner (1891) criticized how German economists tended to be too dismissive of English political economy (Hagemann and Rösch, 2012, pp. 100–101). The institutional and political agenda of the German Historical School was closely related to an important association founded in 1873: the *Verein für Sozialpolitik* (Society for Social Policy), of which Wagner was a member. The founders of the *Verein* were a group that for the most part consisted of university professors who were against both the Manchester School and Marxist revolutionary ideas. These reformist thinkers were derogatorily named *Kathedersozialisten* (socialists of the chair). After a period of pacific coexistence with liberal stances towards economic matters, in 1879 the protectionist position, which associated higher tariffs with the necessities of German industry, became a predominant current of thought within the *Verein*. Bismarck's shift towards a protective trade policy in the same year was the background for Gustav Schmoller's defense of high tariffs in the 1879 meeting of the Society.[5]

Wagner's most comprehensive book in the field of economic theory was the *Fundamentals of Political Economy* (*Grundlegung der Politischen Ökonomie*), which was published for the first time in 1876 in German, and received a

French translation in 1909. Following Rau's scheme, this textbook had "political economy" in the title, but its first part dealt with "The fundamentals of *Volkswirtschaft*."[6] Roberto Simonsen mentioned this book in his 1935 speech: as he did not read German, he probably had access to the French version, which circulated in São Paulo at the time.

Rui Barbosa, in turn, had in his library two translated versions of Wagner's treatise on public finance, *Finanzwissenschaft* (first edition: 1871–1872), as well as the original German version of the *Handbuch der politischen Ökonomie* (*Handbook for political economy*), edited by Gustav von Schönberg and published for the first time in Tübingen, in 1882. In conformity with the German textbook tradition, the first part of this handbook was dedicated to *Volkswirtschaftlehre*. This volume consisted of contributions from different authors, such as Hans von Scheel, Erwin Nasse, Adolph Wagner, and Gustav Schönberg himself. Wagner wrote the section called "Credit and the banking system"[7] for the volume on *Volkswirtschaftlehre*. According to Hagemann and Rösch (2012, p. 113), this handbook was the first of its kind published in the German language area comprising the full area of political economy; it was also very successful, having received three expanded re-editions (1885–1886, 1890–1891, 1896–1898) after the original one. The fact that an exemplar eventually reached Barbosa's library in Rio de Janeiro corroborates this view, suggesting a favorable international reputation for the *Handbuch*.

Rui Barbosa and the challenges of the republican transition (1890–1892)

Rui Barbosa (1849–1923) was one of the founding fathers of the Brazilian Republic and certainly one of the most distinguished intellectuals of Brazil in the late nineteenth and early twentieth centuries. He played a major role in the political, juridical, and economic organization of the new regime. Barbosa began his law studies in Recife and concluded them in 1870, in São Paulo. After some years working in his hometown of Salvador (Bahia), he moved to Rio de Janeiro, where he worked as a lawyer and started his career as a politician of national relevance. He was an advocate for the abolition of slavery and for the federalist system. When the Republic was proclaimed in 1889, he became Finance Minister, and remained in office until January 1891. Elected Senator representing his native state, Barbosa played an important role as a jurist during the constituent assembly that formulated the first republican constitution of Brazil, promulgated in 1891.

Rui Barbosa had a predominantly Anglo-French intellectual background: his references to France and particularly to Britain as cultural models were recurrent. However, the Germanic universe was in no way absent from his education. In the preface to a book published in 1921, Rui Barbosa ([1921], 1947, p. xiii) mentioned that in the year before he reached 16, the age at which he could enroll in a university, he had perfected his German, following his father's advice. Moreover, upon his arrival in Rio de Janeiro, he was commissioned to translate into Portuguese the book *The Pope and the Council*,[8] by Johann Joseph Ignaz von Döllinger, a prominent German Catholic theologian who refused to abide by the doctrine of papal infallibility (Vianna Filho [1941] 1987, p. 60 and pp. 68–76).

Though not committed to an agenda of research in economic matters, Rui Barbosa was certainly in contact with economic concepts. The texts in which he discusses his policymaking as a Minister provide evidence that he was informed by economic ideas coming from various lineages of thought. The fact that he mentioned ideas drawn from works of economists in order to address his audience shows that these concepts circulated in Brazil at the time, and that Rui Barbosa had enough reasons to mobilize them for his inter-related political and intellectual purposes.

Another relevant indication of this proximity to economics is the fact that his library, a famous collection for Brazil at the time with more than 37,000 volumes, included the works of a wide range of economists.[9] From the British tradition of political economy, the most famous authors were represented: Adam Smith, David Ricardo, John Stuart Mill, and Alfred Marshall, among others. From Germany, Wilhelm Roscher, Karl Bücher, Gustav Schmoller, Lujo Brentano, and Adolph Wagner. And from France, Jean-Baptiste Say, Paul Leroy-Beaulieu, and Léon Say. Many of these books have passages marked by Rui Barbosa – and some of them are quoted in Barbosa's texts dealing with economic matters.

From a general perspective, Rui Barbosa's "anti-bullionism" (or his *papelismo*[10]) can be regarded as the theoretical foundation for his policymaking as Finance Minister, which would become associated with the period of speculation and economic instability in Brazil known as *Encilhamento* (Triner and Wandschneider, 2005). Rui Barbosa's initial monetary policy, inspired by the federalist mood and conditioned by the increased demand for money that characterized the republican transition in Brazil, consisted in establishing regional banks that could issue paper money backed by either gold or public debt bonds.[11] The difficulty in obtaining gold in international markets gave rise to emissions that were based on public bonds. This scheme, instituted by a decree in January 1890, proved to be unstable: emissions soared, speculation took over the stock market, and the local currency devaluated. In an attempt to tackle this problem, Barbosa changed the course of his policy at the end of 1890, unifying emissions by merging two pre-existing issuing banks into one centralized note-issuing national bank: the "*Banco da República dos Estados Unidos do Brasil*" (BREUB).

Before turning specifically to Rui Barbosa's references to Wagner, it is worth registering that both men had a very similar approach to the usage of paper money. An important idea advanced by Wagner in "Credit and the banking system" was that paper money had many advantages over metallic currency: saving transport expenses and reducing costs in general, for example. Furthermore, only the emission of banknotes would be able to "adapt to the mutable state of credit, i.e. to the general state of confidence." The circulation of paper money issued by banks was also the only means of payment capable of adjusting well enough to "the temporal and local changes in the demand for means of circulation, so as to prevent disturbances in the general movement of the economy" (Wagner, [1882] 1889, p. 435). Rui Barbosa and Wagner both recognized the importance of nonmetallic monetary circulation, especially as a response to an increased demand for means of payment.

Rui Barbosa's appropriation of Adolph Wagner was not restricted to monetary matters: apart from this speech on policymaking, he referred to Wagner in other opportunities. In the "Report of the Finance Minister," which he drafted upon leaving office, he used Wagner to discuss fiscal issues raised by the establishment of the Federal Republic. The new constitution of Brazil transferred from the federal government to the states the revenues from duties on exports. This transfer urged the federal government to seek other sources of funding. One alternative was the income tax, which was supported by Wagner, particularly because it enabled national treasuries to count on a reliable source of revenue in critical situations. As mentioned above, Barbosa had read Wagner's treatise on financial science (*Finanzwissenschaft*), both in its French and Italian translations.[12] The second volume of the French translation bears Rui Barbosa's reading marks in its section on the theory of taxation. In the Report, Barbosa ([1891] 1949, pp. 33–34) quoted not only Wagner's treatise, but also another author who had himself referenced Wagner's arguments: the Italian economist Giuseppe Ricca Salerno (1849–1912).[13]

Moreover, in general intellectual terms, Barbosa considered the specificity of historical contexts and the importance of particular experiences to be essential in economic analysis. By including Wagner among his references, he engaged with an economist who cared about the adequacy of economic institutions to specific historical periods and national contexts. Wagner's ideas were handy for him in order to make the point that, if his policies were now under criticism for being too "unorthodox" or "dovish," they had been an attempt to construct a monetary framework that was adequate to the Brazilian reality. The following excerpt, which closes the comparison Wagner draws between banking centralization and decentralization, summarizes this idea.

> It follows hence that it is advisable, for practical banking organization, that the point of departure for reforms should be what happened historically in each context and what was essentially preserved; and that one should only reform the prevailing banking system according to necessity, instead of transforming it completely according to a doctrinal model.
>
> (Wagner, [1882] 1889, p. 453)

In a talk published as "Paper money and the decline of the foreign exchange rate,"[14] given before the Senate on November 3rd, 1891, after Barbosa had already left the Ministry, he argued that the economic policy carried out during his incumbency was not the main culprit behind the exchange rate devaluation that took place in 1890 and 1891 (Barbosa, 1892). In order to give a theoretical basis to this argument, Rui Barbosa resorted to an idea concerning the velocity of circulation of money in order to reinforce the argument that paper money emissions should not be dependent only on the availability of bullion. They should be determined according to circulation needs, i.e., the amount of transactions that businesses needed to perform. In the case of Brazil, a country with transport deficiencies, a backward economy, and primitive transaction mechanisms, there were serious hindrances to a smooth process of circulation, leading to a lower velocity of monetary circulation. In that sense, taking the specificities of a backward economy into account, paper money should be issued in larger amounts than what was necessary to carry out the same transactions in a rich, developed country: "The less advanced a country is, the more slowly money circulates – and the larger is thus the sum required to perform the same number of operations" (Barbosa, 1892, p. 72).

If it is theoretically possible that issued paper money does not come into circulation in its entirety, and if there is a part of issued currency that "for the special circumstances of certain countries hibernates in the hands of its possessors," the causal relationship between monetary expansion and currency devaluation does not necessarily hold true anymore (Barbosa, 1892, p. 68). The state of the exchange rate would have nonmonetary determinants, such as the situation of the balance of payments and the prosperity of national businesses. This argument, developed in the course of his speech in November 1891, should be enough to refute the direct theoretical association between Rui Barbosa's policy as a Minister, which had increased the amount of monetary assets available in the economy, and the devaluation of the *milreis* against foreign currencies that had intensified in 1890.

A few months after "Paper money and the decline of the foreign exchange rate," Rui Barbosa gave another speech in the Senate on January 12th, entitled "Issuing banks – the official bill."[15] One of the goals of the talk was to continue defending his economic policy as a Minister from public discredit. In this intervention, Rui Barbosa quoted speeches by Otto von Bismarck in order to justify the change of course in his economic policy: "I would shame myself politically, if I were part of the 'rabble' of individuals who, in their entire lives, have known nothing but one single idea, with which they have never set themselves in contradiction" (Barbosa, 1892, pp. 154–155).[16] The sentence referred to the change in Rui Barbosa's stance towards monetary emissions: if he had implemented plurality of emissions at the beginning of his term by means of the regional banks, he now defended the centralization of banking, as it had been established shortly before he left office with a centralized issuing bank (Barbosa, 1892, p. 156). In the course of his speech, Barbosa sought to justify in many ways his change of course in banking policy: he resorted to arguments that could provide legitimacy for the existence of a centralized national bank, and hence invoked Adolph Wagner.

The first of Wagner's excerpts cited by Rui Barbosa in the speech on issuing banks brought forward a historical comparison between centralized and decentralized banking systems. The Scottish system was mentioned because its decentralization enabled it to tackle the need for means of circulation coming from the "social economy." This system, nevertheless, did not enjoy a great advantage over centralized banks, whose net of disperse affiliates can also meet the scattered local demands for means of circulation, according to the necessity of each place. Large banks are therefore seen as more desirable for being capable of "withstanding the storm" during critical times. Wagner refers to the history of some "national" centralized banks in order to reinforce his argument. He mentions the Bank of England in the "commercial crises" of 1825, 1847, 1857, 1866; the Bank of France in the years 1848, 1866, 1870, and 1871; the Bank of Prussia in 1857, 1866, and 1870; and lastly, the Austrian Bank in 1873 (Barbosa, 1892, p. 159 and Wagner, [1882] 1889, p. 436).

The next fragment of Wagner's quoted by Rui Barbosa reinforces the argument with the idea that, when there is a centralized issuing bank, runs on the bank to present notes for exchange are rather infrequent. Large centralized banks are able to bridge the gap that appears in the whole credit system when there are crises, so as to overcome them "in the true interest of the social economy" (Barbosa, 1892, pp. 159–160 and Wagner, [1882] 1889, pp. 451–452). This would be their greatest, most decisive advantage, advocating in favor of monetary centralization instead of multiple emissions. The historical comparison (sketched through examples) stressed the point once more: according to Wagner, the lessons of banking history were favorable to centralization. To sum up and conclude, Rui Barbosa quoted Wagner: "In great State catastrophes, the possibility of having the support of a large central bank, powerful and well-managed, is of high political and social economic interest" (Barbosa, 1892, p. 160 and Wagner, [1882] 1889, p. 452).[17]

The expression "social economy" and its adjective form in the phrases "in the interest of the social economy" and "social-economic interest" correspond to "*economia social*," the Portuguese translation given by Rui Barbosa for the German term *Volkswirtschaft*. It is worth noting that Rui Barbosa was proficient in the German language and certainly understood the meaning of the word *Volk* (people), as well as the usual French translation of the concept of *Volkswirtschaft*. In the very Introduction to Wagner's *Finanzwissenschaft*, or *Traité de la science des finances*, one can find examples of *Volkswirtschaft* translated as "*économie nationale*" – and Barbosa read his French copy, as the reading marks indicate. The point is that, in his translation, Rui Barbosa probably chose not to emphasize the national aspect of the concept, but only the fact that large issuing banks would be beneficial for the whole of society.

This procedure seems to be related to a historical context in which one of the goals of the new republican government, to which Rui Barbosa belonged, was to overcome the monarchical legacy and to empower the Brazilian states. According to Emília Viotti da Costa (1977, pp. 309–317), the federalist idea gained support in Brazil as the end of the nineteenth century approached. From a socio-economic point of view, Costa argues, Brazilian problems related to modernization, particularly in the cities, came to be associated with the excessive centralization of the monarchical regime. The political context also favored federalism: the institutional framework of the Monarchy did not allow for a proportional parliamentary representation by new powerful economic groups, such as coffee-producers employing free labor instead of slaves, capitalists involved in the import-export business, and industrialists. These groups were particularly influential in São Paulo, where not only federalism, but also separatism, were invoked in this context. In the end, the political arrangement of a federative republic proved to be more viable, as it accounted for regional interests without breaking with national unity.

Therefore, although Rui Barbosa resorted to the ideas of an author affiliated with a lineage of economic thought known for its nationalist inclinations, he did not incorporate them indiscriminately: rather, he adjusted them to his own contemporary political context. To change the very wording of a concept through a (mis)translation that concealed its nationalist implications can be regarded as a strategy of conceptual appropriation by means of a convenient linguistic adaptation. This alteration made the concept more appropriate to be mobilized in the political context of the republican transition in Brazil.

The usage of the term "social economy" might also be related to an attempt to employ a terminology that was associated with a more Western-European tradition, especially the French one, represented by Jean-Baptiste Say. Rui Barbosa owned Say's booklet *Économie politique*, published posthumously in 1888. Barbosa also had a volume written by J.-B. Say's grandson, Léon Say, entitled *Économie sociale*. This book was actually a report of the "Social Economy Group," that was part of the Paris *Exposition Universelle* of 1889: it featured the results of a contest among participant delegations from different "sections" of the economy, including public hygiene, housing for the working class, insurance against accidents, and large and small industry, among others (Say, 1891). Ultimately, the translation of *Volkswirtschaft* as "social economy" wiped out its possible nationalist implications, and favored others that were more suitable to federalism and to the claim that issuing banks were politically neutral and beneficial to society. A few decades later, Roberto Simonsen would shift the emphasis of his appropriation to the national aspect of the concept, as shall be discussed in the next section.

Roberto Simonsen and the *Aspects of national political economy* (1935)

Roberto Simonsen (1889–1948) was an influential businessman and economic historian in early twentieth-century Brazil. He graduated from the São Paulo Polytechnic School as an engineer and started his career in the building industry, which was his focus until the mid-1920s. As industrialization gained momentum in Brazil, Simonsen became an important leader representing the industrial bourgeoisie from São Paulo state, which was the most important locus of Brazilian industrial development at the time. In the 1930s, Simonsen taught economic history at the São Paulo Free School for Sociology and

Politics,[18] giving a course that resulted in a book called *Economic History of Brazil* (published in 1937). This book would eventually become a founding achievement in Brazilian economic historiography. Apart from his intellectual reputation as an economic historian, Simonsen gained recognition for his advocacy of protectionism and of economic planning.

Simonsen's ideas on protectionism were influenced by Friedrich List, as well as by the Rumanian economist Mihail Manoilescu, the translation of whose book Simonsen sponsored on behalf of the Center for the Industries of São Paulo, having himself prefaced the volume (Love, 1996; Rodrigues, 2005). In a lecture delivered in 1931, Simonsen recognized Friedrich List as an important source of inspiration and also declared himself an affiliate of Manoilescu's protectionism. In the same lecture he referred to information collected by the Russian-German-American economist Wladimir Woytinsky as a means to prove the point that industry is in general more productive than primary sectors (Simonsen, 1931; Bruzzi Curi and Saes, 2015). As the most productive economic activity, industry should be made to prosper in backward economies, according to Manoilescu, so as to elevate their national productivity.

Simonsen became associated with the foundation of a heterodox economic thought in Brazil for his contributions to the so-called "controversy on economic planning" from 1944 to 1945: indeed, the controversy can be considered as a sort of synthesis of his economic ideas. Simonsen criticized the approach adopted by his opponent, Eugênio Gudin, arguing that it presupposed a crystallization of economic laws, which were regarded as valid for all countries in the world (Simonsen, 1945).[19] According to Simonsen, this view was incorrect: Brazil's position as an agrarian economy could not be attributed to its natural endowments as a tropical country, but to the specific historical path that the country had followed. If its backward position was the result of historical evolution – and not of an inescapable fate determined by universal laws governing the economy – it could be reverted in the course of history, if other strategies of economic development were adopted. History could be changed, and planning for integral industrialization was the way to do it.

Simonsen's text, *Aspects of national political economy* (1935), is relevant to this analysis inasmuch as it provides evidence of his contact with German economic thought. It was originally written as an address to the Federal Chamber of Deputies in order to oppose the ratification of a Free Trade Treaty between Brazil and the United States. It is part of the Transcripts of the Brazilian Congress, and Simonsen himself published it in Portuguese and in English, probably as a way to make the arguments against the Treaty available to both Brazilian and North-American authorities and negotiators. It is important to point out that Roberto Simonsen was very favorable to Brazilian-American political relations. He considered many of the United States' economic policies, such as the elevation of tariffs in order to protect industry, as examples to be followed. The translation can thus be seen as an attempt by Simonsen to show that he was in no way an anti-American, but only against the kind of free trade policy implied in the Agreement, which he deemed harmful to Brazil (Lima, 2013).

In the introductory section of his address, suggestively named "National Economy," Simonsen indicated the current of economic thought to which his arguments were attuned. He started by strongly criticizing the supposed inter-dependence between political liberalism and free trade theories. Following Simonsen's "Listian" reasoning, the free trade idea meant the predominance of the strongest and best organized in economic terms, whereas political lib-eralism implied the equality of political rights for individuals and, in a geo-political sense, respect for the political rights of each nation. In these terms, political freedom is relatively incompatible with liberalism when it comes to trade. Simonsen acknowledged the merits of Adam Smith, but attacked his fol-lowers for worshipping classical liberalism and overlooking the disturbances that free trade could inflict on economic activities carried out domestically.

He then described the kind of thought which he favored, referring to "socialistic" teachers whose ideas were more "in accord with reality" than those defended by liberal thinkers. Karl Rodbertus was praised for putting the Smithian concept of the division of labor in correct terms, "in an endeavour to emphasize its social aspect [of the division of labour], the organic basis of States, their process of historical formation and the preponderant part which was reserved to them in the exercise of social rights" (Simonsen, 1935, p. 8). The following mentions were to Friedrich List and "those of his school," who had associated their concept of the economy – "*economia nacional*" in Portuguese and "national political economy" in English – with the existence of nations, each of which was a distinct entity, resulting from a specific pro-cess of historical formation (Simonsen, 1935, p. 9).

Simonsen went on to point out that the evolution of economic studies had demonstrated that the division of labor operates socially: the greater the divi-sion of labor, the more civilized a nation is. The result of this evolution was that economists came to understand the importance of "national political economy," which had the purpose of "satisfying the necessities of countries, of the social groups and of the individuals who compose them." Simonsen concluded this doctrinal introduction by praising Adolph Wagner as the author who first and best established the concepts of "national economics," "national capital," and "national income." According to Simonsen, Wagner's theory was universally accepted (Simonsen, 1935, p. 9).

Simonsen reputed three German authors – List, Rodbertus, and Wagner – as representatives of the most up-to-date and realistic current of economic thought. As the references were made during a speech, they had the purpose of giving intellectual legitimacy to the arguments presented: in that case, they should corroborate the idea that Brazil should *not* ratify the Free Trade Treaty with the US. Indeed, Simonsen's protectionist arguments and proposals in 1935 were quite attuned to what List, Wagner, and Rodbertus had written years before.

Friedrich List (1789–1846) was famous for his *National System of Political Economy* (1841), and Simonsen had cited his authority in other opportunities, such as the foundation of the Free School for Sociology and Politics. On this occasion, he advanced the argument that List was responsible for taking political economy beyond its academic boundaries, making it a more concrete and realistic discipline through the application of the comparative method in economic history (Simonsen, 1935, p. 20). The key argument that made List known in Brazil was the metaphor of the infant industry, which should be protected by high tariffs in backward countries until it reached the stage of development prevailing in the most advanced nations. In a speech supposed to avoid the ratification of a Free Trade Treaty, it certainly made sense for Simonsen to evoke the authority of Friedrich List. Scholarship has demonstrated that List was an important influence not only on Simonsen, but also on Brazilian debates concerning protectionism and tariffs since the end of the nineteenth century, even though industrialists tended to ignore an important facet of List's thought – his pronounced skepticism towards industrialization in the tropics.[20]

Karl Rodbertus and Adolph Wagner are not as known as List, especially in what concerns the diffusion of their ideas in Brazil, but the reference to their work was quite coherent with Simonsen's ideas. According to Schumpeter, Rodbertus' ideas were rediscovered and brought to the center of economic debate in Germany as Adolph Wagner republished his fourth letter to von Kirchmann in *Das Kapital* (1899) (Schumpeter, 1954, p. 507).[21] These connections suggest that Simonsen was attuned to authors individually, while also keeping abreast of a cluster of economic ideas that had their origins in Germany: not only did he praise Wagner's theory as the apex of national political economy, but he also cited Rodbertus, an author who had been studied by Wagner.

In the doctrinal introduction to *Aspects of national political economy*, Simonsen mentioned Wagner's *Fundamentals of Political Economy*, his *Grundlegung*. The title of the book was the only precise information given by Simonsen: he gave no further clue of the specific arguments that interested him in this comprehensive piece. Nevertheless, from his speech and from other works, such as *Economic history of Brazil*, it is possible to infer that at least two aspects of Wagner's *Grundlegung* were appropriated by Simonsen: the theory of trade, and the national aspects of the concept of *Volkswirtschaft*, or "*économie nationale*," the French version of the term which was probably familiar to Simonsen.

Wagner's considerations on international trade were moderate, inasmuch as he did not intend to completely deconstruct the liberal arguments proposed by English economists. However, he tried to qualify the idea that free trade necessarily benefited all parties involved; for him, there was no absolute justification for liberalism in world trade, only relative ones. He resorted to history to argue that the development of one national economy could hinder that of others, if they were commercially integrated. The example given was the post-Civil War United States, which would change the world economic scenario, influencing many other nations and competing with them. Another factor that could diminish the possible benefits of free trade was uncertainty: the supply of important inputs was not assured if they were imported. In this case, the historical example was the "cotton famine" that affected British industry during the shortage of input caused by the American Civil War.

Wagner further stated that when one deals with issues such as trade and questions relating to labor, industry, and agriculture, both a national and a cosmopolitan point of view must be taken into account: "Physiocratic-Smithian economics tends too much to a cosmopolitan conception, whereas mercantilist-protectionist economics sometimes exaggerates the national point of view. Yet in principle and ultimately the latter is more correct" (Wagner, [1876] 1909, pp. 36–39). Needless to say, in order to argue against free trade, such a theoretical background was really useful to Simonsen.

As for the conceptualization of national economy (*Volkswirtschaft*), the object of "national political economy" (*Volkswirtschaftslehre*), the definition presented by Wagner and praised by Simonsen as the "best" available was aligned with the German Historical School (Schmoller, 1900, p. 6). Wagner proposed a historic-sociological typology for the evolution of economies, according to which all human communities went through the following stages: race, gender, tribe, and finally *Volk* (the French edition kept the German word for people/nation). This national economy (*Volkswirtschaft*) was understood not as a "mechanical juxtaposition of individual economies," but as an organic combination whose existence could be guaranteed by the state or by economic rules established by a sort of state, as in the German *Zollverein* (Wagner, [1876] 1909, p. 20). This typology of development is clearly related to the more general German context of the nineteenth century, in which regional fragmentation was an obstacle and economic development was a corollary of national unification.

Simonsen's appropriation of the term "*économie nationale*" emphasized the national aspects of the concept: he mobilized this idea in order to imply that national economic interests – which Simonsen associated with the interests of the Brazilian industrial sector – should prevail over the eventual benefits brought by a Free Trade Agreement. The idea that it was necessary to build the cultural and social foundations of the nation in order to foster economic development underlay not only the parliamentary address in which Simonsen referred to Wagner, but most of his economic thought from the late 1920s onwards. At the very beginning of his *Economic history*, in the part corresponding to a lecture delivered on April 8th, 1936, he stated that the aim of the book was to contribute to the construction of a national conscience. Peoples in the vanguard of civilization, argued Simonsen (1937, pp. 53–54), were those who had liberated themselves from disorganization – and the first manifestation of these peoples' strength was the establishment of a national conscience of their needs and aspirations.

Final remarks

This chapter approached the way in which the German concept of *Volkswirtschaft*, present in the works of the political economist Adolph Wagner, was appropriated by two Brazilian thinkers: Rui Barbosa and Roberto Simonsen. Coined at the moment when Smith's *Wealth of Nations* was received in Germany, at the beginning of the nineteenth century, the conceptual pair *Nationalökonomie-Volkswirtschaft* gained a nationalist connotation that made it suitable for the intellectual and political purposes of the German Historical School of economics. The prestige of this designation reached its peak at the beginning of the twentieth century, and it was the standard designation for "economy" in Germany – *Volkswirtschaftlehre* corresponding to the name of the science, as in "economics." The nationalist connotation of term fell into discredit after World War II, when the whole German idea of nationality experienced a crisis.

In Brazil, the concept was mobilized in very different contexts, even receiving different translations: "social economy" at the end of the nineteenth century, and "national economy" (or "national political economy," for the science), in the 1930s. As described earlier, the political intentions, as well as the intellectual backgrounds of Rui Barbosa and Roberto Simonsen, were very different from one another – these factors certainly shaped their divergent approaches to the same concept. Rui Barbosa wanted to justify his attempt at banking centralization in Brazil in a context of strong federalist claims, so he attenuated the national connotation of the concept. Simonsen, on the contrary, integrated the idea of "national economy" into a protectionist speech in order to oppose a Free Trade Agreement, emphasizing the importance of the national aspect. From these two historical situations, it becomes clear that the international diffusion of economic thought is a complex process, which may involve not only absorption, but also a creative process of adaptation of ideas that fosters an original intellectual production.

Acknowledgments

For valuable comments I thank Jean-Pierre Potier, Harald Hagemann, Céline Bouillot, and the anonymous reviewer; I also acknowledge Bruno Betat's careful revision of the draft. The usual disclaimers apply.

Notes

1 See, for example, Dorfman (1955) and Yanagisawa (2001).
2 It is worth noting that Alexandre Cunha (2013) questions the primacy of the idea of *Staatswirtschaft* as a way of framing Justi's *oeuvre* as a whole. Cunha argues that the core of Justi's intellectual contribution can be found within the realm of *Polizeiwissenschaft*, i.e., to his ideas relating to economic policymaking, in cameralistic terms.
3 For the various alterations in the way of conceiving the society, which took place in Germany in this context, see also Koselleck (1979).

4 The discussion about the history of the concepts *Nationalökonomie* and *Volkswirtschaft* in nineteenth-century Germany benefits from the entry "Wirtschaft" in the lexicon *Geschichtliche Grundbegriffe*. Most of the text of this entry was written by Johannes Burkhardt. See Burkhardt (1991).

5 For a detailed account on the origins and institutional vicissitudes concerned with the *Verein*, see Hagemann (2001).

6 The book was published for the first time as a revision of K. H. Rau's textbook, with the title *Allgemeine oder theoretische Volkswirtschaftslehre*. See Meyer (1968).

7 In German: "Der Credit und das Bankwesen."

8 The original book, *Der Papst und das Concil*, was published in Leipzig in 1869, under the pen name "Janus." See Janus (1869 and 1877).

9 Shortly after Rui Barbosa's death, the Brazilian federal government acquired his house in Rio de Janeiro, where he kept his library, with the clear purpose of turning it into a museum. As a result, the library has been preserved since 1923 exactly as Rui Barbosa left it.

10 "*Papelismo*" is the Brazilian name for the current of monetary thinking and policymaking that defended the emission of paper money, not always backed by bullion. The word is associated with the debates held in the nineteenth century: these discussions, between "*papelistas*" and "*metalistas*" share common features with the English controversies of that time. See Fonseca and Mollo (2012).

11 The abolition of slavery in Brazil, in 1888, associated with the arrival of an expressive contingent of European immigrant workers (about 200,000 between 1888 and 1890), as well as favorable results from foreign transactions were factors increasing the demand for currency. See Franco (1990, pp. 21–22).

12 The original *Finanzwissenschaft*, published in 1871–1872, was a revised edition of K. H. Rau's *Lehrbuch der Finanzwissenschaft*. The book went through successive editions from 1877 to 1901. The French translation, *Traité de la science des finances*, published by Giard & Brière in five volumes from 1909 to 1913 was an abridged version of Wagner's work. According to the Preface to the first volume (1909), it is a selective translation, which focuses on the topics relevant to the French reader. The "Preface to the French edition" of the third volume (1912) stated that the book on public credit was absent from the original German version of *Finanzwissenschaft*. The volume was a translation of the section on public credit in Schönberg's *Handbuch*. See Meyer (1968).

13 Rui Barbosa's marked volume of the *Traité* was the second one, published in 1909 which comprised "Théorie de l'imposition, théorie des taxes et théorie générale des impôts." The text by Ricca Salerno quoted by Rui Barbosa was: *L'imposta sull reditto*.

14 The original title in Portuguese is "O papel e a baixa do câmbio."

15 The original title was "Bancos emissores – o projeto official."

16 The quotation made by Rui Barbosa is Bismarck's.

17 See also Gremaud (1997, p. 111).

18 This institution, "Escola Livre de Sociologia e Política" in Portuguese, was founded in 1933 by entrepreneurs and intellectuals of São Paulo in order to offer undergraduate courses with an emphasis on applied social sciences and a theoretical influence from North-American sociology. See Limongi (1989).

19 Eugênio Gudin (1886–1986) was a very influential economist in Brazil, committed to a liberal political agenda.

20 The selective reading of List's arguments by industrialists was highlighted by Fonseca (2000) and Boianovsky (2013) developed the argument further. For the debates on protectionism in Brazil see Luz (1975), Bielschowsky (2000), and Rodrigues (2005).

21 In 1850–1851, Rodbertus wrote his four *Social letters to von Kirchmann* (*Sociale Briefe an von Kirchmann*), in which he exposed his economic theory. The fourth letter was republished in Berlin by Adolph Wagner in 1899, with the name *Das Kapital*. This book was translated into French in 1904 as *Le Capital* and it eventually circulated in Brazil. For Rodbertus's thought see Cole (1957, pp. 58–62); for a Marxist stance on his socialist ideas see Engels (1884).

References

Primary bibliography

Barbosa, Rui. (1891) 1949. *Relatório do Ministro da Fazenda*. Rio de Janeiro: Ministério da Educação.

Barbosa, Rui. 1892. *Finanças e política da Republica – discursos e escriptos*. Rio de Janeiro: Companhia Impressora.

Barbosa, Rui. (1921) 1947. *Queda do império; diário de notícias*. Rio de Janeiro: Ministério da Educação.

Engels, Friedrich. 1884. "Préface à la 1ère édition allemande." In: Marx, Karl. (1847) 1961. *Misère de la philosophie*. Paris: Éditions Sociales.

Janus (pen name for Döllinger). 1869. *Der Papst und das Concil*. Leipzig: Steinacker.

Janus. 1877. *O Papa e o concilio por Janus. A questão religiosa. Versão e introdução de Ruy Barbosa*. Rio de Janeiro: Brown & Evaristo.

Say, Léon. 1891. *Économie sociale*. Exposition Universelle de 1889, Groupe de l'Économie sociale, Rapport Général. Paris: Guillaumin.

Schmoller, Gustav von. 1900 (vol. 1) and 1904 (vol. 2). *Grundriss der Allgemeinen Volkswirtschaftslehre*. Munich and Leipzig: Duncker & Humblot.

Simonsen, Roberto. 1931. "As finanças e a industria." In: Simonsen, Roberto. 1932. *Á margem da profissão*. São Paulo: Ed. São Paulo.

Simonsen, Roberto. 1935. *Aspects of national political economy: address delivered in the Federal Chamber of Deputies on the 11th September 1935*. São Paulo.

Simonsen, Roberto. 1937. *Historia economica do Brasil* (2 volumes). São Paulo: Companhia Editora Nacional.

Simonsen, Roberto. 1945. "O planejamento da economia brasileira – Réplica ao Sr. Eugênio Gudin." In: Simonsen, Roberto; Gudin, Eugênio; Von Doellinger, Carlos. 2010. *A controvérsia do planejamento na economia brasileira*. 3rd edition. Brasília: IPEA.

Wagner, Adolph. (1876) 1909. *Les fondements de l'économie politique*. t. II. Paris: V. Giard & E. Brière.

Wagner, Adolph. (1882) 1889. "Der Credit und das Bankwesen." In: Schönberg, Gustav (ed.). *Handbuch der politischen Ökonomie*. 3. Auflage. Tübingen: Laupp. (Band 1: "Volkswirtschaftslehre").

Wagner, Adolph. 1891. "Marshall's *Principles of economics*." In: *Quarterly Journal of Economics*, v. 5.

Wagner, Adolph. 1909 (vol. 1 and 2), 1912 (vol. 3), and 1913 (vol. 4 and 5). *Traité de la science des finances*. Paris: V. Giard & E. Brière.

Secondary bibliography

Anderson, Perry. (1974) 2013. *Lineages of the absolutist state*. London: Verso.

Bielschowsky, Ricardo. 2000. *Pensamento econômico brasileiro: o ciclo econômico do desenvolvimentismo*. Rio de Janeiro: Contraponto.

Boianovsky, Mauro. 2013. "Friedrich List and the economic fate of tropical countries." In: *History of Political Economy*, v. 45, n. 4.

Bruzzi Curi, Luiz Felipe; Saes, Alexandre Macchione. 2015. "Cuestionando las ortodoxias: Roberto Simonsen y Wladimir Woytinsky en el ambiente intelectual del período de entreguerras." In: *Investigaciones de Historia Economica*, v. 11, n. 3.

Burkhardt, Johannes. 1991. "Wirtschaft." In: Brunner, Otto; Conze, Werner; Koselleck, Reinhart. (eds.). *Geschichtliche Grundbegriffe*. Stuttgart: Klett-Cotta.

Cardoso, José Luís. 2009. "The international diffusion of economic thought." In: Samuels, W. J.; Biddle, J. E.; Davis, J. B. (eds.). *A companion to the history of economic thought*. Malden, MA: Blackwell.

Cole, D. H. 1957. *Historia del pensamiento socialista*. México: Fondo de Cultura Económica.

Costa, Emília Viotti da. 1977. *Da monaraquia à república: momentos decisivos*. Sâo Paulo: Grijalbo.

Cunha, Alexandre Mendes. 2013. "Johann Heinrich Gottlob von Justi (1717–1771) e o pensamento econômico cameralista." In: *41º Encontro Nacional de Economia*. ANPEC: Foz do Iguaçu, online.

Cunha, Alexandre Mendes; Cardoso, José Luís. 2012. "Enlightened reforms and economic discourse in the Portuguese-Brazilian Empire (1750–1808)." In: *History of Political Economy*, v. 44, n. 4.

Dorfman, Joseph. 1955. "The role of the German Historical School in American economic thought." In: *The American Economic Review*, v. 45, n. 2.

Fonseca, Pedro C. D. 2000. "As Origens e as Vertentes do Pensamento cepalino." In: *Revista Brasileira de Economia*, v. 54, n. 3, 333–358.

Fonseca, Pedro C. D.; Mollo, Maria de Lourdes. 2012. "Metalistas x papelistas: origens teóricas e antecedentes do debate entre monetaristas e desenvolvimentistas." In: *Nova Economia*, v. 22, n. 2. Belo Horizonte.

Franco, Gustavo. 1990. "A Primeira Década Republicana." In: Abreu, Marcelo de Paiva (ed.). *Ordem do progresso; cem anos de política econômica republicana 1889–1989*. Rio de Janeiro: Elsevier.

Gremaud, Amaury Patrick. 1997. *Das controvérsias teóricas à política econômica: pensamento econômico e economia Brasileira no segundo império e na primeira república (1840–1930)*. São Paulo: FEA/USP.

Hagemann, Harald. 2001. "The Verein für Sozialpolitik from its foundation until World War I." In: Augello, M.; Guidi, M. (eds.). *The spread of political economy and the Professionalisation of economists: economic societies in Europe, America and Japan in the nineteenth century*. London and New York: Routledge.

Hagemann, Harald; Rösch, Matthias. 2012. "Economic textbooks in the German language area." In: Augello, M.; Guidi, M. (eds.). *The economic reader: textbooks, manuals and the dissemination of the economic sciences during the nineteenth and early twentieth century*. London and New York: Routledge.

Koselleck, Reinhard. 1979. *Vergangene Zukunft: zur Semantik geschichtlicher Zeiten*. Frankfurt am Main: Suhrkamp.

Lima, Danilo Barolo Martins de. 2013. "A conformação dos grupos de interesse no debate sobre o Tratado de Comércio Brasil-Estados Unidos (1935)." In: *História econômica & História de empresas*, v. 16, n. 2.

Limongi, Fernando. 1989. "A Escola Livre de Sociologia e Polítca em São Paulo." In: Miceli, Sérgio (ed.). *História das ciências sociais no Brasil*. São Paulo: Vértice/ IDESP.

Love, Joseph. 1996. *Crafting the third world: theorizing underdevelopment in Rumania and Brazil*. Stanford: Stanford University Press.

Luz, Nícia Vilela. 1975. *A luta pela industrialização do Brasil: 1808–1930*. 2nd edition. São Paulo: Alfa-Ômega.

Meyer, Gerhard. 1968. "Wagner, Adolf." In: *International Encyclopedia of the Social Sciences*, online.

Richter, Melvin. 1990. "Reconstructing the history of political languages: Pocock, Skinner, and the Geschichtliche Grundbegriffe." In: *History and theory*, v. 29, n. 1.

Rodrigues, Carlos Henrique Lopes. 2005. *A questão do protecionismo no debate entre Roberto Simonsen e Eugênio Gudin*. Campinas: Unicamp.

Schumpeter, Joseph A. 1954. *History of economic analysis*. New York: Oxford University Press.

Tribe, Keith. 1988. *Governing economy: the reformation of German economic discourse 1750–1840*. Cambridge: Cambridge University Press.

Triner, Gail; Wandschneider, Kirsten. 2005. "The Baring Crisis and the Brazilian Encilhamento, 1889–1891: an early example of contagion among emerging capital markets." In: *Financial History Review*, v. 12, n. 2.

Vianna Filho, Luís. (1941) 1987. *A vida de Rui Barbosa*. 11th edition. Rio de Janeiro: Nova Fronteira.

Yanagisawa, Osamu. 2001. "The impact of German economic thought on Japanese economists before World War II." In: Shionoya, Yiuichi. *The German historical school: the historical and ethical approach to economics*. London: Routledge.

Part IV

Doing political economy in Latin America

10 An outline of the economic thinking of Joaquim José Rodrigues Torres and the economic policy of the Brazilian Empire (1848–58)

Thiago Fontelas Rosado Gambi

Introduction

The time frame examined by important studies concerning Brazilian economic thinking usually only considers the time period after the twentieth century, starting from the 1930s.[1] Therefore, before actually entering the main topic of this chapter, it is necessary to minimally justify the study of Brazil's economic ideas from the nineteenth century. We would like to propose that the study of the nineteenth century may be relevant to understand, generally speaking, the formation of economic thinking on the periphery of capitalism and, more specifically, its influence on the economic policies effectively adopted during the Brazilian Empire. In this sense, we agree with Beauclair (2001), who criticizes economists who disregard the nineteenth century as a relevant period in the history of Brazilian economic thought.

Brazilian thinkers have not generally been praised for their contributions to economic thought. However, researchers have underlined their originality in adapting the general principles of classical political economy and the foreign monetary and banking debates to fit the native experience. Leaving aside the standpoint of 'original' economic theory, usually emanating from the center, it would be more appropriate to focus on a concrete and adapted thought, resulting from the clash of ideas assimilated from abroad with the domestic reality of an agricultural, commercial and slave economy. The combination of advanced 'central' ideas with the conditions prevailing in the periphery may have produced in Brazil, and in other peripheral countries, an economic thought born from late capitalism, and based on original adaptations (Cardoso, 1989, 1997, 2001, 2009; Hugon, 1994; Gremaud, 1997).

Politicians such as Joaquim José Rodrigues Torres, the Viscount of Itaboraí, elaborated their economic ideas through such original adaptations, bearing in mind the economic policies that could soften the contradictions that moved the commercial and slave-based economy of the Brazilian Empire. The purpose of this article is to analyze the economic ideas of Rodrigues Torres between 1848 and 1858, a period that begins with his rise to the post of finance minister, following the liberal period experienced under Bernardo de Souza Franco as Head of the Treasury, and ends with his return to the presidency of *Banco do Brasil* (Bank of Brazil).

This is an interesting time to evaluate his economic ideas, since Rodrigues Torres' activities can then be observed both as a minister and outside the ministry. His economic ideas, discussed in this chapter, were taken from his parliamentary speeches, the ministry of finance reports and the minutes of the State Council's treasury sessions. The first section of this chapter provides a brief political biography of Rodrigues Torres. The second section traces an outline of his economic ideas and discusses the adaptation of foreign economic theories to the Brazilian context. In the third section, we specifically study the matter of the issuing banks, in order to evaluate the consistency between Rodrigues Torres' ideas and the economic policy implemented in mid-nineteenth-century Brazil. In the concluding remarks, we examine the coherence of Rodrigues Torres' economic ideas.

Joaquim José Rodrigues Torres, Viscount of Itaboraí (1848–58): a brief political biography

Usually when we propose to study the ideas of a thinker, the first path we take is to the library. We look for the works that materialize and perpetuate the ideas of the author who we want to study. That is what most historians of economic ideas do, as they usually deal with thinkers who exposed their ideas in books. Rodrigues Torres, however, did not write a single book. For that reason, he cannot be considered an author in the field of economic thinking, although that does not mean he did not have economic ideas that, in one way or another, influenced the economic policy of the Brazilian Empire, and thus the historical path of the country. If the conservatives,[2] the so-called '*saquaremas*,' were for a time the guides of the Brazilian Empire (Mattos, 1990), Rodrigues Torres was their exponent on the crucial field of political economy.

However, since Rodrigues Torres did not leave us any books through which to study his ideas, a different source must be used: the archives. His ideas were materialized and perpetuated in documents written throughout his political career, especially in his interventions in the legislative assembly as a representative and, later on, as a senator of the Brazilian Empire.

At first, it may sound strange that a work on the history of economic thought dealt so specifically with a character that left no books, nor became famous for his economic ideas. In doing so, it seems our purpose would be to study and comment on the ideas of an obscure economist, something O'Brien (2000) would call a 'lucky dip.' The case is made even worse when we consider that Rodrigues Torres was not an economist by education, and that we are dealing with economic ideas produced in the periphery of the nineteenth-century capitalism, in the heart of a monarchic regime and an agrarian, slave-based economy.

Undoubtedly, some historians of economic thought would consider Rodrigues Torres as a 'lucky dip.' However, he was one of the brightest politicians of the Empire, especially when it came to economic issues. Calógeras (1960, p. 75), for example, considered him "one of the most eminent financiers" of the Empire. More recently, Peláez and Suzigan (1981, p. 73) qualified him as "the most important [monetary] policy technician of the Brazilian monarchy." His expertise on economic issues was recognized even by his opponents (Sáez, 2013, p. 124), despite his austere style and a small speech impairment.

According to Baron Smith de Vasconcellos, by the end of his political career, Rodrigues Torres had gone through ten ministerial terms, which indicates his public prominence. In the 1830s, he took on the ministries of Navy and War during a regency period that was turbulent both politically and militarily. In 1832, he temporarily took on the Ministry of Finance. But Rodrigues Torres' political appointments were not restricted to ministries. He was a representative for the province of Rio de Janeiro from 1834 to 1844, and its first president between 1834 and 1836.

In 1837, he moved from the liberal to the conservative party, following the footsteps of Bernardo Pereira de Vasconcellos, who had made the same move a year before. He became one of the party's main leaders and part of the so-called 'Saquarema Trinity,' together with Eusébio de Queirós and Paulino José Soares de Souza, the Viscount of Uruguai. If Eusébio was the leading figure in the field of law, and Uruguai was an authority in administration and diplomacy, Rodrigues Torres led the charges in the economic area.

However, despite the fact that he later became Pedro II's trusted financier (Nabuco, 1997, p. 761), economic issues were not his strong suit from the very beginning. According to Macedo, Rodrigues Torres only got in deeper touch with economic issues right before becoming Minister of Finance for the second time, in the 1840s. In the words of Alberto de Faria (1933), he became a financial expert through a *droit de conquête*.

While in the conservative party, he took on the ministries of Navy, War, Empire and Finance, becoming the Chief of Staff on two occasions, in 1852 and 1868. In the Ministry of Finance, he served the longest term of all imperial ministers. Chosen by the Emperor, he became a Senator in 1844 and member of the State Council in 1853. During his tenure in the Council, he could be considered as the main representative of agricultural interests, and one of the ideologues of slavery (Escosteguy Filho, 2010). Unlike other council members, who claimed 'Senator' as a profession, Rodrigues Torres declared himself a 'landowner,' because, in fact, he owned real estate in the regions of Itaboraí and Saquarema (Martins, 2005).

In 1854, he received the title of Viscount of Itaboraí. Already a viscount, he served twice as the president of *Banco do Brasil* (Bank of Brazil), which was conceived and created by Rodrigues Torres himself. He was a General Inspector for the court's primary and secondary instruction programs, and the Vice-President, between 1856 and 1858, of the Brazilian Statistics Society (*Sociedade Estatística do Brasil*) – whose purpose was, in addition to "collecting, organizing, and publishing" statistics for the Empire, to promote the teaching of political economy in Brazil (Macedo, 1876; Vasconcellos and Smith de Vasconcellos, 1918; Sisson, 1999; Martins, 2005). Hence, Rodrigues Torres has enough credentials for his ideas to be at least evaluated as a possible research subject within nineteenth-century Brazilian economic thought.

Rodrigues Torres' political relevance amplified the influence of his economic ideas. Even if not materialized in books, they were carved in the economic policy implemented by the imperial government during the mid-nineteenth century. He played a key role in the economic debates held at the time, and his interventions illustrate how foreign economic ideas, especially regarding money and banking, were received in the country. Therefore, when one takes into account the relevant historical context, it should become clear that the study of Rodrigues Torres' thought is far from a 'lucky dip.'

Adaptation of foreign economic ideas and economic policy: an outline of Rodrigues Torres' economic thought

Despite his education in mathematics, in 1832 Rodrigues Torres provisionally took on the Ministry of Finance. However, as said before, he only got in deeper touch with economic matters after 1840 (Macedo, 1876). In the face both of his personal knowledge and political position, "Itaboraí's financial authority was usually respected" (Calógeras, 1960, p. 114). In fact, in 1848 Rodrigues Torres rose to the Ministry of Finance, and in 1854, in the words of Hélio Viana (1968, p. 132), the Viscount of Itaboraí's "prudent financial ideas" ruled the country.

Rodrigues Torres, therefore, also figures in more contemporary works on the economic policies of the Brazilian Empire, and analyzing the way such works depict him can help better define the outlines of his economic ideas. With the exception of Normano (1939), who wrongfully describes him as a "credit propagandist," Rodrigues Torres is presented as a supporter of *metalismo*[3] and currency stability (Cavalcanti, 1893), or at most as an eclectic in financial matters, as described by Peláez and Suzigan (1981). The latter description may be due to a certain underlying ambiguity in his discourse regarding the need to balance his economic policy between the dual goals of a stable currency and the supply of credit to trade and farming.

During the period in which Rodrigues Torres headed the Ministry of Finance and was a key leader in the conservative party, the economic debate laid emphasis on monetary and financial matters, leading Joaquim Nabuco (1997) to coin the expression "financial cabinets." In fact, the Brazilian government faced these issues since the extinction of the first Bank of Brazil in 1829, as reflected in the monetary reforms of 1833 – designed to heal the imperial currency, 'contaminated' by copper coins – and 1846 – legally establishing the parity of the *mil-réis* against gold.

It is easy to see that the ideas of Rodrigues Torres were influenced by the economic thought produced at the vanguard of capitalism, more specifically by the British debate between the monetary and banking schools. This controversy was disseminated throughout Brazil, and to judge from the discussions held in the parliament, it was assimilated by the politicians charged with dealing with the Empire's economic concerns. The economic theories defended by each school were known to Brazilian politicians, and very often harshly criticized. However, there was no simple transposition of ideas in play.

It was one thing to discuss the centrality or plurality of issue in an industrializing nation such as Britain, another very distinct to do so with respect to an essentially agrarian society. It was one thing to debate convertibility or inconvertibility in an economy based on manufactures and wage labor, another to inquire into the same topic in a commercial and slave-based economy. Despite the prevalence of monetary theories designed in Europe, the gold standard in particular, it was well known that adjustments had to be made to these theories before they could fit into the Brazilian economic reality.

Rodrigues Torres' economic ideas followed the path of the British monetary school. One of his main concerns was maintaining the value of the currency, either for doctrinal reasons, since he accepted the quantity theory of money, or for political reasons, given the need to ensure a stable currency in the Empire. His ideas were closely related to matters of currency and credit. He defended granting the monopoly of issue to a large banking institution, which could be public or private, but always supervised by the government, given the public aspect of the enterprise. Its public nature would be revealed by the consequences of a rise in the monetary supply to the economy as a whole. Convertibility to metal was a requirement. At first, Rodrigues Torres advocated the currency should be backed exclusively by gold, but he was forced to concede to the reality of the Brazilian economy and also admit, in practice, convertibility in treasury notes issued by the government.

However, this was not simply a passive absorption of foreign ideas, since it was necessary to adapt them to the national reality before they could become feasible economic policies. Such a process of adaptation can be seen, for instance, in concessions made to the *metalista* orthodoxy upon the creation of the second Bank of Brazil, in 1853. Between 1852 and 1853, the government ran a budget surplus, the trade deficit was reduced, and the exchange rate fluctuated above 27d. parity, indicating that the time to create a national bank of issue was arriving. However, the positive fiscal results were not followed by a reduction of treasury notes in circulation, a condition established by Rodrigues Torres for the creation of the bank. On the contrary, the increase in the proportion of coins in circulation signaled, according to the minister, the need for a greater volume of paper money to accommodate the growth of transactions (Brasil, 1853b). When faced with the choice between holding back economic growth in order to control monetary circulation, and allowing for an economic expansion in spite of such circulation, a *metalista* would go for the first option. Rodrigues Torres, however, was not strictly committed to the *metalista* ideal, which did not seem to fit the Brazilian reality, and therefore required adapting.

The project for the new Bank of Brazil offered yet another instance of the same process at work. The bank's issue should be backed by metal or paper money i.e., banknotes could be exchanged for either metal or inconvertible treasury notes. Therefore, the maintenance of the 27d. parity established in 1846 did not mean that the circulating medium was necessarily backed by metal at all times. In practice, the gold standard did not become fully effective, although it was clearly implicit in the spirit of the law, as conceived by Rodrigues Torres, that the exchange in paper money presupposed that banknotes were issued against gold. Not requiring the full convertibility of the currency amounted to a concession to local economic reality.

These two examples illustrate the bending of *metalista* doctrine, and how it was adapted to the possibilities of the Brazilian economy at the time. As noted by Saes (1986, p. 28), European monetary thought did come to Brazil, "but it was already processed in a way that reflected the particular problems of the Brazilian economy." Rodrigues Torres was aware that, in many cases, foreign experience did not serve as a model for Brazil (Brasil, 1870), an agrarian, commercial and slave-based economy often beset by metal shortages. In the minister's perspective, when it came to monetary matters, it was not possible to apply the European and North American experiences to Brazil, since the adequate amount of circulating money depended on the economic conditions of each country.

It is true that the contents of the statements found in the minutes for the State Council treasury sessions may not be attributed exclusively to Rodrigues Torres, as they were signed by all council members. Nevertheless, the ideas recorded in these documents from 1853 onwards, when he entered the board, may be largely attributed to him, for a number of reasons: first, due to his great influence on economic matters; second, because he was usually the rapporteur for the proceedings; and third, because diverging opinions were recorded in the minutes. If the conclusion was not unanimous, the losing vote would necessarily be reported separately, and one could thus identify his ideas in case of disagreement with other members of the session. Considering, then, that the opinions of the State Council express, to some extent, the thoughts of Rodrigues Torres, it is worth highlighting a passage emphasizing the specific character of the national economy:

> Wrong, however, would be the Statesman who could be satisfied with the mere abstract or theoretical knowledge of the principles of the economic or administrative science … *Just like the needs, the laws that rule the individuals in different times of their existence are not the same; as also the needs and laws that rule the nations in different times of their politics and industrial existence cannot be the same* [emphasis added].
>
> (Brasil, 1870, p. 397)

The minutes of the treasury sessions also contain an interesting excerpt from a discussion at the high council about a customs project, in which the Viscount of Jequitinhonha cites John Ramsay McCulloch to support his position, while Rodrigues Torres defended the project using arguments, in the words of the Viscount of Maranguape (one of the present), "mainly extracted from the specialty of our circumstances" (Brasil, 1870, p. 437), a slave-based mercantile economy without industries. In short, the Brazilian reality demanded that Rodrigues Torres adapted his economic ideas to the prevailing conditions, so that his economic policies would become feasible.

Based on the quantity theory of money, Rodrigues Torres argued that the amount of currency in circulation should be such that it would maintain its stable value, for that was what the "masters of economic sciences" demonstrated (Brasil, 1870, p. 268). Therefore, the stability of the exchange rate was one of his greatest concerns. The conservative party was aligned, above all, with the interests of Rio de Janeiro's coffee producers, while Rodrigues Torres himself was married to the daughter of one such farmer. These theoretical and political allegiances were both reflected in his economic policy, more concerned with the foreign sector to which the imperial economy was inextricably linked. He considered the stability of the currency and exchange rates a requirement for increasing the national wealth. In the 1849 Ministry of Finance report, he pointed out the problems of currency and exchange rate instability, and argued that the government should use all available resources to stabilize such values, including, if the time was right, the creation of a bank that could control the supply of currency throughout the Empire – an idea that would become reality in 1853 with the creation of the second Bank of Brazil.

In the passage transcribed below, he refers to the maintenance of the parity set by the 1846 law as a solemn commitment between the state and the country. Its defense was thus imperative, and even more so for Rodrigues Torres, who considered the law one of the most reasonable acts passed by the Brazilian legislature. He wrote:

> It is therefore the most rigorous duty of Power, who is responsible for looking after the interests of society, to employ all the means that are available to give stability to the currency; and this is of utter urgency because, approving the Law of September 11th, 1846, the Legislative solemnly contracted this imperative duty with the country. This law that had so many detractors, and still does, is to my understanding one of the most judicious acts of Brazilian Legislature.
>
> (Brasil, 1850c, p. 35)

The following year, Rodrigues Torres demonstrated to the House of Representatives his concern with the depreciation of the exchange rate. According to his diagnosis, the exchange rate instability indicated that the country did not have a "financial system based on solid grounds," and that was restricting industrial and commercial development. The "solid grounds" referred to were stable currency and exchange rates.

Such concerns appear in a statement of the State Council treasury session from March 1858 (Brasil, 1870, p. 258). We have mentioned that the authorship of these statements cannot be exclusively attributed to Rodrigues Torres; however, they reflect his economic ideas as well as his political position, as made especially clear in this statement. Inquiring about the causes of the low exchange rate to London, the treasury session explicitly stated that the failure to exchange Bank of Brazil's notes against gold was the root cause of the currency depreciation, and that this was connected, in its turn, to the excessive expansion of its operations – i.e., the issue of bank notes over and above the needs of the economy – and to the reduction of interest rates in a scenario that already forecasted a low exchange rate.

The relationship between increased money supply and a lower exchange rate established in the statement is evident, and the criticism of the economic policy carried out by Souza Franco, the current finance minister, is also noticeable. The open criticism of the Bank of Brazil's imprudence was, in fact, an indirect criticism of Souza Franco's economic ideas. The disasters then threatening the country, according to Rodrigues Torres, were related to the 'disastrous' effects of an increased issue: the depreciation of the exchange rate and, above all, the inflation that would make consumer goods more expensive, and thus increase poverty.

Initially, then, there was no concession on the convertibility into metal. The currency should be either metallic or completely backed by metal. Rodrigues Torres defended the strength of the currency and the safety it brought to business:

> It is not unknown, Mr. President [of the House of Representatives], that some theoretical economists, among which let me mention the name of Ricardo, understand that the most perfect currency is the paper; but I ask the House to note that these economists speak of realizable paper, paper with solid guarantees, not the paper money we have. Moreover, while it is inconvenient to move capital from productive employment to be used as a circulation tool, it is also beyond doubt that the peace and security of trade deals require that this instrument have real and intrinsic value.
>
> (Brasil, 1850b, p. 93)

In this case, the metal supply should be proportional to the volume of transactions so that there would be enough money to effect them. However, this was an illusion in the Brazilian context, where scarcity of metal was the norm.

Following the line of Rodrigues Torres, the Brazilian government invariably tried to ensure the convertibility of its bonds into metal – most of the time unsuccessfully, as shown by the experiences of the first Bank of

Brazil and of the 1833 reform, although the latter contributed to improving the state of the currency at the beginning of the regency period. The 1846 reform broke the monetary standard again and established a new parity for the *mil-réis* against the British currency, in order to make the Brazilian currency convertible into gold, and thus ensure the stability of prices and exchange rates.

However, if full convertibility was implemented, the shortage of metal would lead to insufficient currency, and possibly paralyze transactions. The choice that presented itself was whether to curtail transactions or to keep the metallic backing of the currency. As previously mentioned, the theoretically adequate option for a *metalista* would be the first one. The *metalistas* in the Brazilian Empire, however, found an alternative to keep business flowing, even if this could somehow compromise the value of the currency. This was adopted so extensively that, when defending the proposed creation of the Bank of Brazil, Rodrigues Torres indicated two – apparently contradictory – goals for the institution: to help the government improve the currency, and to promote credit and national wealth.

In the House of Representatives, Rodrigues Torres defended his proposal by saying that his main purpose was not to improve the currency, but to "offer development and credit expansion, and by means of this, to help commercial and industrial operations" (Brasil, 1853a, p. 259). However, he continued, "as the improvement of the currency is, in my view, a public need ... I understand that it is also appropriate to call the concourse of the institution that we intend to create in aid of this improvement." As shown above, he thought that stability of the currency was a prerequisite for development and credit expansion. Therefore, the bank he idealized would first be concerned with currency, and only then with credit. The harsh criticism directed against the aforementioned reduction in the Bank of Brazil discount rate between January and February, 1858, in the context of the crisis begun the previous year, was an example of that order of priority.

According to the monetary principle, the money supply was connected to inflation and, consequently, to the exchange rates. As the exchange rates were determined by the amount of money in circulation, they were the variable that would signal the need for adjusting the money supply. If that amount was higher than the volume of transactions, the exchange rate would fall and signal an excessive issue, requiring the government to soak up the excess of currency. However, the consequences for commerce of such interventions were frequently considered in governmental decisions.

Furthermore, in the 1849 report, Rodrigues Torres wrote the section "Means to protect the industry," where he stands up against the unlimited freedom of trade and industry, and advocates incentives and protection for domestic industries that could more efficiently produce goods that were currently imported. However, he also made clear that these incentives had to be limited and cautious, in order not to generate too much of a cost and sacrifice to agriculture. The protection of domestic manufactures should be aligned with agricultural interests (Brasil, 1850c). Rodrigues Torres frequently mentioned the importance of credit, trade and manufacturing for the country, but he was, above all, a defender of the currency and of agricultural and trade interests.

This apparent ambiguity was also present in speeches in which, pressured by credit demands, he denied being an enemy of paper money. As it happens, Rodrigues Torres always referred to convertible paper money. Like Ricardo, he had nothing against the use of this instrument of circulation *per se*, although he was fiercely opposed to the issue of inconvertible paper money, such as the one circulating in Brazil at that time (Sáez, 2013).

Banks and monopoly of issue: the consistency of Rodrigues Torres' economic ideas and his economic policy

Coherently, in banking matters, Rodrigues Torres was contrary to plurality of issue, as he believed this would compromise control of the money supply. He reaffirmed this theory in the early 1850s, when the two main banks of Rio de Janeiro, the *Banco Commercial* (Commercial Bank) and Mauá's Bank of Brazil, began competing through increased issues and reductions in their discount rates. As the notes of the issuing banks circulated like currency, there was a downward pressure on the value of the *mil-réis*, thus threatening the legal parity. Moments of credit expansion, moreover, were usually followed by financial contractions and crises.

It is worth stating that Rodrigues Torres only objected to issuing banks, not deposit and discount banks, since in his view the latter would not be capable of creating money. Generally, *metalista*s did not regard deposit and discount banks as currency creators. This is demonstrated by the authorization, given by minister Torres Homem in 1859, for the creation of many such banks in a moment when the reduction of the currency volume was a stated purpose. In the March 8th session, in response to Souza Franco, Rodrigues Torres said he did not doubt that

> to some extent banks facilitate the movement of trade operations; but if they are somehow facilitated by the banks, they could be considerably harmed, giving them dangerous excitement, enabling the start of operations, both of the industry and of trade, that have no probability of being successful. I don't mean by that that I am an enemy of the banks, I repeat that I am not; but under the country's circumstances, when our currency is paper money, I can't defend issuing banks, for the only advantage I see in such institutions, the only thing they are good for, which can't be supplied by discount banks, is the replacement of part of a costly instrument of circulation with a less costly one; but if our circulation instrument is not a metal, if it's not expensive, what benefit can we get from issuing banks?
>
> (Brasil, 1850b, p. 100)

If someone read only these words from the minister, they would never imagine that three years later he would become the mentor behind the creation of an issuing bank, precisely with the purpose of replacing the government's paper money with its bonds. As was well observed by Pacheco (1979), although he criticized banks of issue at the time, Rodrigues Torres had left the door open for their creation.

However, although he did not declare himself against banks, Rodrigues Torres showed at least some suspicion about their actions when describing the process that took such an institution from a boom to a crash. In fact, his point was indeed the increase in the currency value. There was nothing specifically against banks in his discourse, but much regarding the moment in which they were created. As he said during the sessions of April 25th and 26th:

> [On April 25] It has been said and repeated more than once, that I plan to mess with the development of public credit, because I oppose the organization of banks. Gentlemen, I believe I have on another occasion announced to this House an opinion that I am convinced of, and it is that banks are not organized when the government or the legislative body wants them.
>
> (Brasil, 1850a, p. 485)

> [The next day] Gentlemen, if in our country there were other currencies that were not paper money; if we had a money supply consisting of precious metals, I would be the first to say to the honorable representative [Souza Franco]: – let's see to it that banks are created.
>
> (Brasil, 1850a, p. 498)

In a similar vein, the excerpt from the Ministry of Finance report of 1849 in which Rodrigues Torres summarized his position regarding banks, and their use for assisting the government to rescue paper money, gained notoriety:

> I am not against banking institutions: I acknowledge the great services they can offer to Brazil: I hope that banks of deposit and discount will be created in all our provinces, that they will unite the economies and dormant capitals, and lend them under interesting conditions to whom may employ them usefully: they will contribute to fertilize the industry and enrich the country; *but I cannot conceive for now what use could issuing banks have, nor how it could be possible to combine their existence with the reduction of the currency mass, the way it is essential to stabilize its value* [emphasis added].
>
> (Brasil, 1850c, p. 36)

Besides pointing out the problems that banks of issue could occasion for the stability of the currency, Rodrigues Torres also drew attention to the fact that the Brazilian Empire did not gather the minimum necessary conditions for the operation of such banks by the private sector. According to him,

> So that banks can be organized the existence of available capitals that apply to this kind of trade is necessary; individuals who wish to compete against these capitals are necessary; desire from the capitalists is necessary, and only when this desire exists, when individuals show they have means to create such credit establishments, a reasonable government must consent in their creation and give them the necessary and fundamental privileges, without which they cannot be organized.
>
> (Brasil, 1850b, p. 99)

The above speech, given by Rodrigues Torres in March 1850, sounds quite strange. It is true that the abolition of traffic, which would release the capitals promised by the minister to be applied in different activities, including the banking sector, would only become a reality in September. The 1840s, however, witnessed the creation of commercial banks in many Brazilian provinces, indicating interest on the part of the fund holders. One must bear in mind, though, that speeches are often proffered by actors who are directly involved in the issues at stake, and can thus manipulate information in order to suit their interests. Before analyzing the records, therefore, it is important to identify who authored the speech, to what purposes, and with which audience in mind. One cannot separate this excerpt of a speech made by Rodrigues Torres, as Minister of Finance, to an assembly of representatives, from his wider perspective on banks. Reality, it seems, was sacrificed in the name of his beliefs. Souza Franco went straight to the point when he said that

> all the fear of the minister in relation to banks is not because they can break or they don't aid the industry, *but because their role might mess up with the government's role: here lies all the matter.* Not to belittle the role of the government, let credit die everywhere, do not gather dead capitals, dispersed, unemployed, nor try to favor the industry! [emphasis added]
>
> (Brasil, 1850b, p. 106)

It is true that, although Rodrigues Torres did not agree with the immediate creation of issuing banks, he did envision a time when they could become useful for the country. That moment would arrive when their issue could be backed by precious metals. The crucial problem for the minister was his fear that bank bonds would start circulating as paper money – which in fact happened, contributing to depreciate the *mil-réis*. In his view, by concurring to depreciate the currency, the competition between bank notes and government notes would do harm to the national economy. It is worth noting once again that his concern was first and foremost with the stability of the currency, and only second with the supply of credit. In 1852, given the large volume of loans stimulated by the low prevailing interest rates, the two largest Brazilian banks were forced to raise interest rates in order to contain the euphoria, leading to a small liquidity crisis. Amidst a legislature entirely dominated by the conservative party, Rodrigues Torres chastised the seemingly boundless competition between the two Rio de Janeiro credit institutions when addressing representatives on July 20th, 1853:

> The competition between the banks has been the main cause of almost all commercial crises ... *it is the rivalry between the banks that powerfully contributes to produce the breakdown, the ruin, the despair of thousands of families, when the day comes when this phantasmagoria disappears* [emphasis added].
>
> (Brasil, 1853a, p. 260)

As State Councilor, moreover, Rodrigues Torres subscribed to opinions contrary to the creation of new banks, claiming that competition between banks of issue encouraged irresponsible and immoral administration, thus generating negative effects on the national currency and the economy as a whole (Brasil, 1870, p. 279). A good example is the statement from the September 30th, 1858 treasury session, regarding the establishment of the *Banco do Ceará* (Bank of Ceará), which illustrates the consistency of the Rodrigues Torres' economic ideas over time, and also highlights one of his main theoretical influences: John Ramsay McCulloch, a supporter of the English currency school (Brasil, 1870, p. 268).[4]

In this statement, the session did not recommend that the new bank assume issuing functions, and it also opposed the proposal of using government bonds or railroad shares (with interest payments guaranteed by the government) as a collateral for eventual issues. The reason offered was based on *metalista* principles and a criticism of 'free-banking.' It is worth stressing that the reference to McCulloch indicates the session was up-to-date with foreign ideas on financial affairs, since the relevant text – *Treatise on Metallic and Paper Money and Banks* – was written for the Encyclopedia Britannica in 1858, the same year when the session statement was compiled. It also stated that the proposal of issuing privileges for the Bank of Ceará was an 'imitation' of the free-banking model born in the United States – a system that had proved ineffective at ensuring convertibility, as evidenced by recent events in that country. This indicates that the treasury session was also up-to-date with international financial practices.

It was in the context of bank competition and expansion of issue that the then Finance Minister envisioned the centralization of issue in a new Bank of Brazil, resulting from the merger of the two aforementioned institutions. The excerpt from the report in which the minister announced the time was ripe for the creation of a bank of issue in Brazil has also become famous: "It appears the time has come to create an issuing bank, which assists the government not only in the rescue of paper money, but also in the progressive increase in credit and national wealth" (Brasil, 1853b, p. 14). In this endeavor, he could count on Dom Pedro II's support. In his speech at the opening of the legislative session in 1853, the emperor, probably influenced by Rodrigues Torres, stressed the time had come to create a bank that could provide for commercial and industrial demands. According to the emperor, given the circumstances prevailing in the country, such a bank would be "an indispensable element of our economic organization" (Brasil, 1889, p. 476).

However, despite the reasons presented by the minister and the emperor's support, one must not forget that the favorable state of the public finances and exchange rates coincided with the expansion of issue by the Rio banks, and the consequent increase in competition between them. This competition, which became manifest the year when the finance minister's proposal was elaborated, was interpreted by the government as harmful to the national economy, thus requiring corrective measures.

Some legislators, such as Senator Manuel de Assis Mascarenhas, believed it was precisely the competition between the Rio banks that was bringing about the favorable conditions, and that this was the true motivation behind Rodrigues Torres' project. During the Senate session in which the project was discussed, Mascarenhas argued that the scenario had not changed sufficiently to convince the minister that it was now time to create a bank of issue. Instead, he stated that "one of the reasons for this project is the desire of the Minister, who is opposed to the country's banks, with no exception, to ruin them" (Brasil, 1853c, p. 152). The proposal to create a bank with a monopoly of issue fitted this context very well, mixing the political practice of Rodrigues Torres, as a Saquarema leader, and his economic ideas, as an advocate of *metalista* principles – even if adapted to the national reality.

The second Bank of Brazil, established in 1853, became operational the following year, and acted towards minimally guaranteeing the convertibility principle idealized by its mentor until the complete abolition of the monopoly of issue in the Brazilian Empire, in 1866. In his work with the State Council during this period, Rodrigues Torres continuously opposed requests for new issues filed by several institutions, such as savings banks. In addition, he supported an initiative for the provincial emission of currency – approved in 1850, but only effective later – through which the Bank of Brazil would branch savings banks. He defended this strategy by not approving the creation of new local banks in places such as Bahia, Rio Grande do Sul and São Paulo (Brasil, 1870, pp. 260, 318, 446).

The new Bank of Brazil struggled, of course, to achieve the desired convertibility, and lived through moments of ambiguity, shifting gears between a stable currency and the supply of credit. The expansions in the bank's issue to meet the demand for credit, including when Rodrigues Torres was its president, gave concrete expression to this ambiguity. This is perhaps why Normano (1939) called Rodrigues Torres "the famous credit propagandist" – after all it was him, as chairman of the bank, who requested that the issue limit be maintained at three times the volume of available funds, and in fact increased issues during the bank's early years.

Was there a contradiction between these policies and Rodrigues Torres' economic ideas? Nabuco (1997, p. 310), for instance, argued that one should not call the defenders of monopoly austere, since their representatives authorized the enlargement of the Bank of Brazil's issues. In subsequent parliamentary speeches, the liberal Souza Franco made similar charges. However, several clues suggest this was not the case.

First, as clearly evidenced in the Paraná ministerial report,[5] the bank did not ask for an enlarged issue limit in order to its operations, but to rather to guard itself against the possibility of exceeding the limit given the frailty of its reserve fund. Second, the demands and difficulties associated with a slave-based market economy challenged the implementation of conservative economic policy, given the dual pressure arising from, on one hand, the demand for credit by merchants and farmers, on the other, the difficulty of securing metals from abroad to back the monetary issue. The Brazilian economic reality ensured that the currency would have to yield to credit, and the challenge became to meet the needs of the economy without compromising the convertibility and stability of the currency. Despite the relaxation thus imposed, the government was fighting to maintain its policy – so much so that, in the fifth article of the decree granting the bank's request, the government reserved the right to, when necessary, "reestablish all or some of the definitions of the statute of the Bank of Brazil and of its branches, changed by this decree." The same cautionary measure had also been adopted in the previous decree, which increased for the first time the issue limit from two to three times the bank's available funds. Finally, even at a high cost for itself, the bank continued to partially back its currency issue with reserves of precious metals.

The concessions made by the government to the bank were seen by Calógeras (1960, p. 106) as "acts of weakness." The government, however, needed to help the bank in its attempts to balance the ideal of a fully metallic circulation with the reality of a credit-starved slave-based market economy. This was how, despite recurrent concessions, the conservative economic policy conceived by Rodrigues Torres kept trying to impose itself over the reality of the Brazilian economy. It is undeniable that issues increased during that period, but so did the reserve funds too, guaranteeing that total issues always remained within the legal limit established by the bank's statutes. The maintenance, between April 1854 and November 1857, of the exchange parity set by the 1846 law also reveals the government's commitment to this economic policy (Villela, 1999, p. 228).

In short, the demands from the bank and the government's response show that there was an arena where the bank fought to push the limits of its actions, whilst the government, in turn, tried to defend its economic policy. This was a conflict that caused tensions, but never a rift between the government and the bank. Another conflict took place between the ideal of the Saquarema economic policy as designed by Rodrigues Torres – based on the gold standard, though adapted to the national circumstances – and the reality of the Brazilian slave-based market economy, which demanded an ever increasing volume of currency to honor transactions, speculative or not, in a context of expansion and euphoria. By the beginning of 1857, the government, with Rodrigues Torres either in the Treasury or in the Bank of Brazil, gave way to reality in some moments, but held strongly to an orientation that privileged the centralized control of the money supply and a stable currency. Rodrigues Torres did not neglect credit, but this never came at the expense of monetary stability in the implementation of his economic policy. His ambiguities can be largely attributed to the adjustments required by the peculiarities of the Brazilian economy.

Concluding remarks

Rodrigues Torres is an important character in the political history of the Brazilian Empire, and his ideas deserve attention in the reconstruction of the history of nineteenth-century Brazilian economic thought, not only due to his work as Minister of Finance and President of the Bank of Brazil, but also because of the theoretical background he brought to the conduct of economic policy. As a representative of landed interests, Rodrigues Torres crafted policies inspired by the British monetary school, but adapted to the Brazilian reality, and consistent with the centralizing political project advanced by the conservative party, which aimed at preserving order in a slave-based market economy.

It is clear from the documents mentioned that, between 1848 and 1858, his main concerns were matters of currency and credit. This bears testimony to the practical bent of his economic ideas, grounded in Brazilian economy reality and focused on the development and implementation of economic policy. The adaptation of the principles of the British currency school to fit Brazilian reality put in evidence the consistency of his ideas on these topics, which became a crucial source of guidance for Brazilian economic policy during the mid-nineteenth century – in particular between 1853 and 1866, when the Bank of Brazil held the monopoly of currency issues in the Empire.

The economic policy of this period was based on Rodrigues Torres' 'adapted' brand of *metalismo*, striving to strike a delicate balance between the stability of the currency and the supply of credit to trade and agriculture. In short, Rodrigues Torres' economic thought and policy encapsulated the contradiction inherent in the ideal of a fully convertible currency when applied to the commercial and slave-based economic reality of the Brazilian Empire.

Notes

1 That is the case of the classic books by Mantega (1985) and by Bielschowsky (2004), and also of the studies done by Szmrecsányi and Coelho (2007) and Ganem (2011).
2 There were two parties in Brazil at that time: Conservative and Liberal.
3 *Metalismo* and *metalistas*, according to Villela (1999, p. 42), "would come to designate advocates of convertibility and, more generally, of hard money, i.e., monetary restraint and a high exchange. Conversely, their ideological foes, *papelistas*, sided

with expansionist monetary policies, a slipping exchange and, at times, fiduciary paper."

4 McCulloch is linked to the British currency school in particular due to his support for the Peel Act, in 1844. However, his association with the school must be made cautiously. Cf. O'Brien (2003, p. 188).

5 Honório Hermeto Carneiro Leão, Marquis of Paraná, was the minister of finance between 1853 and 1856.

References

Documents

Brasil. Câmara dos Deputados. 1850a. *Anais da Câmara*, Sessions on April 25 and 26.

1850b. *Anais da Câmara*, Session on March 8.

Brasil. Ministério da Fazenda. 1850c. *Proposta e relatorio apresentados á Assembléa Geral Legislativa na Primeira Sessão da Oitava Legislatura do anno de 1849 pelo Ministro e Secretario d'Estado dos Negocios da Fazenda Joaquim José Rodrigues Torres*, Rio de Janeiro, Typ. Nacional.

Brasil. Câmara dos Deputados. 1853a. *Anais da Câmara*, Session on June 20.

Brasil. Ministério da Fazenda. 1853b. *Proposta e relatorio apresentados á Assembléa Geral Legislativa na Primeira Sessão da Nona Legislatura do anno de 1852 pelo Ministro e Secretario d'Estado dos Negocios da Fazenda Joaquim José Rodrigues Torres*, Rio de Janeiro, Typ. Nacional.

Brasil. Senado. 1853c. *Anais do Senado*, Session on May 28.

Brasil. Conselho de Estado. 1870. *Imperiais resoluções do Conselho de Estado na Secção de Fazenda (1850–55)*, Rio de Janeiro, Typ. Nacional, v.3.

Brasil. 1889. *Fallas do Throno desde o anno de 1823 até o anno de 1889*, Rio de Janeiro, Imprensa Nacional.

Bibliography

Alencar, J. 1866. *Ao visconde de Itaborahy. Carta de Erasmo sobre a crise financeira*, Rio de Janeiro, Typ. de Pinheiro e Cia.

Almodovar, A.; Cardoso, J. L. 1998. *A History of Portuguese Economic Thought*, London, Routledge.

Beauclair, G. M. O. 2001. *A construção inacabada: a economia brasileira (1820–1860)*, Rio de Janeiro, Vício de leitura.

Bielschowsky, R. 2004. *Pensamento Econômico Brasileiro: o ciclo ideológico do desenvolvimentismo*, Rio de Janeiro, Contraponto.

Caldeira, J. 1995. *Mauá: empresário do império*, São Paulo, Cia das Letras.

Calógeras, J. P. 1960. *A política monetária do Brasil*, São Paulo, Cia Editora Nacional.

Cardoso, J. L. 1989. *O pensamento econômico em Portugal nos finais do século XVIII (1780–1808)*, Lisboa, Editorial Estampa.

Cardoso, J. L. 1997. *Pensar a economia em Portugal. Digressões históricas*, Lisboa, Difel.

Cardoso, J. L. 2001. *História do pensamento econômico português. Temas e problemas*, Lisboa, Livros Horizonte.

Cardoso, J. L. 2009. Reflexões periféricas sobre a difusão internacional do pensamento econômico. *Nova Economia*, vol. 19, n. 2, 251–265.

Cavalcanti, A. 1893. *O meio circulante nacional (1836–1866)*, Rio de Janeiro, Imprensa Nacional.

Escosteguy Filho, J. C. 2010. *Tráfico de escravos e direção saquarema no senado do império do Brasil*, Dissertação de Mestrado, Universidade Federal Fluminense.

Faria, A. de. 1933. *Mauá*, São Paulo, Cia. Ed. Nacional.

Ganem, A. 2011. Reflexões sobre a história do pensamento econômico brasileiro. *Análise Econômica*, vol. 29, n. 56, 131–152.

Gremaud, A. P. 1997. *Das controvérsias teóricas à política econômica*. Tese de doutorado. Universidade de São Paulo.

Hugon, P. 1994. A Economia Política no Brasil. In: Azevedo, F. (org.), *As Ciências no Brasil*, Rio de Janeiro, Editora UFRJ, v. 2.

Macedo, J. M. 1876, *Anno Biographico Brazileiro*, Rio de Janeiro, Tipographia e Lithographia do Imperial Instituto Artístico, v. 3.

Mantega, G. 1985. *A economia política brasileira*, São Paulo/Petrópolis, Vozes.

Martins, M. F. V. 2005. *A velha arte de governar: um estudo sobre política e elites a partir do Conselho de Estado (1842–1899)*, Tese de doutorado, Universidade Federal do Rio de Janeiro.

Mattos, I. R. 1990. *Tempo Saquarema. A Formação do Estado Imperial*, São Paulo, Hucitec.

Nabuco, J. 1997. *Um estadista do império*, Rio de Janeiro, Topbooks.

Normano, J. F. 1939. *Evolução Econômica do Brasil*, São Paulo, Cia Editora Nacional.

O'Brien, D. P. 2000. History of economic thought as an intellectual discipline. In: Murphy, A.; Endergast, R. (Eds.), *Contributions to the History of Economic Thought: Essays in Honour of R. D. C. Black*, London and New York, Routledge.

O'Brien, D. P. 2003. *McCulloch: A Study in Classical Economics*, Oxon, New York, Routledge.

Pacheco, C. 1979. *História do Banco do Brasil*, Brasília, Banco do Brasil.

Peláez, C. M.; Suzigan, W. 1981. *História monetária do Brasil. Análise da política, do comportamento e das instituições monetárias*, Brasília, UNB.

Saes, F. A. M. 1986. *Crédito e bancos no desenvolvimento da economia paulista 1850–1930*, São Paulo, IPE/USP.

Sáez, H. 2013. *O tonel das Danaides: um estudo sobre o debate do meio circulante no Brasil entre os anos de 1850 a 1866 nas principais instâncias decisórias*, Tese de doutorado, Universidade de São Paulo.

Sisson, S. A. 1999. *Galeria dos brasileiros ilustres*, Brasília, Senado Federal, v. 1.

Szmrecsányi, T.; Coelho, F. S. (orgs.). 2007. *Ensaios de História do Pensamento Econômico no Brasil Contemporâneo*, São Paulo, Atlas.

Vasconcellos, B.; Smith de Vasconcellos, B. 1918. *Archivo nobiliarchico brasileiro*, Lausanne, Imprimerie La Concorde.

Viana, H. 1968. *Vultos do império*, São Paulo, Cia Editora Nacional.

Villela, A. A. 1999. *The political economy of money and banking in Imperial Brazil 1850–1870*, Tese de doutorado, London School of Economics and Political Science.

11 From free banking to paper money

Ideas behind the building of a National Bank in Colombia at the end of the nineteenth century

Andrés Álvarez

1 Introduction

Very little has been studied about Colombian economic thought during the nineteenth century, and even less about the monetary ideas developed in the country at the time. In one of the few attempts to make a history of economic ideas in Colombia, A. Espinosa (1942) asserts that, with respect to monetary thought, "there are only poor ideas on the subject. The subject could be covered only giving two or three quotations, and a couple of comments..." (p. 132). This perception can be partly explained by the confusion between the slow development of the Colombian monetary system, on one hand, and the production of related ideas on the other. Monetary history is, of course, strongly related to monetary thought. However, it is precisely because monetary institutions took a long time to be developed in Colombia that monetary thinking and debates on the subject were richer than usually acknowledged. This is what this chapter will try to show.

Scholars usually summarize the monetary architecture of Colombia during the nineteenth century using two distinct images: the chaotic and anemic circulation of sound money since the beginning of the republican period (1820s), followed by high inflation related with the adoption of paper money issued by a monopolist National Bank by the turn of the twentieth century. Against this background, rather sad and uninteresting at first glance, one might think the ideas of politicians and intellectuals who participated in these events did not reach significant analytical heights. The disorder of monetary institutions should rhyme with poor knowledge and lack of development of monetary ideas. This sentiment was also present among contemporary authors. An important witness and prominent author of the period thus summarized it: "How I would try to write a good treatise on banks if there are no banks or statistics, or changes, or trade?" (Galindo 2014 [1869]: 10).[1]

However, the reality of monetary debates in the country during the nineteenth century was different. Colombian intellectuals and politicians from all sides had a more acute awareness and deeper knowledge of the problems than usually acknowledged. Their concern with learning about the most developed and desirable forms of organization for the national monetary system resulted in fertile ideas, even if the facts were not as auspicious.

The intellectual debates concerning the institutional design of the financial and monetary system during the first part of the nineteenth century were closely related to public debt and finance. The piteous condition of the State budget after the independence and successive civil wars led to a vicious circle of weak government power and a weak capacity to raise taxes and credit. As a consequence, even the public debt accounting system was disastrous. This chapter will show how such concerns with public management were the main reason to consider a national bank as the solution for both monetary and public financial problems.

The monetary history of Colombia during its first century as an independent republic begins with the first Constitution in 1821. Since that period, Colombian political and intellectual elites tried to build up a coherent monetary and financial system according to a modern democratic and capitalist utopia. However, it was not until the early years of the twentieth century, by the end of the main civil war of the period (1902), that a modern central bank was finally considered as a possible solution. In the meantime, a key period in Colombian financial history concerned the adoption of a free-banking system between 1865 and 1885. The free-banking experience was wrecked by the creation of a National Bank with a monopoly power of note issue. Our main interest in this chapter is to show how this radical transformation from a decentralized and market-oriented system towards a centralized and purely public-oriented system made an imprint in Colombia's monetary thought. This chapter shall not deal with free-banking ideas directly, but only with the influence of this experience on the establishment of the first National Bank and a paper money regime (1885–1898).

The desire to create a modern banking system was a chimera accompanying the construction of republican institutions just after independence in the 1820s. The first constitutional attempts already contained a reference to the creation of a National Bank of issue. However, every private and public attempt to build a stable financial and monetary system failed until well into the second half of the first century of Colombian republican history. The nineteenth century ended with a resounding institutional collapse in the longest civil war of the republican era, the so-called 'Thousand Days' War' (1899–1902). The political turmoil and economic weakness of the State provided the best reason, and the best excuse, to use paper money as the main mechanism to finance war.

A period of disastrous management of paper money, brought about by a government who initially promised to get rid of the evils of paper money, immediately followed the bad experience of the National Bank. This episode left a deep imprint on monetary ideas during the twentieth century, as the Colombian political elite came to consider the National Bank and the very idea of paper money as intellectual impostures. As a result, few scholars were interested in the ideas underlying them, nor in the debates between partisans of a national bank and the liberal thinkers promoting free banking. Nonetheless, these debates are crucial to understand the choice made in 1923 of creating a modern central bank inspired by the young Federal Reserve experience in the US. Beyond the paramount influence of Edwin Kemmerer as a money doctor, and the example provided by international experience, Colombians decided to adopt a central bank with a very conservative monetary supply rule based on gold standard prescriptions and independent governance. This resulted in a fair compromise between quasi-fiduciary means of payments (central bank bills) and the aversion to paper money. This chapter thus aims to show how, during the first century of its independent political existence, Colombia struggled to create an economically and politically sound monetary system, and how both good and bad experiments are crucial to understand the modern monetary ideas and institutions prevailing in the country.

In order to reconstruct the intellectual debate on money, we will refer to the published opinions of the main characters involved in the political and intellectual debates of the period. During the second half of the nineteenth century there appeared a few newspapers specializing in economic topics, and several articles about economic institutions were published in the more generalist press. Additionally, the discussions of economic issues and the arenas of debate were extended to schools of Law. The *Chair of Political Economy* was adopted both in elite secondary schools, and in institutions of higher education. The teaching of political economy included the study of the monetary system, banks and the fundamentals of the rate of interest concept. In several recently found notebooks[2] and syllabi from the second half of the nineteenth century, one can see that at least 7 out of the 16 chapters composing a one-year course in political economy were related to money, credit and banking.

Colombian policy makers and intellectual elites were well aware of the modern forms of organization of monetary and banking systems in the more developed countries, including the ideas there produced. This is a typical feature of Latin American intellectuals and policy makers: having a good knowledge of the most advanced intellectual and institutional developments of the moment, but feeling incapable to transform their own countries into developed nations.

As an example of such 'tropical money doctors,' we can mention the works of Anibal Galindo, already quoted above. Galindo is considered one of the best Colombian economists from the second half of the nineteenth century. A politician, lawyer and minister of Finances and Treasury, in 1865 he was commissioned by the liberal government to go to Europe in order to study the French and English monetary and financial systems. He spent more than a year visiting the Bank of England in an 'ethnographical stage,' and published an interesting treatise on the institutional and economical principles of the English system in comparison to its continental (mainly French) counterpart (Galindo 2014 [1869]). The Colombian monetary experiences from this period, and particularly the country's institutional backwardness, were felt more harshly by those, such as Galindo, who not only understood the importance of a sound monetary system, but also had an intellectual understanding of its underpinnings.

The debate on monetary ideas extended beyond the political arena. The lack of an organized tax system limited Colombian governments because of a constant sentiment of imminent State bankruptcy. The situation led thinkers of different ideologies to focus on international experiences and ideas in order to find a way to solve the problem that could supplant internal disputes. Different interpretations were developed in the search for means to adopt and adapt concepts such as credit, private banks, bank notes, interest rates and securities' discount, among others. A consensus on the need to establish a sound monetary and financial system sometimes even blurred the political divides that separated political parties during the early nineteenth century. Most of the authors, from 1821 to 1865, proposed to create a National Bank following the model of the Bank of England or the Bank of France. However, civil wars and trial-and-error methods of institutional building led to the establishment of a free-banking system between 1865 and 1885.[3] This experience proved to be a turning point in Colombian monetary thinking. The adoption of a system based on a free market organization of fiduciary means of payment brought more theoretical elements into an already politicized debate. Among the issues at stake, the relationship between public finance and monetary policy occupied the center of the debate.

The monetary problem was never completely separated from fiscal issues and, in general, proposals for modernization and the promotion of economic growth. The majority of the proposals and discussions one can find throughout the nineteenth century on the creation of banks or the organization of the monetary system were associated with problems of public debt and the abuses of informal and profiteering moneylenders who dominated the precarious financial intermediation, imposing high interest rates.

Besides the difficulties surrounding the consolidation of a powerful and stable State, another important feature of the historical context was frequently mentioned in intellectual debates: the scarcity of means of payments, meaning the scarcity of metallic money, the only legal tender at the time. Since its independence from the Spanish crown, Colombia was unable to organize its domestic metallic circulation and to develop stable fiduciary forms of money. In this context, banks were frequently presented as a solution to both problems, public finance and circulation, as suppliers of non-metallic means of payment, on one hand, and credit to private and public agents on the other.

This chapter will explore the resulting intellectual production in late nineteenth-century Colombia, in order to demonstrate the value of the long-time neglected debate on banks and money during this period. We aim to show how these ideas mobilized theoretical concepts and first-hand experience about the most developed forms of money and banks (England, France, US), trying to adapt them to the Colombian precarious situation. Three main issues underlie the analysis: the pragmatic inquiry on the nature of bank notes as money; the public nature of money, contrasted to the necessity of allowing for its independent or even private management; and finally, the promise of a National Bank as a way to organize public finance and the administration of the State.

As mentioned at the beginning of this introduction, the monetary thought of nineteenth-century Colombia has been ignored or disdained by historians of economic thought. A collective effort to take past economic ideas seriously has been recently published (Álvarez and Correa 2016). Half of this volume is devoted to banking and monetary ideas. Although Acosta's (2016) contribution bears close relation to the third section of this chapter, it focuses only on the National Bank before 1880, without explicitly exploring the changes in the intellectual debate produced during the free-banking period (1865–1885). In the same volume I published a chapter on the free-banking experience, centered on the role of French liberalism as a source of political ideas for the supporters of private money issue (Álvarez 2016b). The present chapter focuses mainly on the debates developed during the transition from one system to another – that is, from free banking to the national bank.

The documents discussed in sections 2 and 3 below were recently collected and published through a joint effort of the *Universidad de los Andes* and the *Banco de la República* (Colombian Central Bank). They are now all available online (www.banrep.gov.co/es/libro-ideas-monetarias-siglo-xix). When a document belonging to this compilation is quoted, the original date is given between brackets. Another important source of documents used in this chapter is the compilation of economic texts by Rafael Núñez organized by R. Junguito (2014), also available online (www.banrep.gov.co/es/libro-escritos-economicos-nunez).

Three other sections and some concluding remarks follow this introduction. Section 2 deals with the historical context and the evolution of the Colombian monetary system during the period 1820–1870, and the way this changed perceptions on the necessity of establishing a National Bank. Section 3 presents the ideas developed at that moment on the relationship between the State and the National Bank. Section 4 is devoted to discussing the ideas of a crucial political and intellectual figure, Rafael Núñez. The special treatment is fully justified, as Núñez was responsible for the establishment of the first institution with a public monopoly of note issues, the National Bank created in 1880. Finally, a last section with final remarks concludes the chapter.

2 The ideal of a National Bank, and the practice of free banking

The sluggish path in the development of a banking system in Colombia, compared to other Latin American countries, accentuated the concerns of local intellectuals. Debates on political and economic ideas during the first half-century of the republican era often referred to the difficulty of organizing the means of payment and the 'public credit.' Overall, the discussion on the need for a banking system did not distinguish between these two problems. This finds expression, in particular, in two goals that oriented many of the proposals: to reduce the shortage of means of payment, and at the same time support public debt.

Contrary to what is commonly stated by historians of the period, the prevailing consensus was not on the adoption of a free-banking system (see Echeverri 1994). On the contrary, the idea of a monopoly power over money was dominant between the 1820s and 1860s. The debate focused mainly on the relationship between a bank of issue and the government. Public ownership, and the possibility of the bank being 'captured' by government forces, were the issues at stake.[4]

2.1   Learning about the virtues of non-metallic means of payment

Proposals for a national bank of issue had been on the table since the first constitutional attempts of the new republic (1823).[5] Two main issues were addressed in the first official project to create a National Bank. The first and most urgent concern was to bring order to the management of public debt. It was thus proposed that public debt bonds were turned into shares of the new National Bank, and that a department of Public Debt would be created, in charge of collecting taxes, as a means of supplying the bank's money stock. The second goal was to complement, and even replace metallic circulation with instruments issued by the Bank – not only through convertible notes, but also using the bank as a clearing-house for merchants to obtain liquidity in their local and foreign trades.

This project did not come to fruition, and all along the period 1830–1865, almost every new government tried to establish a National Bank. The main difficulty encountered was convincing investors to accept putting their capital in the enterprise. Another obstacle also gradually emerged: the civil wars that pitted regional powers against a centralized government.[6] The most important turning point in this sequence of conflicts was the victory, in 1862, of the radical faction of the Liberal Party over the conservatives. The former championed deep liberal economic reforms and a federalist political organization, whereas the latter tried to preserve a centralized national government. The increasing economic and political importance of local elites finally led to the constitution of a federal system with a strongly liberal constitution in 1863, putting an end to almost half a century of confrontations between centralists and federalists. In this meantime, central government and the national public finances had been constantly in disarray since the independence wars. The new political unit that emerged in 1863, the United States of Colombia, made it virtually impossible to organize a centralized National Bank. This prevented, in particular, the adoption of a nationwide monopoly of bank notes, thus making it even less attractive for private capitalists to invest in such an enterprise (Álvarez 2016b; Correa 2016).

This led to the emergence of a federalist solution promoted by the Radical Party: the creation of regional private banks of issue. This system sought to regulate the means of payment through market competition among private banks. The ideal of a banking system functioning under free competition among both banks and regions, and only disciplined by the convertibility of notes into the legal metallic currency, was an ideal appealing to some liberals (Álvarez 2016a). The era of free banking, covering the period 1865–1885, was to become the origin of a modern banking system, and at the same time a source of new facts that fueled the debate on the appropriate forms of monetary organization.

The first private equity bank was only established until 1864: the Bank of London, Mexico and South America. Although the institution quickly went bankrupt, the terms of the contract between this private bank and the Colombian State became *de facto* a charter for the establishment of a free-banking system since 1865. However, less than three decades later, a deep political change brought an end to the free-banking experiment. A conservative alliance forged by the so-called Regeneration Party created a *National Bank* funded with government capital in 1880. In 1885, the notes issued by this institution were imposed as the only legal circulating currency, and a few years later they were officially declared legal-tender unconvertible paper money. Along the spectrum that separated these two radically opposed institutional arrangements, ideas were less radical.[7]

The ideas sustaining the free-banking system were initially very incomplete. A group of young radical liberals, highly influenced by French liberalism,[8] clearly supported a system of purely private and convertible bank notes as the best alternative to organize a non-centralized monetary system. They advocated a free-competitive market system as the most effective way to discipline monetary supply. In this chapter we shall not deal specifically with these notions.[9] Our main interest here is to understand the ideas behind the creation of a National Bank, and how they evolved along the nineteenth century. The free-banking period, however, is of great importance as a historical background. The experience with such a monetary architecture nourished ideas and contributed to changing some of the arguments for or against a National Bank and paper money.

As mentioned above, the free-banking era emerged almost as a non-intentional solution to the absence of a banking system and the scarcity of metallic money. After several failed attempts to establish a National Bank supported by local capitalists, calling on foreign investors was perceived as a possible solution. However, the Bank of London, México and South America remained open for only a few months before shutting down its operations due to poor risk management, occasioned by inexperience and ignorance of the local market. This first experiment with a private bank issuing fiduciary money backed by metallic reserves appeared as an alternative to remedy the scarcity of metallic means of payment, thus showing that a public National Bank was not the only solution available. However, its concrete implementation required a process of trial and error.

Before 1865, proposals defending the creation of a National Bank stressed the necessity to complement metallic circulation. Even if Colombia, in particular its Western regions (Antioquia and Cauca), were rich in gold and silver, high international prices for these precious metals guaranteed that they were mostly used as export goods, rather than being minted. Internal monetary circulation thus consisted in poor quality money, according to a particular form of Gresham's law.[10] This situation pushed local policy makers and intellectuals to advocate for bank money.

2.2 *Bank notes: more than a representative of real money*

An interesting feature of the arguments in favor of bank notes (or non-metallic money in general) before the 1870s in Colombia was the salient absence of a discussion of their 'monetary nature.' An important debate among French liberals regarded whether bank notes were actual money, or merely its representative signs. This would become an important intellectual influence on young Radical Liberals, who would later champion the free-banking system between the 1870s and 1900s. Nevertheless, older intellectuals writing between the 1830s and 1860s barely mentioned this issue. This illustrates how, before French-liberal economic ideas became dominant in Colombia, intellectuals had a more empirical, eclectic and pragmatic view about the solution to monetary problems.

Two emblematic writings are worth mentioning in this connection. The first is the work (already mentioned above) of William Wills (1805–1875), an eccentric English businessman and pamphleteer very active in Colombian economic life during the 1850s. Wills wrote several documents promoting the creation of bank money.[11] In his *Proposal for a National Bank in the Nueva Granada* (*Proposal* henceforth) (Wills 2014 [1854]: 172), he explained the merits of bank notes as substitutes for gold and silver:

> In all civilized countries it has already been largely replaced the use of paper money to gold and silver, because that is the best substitute for these metals that has been discovered so far. In those countries, the largest payments are made almost exclusively in bonds or notes, payable on demand, or short-term. As these notes, or drafts, passed from hand to hand as well as money costs, risks and time are saved. So a reputable bank does not even need its cash advances, because their notes have the same value as gold and silver coins …

The main argument related to the capacity of fiat money to substitute metallic currency, thus liberating precious metals to be used in international trade. Wills, as well as Anibal Galindo (2014 [1869]), aimed to demonstrate the superiority of fiat-money circulation using the Bank of England as the best example of this ideal system. Galindo frequently recalled the success of this institution in managing the circulation of unconvertible paper money for long periods, without the expected abuses of an excessive supply.

Galindo explained the virtues of the 1844 act leading to the separation of the issue and discount departments in the Bank of England. Interestingly enough, the main reason to support this organization, in his view, was the capacity to create confidence, not to control supply. Galindo went beyond the English experience and proposed an adaptation of the Bank of England to Colombia, allowing more flexibility in the rules of the issue department due to the lack of an active commerce in the country. He considered that a National Bank should initially constitute an "engine for the commerce," since the scarcity of means of payments and credit put Colombian economic reality distant from the advanced stage of England.

A National Bank adapted from the Bank of England example had to provide liquidity to the economy, first of all by transforming public and private debts into the more reliable debt of a solid bank. Metallic reserves were a secondary source of leverage for fiduciary circulation, since the scarcity of metallic money should not be made worse by a complete removal of all metallic coins from circulation. Galindo thus proposed to manage the National Bank of Colombia as a discount bank with a capital composed of the entire floating public debt – clearly independent from government spending, but fulfilling a key role in the organization of public finance.

Bank notes were thus considered as a complement for metallic money – neither its substitute, nor its mere representative. Fiat money could function as money as long as correct bank management secured confidence in it. Contrary to these early views, the first experiment of this nature was a disaster. There is a consensus in Colombian scholarship regarding the failures of the experience with a National Bank and paper money between 1880 and 1890. The picture found in recent literature on the National Bank is very hostile, but there is almost no discussion of the reasons and ideas behind its creation. It is time to move beyond prejudices, and try to explore from a different perspective the intellectual perspectives on national banks that existed before the free-banking era.

3   National Bank and public finance

Beyond the debates about the necessity to organize and boost the supply of means of payment, another issue was at stake in the discussions: the organization of public finance. This type of argument can appear unusual to scholars used to study modern monetary debates. However, historians of the Bank of England, Bank of France and the First Bank of the United States know it well: all these institutions were created, at least partially, in order to support government spending or contribute to the management of public debt.

Not only the sustainability of public finance was important, but also a serious management of accounting and the reliability of records were at stake. Colombian intellectuals from the early nineteenth century knew this just as well, and the first idea invoked in order to solve these problems was the creation of a National Bank, following the above-mentioned international examples.

3.1   *Money is a public matter but better managed by privates*

Already in the Cucuta Constitution (1821), it appears clearly stated that a national bank was not a bank like the others. It was considered that a bank of this nature could not be established by any individual, but only by a special agreement among public and private forces. Furthermore, such a bank was considered as part of a larger reform that included determining the name and characteristics of the national currency – a function pertaining to the government. The establishment of a national bank disappeared from constitutional texts after 1830, but the projects presented during the period between 1821 and 1863 preserve this close relationship between money, banking and public administration.

An important example of a National Bank project relating fiscal and monetary problems was José Rafael Revenga's draft act on the establishment of a National Bank (2014 [1826]). In this project, it is clear what the relationship between Bank and government should be. First, the government could participate as one of the bank's shareholders, holding up to 5 of the 25 million pesos proposed as capital. Second, the executive power, under Parliament's approval, would appoint the president and 3 of the 12 bank directors. According to Revenga, this was the only intervention the government would exert in the workings of the bank, considered important in order to strengthen the confidence of shareholders (Ibid.: 10). Third, the Bank would manage public debt and tax collection. In return, the government would grant the Bank a monopoly on the issue of bank notes payable on demand for 21 years.

Revenga aimed essentially at ensuring that the government's creditors joined in as bank shareholders. They could only subscribe shares by paying with government bonds. Foreign private investors, in particular, should have a participation of up to 5 million pesos in the bank's capital in order to bring that debt into the country, and thus reduce the outflow of metallic money. Revenga also proposed a mechanism whereby the bank would be responsible for making the corresponding repayment of national debt payments. The obligation created on behalf of the government by its 5 million contribution to the bank's capital would be paid up to 5 percent of the profits made by the bank. The rest would be used to buy bonds on foreign or domestic debt, at the will of the Executive, the President, the Commission on Credit and the bank directors (art. 21).

Revenga's proposal was thus especially centered on the role of the Bank as an 'instrument of credit' for the government, rather than as a monetary institution. Public and private credit were nonetheless considered as forms of attaining fluidity in the payments system. This was essential for the Colombian economy, due both to the scarcity of metallic means of payments and the backwardness of the internal market at the time. Other early projects, however, were more detailed on the monetary role of the National Bank.

In 1829 (Acosta and Álvarez 2014) Juan Garcia del Rio proposed the idea of a National Bank closer to the government, who could also be its shareholder. First, the Bank would be responsible for the payment of government debts. This would be implemented by establishing a central office "where you take an account of all branches of government revenues and all overhead costs." Second, the bank would facilitate the government obtaining resources, for instance by extending loans backed by public revenues (Ibid.: 194). In both cases Garcia del Rio presented the Bank of England and the English state as an example of how this relationship worked. In addition, he also insisted that this was a win-win situation for both parties involved.

García del Río proposed better institutional governance rather than a purely private ownership. To him, the participation of the State, playing a leading role as both investor and privileged client, was not incompatible with good governance. The bank must play a fundamental role managing public finance and providing liquidity to the State in exchange for the monopoly of bank note issues.

3.2   The liquidity of public debt and good practices in public administration

Beyond this apparent consensus on the relationship between government and the National Bank, there appeared a few opposing liberal voices. A central figure of the Radical Liberal Party, Florentino Gonzalez, moved away from previous authors by proposing to limit government involvement with Bank governance, and thus avoid transforming the Bank into the government's creditor at will (2014 [1847]). The central idea behind this proposal mixed the consolidation of a liberal project for expropriating Catholic Church lands (*'bienes de manos muertas'*) with obtaining revenues to back and pay government debt. It also aimed at a complete transformation in the uses of land. Church land should put in the market for people to buy and sell it freely, and thus transform it into a productive factor. This could allow the consolidation of public debt, and also ensure future revenues for the State not only to fulfill its functions as a provider of public goods, but mainly to extinguish short-term debt.

The main goal of this proposal went beyond the management of public debt. Gonzalez considered the lack of confidence (credit) on the national debt to be the worst evil in the Colombian economy. 'Credit' needed to be restored in the country so that investment from national and foreign capitalists could find a good environment in which to flourish. A National Bank, based on private management, was a necessary condition to achieve this purpose.

Gonzalez believed it was better "to trust private management" rather than public goals. The government would give the bank privileges for 30 years, including to right be the only facility of its kind, and the power to issue notes payable on demand, which would be admitted as hard cash in payment for taxes. In terms of oversight, the government would appoint the governor, which would be recommended by the general meeting, and periodically revise bank records in order to ensure that it fulfilled its obligations (Ibid.: 76, art. 15). The government might also act as a regulatory authority. Gonzalez thus envisaged the bank guided by private interests and protected from legal arbitrariness.

This proposal represented an alternative point of view regarding the relationship between public finance and private banking. It considered that progress in private banking and finance should contribute, directly and indirectly, to overcome the lack of liquidity of public debt. Nevertheless, Gonzalez clearly opposed allowing for an increase in public debt, and proposed instead to aim at a zero public deficit policy. The circulation of public debt bonds might increase if the whole economy and the private industry flourished. The National Bank, for Gonzalez, was an instrument necessary for boosting the private economy, rather than public finance.

In his *Proposal*, William Wills continued on the path started by Gonzalez, and also noted that private interest was the best guide for the national bank (Deas 1996: 206). The fundamental role of government was to monitor, when deemed appropriate, the bank's operations, and to provide the necessary privileges for the bank to work, along with legislation to protect it from defaulting debtors and to allow for quick selling of its property. The government would give the bank, among other privileges, the right to be the only institution of its kind, and the power to issue notes payable at sight that would be accepted as money in payments made to government, as well as having the public revenues deposited with it.

Contrary to Gonzalez's ideal of a zero deficit policy, in Wills' *Proposal* the organization of national credit, the payment and nationalization of part of the debt, and the establishment of a national bank are closely linked. Wills' plan was to organize national credit so that the government could obtain a new loan backed by the income from the monopoly of salt mines, and require that part of this loan be used to buy foreign debt bonds. This ensured that at least part of the foreign debt would be nationalized, as it was also required that 3 of the 4 million pesos constituting the bank's capital were in the form of new debt backed by the salt mines revenue. The purpose was to make the National Bank capable of providing liquidity to public debt, as long as this was made within the limits of a private profitable business. Rather than banished, as was Gonzalez's ideal, government debt was thus limited by private initiative.

Finally, it is worth noticing that these thinkers all agreed on one thing: a National Bank would help solve the problem of the chaotic management of public accounts and tax collection. Simple as they might seem, the government's bookkeeping procedures needed to be improved. A National Bank would bring with it more sophisticated accounting procedures, and the independence of bank officials could contribute towards avoiding corruption on the very management of public accounting data.

The above-mentioned projects illustrate the characteristic relationship between a national bank and the government. Even if there are differences in details, almost all of them proposed banks with close relations to the government (excepting the radical ideas of Gonzalez). In this regard, the government should receive two major benefits: liquidity and the good management of public debt. The increase in liquidity should be obtained in three ways. First, if the government were itself a shareholder, it would be entitled to a profit for its participation. Second, the government could obtain loans and advances on income. And finally, credibility (or 'credit') was boosted by better economic conditions and a developed financial system. Thus, the establishment of a national bank would help address the government's continuing fiscal difficulties, either directly or indirectly.

The last important element behind the ideal of a national bank as a provider of liquidity has to do with good accounting and management practices in public financial affairs. We could even say this was actually the most valuable benefit the government could obtain from its relationship with a national bank. If the national bank was responsible for making government payments, including the national debt, this solved a large problem in public administration. Complaints about the difficulty of administering national revenues in an orderly fashion were a constant in the Proceedings of Finance from this period: the number of staff was inadequate (sometimes more than necessary, sometimes less), the functions of some units were unclear, aggregated accounts required a long and tortuous process, etc. A bank needed to manage its business in the most orderly manner, with responsible accountants, since this reflected heavily on profits. It could thus manage public accounts and debt in the very same way.

This was particularly important in the management of debt, for two reasons. First, because disorder in such matters was costly for the government. There were many debt papers with no centralized control over their repayment, opening the door to all kinds of fraud (Galindo 2014 [1869]: 111). Second, this constituted a firm step forward in the establishment of the 'national credit,' meaning the credibility of Colombia and its government before foreign investors. Even for Wills, who stated that 'national credit' was a prerequisite for the establishment of the National Bank, further good handling of debt would strengthen confidence in the government. More confidence in the government would, in its turn, result in greater ease for obtaining resources and a lower rate of interest, which would also help alleviate fiscal constraints. Moreover, increased confidence also had a positive effect on the value of government debt papers, which circulated at a greater or lesser discount, thus helping to reduce the shortage of cash. Finally, this should foster a good environment for private business.

Authors did not forget that government needed to play an active role in creating and enabling an environment in which the Bank could operate and provide liquidity and order to its business. If the public had no confidence in the Bank or its notes, they would not circulate, and so the benefits accruing to the government would be at risk. Under these circumstances, notes and draw-ings on the government's account would be changed into metallic currency as soon as possible. A bank subject to such constant pressures would quickly find itself in crisis, and instead of being part of the solution would become a new problem. If the government wanted to obtain the benefits the bank could offer, it needed to ensure the public trusted the bank and saw its bills as an additional means of payment, as reliable as coins.

An important step in this direction was securing that notes issued by these banks would be accepted as payment in any transaction with the government, especially for taxes. This created demand for banknotes and increased the likelihood that they would remain in circulation, since this reduced the metal-lic drain on the Bank. The demand created by the government, together with the promise that these notes could be exchanged for metallic coins at any time, were the basis on which the circulation of banknotes would be built. Banknotes would not circulate because the government imposed it, as in the case of forced and decreed course. Rather, fiduciary money was easier to han-dle and could function as a better technology for payments. They would be accepted on the confidence that someone else would also receive them later, and that they could be turned into metallic coins whenever necessary.

Furthermore, these proposals aimed to create a compatibility of incentives for the interaction between the government and the Bank. It should be in the interest of the former to protect the interests of the latter. However, in order to avoid any unwarranted privileged treatment leading to an excessive supply of banknotes, the government should also exercise regulatory functions, in particular to guarantee that convertibility of banknotes was always possible. Both policies were essential for the stability of the system.

Several authors noted how confusing the judicial system was, and how diffi-cult it was to collect from delinquent debtors. This would, of course, generate great difficulties for the bank. If it was not possible to sell securities and man-age the legal treatment of defaulting debtors, the bank could not maintain its liquidity and eventually might not be able to guarantee the convertibility of its notes. The authors discussed clearly understood the mechanisms generat-ing credibility, and their projects contained ideas about the management of the bank's liquidity, such as protecting bank deposits, and granting privileges to implement legal actions against debtors who defaulted on their payments.

There was a consensus among the authors writing between the 1820s and 1860s that the government must be given at least an important role in monitor-ing the bank's operations. Confidence on the bank depended on this, although government supervision was a complex issue. Too much monitoring could be perceived as interference with current bank management. The government should ensure the bank was not behaving irresponsibly, but without directing its operations. The projects, accordingly, insist on bank independence. The ideal bank should be mainly guided by private interest, but it was not easy to harmonize this with the work of government surveillance. In Revenga's project, for instance, it was proposed that some of the members of the bank's board of directors should be appointed by the government as a way to ensure close monitoring.

However, as more liberal ideas appeared, criticism against the idea of public direct influence or close supervision of banks emerged. Some intellectuals considered this was perhaps too large a degree of interference with the bank's business, and the idea was accordingly abandoned. Revenga's was thus the last project in which the government should be responsible for appointing directors and supervising records, and where it had permanent presence in the decision-making process.

The idea of an intrusive supervision by the government was substituted by a more liberal notion of a bank regulated by a chart and legally protected by public powers. A national bank, following the example set by the Bank of England, should be independent and yet close to the State. Private business goals should guide its actions in order to ensure that it becomes a good 'instrument of credit.' Such was the ideal proposed by Galindo (2014 [1869]) in one of the most advanced treatises on the theory of a national bank from that era, based on his first-hand experience of more than three years in the Bank of England.

Galindo's treatise arrived, however, a bit too late. It was published right at the dawn of the free-banking era in Colombia. It was thus mostly overlooked by his contemporaries, and later ignored by historians. This project, however, was one of the most intelligent assessments of the possible adaptation of the Bank of England's institutional architecture into a Colombian National Bank. The treatise was full of pragmatic ideas, rather than deep-rooted theories and utopias. However, theoretical utopias were an important influence for those who would become the champions of free banking, and also for the second wave of advocates for a National Bank, whose main figure was Rafael Núñez. During his young years as a politician, Núñez belonged to the liberal party, but by 1870 he radically changed his views on economic matters. He then became the leader of a coalition of conservatives and nationalists (meaning defenders of centralism against federalists), and subsequently won the 1880 presidential elections against the Radical Party.

4 Rafael Núñez and the natural experiment of a National Bank against free banking

During the electoral round of 1880, Nuñez[12] became the main representative of conservative, catholic and centralist ideas against the liberal, anticlerical and federalist views of the liberal Radical Party. His proposal for a National Bank became reality in 1880. This mixed-capital bank was intended to be a competitor to other purely private banks of issue created during the free-banking era. However, due to private investors failing to buy its shares, the bank became a purely public establishment. In 1885, private banknotes were banished from circulation and the National Bank's notes were declared legal tender. A few months later, inconvertibility was imposed under the pretext of a civil war, and a regime of pure paper money began.

In this final section we will briefly present the ideas advanced by Nuñez that were behind this (failed) experiment with a National Bank. Our goal is not to go into the controversy about how and why he changed his mind so drastically from his early career as a young radical liberal (1850s–1870s), to a later phase as a conservative championing state intervention and the centralization of political and economic power in Bogota. On these matters, we simply follow the thesis formulated by Junguito (2014), who portrays it as a pragmatic political change intellectually motivated by Núñez's experience in the US around the 1870s.

4.1 A National Bank as a political weapon

Núñez's economic thinking was initially nourished by French liberalism. He gradually came to realize, however, that this was a utopian point of view leading the country towards a chaotic federalism, while weakening the central government and allowing the merchants' corporation to capture all economic privileges at the expense of artisans and farmers. As Bergquist (1976) and Bushnell (1993) showed, the political triumph of national conservatism during the two last decades of the nineteenth century in Colombia owes a lot to the monetary debate. Nuñez and his intellectual and political companion M. A. Caro succeeded in convincing artisans and farmers of the evils of free banking as a system controlled by merchants, who monopolized the whole metallic reserves and exported them for their own transactions, lending money only between themselves and thus controlling the means of payment.

Along with this appraisal of the free-banking system, Núñez also added the notion of a discretionary public management of the money supply. His main concern was to oppose a socially oriented credit system against the corporatist (from his point of view) penchant of the private banks of issue. Núñez developed the ideal of a credit and monetary supply based on the 'needs' of society, rather than on private profits. M. A. Caro contributed to this idea by putting it into a catholic wrapping so as to attract a conservative constituency.

Caro proposed to conceive money on the same footing as time, from a scholastic point of view. Money was a form of time, as it represented a promise of future payment. As time could not be a private property since it belonged to God, money consequently belonged to the whole social body. Money was conceived as a promise backed by the whole social fabric, not only by precious metals. This allowed Núñez to propose abandoning the ideal of a metallic standard, and substituting for it the public confidence on government management. However, Caro wanted to go further and suggested the possibility of offering as much money as society needed in order to produce goods. Núñez never went that far, and even if he encouraged a discretionary supply of money, he was well aware of the inflationary risks of an excessive supply.

4.2 Managing paper money and the balance of trade

The economic writings of Rafael Núñez during the 1880s focused on coin shortages, the rise in the exchange rate, and the desirability of making more intensive use of the paper money issued by the National Bank. "The High Price of Change" (1883-Change) is one of the writings that illustrate Núñez's knowledge of mainstream economic theories. He developed the reasons that, in his view, had led to the high price of exchange letters (currency depreciation). He argues that the high price of foreign money (not all prices) had its origins in the fall of exports rather than an excessive money supply, contrary to what private bankers argued. He based this assessment on the fact that major export products such as quinine and coffee had fallen in price in international markets; as a result, there had been a large imbalance between exports and imports. Núñez thus considers that the devaluation of Colombian currency was mostly due to the reduction in the demand for letters of exchange, combined with a growing demand for foreign currencies.

According to Núñez, a real cause was behind the depreciation of the Colombian currency, rather than purely monetary reasons. The National Bank was not responsible for this real commercial imbalance. According to him, a contraction in the international markets for Colombian goods was to blame, while the increased supply from Asian countries contributed to the reduction in commodity prices.

By June 1883, Núñez published a paper on the subject of economic crisis and gold production (1883-Gold), addressing more directly the exodus of metallic coins and the depreciation of Colombian currency. He discussed the depreciation of the metallic content of the currency as a possible solution to the problem. However, he did not support this idea since it did not address the real problem, and even tended to make it worse. His opinion was that currency depreciation, as already mentioned, was due to the price of Colombian exports. He then proposed to develop a productive system that would allow the country to diversify its production and develop agro-industrial sectors. This led him to emphasize the importance of credit as a mechanism for stimulating production, and the important role played by the National Bank in promoting low interest rates. In his reasoning, he completely deviated discussion towards the issue of interest rates, and blamed the evils of the whole economy on private bankers rather than on paper money.

In 1884, when Núñez was elected for a second presidential term, the economic situation was deplorable. He published an article entitled "An Agreement on Trade Crisis" (1884-Trade), where he acknowledged the bad conditions of the economy but insisted the problem had its origins in the trade balance. Now, however, he underscored that exports also had an impact on the fiscal situation, as they impacted the ability to import, thus reflecting in customs and other sources of revenue during a commercial crisis. The conclusion to this argument was that the powers of the National Bank – in particular its power to lend money to the government – need not be limited, but rather enhanced.

4.3   Paper money as the "final solution"

These arguments added to the political turmoil, and the consequent civil war of 1885 finally triggered the decision to declare legal tender and to create a paper money regime based on the National Bank. Núñez already anticipated this decision in a crucial article on the currency crisis entitled "Signs of Time" (1884-Signs), where he recognized the depth of the monetary crisis, stating: "The currency crisis is thus complete." He added that, having no hope for improvement in the current account balance, and given the reduction in the productivity of mines of precious metal, the scarcity of gold and silver was inevitable. To Núñez, the Colombian economic system was walking towards an inevitable failure if a different rule was not adopted for managing the monetary system. Paper money thus became the only solution.

Paradoxically, in the same article he recognized the flaws of paper money when maintained for long periods. To impose inconvertibility was thus a temporary solution, as had also been the case in particular situations in other countries, including England. He then postulated:

> The regime of paper money is, as everyone knows, one with permanent price fluctuations, which makes impossible any precise calculation in industrial operations and is a danger ... If gold and silver have been chosen for the manufacture of the coin, it was precisely because of the relative stability of its intrinsic value. The paper currency is the reverse of that stability and may only occur in hours of despair and may allow fictitious transactions.

The main point of this rather orthodox perspective was to explain that, based on a weak version of the *real-bills doctrine*, the Bank could manage inconvertible money supply during exceptionally difficult periods. Even if paper money was a potentially unstable system, the aggregate results depended on how the National Bank accomplishes the discount of private and public debt. Good management could entertain confidence on public debt.

In a subsequent letter from May 1885, Nuñez again referred to the issue of paper money (1885-Paper Money). This document discussed the role of money in the economy and the advantages and disadvantages associated with paper money. It stated that no one wants money in itself but rather for its services, emphasizing its character as a medium of exchange above that of store of value. The role of money as a medium of exchange, in its turn, was based on confidence. He then argued that distrust in the National Bank was unfounded, and that government revenues backed the national bank notes. He recognized, however, that economic crises could destabilize foreign trade and thus adversely affect the availability of coins, but emphasized, above all, the importance of paper money for the well-functioning of domestic trade. In this regard, he recognized that paper money might face three major risks: inducing excessive emissions, draining the nation's metallic reserves, and lacking an automatic mechanism for the adjustment to commercial fluctuations. Núñez pondered the potential dangers of the absence any natural control of the paper money circulation, especially during periods of booms and busts of foreign trade cycles. This argument shows that his main purpose was not stability or the reduction of economic fluctuations, but rather the availability of means of payment in a transitory situation of metallic scarcity. He finally noted that money supply had to remain within a limit of prudence, justifying this idea through a quotation from Stanley Jevons: "Many examples show that an inconvertible paper money, can preserve their value, if the amount of issue is carefully limited."

In August 1885, Nuñez referred to the necessity of temporarily declaring paper money as legal tender (1885-Legal Tender). As an introduction to the subject, he pointed out: "We are not supporters of legal tender or issuing currency of low quality." However, he added that, given the circumstances of the economy and the war, it was important to check the conditions that had led to the adoption of legal tender elsewhere in the world, thus prompting a tour of such episodes as had taken place in other countries. A historically based argument was thus developed: since other countries had already done it, why not us?

Núñez listed the experiences of other Latin American counties. Brazil adopted legal tender paper money since the eve of its independence. He recognized that in Argentina the system had been a disaster, as highlighted by Jevons himself. However, the case of Chile was not entirely unsuccessful. He went on enumerating good and bad experiences and showed how, in almost every country, civil war was the starting point for the adoption of paper money. In many such cases paper money actually permitted the stabilization of public deficit, and it was only due to subsequent abuses that the systems collapsed.

According to his ideas, the correct way to manage paper money was by transforming it into an instrument to reduce the cost of credit. Nuñez came back to his central proposal: a National Bank was a way of promoting the production of artisans and farmers, and of achieving financial independence for the government. The National Bank was thus conceived as a political weapon – one which, through general economic growth, acted against the merchant corporatism enabled by private banks.

Concluding remarks

This chapter aimed to show how the monetary debates that took place in nineteenth-century Colombia were intellectually rich, in spite of a backward economic situation. It was precisely because of the structural difficulties faced by both policy makers and businessmen that an original, and perhaps eclectic, economic debate flourished in the country. The analysis of economic ideas in such a historical context requires one to understand how contemporary economic theories on money and banking were adapted to a pressing reality.

Economic historians have shown how the Colombian economy was stuck in a Malthusian trap all along the first century of the republican era. The political rupture with the old colonial regime was not immediately followed by the development of a modern economic system. In this regard, the political economic problems involved in the building of monetary institutions were an obstacle that eventually divided the political spectrum and regional powers. Civil wars, the secular weakness of the State, and the insufficient provision of public goods hindered the development of infrastructure, education and a developed financial system. It is thus easy to understand why discussions about the organization of a monetary system were tightly linked with concerns about public finance.

Even if a small group of radical liberals succeeded in implementing a free-banking system around the 1870s, the general consensus since the beginning of the period under analysis converged on the need to establish a National Bank. A free-banking system was not considered as an immediate solution to the problems of public debt management, but it was an adequate answer to the insufficiency of the means of payment. A more general agreement among intellectuals regarded the necessity of complementing metallic monetary circulation with banknotes. Supporters of free banking pointed towards the ideal of a gold-standard metallic money and convertible banknotes. More pragmatic thinkers, on the other hand, embraced proposals for a monopolistic National Bank issuing banknotes backed by public and private debt – a fiat money system.

The bad experience with the National Bank by the end of the nineteenth century introduced a turning point in the early consensus about the virtues of non-metallic money. The abuses and oversupply of paper money amidst political turmoil led towards a new dominant perspective, closer to the ideas adopted by supporters of free banking: money supply required the discipline of metallic circulation. The National Bank was thus considered, at the beginning of the twentieth century, to be the worst idea bequeathed by the nineteenth century. A different approach was needed: Kemmerer's idea of a Central Bank based on a gold standard rule. The *Banco de la Republica* was thus established in 1923 as a system free from the sins of the deceased National Bank. This, however, is another part of the story.

Notes

1 I will use the original year date in square brackets for references to original bibliographical sources from the nineteenth or early twentieth century recently republished or reprinted.
2 See the compilation of three different manuscript notebooks found and edited by Universidad Externado de Colombia (Pérez 2004).

3 See Álvarez (2016b) for a detailed explanation of the historical events behind the creation of the free-banking experience in Colombia.
4 At the beginning of a pamphlet published by William Wills (2014 [1854]) advocating the establishment of a National Bank, he acknowledged the caveats people expressed about such an institution. We will come back later to this proposal and to the way Wills dealt with these issues.
5 See Revenga (2014 [1826]).
6 The federalist ideas promoted by economic and political regional elites were well present since the beginning of the republican era. As López and Kalmanovitz (2016) show, the intellectual hesitation among policy makers and regional political leaders made it difficult to organize a stable national tax system and a liquid market for public debt.
7 For a full history of the Colombian banking system see Sánchez (1994).
8 The main intellectual influence on Colombian liberal thinkers comes from Jean-Gustave Courcelle-Seneuil Works on free banking and his Chilean experience as a money-doctor around the 1850s. See Alvarez (2016a).
9 See Álvarez (2016a) for a detailed study on free-banking ideas in Colombia.
10 See Acuña and Álvarez (2014).
11 For a detailed and fascinating intellectual biography and anthology of Wills' works see Deas (1996).
12 All the references to Nuñez's writings are followed by the year of publication and a keyword from the title. They are all available in Junguito (2014), in chronological sequence.

References

Acosta, J. C. 2016. "Sobre la discusión en torno al establecimiento de un banco nacional en Colombia, 1821–1870," chapter 6, pp. 183–220, in Álvarez and Correa (eds.).

Acosta, J. C. and Álvarez, A. 2014. *Ideas monetarias del siglo XIX en Colombia*, Banco de la República – Bogota, available online (last visited: November 11th 2015): www.banrep.gov.co/es/libro-ideas-monetarias-siglo-xix.

Acuña, K.-V. and Álvarez A. 2014. De La Moneda Metálica al Billete de Banco en Medellín y Bogotá (1871–1885): Complementariedad y Sustitución de Medios de Pago en un régimen de Banca Libre, *Revista Tiempo & Economia*, No. 1. Available at (last visited October 10th 2015): http://ssrn.com/abstract=2585760.

Álvarez, A. 2016a. "Nineteenth century monetary utopias in Latin America: the influence of French liberalism on the Colombian free-banking experiment," chapter 10, pp. 159–172, in García-Molina, M. and Trautwein, H.-M. (eds.) *Peripheral visions of economic development: new frontiers in development economics and the history of economic thought*, Routledge, New York.

Álvarez, A. 2016b. "Banca Libre, federalismo y soberanía monetaria regional en el siglo xix en Colombia," chapter 5, pp. 155–182, in Álvarez and Correa (eds.).

Álvarez, A. and Correa, J. S. (eds.) 2016. *Ideas y políticas económicas en Colombia durante el primer siglo republicano*, Ediciones Uniandes – Editorial CESA, Bogota.

Bergquist, Ch. 1976. The political economy of the Colombian presidential election of 1897, *The Hispanic American Historical Review*, Vol. 56, No. 1, 1–30.

Bushnell, D. 1993. *The making of modern Colombia: a nation in spite of itself*, University of California Press, Berkeley.

Correa, J. S. 2016. "Moneda y nación: la política económica y los debates sobre el Estado 1865–1899," chapter 7, pp. 221–242, in Álvarez and Correa (eds.).

Deas, M. 1996. *Vida y Opiniones de Mr. William Wills*, Banco de la República, Bogota.

Echeverri, L. M. 1994. "Banca Libre: la experiencia colombiana en el siglo XIX," chapter 7, pp. 305–330, in Sánchez, F. (ed.) *Ensayos de historia monetaria y bancaria de Colombia*, Tercer Mundo editores, Bogota.

Espinosa, A. 1942. *El pensamiento económico y político en Colombia: apuntes sobre su evolución*, Imprenta del departamento, Bucaramanga, Colombia.

Galindo, A. 2014 [1869]. "Organización del Banco de Inglaterra," chapter 10, pp. 497–568, in Acosta and Álvarez (eds.).

Gonzalez, F. 2014 [1847]. "Informe presentado por el Secretario de Estado del Despacho de Hacienda del Gobierno de la Nueva Granada a las mui Honorables camaras legislativas en sus sesiones de 1847," chapter 6, pp. 226–272, in Acosta and Álvarez (eds.).

Junguito, R. 2014. *Escritos Económicos de Rafael Núñez*, Banco de la República, Bogota.

López, E. and Kalmanovitz, S. 2016. "La idea federal en el nacimiento de la República colombiana 1810–1828," chapter 4, pp. 123–154, in Álvarez and Correa (eds.).

Pérez, S. 2004 [circa 1880]. *Economía Política i Estadística*, Editorial Universidad Externado de Colombia, Bogota.

Revenga, J.-R. 2014 [1826]. "Informe de la Comision Primera de Hacienda de la Camara de Representantes sobre el presupuesto de gastos la Republica de Colombia para el año de 1825. I proyecto de establecimiento de un Banco Nacional en la misma Republica, con informe de la espresada Comision," chapter 3, pp. 51–74, in Acosta and Álvarez (eds.).

Sánchez, F. (ed.) 1994. *Ensayos de historia monetaria y bancaria de Colombia*, Tercer Mundo editores, Bogota.

Wills, W. 2014 [1854]. "Establecimiento de un Banco Nacional en la Nueva Granada," chapter 6, pp. 272–403, in Acosta and Álvarez (eds.).

12 The economic redefinition of Peru

The turn to liberalism through the 1845–54 debate

Alvaro Grompone Velásquez

Introduction

"No Country in South America, since the declaration of independence, has suffered more anarchy than Peru." Charles Darwin (1890, p. 266) used these emphatic words to describe the country's condition during what is commonly known as the *Periodo Caudillista* (1821–45). The subsequent boom in guano trade – which provided enormous economic resources – and the *Pax Castillista* (the Ramon Castilla government) – a period of relative political stability – transformed the Peruvian state completely, so that it could finally begin to address some of the serious problems that had existed since the formation of the Republic in 1821. This context was the perfect setting to start discussions about constructing and redefining the identity that the fledgling nation should pursue; the country's economic policy, which had been strongly protectionist during the first two decades of the Republic, was also called into question following the export-led economic boom.

This chapter seeks to summarize the economic debates that took place in Peru between 1845 and 1854. In particular, the chapter focuses on the dilemma over selecting the economic policy that was better suited for the country's future progress – protectionism or free trade. On examining this time period, it can be seen that a first phase of protectionist preponderance was followed, after 1850, by free trade hegemony in the following decades. However, the main objective of this chapter is the analysis of the economic discussion in itself, particularly the arguments used by those involved in it. The chapter uses the *Critical Discourse Analysis* (CDA) framework, with particular emphasis on Van Dijk's concept of the *ideological square* (1993, 1997, 2008). It is expected that the analysis of the arguments over economic policies can provide new insights for understanding the economic shift that took place during this period.

Two issues seem to be particularly relevant to this discussion. First, the construction and redefinition of the national economic identity played a key role in the debate. This can be divided into two aspects: (i) the opposition to Spanish colonial rule was used equally by the two opposing groups to defend their arguments; and (ii) both groups of participants advocated a clear and distinct economic identity for Peru, that would lead to a consistent national economic policy. Second, the participants in this debate resorted to the use of political economy concepts as the only valid attempt to provide scientific validity to their opinions. This led to what could be considered as the first attempt of technocratic debate in the young Republic. These three elements were important to both sides of the debate, though their contents were obviously quite distinct.

A couple of caveats are also important. Throughout the discussion, the liberals and the protectionists are presented as two distinct blocs, when, in reality, it is difficult to ascribe a single and developed ideology to those involved in the debate. In addition, even if it could be said that representatives from the *sierra* region tended to be more protectionist than those from Lima, that would be a rather rough generalization. Actually, there is no clear pattern and no distinction can be easily made regarding the economic position of the participants in the debate. Instead, we have identified the two opposing views according to which we could situate their arguments, focusing on the economic opinions usually advocated. Moreover, since we are interested in the debates in themselves as a key source, we have given special significance to direct quotations from the participants; thus, these quotations are organized – aiming for consistency among them – to better reflect the spirit of the moment. This was achieved through the use of the Peruvian national daily newspaper *El Comercio*, which reproduces full extracts from the sessions of the *Cámara de Diputados* (House of Representatives) and *Cámara de Senadores* (the Senate), Congressional and presidential decrees, prefectural circulars, official communications, etc.[1]

The chapter is divided into six sections, including this introduction. The second section briefly contextualizes the time period of our study. The third section outlines the evolution of trade policies during the period under study. The fourth section shows the conceptual tools of CDA that were used for analysis in this chapter. The fifth section focuses on the arguments of the debate, with particular emphasis on the three aspects discussed above. Finally, the sixth section includes the discussion and conclusions of the chapter.

The historical context: the beginning of the guano boom

Before directly addressing Peruvian commercial policies *per se*, a brief historical background seems necessary. Since the Peruvian independence, the country had been characterized by high political instability (which is clear considering that it had nineteen presidents and five constitutions in fewer than twenty years) and economic stagnation, showing no improvement in most measures of socio-economic development; this was denominated the *Periodo Caudillista*. Regarding the economic situation, the independence had had disastrous consequences: mining and agricultural production, as well as foreign trade had sharply declined, while foreign and domestic debt were steadily raising (Contreras, 2011). In short, the Peruvian economy was based on the extraction of primary resources, with mining still the main activity, complemented with limited but still significant linkages with international markets (Deustua, 1986; Quiroz, 1987, p. 21). The dominant economic policy during this period had a strong protectionist orientation, with restrictions quite similar to those of the colonial period, based upon the interest of key economic actors and the precarious fiscal situation (Gootenberg, 1997). A clear example of this strong protectionism is the *Ley de Prohibiciones* (Prohibition Law) of 1828, which forbade the importation of any commodity similar to those produced locally for eight to ten years (Basadre, 2005, p. 265). Given these kind of rules, it is not strange that policies that today could be considered rather protectionist were actually viewed as far more liberal in that period.

This scenario would later radically change with the emergence of guano as a valuable resource for export. The economic boom was spectacular. The guano exports in 1870 were twenty-five times those of 1845, and the State managed to keep around 50–60 percent of the guano revenues (Hunt, 1984). In that sense, fiscal revenues grew more than ten times during the same period, which undoubtedly meant a fiscal revolution for the country. Nonetheless, the end of this period was dramatic: economic crisis at every level, the second highest foreign debt in the world, a lost war against Chile, etc. Extravagant spending, the absence of a capable elite, the impossibility of creating a domestic market, speculative trade, among others are the standard explanations to address this failure.[2] At the same time, the economy became extremely dependent on the guano resources, while the rest of the activities remained stagnant. For example, the taxes collected from the guild of *Consignatarios del guano* (Guano consignees) represented 11.2 percent of the total taxes collected from all Lima guilds in 1842, rising to 36.4 percent in 1859.[3]

It is important to stress, however, that even if the 'guano period' started in 1840, the precarious fiscal and economic situation was not solved until the following decade. Therefore, our period of analysis shows the transition from a situation of deep structural imbalances to a period of greater availability of economic resources. For instance, public finances, which were extremely disorganized until the end of the 1840s, became more efficiently managed when the Congress enacted the first National Budget for the years 1848–9.[4] Nevertheless, economic resources were still scarce; in fact, the main concern with this budget (as for the next few years) was the tremendous fiscal deficit, and the need to obtain resources in every possible way.[5] This situation would change dramatically when the guano exports rose from an annual average of US\$4.4 million between 1845 and 1849 to US\$16.6 million between 1850 and 1855. As an example of this transformation, we can see congressmen in 1853 stating that "the nation currently possesses enough resources as to face its ordinary expenses."[6]

With regard to the political arena, there was an important transition taking place as well. In fact, the economic gains from the guano trade permitted relative political stability in the subsequent period, starting with the Presidency of

Ramon Castilla (1845–51), the first President to complete his six-year term. This transition was widely acknowledged. For example, a contemporary editorial from *El Comercio* (December 1849) on the constitutional presidency and Congress stated:

> not long ago these bodies were for many people an exotic plant that would have never acclimatized to our soil, and never would provide useful fruits: today, we all recognize that they are indispensable for the maintenance of public order.[7]

In fact, in this period we can see a Legislative Branch with a higher degree of institutionalization and coordination with the Executive Branch than in the previous decade.

As we will see, this juncture of deep transformations would have important consequences for Peruvian economic policy, especially concerning the debates around liberalism and protectionism. This kind of discussion was not unique in Peruvian history. For example, O'Phelan (1988) contrasts the eighteenth-century position of José Ignacio Lequanda, who stated that every *obraje* had to disappear in order to permit the introduction of foreign textiles and free labor to work in the mining settlements,[8] with the ideas of Alonso Carrió de la Vandera on the need to protect and foster the textile production, using *vicuña* and *alpaca* fur as raw material. However, an interesting feature of the intense debates and discussions of our period is that they were more systematic and elaborated. It is also important to note that the latter deeply affected economic policy. This precise issue is what we outline in the following sections.

The evolution of trade policy during 1845–54

This section charts the evolution of economic policies and related discussions during the period under study. The analysis is divided into two subsections; the first covers the period between 1845 and 1849, when protectionism held sway, while the second discusses the move towards liberal hegemony from 1850 onwards.[9] This separation has already been convincingly addressed by Gootenberg (1990), but our analysis emphasizes certain additional aspects of these two periods.

Phase I: The protectionist move, 1845–9

As stated earlier, the first half of this period was characterized by protectionist economic policies, with emphasis on the promotion of national industries. The economic policies of the 1840s were visible in the *Reglamento de Comercio* (Trade Regulation) of 1840.[10] The *Reglamento* replaced the aforementioned *Ley de Prohibiciones* of 1828 (with more moderate policies), but continued earlier practices regarding the importation of several foreign goods and the prohibition of others.[11] However, the pressure to increase import tariffs was also relentless during the next five years.

The strength of the protectionist initiatives is visible in four proposals presented to the *Cámara de Diputados* between July and October, 1845. These sought to: (i) prohibit the importation of products that were manufactured in Peru;[12] (ii) restore the *Ley de Prohibiciones*;[13] (iii) grant exclusive rights to the national textile industry;[14] and (iv) raise import duties on wheat flour.[15] These protectionist demands also had the full support of the Executive branch. The latter repeatedly recognized the 'duty' of the government to protect, encourage and promote the development of the national industries.[16] This is clearly reflected in a memorandum from the Minister of Foreign Relations, José G. Paz Soldan, to government prefects:

> After giving thought to the issue of restoration of law and order, the government believes that there cannot be another subject that deserves more preferential attention than expanding the types of industry known to exist in this country, or introduce new kinds [of industries] ... Nations without Industry, besides being in misery, develop the propensity for social movements and creating social disorders.[17]

The last statement is particularly interesting, as it was part of instructions to prefects on the introduction of silk production in Peru. This endeavor to produce silk was one of several 'experiments' to achieve industrial progress during the late 1840s. Thus, the environment was such that the Presidency, most members of Congress and industrialists considered the promotion of manufacturing indispensable for national economic development. Among various efforts, Carrasco (1849, pp. 82–3) highlights initiatives geared to promoting the production of cotton yarn and fabric, silk fabric, glass, paper, candles and wax bleaching, as well as workshops for browning and plating of all types of metals, all of them established between 1847 and 1848.

The uniqueness of these initiatives resides in two aspects: (i) they were broader attempts, compared to previous decades, at industrial experimentation;[18] and (ii) there was constant support of public officials towards these undertakings, through material and symbolic measures.

An essay by Juan Norberto Casanova (1849), a business partner in a cotton factory, illustrates the first aspect. The author proposed that the state should combine moderate import duties with financial incentives – drawn from guano resources – for the national industry. Gootenberg (1990, 1998) argues that Casanova had a fully developed vision of industrialization and called it "transforming guano to factories."[19] In fact, the *Cámara de Diputados* did approve a loan amounting to the monetary equivalent of 20,000 tons of guano in September 1849, but the funds ended up not materializing due to other fiscal reasons.[20]

The second characteristic is visible in the seemingly boundless enthusiasm for industrialism within the state apparatus during this period. A few examples: (i) granting exclusive rights for the establishment of a paper mill;[21] (ii) the Congress increasing the import duty on *tocuyo* (coarse cloth made of cotton) and paper by 40 percent;[22] and (iii) leasing of the San Pedro building in Lima on favorable terms for the development of silk industries.[23] An announcement from Minister José Dávila addressed to the *tocuyo* factory owners clearly reflected the sentiments of the incumbent government:

> Your excellency [i.e., Ramón Castilla], who has great interest in the development of the industries since he is convinced that in this lies the happiness of the nation, hopes that this industry is not discouraged in its noble endeavour; and that instead it will redouble its efforts to overcome the obstacles that, as to all the various improvements that are tried, may obstruct and hinder the work and advancements of this important mission.[24]

This convergence of interests became stronger towards the end of the decade into what Gootenberg (1990) termed "the protectionist offensive." A key role in this process was played by artisanal craftsmen, who stated that progressive liberalization had led to their ruin (ibid.).[25] The increasing pressure from various quarters, anticipating the imminent elections, led to the passing of the *Ley de los Artesanos* (Craftsmen Law) on December 21, 1849. The law amended the *Reglamento de Comercio* of 1840 and imposed a 90 percent duty on any foreign commodity that could generate significant competition for domestic producers; this law was considered the most radical protectionist policy from this period. The 'offensive,' however, was one of the last protectionist acts before the liberal bloc began an aggressive counter-attack for reform.

Phase II: The liberal response and triumph, 1850–4

As mentioned earlier, the increasing strength of liberals after 1850 led to economic policies consistent with their ideology.[26] Faced with the radical offensive of the artisans, the free market advocates decided to remove from Peru every possibility of protectionist contagion (Gootenberg, 1998, pp. 87–8). This would give way to strong anti-industrial sentiments among civic groups, the press, and especially in government policies. This subsection shows the shift that led to the consolidation of the free trade position in subsequent decades. We are not implying, however, that free trade voices had been completely absent or an exception during the previous phase. In fact, many Representatives opposed the protectionist projects mentioned earlier using liberal arguments,[27] but their opposition did not prevail nor curb the advance of protectionism.

The situation changed after 1850 when, in response to the *Ley de los Artesanos* of 1849, the free market advocates not only successfully prevented the enactment of the law, but also managed to pass a comprehensive reform of the *Reglamento de Comercio* of 1840. After a first round of reforms by the *Ministerio de Hacienda* (Ministry of Finance) that simplified processes while maintaining several import duties,[28] many called for deeper reforms in the tariff structure. Newspapers editorials and articles illustrate this 'campaign,' arguing on several occasions that trade liberalization was fundamental for sustained progress, while restrictions favored only a handful of industrial entrepreneurs at the expense of the general population.[29]

The views of the *Consejo de Estado* (State Council) also veered in this direction. The *Consejo* argued that protectionist restrictions were not only inherently annoying, but also inappropriate since there was no industry to protect within the country, and would thus only generate backwardness. It also stated that "all tariff duties that exceed 20 percent seem excessive," and instead proposed the establishment of a standardized *ad valorem* tax.[30] The *Consejo* reiterated its position the following year, arguing that such restrictions were useless, impractical, did not benefit the industries, and were detrimental to the majority of the population and the Treasury. Instead, the purpose of the *Reglamento de Comercio* should be to "allow freedom and entrepreneurship, and protect and secure trade with all nations of the globe."[31]

From this point on, the free trade position demonstrated remarkable and rapid progress, quickly becoming the hegemonic economic position. The rise to power of José Rufino Echenique, who employed a strong liberal discourse, was an important catalyst for its advancement. As President, Echenique declared:

> I find absurd the protection given to sustain those fictitious industries that are not consistent with the normal conditions of the [Peruvian] people, which results in us having to pay a lot for what one can buy cheaply, and imposes a burden on many for the benefit of the few ... The same principles also make me think that freedom of trade, ease of transactions, simplification of customs operations, and a moderate tariff are overriding requirements in our trading situation .... It is not possible to comprehensively monitor a country with long and unprotected coastline; that does not have any manufacturing interests to protect; and [for whom] customs earnings are one of its main incomes. The high and prohibitive duties are, at the least, a contradiction.[32]

With the support of the *Consejo de Estado* and President Echenique, the Congress got to work quickly towards creating a more liberal trading system. As early as July 1850, the *Cámara de Diputados* presented a proposal to repeal the *Ley de Artesanos* of 1849 and formulate a new trade regulation, including the reduction of import duties.[33] This initiative was welcomed by various sectors, as indicated by an editorial in *El Comercio*: "The industry whose products cannot compete with imports should disappear; taxing foreign products that resemble those produced in the country represents a burden on the public in favor of the few."[34] In turn, the *Cámara de Senadores*, with the lone exception of Senator Ugarte,[35] applauded the initiative to "approve the most liberal trade regulation since the beginning of the Republic."[36]

The previous 'protectionist' coalition of the Executive, most of the Congresspersons, new industrialists and artisans had ceased to exist. The Executive and the Congress, together with the press, had turned sharply in favor of free trade. For their part, the industrialists and artisans were powerless against this shift: they were unable to prioritize and articulate their demands, which appeared contradictory (Gootenberg, 1990, pp. 264–7). Hence, every consideration regarding the 'duty' to encourage industry vanished to make way for those that promoted free trade as an imperative.[37] In fact, a series of free trade measures were included in the new *Reglamento de Comercio* of March 1852, the most liberal of its kind so far.

As opposed to the excitement of the previous five years, discussions on economic issues virtually disappeared; further amendments to reduce privileges and tariffs were approved without major deliberations. Like any debate, it ended when a consensus was reached, and in this case, the consensus was strictly liberal – the first of many to follow in Peru. Faced with the liberal counterattack, any attempts by protectionist industrialists were, regardless of their claims, quickly crushed; and this also duly discouraged similar attempts in the future. Renewed protest by artisans appeared in 1858, but the free trade vision held its course in the following decades (Hunt, 1984).

The conceptual approach: Critical Discourse Analysis

Having understood the evolution of trade policy during the period under study, we now move to the main purpose of this chapter: the analysis of the arguments used in the economic discussions of the period. In order to do so, we have adopted some of the tools provided by CDA, focusing mainly on the work of Teun A. Van Dijk. As indicated earlier, rather than attempting a rigorous review of CDA, the chapter focuses on a few concepts relevant for this analysis.

Under CDA, language is understood as a social practice. Thus, it is conditioned by social institutions and structures in which it is framed, while at the same time influencing these social institutions and structures (Fairclough and Wodak, 1997; Jäger and Maier, 2009). In other words, language users employ discourse as members of specific social classes, groups or communities, while constructing, exhibiting and activating these same identities or roles through the use of discourse itself (Van Dijk, 1997). Thus, discourse influences society and culture by constructing socially shared representations of the world, interpersonal and social relations, and personal and social identities. In that sense, discursive practices could be persuasive and manipulative, leading to the (re)production of dominance relations; CDA seeks to reveal these coverings and the manipulation of discourse in the attainment of power (Reisigi and Wodak, 2009).[38]

Discourses are thus vehicles of *Knowledge* (in the Foucauldian sense), due to the fact that they try to influence how individuals interpret and organize society, i.e., they guide the creation of individual and collective realities (Jäger and Maier, 2009). The latter explains the strong ideological character of discourse, since it builds and strengthens specific views that are presented as consensual, with significant consequences for social relations of inequality (Reisigi and Wodak, 2009). Likewise, the perceptions, interpretations or social practices of one group could be fostered over those of others depending on the group's interest (Van Dijk, 2008). Thus, CDA focuses on ideological strategies of domination, seeking to make them more transparent and revealing what is hidden behind their seemingly neutral character (Van Dijk, 1993; Wodak and Meyer, 2009).

This analysis uses only a few of the tools provided by CDA. For example, Gee (1999) proposes the concept of 'Conversations,' which refers to discussions, debates and issues that have been carried out in society, and are relatively similar across all ideological positions. Therefore, Conversations embody values and beliefs shared by society, as well as common ways of thinking about these debates. This is consistent with the proposal of discourse as a historical construction that only makes sense if we insert elements of the past to which it refers (Fairclough and Wodak, 1997).

In addition, our main interest is in the argumentative strategies used in discourse to justify the pursuit of self-interest. According to Renkema (2004), when introducing an argument, one can opt for (i) justification of motivation (state that it benefits the receiver), (ii) justification from authority (credibility of the source), or (iii) substantive justification (draw generalizations from one case). In each of these situations, one must distinguish between persuasion by the central route (reflection on the arguments provided) and the peripheral route (convinced due to emotional reasons), where neither is necessarily more powerful than the other (ibid.). For its part, Reisigi and Wodak (2009) suggest five types of discourse strategies to consider within CDA: (i) nomination (build the social actor, object or phenomenon); (ii) predication (describe using allusions, evocations, etc.); (iii) argumentation (justify and question statements); (iv) perspectivation (positioning the source); and (v) mitigation/enhancement (through hyperbole, nicknames, speech acts, etc.). In the case of political discourse in particular – with its unique rhetorical, persuasive and manipulative character – Chilton and Schäffner (1997) offer various strategic functions, which are based on creating the image of a single source of knowledge and authority for general welfare. This involves building (so-called) consensus around certain assumptions and presenting them as having the support of the whole nation – 'We' versus an isolated opposition.

Within these multiple forms of argumentative and rhetorical strategies, Van Dijk's proposal of the "ideological square" (1993, 1997, 2008, 2009) is especially interesting. In short, it refers to the creation of an ideological polarization between 'Us' and 'Them' through the use of multiple mechanisms of discourse: the building of a positive self-representation along with a negative representation of the 'Other.' This implies extolling 'Our' virtues and 'Our' good deeds, while emphasizing the bad actions and damages caused by 'Them.' Conversely, 'Our' misdeeds are mitigated or left implicit, as are 'Their' virtues. Clearly, it tries to polarize using concepts of good ('Us') and evil ('Them') as something univocal, building the 'Other' as the real enemy, while 'We' are victims or the disregarded. This can occur through different strategies, including semantic shifts (denial, empathy or apparent concession), transfer, dichotomization, etc. (ibid.; Van Dijk, 1998). Additionally, group polarization is visible at different levels: (i) syntax (emphasize or reduce agency); (ii) lexicon (negative terms for 'Them' and positive for 'Us'); (iii) local significance (vagueness about 'Our' bad attitudes and detailed information about 'Theirs'); and (iv) rhetorical devices (hyperbole, euphemisms, metaphors), among others (Van Dijk, 2008). Overall, Van Dijk's "ideological square" is intended to bolster one's own position with respect to opposing groups, which represents a clear ideological operation.

The key debates: national identity and political economy

This section discusses the factors, from the debates in themselves, that influenced the shift of economic policy from protectionism to liberalism during the period under study. It is interesting to note that this shift occurred concurrently in several Latin American countries. In that sense, we need an explanation that transcends the strictly national context. Specifically, we propose that a key role was played at the conceptual-ideological level, emphasizing two aspects: the attempts to build a new national identity (present in all the new Latin American republics), and the growing influence of Political Economy (as a process throughout the region around the same years). This was complemented by the large increase in commodity exports (Peru being the typical case), creating the perfect recipe for consensus.

To support this hypothesis, we provide an in-depth analysis of the arguments used in the various debates mentioned in the third section, based on especially illustrative fragments. Three argumentative resources are found to be particularly relevant: (i) the opposition to the colonial economic policy; (ii) the definition of an infallible economic identity; and (iii) the use of political economy as an argument from authority.[39] These three resources were used extensively by both liberals and protectionists, although the former were more articulate and coherent in their ideas. We examine each of these ideas closely in the following subsections.

Opposition to colonial trade policy

Once the new republics were consolidated in Latin America, they developed a strong distaste for the colonial past. This criticism also extended to the discussions about trade policies examined in this chapter. Clearly, this can be related to the previously mentioned concept of Conversations, since any allusion to the colonial period was inserted into the common sense that suggest the undignified past that it represented. Therefore, it was a strategy to strengthen the arguments, appealing to the values and beliefs shared by most of society at that particular time.

From the liberal perspective, protectionist policies were considered as an example of the backwardness of the colonial period, and as the main explanation for the current precarious economic situation of Peru. Thus, it was proposed that "our current backwardness is a result of the system of prohibitions that we have continued since colonial times: that is why we are suffering now that we have entered the path of competitive trade."[40] In that sense, the mercantilist system of the Spanish Empire that dominated Peruvian economic policies for three centuries explained the poor economic performance of Peru:

> Under the crude yoke of Spain, which more than any other nation in Europe continued to trust the petty mercantile system that is uneconomical as well as anti-political, and forced her colonies to also follow the same stupid behaviour that led to their downfall ... Our economic regulations are the offspring of Spanish laws which nourished those ruinous principles of the dominant restrictive system, so that it contains within itself its fatal seed.[41]

The liberal argument is very clear, direct and attractive. The colonial policies "not only exploited our wealth, destroying in its infancy all the elements of abundance that we possessed and that under the atmosphere of freedom could have produced the best fruits,"[42] but also left us with a legacy of an extremely pernicious economic system from which Peru had failed to escape. It is clear that the liberals wanted to employ an *intensification strategy* by linking trade restrictions to colonial subjugation, intending to appeal to the emotions of the recipient (e.g., the reference to "crude yoke"). This relates to a strong *delegitimization* of all protectionist measures by presenting them as an accumulation of past colonial abuses, so constructed that the anti-liberal subject appears solely as a product of the colonial period (*nomination*).

The *ideological square* can also be used to explain the liberal strategy. 'They' (the protectionists) have kept 'Us' within an economic and political system of domination, causing, in addition, deep misery. This is especially clear if one notices the syntactically active role that is assigned to the Colony and protectionism; in contrast, 'We' (the Liberals) are the victims ("Our economic regulations are the offspring") of colonial abuse. At the same time, free trade is presented as the only system analogous to the new independent republic, moving away from such disgraceful past.

This anti-colonial argument was also used by the protectionists, building it around the extractive model that prevailed at the time. This is clear in the statement of Congressman Alegre who claimed that the alleged natural inclination to work in the mines was a result of the fact that "before independence this was the only thing that enthused our oppressors; but now everything has changed sir; and those vindictive ideas that contributed to our current backwardness are being banished."[43] In this explanation, the colonial period is associated with the idea that Peru is essentially a mining country, something 'They' ("Our oppressors"; the liberals) wanted to maintain, while 'We' ("the sons of the country"; the protectionists) want to overcome this barrier to national progress. This advancement required emancipation to proceed hand in hand with industrial progress, an argument that delegitimizes liberalism as a malicious attempt by appealing to the people's emotional judgments.

Destiny and economic identity of Peru

The previous argument proposed by the protectionists brings us to another relevant issue: within the debates, both positions are not only discussing concrete economic policies, but also the Peruvian identity as a whole. What they suggested is that there was an infallible economic destination for Peru, which should be the foundation of economic policies consistent with such identity; in other words, what is at stake is the future economic path of the country in general. Thus, the shift towards liberalism entailed an attempt to comprehensively redefine the basic identity of the country.

The liberal bloc often used this argument, defending the unshakable mining and agricultural vocation of the country.[44] In that sense, the liberals argued that any form of protectionism only disturbed the original nature and economic potential of the country, while liberalism instead would allow maximum deployment of this economic spirit. As an example, in opposition to the protectionist projects of 1845, Representative Tirado argued:

> Our country does not have any natural disposition for factories or manufacturing: our destiny lies in extracting our natural resources from the ground, things that can be exported and changed ... Our industry cannot be other than those that obtain natural products by working the land and mines with care; producing for export. [45]

In the same context, Representative Urrutia was even more direct: "We are called to be only farmers and miners: all peoples of the world have their role: we should be content with ours."[46] For its part, President Echenique also concurred: "Peru is essentially an agricultural and mining country; and it is my wish not only to see that the impediments that obstruct these sources of public wealth are removed, but also it is my desire and purpose, to facilitate its progress."[47]

As is evident, the discussions transcended the conditions prevailing at the moment, and the project under discussion. It was seen as a destiny dictated by the nature of the nation, coupled with the unequivocal belief in the advantages of free trade. In this process, several argumentative strategies are visible. There is the *justification of motivation*, in the suggestion that following a particular economic destiny benefits all members of the nation. As can be seen, it takes a persuasive character to impose a particular position as something that is desirable to the entire country. In fact, it was argued that there were no other plausible alternatives (*concealment*), given that the intrinsic identity of the country was constructed as univocal (*nominalization*). The liberals, in a clear ideological move, attempted to integrate within the national *Knowledge* a consensus based on certain assumptions, in such a manner that particular social representations seemed infallible.

Furthermore, since mining was identified as integral to the country's identity, the liberals stated that the government ought to promote this activity. Various projects during the period support this conclusion,[48] and it is interesting to note the manner in which it was sustained:

> We have passed the period of excitement and doubts that are found in emerging nations, during which they are nervous and waver in their understanding of the most appropriate production techniques given the quality of the soils: the experience and trials of more than three centuries have shown convincingly that mining is the one in which we must affirm our brightest hopes; it presents a future of wealth and power ... If our country is essentially a mining one, if this industry represents the best possibilities of development and growth, we must try to protect, promote, expand and improve it as much as we can, because it is evident that this is in the interests of all partners.[49]

Peru, then, was defined essentially as a country of extractive industries that did not need to continue searching for its engine of economic growth. However, it is interesting to note that this identity was not based on a break with the colonial system, but rather a continuity – the economic identity of the country in the preceding three centuries of colonialism being the same. Be that as it may, it is clear that, for most liberals, the debates were a moment for affirming – and constructing – the national economic identity. Discourse was a compelling mechanism for affirmation, pointing in a predetermined direction, based on the *management/obfuscation of information*. For example, there was no mention of the recurring crises within the mining industry during the colonial period, or of early efforts at economic diversification during the same time. The message, therefore, was brief and attractive: Peru was essentially a mining and agricultural country, without any possibility of ceasing to be one. Therefore, it should abandon its manufacturing ambitions and accept that the exploitation of its natural resources would provide a more comfortable life to its population.

Clearly, this argument was not suitable for the protectionists. They associated the mining-agricultural identity of Peru with the colonial period, and wanted the country to redefine itself as a manufacturing nation (arguing that Peru possessed the conditions for doing so). For example, they claimed:

> [W]hy does the Minister [of Finance] want Peru to retrogress, and to live eternally *sic vos non vobis*, only producing raw materials when the country could export various manufactured products? ... If all nations listened to the opinion of our Minister of Finance, manufacturing industry would never have existed, nor could its progress have found the use for the many raw materials that sustain the livelihoods of millions of families.[50]

In that way, the protectionists argued that the exportation of raw materials was not only undesirable for Peru but also inappropriate, given the state of affairs in the country. It signified retrogression for the economy and the continued perpetuation of Peruvians as a "miserable class of farmers."[51] Representative Ponce suggested sarcastically: "Peru is doomed to eternal nullity, according to the thinking of those gentlemen [i.e., the liberals]: Peruvians should be naked and enslaved, with empty bellies waiting for food and clothing from abroad."[52] Such arguments were meant to contradict the aforementioned *justification by motivation* outlined by the liberals, proposing that the consequences would be the opposite of what the liberals claimed. The protectionists, instead, put forward a *substantive justification*, since they generalized success stories with the purpose of demonstrating that manufacturing was the only possible route to development, while all mining attempts had resulted in notable failures.

In arguing their case, the protectionists employed the *ideological square* to portray a clear dichotomy. It is 'They' (the liberals) who want us to regress, they are the 'Other' as an enemy; meanwhile, 'We' (the protectionists, Peruvians) continue to be their victims, despite 'Our' possibilities to get away from such destiny. It is clear that 'We' bear no responsibility for 'Our' current state, but 'They' are fighting to maintain it. The attempt at dichotomization is clear from the choice of words (e.g., "miserable," "slaves"), syntax (the active role played by 'Them' compared to 'Our' victimization/passivity), and the use of various rhetorical devices. Thus, the protectionists sought to depict the identity of a mining nation in opposition to the progress of the country, arguing that the liberal position was detrimental to the Peruvian population as a whole.[53]

Use of Political Economy as an argument from authority

The first half of the nineteenth century was undoubtedly the highpoint in the history of Political Economy. As a result of the debates on trade policies in Europe – and thereby the principles of economic growth – several notable works were produced, while experts on Political Economy began to play an increasing role in determining national economic policies. Ideas contained within the rubric of Political Economy were often used as arguments from authority by diverse and opposing groups; Peru, and the rest of Latin America, were not outsiders to such trends. Our hypothesis is that the prestige earned by Political Economy was such that it played a crucial role in consolidating the turn toward liberalism that we have outlined – and also that this process has close analogues in other Latin American countries.[54]

The prestige of Political Economy in Peru was recognized by society in general and the government. As proof, one can adduce a deposition from April 1847 that considers Political Economy as essential and "one of the most important sciences for the peoples and governments."[55] Later, another decree proclaimed that the science "is useful and indispensable for all citizens capable of holding public office."[56] Accordingly, works in Political Economy were published in the newspapers, lessons on the science were offered, and European 'economists' were often quoted on various topics.

As expected, the advocates of free trade policies used arguments from Political Economy in a more systematic and coordinated manner than others. This essay from the *El Progreso* diary reflects the importance associated with the science:

> Political economy is the science of the laws whose targeted applica-
> tion gives nations secure access to the abundance of material resources,
> amenities or physical pleasures, social improvement. ... Although politi-
> cal economy, like all sciences, is eternal in the absolute world of princi-
> ples, she had not revealed her secrets until the ruminations of [François]
> Quesnay, Adam Smith and other scholars of the last century gave her a
> scientific character ... In this state of civilization present in today's world,
> the governments in whose hands nations have deposited their fates,
> should make a thorough study and a wise and judicious application of
> the principles by which wealth is produced, distributed and consumed.[57]

In that way, progress within the science of Political Economy provided scientific support to free trade policies. Actually, they proposed that the "advancements within economic science" enabled and facilitated the disappearance of many old theories. It was argued that any policy against industrial freedom was anti-economical, while the principles of free trade were consistently more sane and indisputable.[58] It is immediately obvious how a particular ideology was presented as the only viable and truthful alternative. Additionally, the use of an argument from authority made dominant ideologies appear as neutral, scientific and beneficial for the whole population ("secure access to the abundance"). Following this argument, those who do not make decisions according to the precepts of this new science are condemning their nation to misery by acting unscientifically. Unlike previous instances, there is not an appeal to the emotions, rather the use of specific reasons (*central route*) that obey logical precepts that have been tried and tested.

On further examination, it is possible to observe similarities between the arguments developed by some liberals and ideas from the discipline of Political

Economy. Theories that embraced free trade, for example, were quickly adopted by the liberal bloc by agreeing that the natural advantages should be encouraged.[59] In Peru, Santiago Távara represents the further development of free trade thought. He argued that an increase in trade generates higher profits for both parties, so that it was necessary to promote mutually beneficial trade.[60] He reiterated that the obsolescence of protectionist measures had been proven by the findings of Political Economy: "it has required eminent men centuries of perseverance to tear away the blindfold and show that these measures have hindered and slowed progress."[61] Finally, Távara notes that commerce will better meet the needs of the people, and that self-interest would drive individuals to inevitably discover the means to satisfy them.[62]

Senator Buenaventura Seoane provides another direct reference to Political Economy. The author explicitly quotes Bastiat's *Economic Sophisms* (1859) in developing his argument. Among the refuted sophisms, he highlights: (i) that import duties equalize the production costs of a country with those existing in other countries (Bastiat, 1859, pp. 30–46); (ii) that protectionism increases wages (pp. 73–7); and (iii) that laws improve revenue collection (pp. 189–94), being all of them nothing but absurd. The Senator also stated that

> by looking at the rivalry between the producer who prefers fewer producers so that he can sell at a higher price, and the consumer who very much wants to buy for less – to which side the balance will tilt? ... Let us choose, then, between restriction and freedom, between scarcity and abundance. I am with Bastiat.[63]

In sum, we have tried to show the regularity with which the liberals used Political Economy to build irrefutable arguments. The implications are straightforward and compelling: the debate is no longer about two opposing positions with arguments against each other; on the contrary, liberalism enjoys general and undisputed techno-scientific support, so that any position that opposes it falls into the realm of the anachronistic, absurd and unscientific. This can also be seen from the perspective of Van Dijk's *ideological square*. 'We' (the liberals) possess scientific support (*the credibility from authority*) and unquestionable principles, while 'They' (the protectionists) continue with measures that have been proven to be wrong. In fact, the opposition is clear: between restriction and freedom, shortages and abundance, and obsolescence and scientific discoveries. Evidently, it is an attempt at self-glorification within liberalism, as opposed to the counterproductive effects of protectionism.

The scientific support for liberal arguments attempted to terminate all valid discussions on economic policies. The latter is clear in statements such as "truths and axioms of economics are not disputed today even by the most stubborn opponents of their existence,"[64] or the "incompetence of politics to guide development aside from the principles prescribed by the science of economics."[65] Collier (1979, p. 403) and Centeno and Silva (1998) define a technocrat as someone with a high level of *expertise* and academic specialization in decision making.[66] At the risk of stretching this definition, it can be argued that this was the first systematic attempt of appealing to technocratic arguments in the Peruvian Republic.

The need of using arguments from Political Economy as arguments from authority was also seen, though less frequently, among those who defended protectionist positions. The logic of such arguments, although not explicitly mentioned, followed those proposed by List (1942 [1841]) and other members of the German School.[67] An example is the argument by Representative Ponce in support of reinstating the *Ley de Prohibiciones*: "It is supported within political economy, in the general practice of nations ... the protectionist system is the most common, is the one most adopted and practiced by all civilized nations."[68]

Representative Cavero, in a similar vein, stated that "it is a principle revered by the wisest economists that the domestic industry should be protected and promoted at any cost, promoting domestic products, especially when the factories are in their infancy."[69] Thus, industry and trade, which make nations rich, could not be born or created without the shade of direct and indirect protection, as happened for many decades in England and Jean-Baptiste Colbert's France.[70] At another instance, the same Representative Cavero argued that "even though Smith's theory contains the seeds of some beneficial ideas and is so intimately connected with the principles of social philosophy, it contradicts the current conditions of nations structured under different and even opposite foundations."[71] Hence, according to the protectionists, the problem of liberal doctrine is that it did not reflect the reality and needs of nations like Peru.

Finally, the proposal of the aforementioned Casanova (1849) is also noteworthy for emphasizing that industrial development and the method to achieve it were based on the principles of Political Economy.[72] It stressed, based on a contemporary proposal by Andrés Borrego (1844), that while trade restrictions were certainly undesirable, there should be a system of incentives for a limited time to promote national industry without necessarily harming consumers (Borrego, 1844, pp. 33–7). In this task, the government should take an active role in removing obstacles to progress, contrary to the shameful role of spectator advocated by some liberal economists (ibid., pp. 59–63).

In this case, protectionist arguments were also developed using rational and technical claims, leaving aside all sentimental appeal. In fact, the arguments were based on the indisputable experience of the process of development in advanced countries, and the incontestable principles of Political Economy (it is also interesting that both groups construct their *justification from authority* using the same scientific discipline as a basis for credibility). Additionally, it created the opposites typical of the *ideological square*, where 'We' represents national characteristics, while 'They' use universal formulas that are not appropriate to our national attributes; moreover, this will lead us to ruin because 'Our' situation does not correspond to the international experience in which 'Their' argument is based. This mode of argument is pursued using various devices, such as *apparent empathy* (in the case of Cavero's reference to Smith).

This subsection demonstrated that ideas from the Political Economy literature managed to establish themselves as the only valid arguments. Both liberals and protectionists resorted to using Political Economy to validate their arguments. Similarly, Political Economy itself became the main defence against any proposal that would attempt to break the imposed liberal hegemony in the following decades.

Conclusions

This article analyzed, in depth, the shift that occurred around 1850 towards a more liberal economic orientation, adding new insights to the existing literature. The two phases of economic-commercial policy that were experienced during this period were clearly identified. The first phase (1845–9), with protectionist tendencies, was formed by a coalition of interests involving most members of Congress, the Executive branch, the manufacturing entrepreneurs and the artisans. In response, the second phase (1850 onwards), with a liberal bias, manifested itself when a growing number of economic sectors pushed for reforms in accordance with the principles of free trade. This 'ideology' achieved a dominant position in a relatively short time, leading to a repeal of past protectionist measures and an undisputed liberal order.

The central hypothesis, examined using tools from CDA, argues that part of the reason for this shift can be found in the realm of ideas: the construction of a national identity and imaginary, as well as the growing influence of Political Economy. Regarding the first point, both protectionist and liberal approaches sought to associate the opposite position as an example of colonial backwardness that had to be overcome. Therefore, while the liberals attacked trade restrictions inherited from the colonial times as the cause of the country's backwardness, the protectionists characterized the national identity based on agricultural and mining activities as counterproductive. Second, it is evident that both groups attempted to define the economic identity of Peru in an essentialist manner. While the liberals defended a national identity invariably based on mining and agriculture that would lead to economic progress, the protectionists rejected this label as detrimental and inaccurate. Finally, it is also observed that the prestige gained by the ideas associated with Political Economy during the period allowed it to establish itself as the only source of arguments that possessed a valid authority. Both positions claimed to be based on technical and scientific arguments from known authors in this scientific discipline, a trait that was absent in previous debates on this topic. We propose that this represents the first systematic technocratic debate in the Peruvian Republic.

We wish to make it clear that our hypothesis does not exclude alternatives. In fact, we propose that the guano boom – a structural factor – strengthened the liberal consensus. But it is important to focus on an aspect that is rarely studied: the ideological nature of arguments that pose themselves as an unquestionable, universal and neutral discourse. In fact, it is paradoxical that after more than 150 years, we can see the attempt to build a hegemonic view using the same kinds of arguments, and in very similar terms to those addressed in this chapter – one that is also hostile to any hint of opposition against free trade. Perhaps, Friedrich List's statement about a cosmopolitan economy that ignores the particularities of a country and its historical context is more applicable to certain key sectors of Peruvian reality than one could possibly imagine.

Notes

1 In this case, we rely almost exclusively on official bodies, whereas the discussions that occur in 'Communiques' or 'Submissions' sessions were not taken into account.
2 For the guano period, see Bonilla (1974), Hunt (1984), Quiroz (1987), Contreras (2004), Salinas (2009), and Tantaleán (2011).
3 Source: AGN, H-4: *Libro de matrícula de patentes de los distintos gremios de la ciudad de Lima*, various years.
4 To review the whole National Budget 1848–9, see Dancuart (1903, v. IV, pp. 125–40).
5 See, for example, *El Comercio*, February 1, 1849. This concern is clearly evidenced in the Representative Sessions during that whole month. It will also be an important aspect in economic decision making, like the guano contracts (Matthew, 2009, pp. 120–9).
6 Law Project by Representative Tello, Session of August 5, 1853, *El Comercio*, August 5, 1853.
7 Editorial. *El Comercio*, December 22, 1849.
8 Concerning Lequanda's views on *obrajes*, see Cheesman (2011, pp. 206–36).
9 It is clear, however, that it is in general a period of progressive liberalization compared to previous decades. Furthermore, while the protectionist and free trade positions are observed throughout the period, the policies are inclined initially towards the former, and after 1850 towards the latter.
10 To view the entire trade regulation, see Dancuart (1903, v. III, pp. 106–25).
11 Article 76° specifies the import duties on foreign goods, imposition of 16 percent (plus 2 percent of excise duty) on all articles of silk or lace, of 23 percent (plus 2 percent excise duties) on any item of wool, linen or cotton, 36 percent (plus more than 4 percent excise duty) on noodles and any kind of dough or pastes of flour, etc.; at the other extreme, the introduction of long-haired fabric and washcloths was prohibited. It was also agreed that these import duties would be reconsidered every two years, "leaving open the possibility to include as many items as possible" (Dancuart, 1903, v. III, pp. 116–19).
12 Statement by Representative Ponce, Session of July 7, 1845, *Cámara de Diputados*, *El Comercio*, July 8, 1845.
13 Statement by Representative Cavero, Session of July 7, 1845, *Cámara de Diputados*, *El Comercio*, July 8, 1845.
14 Statement of Representatives Alegre, Larrea and Miota, Session of July 14, 1845, *Cámara de Diputados*, *El Comercio*, July 15, 1845.
15 Session of October 10, 1845, *Cámara de Diputados*, *El Comercio*, October 13, 1845.
16 Decree to be exempt from payment for loading/unloading goods in national ports, *El Comercio*, May 20, 1846. Decree on the abolition of duty on locally produced

tobacco and soap, *El Peruano*, January 9, 1847. Decree of December 4, 1845 on the major port of San Jose, *El Comercio*, December 18, 1845. Circular of the Supreme Government of the Prefects, Maritime Governors and Customs of Callao, Lima, May 20, 1846, *El Comercio*, May 22, 1846. Decree for national vessels to be exempted from paying duty of any kind, *El Comercio*, January 27, 1847.

17 Circular of the Supreme Government to the Prefects. Lima, March 2, 1846, *El Comercio*, March 6, 1846.

18 Dancuart (1903, v. III, pp. 40–2) points out several initiatives between 1840 and 1845.

19 According to the definition from Senghaas (1985), it was an attempt at educative protection, rather than a typical conservative protection.

20 Session of September 26, 1849, *Cámara de Diputados*, El Comercio, September 27, 1849. Session of October 28, 1849, *Cámara de Diputados*, El Comercio, October 19, 1849.

21 Statement by the *Ministro de Gobierno* (Minister of Government). Lima, August 25, 1846, *El Comercio*, 6 September 1846.

22 Session of January 27, 1848, *Cámara de Senadores*, El Comercio, January 29, 1848; Session of February 1, 1848, *Cámara de Diputados*, El Comercio, February 1, 1848. This would eventually be endorsed by Ramon Castilla with the Decree of May 12, 1848, *El Peruano*, May 13, 1848. Session of February 3, 1848, *Cámara de Diputados*, El Comercio, February 4, 1848.

23 Details of lease conditions for the San Pedro building given to J.J. Sarratea. Lima, September 29, 1848, *El Comercio*, October 26, 1848.

24 Communication of Jose Davila of the labor union of workers employed in the cotton yarn and textile mills in the capital. Lima, November 7, 1848, *El Comercio*, November 9, 1848.

25 See also "Representation that elevated the guilds before the Congress Chambers." Press release, *El Comercio*, October 17, 1849.

26 For example, Quiroz (1987, p. 67) argues that "liberal ideas prevailed in economic policy, which is clear in the fiscal management circa 1850, especially in trade regulations, customs and internal debt."

27 For example, statement of Representative Tirado, Session of August 7, 1845, *Cámara de Diputados*, El Comercio, August 8, 1845; Session of February 3, 1848, *Cámara de Diputados*, El Comercio, February 4, 1848.

28 Communication from the *Ministro de Hacienda* to the Presidential Secretaries. *Consejo de Estado*. Lima, July 3, 1850, *El Comercio*, July 8, 1850.

29 See, for example, Editorial, *El Peruano*, July 22, 1850; Editorial, *El Progreso, El Comercio*, August 7, 1850.

30 Report of the Commission of the *Consejo de Estado* on the draft submitted by the *Ministro de Hacienda*. Lima, August 12, 1850, *El Comercio*, August 14, 1850.

31 Protest on the *Reglamento de Comercio* of the *Consejo de Estado*. Session of May 12, 1851, *Consejo de Estado. El Comercio*, May 12, 1851.

32 Message to the Nation of President José Rufino Echenique. Lima, April 20, 1851. *El Comercio*, April 20, 1851.

33 Session of July 3, 1851, *Cámara de Diputados*, El Comercio, July 3, 1851.

34 Editorial, *El Comercio*, July 4, 1851.

35 Session of August 20, 1851, *Cámara de Senadores. El Comercio*, August 20, 1851.

36 Session of September 16, 1851, *Cámara de Senadores. El Comercio*, September 19, 1851.

37 Session of August 21, 1851, *Cámara de Senadores*, El Comercio, August 21, 1851; Congressional Bill of August 12, 1853. *El Comercio*, August 16, 1853.

38 Clearly, this is a Foucauldian view of power, which gives more importance to persuasion than coercion for self-regulation of the subject in the expected terms.

39 Note that these are far from the only arguments that were raised. There were frequent considerations related to the public treasury, the characteristics of the population and the country, etc.
40 Statement by Representative Tirado, session of August 26, 1845, *Cámara de Diputados, El Comercio*, August 27, 1845.
41 "On the causes that determined the fate of Peru, or political and economic essay," *El Progreso, El Comercio*, April 14, 1850.
42 Ibid.
43 Statement by Representative Alegre, session of August 7, 1845, *Cámara de Diputados, El Comercio*, August 8, 1845.
44 It should be noted that others argue that this orientation should exist, at least, momentarily. For example, statement by Representative Garcia Urrutia, session of April 3, 1848, *Cámara de Diputados, El Comercio*, April 4, 1848. See also demonstration against the *Consejo de Estado* regarding the *Reglamento de Comercio*. Session of May 12, 1851, *Consejo de Estado, El Comercio*, May 12, 1851.
45 Statement by Representative Tirado. Ibid.
46 Statement by Representative Urrutia. Session of August 25, 1845, *Cámara de Diputados, El Comercio*, August 26, 1845.
47 Message of President José Rufino Echenique to the nation. Lima, April 20, 1851, *El Comercio*, April 20, 1851.
48 See, for example, the statements by Representatives Mier and Teran. Session of October 9, 1845, *Cámara de Diputados, El Comercio*, October 11, 1845.
49 Bill presented by Senators Bermúdez, Salcedo and Chávez. Session of October 1, 1849, *Cámara de Senadores, El Comercio*, October 2, 1849.
50 Protests by owners of yarn and cotton fabric factories. Lima, November 16, 1849. *El Comercio*, November 17, 1849.
51 Statement by Senator Ugarte, Session of August 19, 1851, *Cámara de Senadores, El Comercio*, August 20, 1851.
52 Statement by Representative Ponce, Session of August 7, 1845, *Cámara de Diputados, El Comercio*, August 9, 1845.
53 They also opposed the liberal approach arguing that regions were very heterogeneous, as well as mentioning manufacturing success stories from the past. See, for example, Statement by Representative Cueto, Session of August 25, 1845, *Cámara de Diputados, El Comercio*, August 26, 1845; Statement by Representative Cavero, session of August 26, 1845, *Cámara de Diputados, El Comercio*, August 27, 1845.
54 For example, Villalobos and Sagredo (1987, p. 61) identify the true influence of liberal economic thought in Chile with the arrival, in 1850, of Juan Gustavo Courcelle-Seneuil, a disciple of Frederic Bastiat.
55 Circular of Minister José G. Paz Soldán to the prefects. Lima, April 22, 1847, *El Comercio*, April 24, 1849.
56 Circular of the Minister of Finance. Lima, 05 September 1850, *El Comercio*, September 9, 1850.
57 "On the causes that determined the fate of Peru, or political and economic essay," *El Progreso, El Comercio*, April 14, 1850.
58 Editorial, *El Comercio*, July 4, 1846; Bill presented by Senators Bermúdez, Salcedo and Chávez. Session of October 1, 1849, *Cámara de Senadores, El Comercio*, October 2, 1849. Statement by Representative Tirado, session of August 7, 1845, *Cámara de Diputados, El Comercio*, August 8, 1845. "On the causes that determined the fate of Peru, or political and economic essay." Editorial, *El Progreso, El Comercio*, May 14, 1850; Editorial, *El Comercio*, July 4, 1851.
59 Congressional Bill of August 12, 1853, *El Comercio*, August 16, 1853.
60 Statement by Santiago Távara, Minister of Finance. Piura, September 27, 1846, *El Comercio*, October 10 and 12, 1846.

61 Ibid.
62 This makes clear reference to the unintended consequences of Adam Smith (1904 [1776]).
63 Statement by Senator Buenaventura Seoane, session of August 19, 1851, *Cámara de Senadores*, *El Comercio*, August 19, 1851.
64 Demonstration against the *Reglamento de Comercio* of *Consejo de Estado*. Session of May 12, 1851, *Consejo de Estado*. *El Comercio*, May 12, 1851.
65 "Emancipation of industry" by José Simeón Tejada, *El Comercio*, October 15 and 19, 1852.
66 Quoted in Dargent (2014).
67 He emphasized the importance of considering the particular characteristics of each nation to the detriment of universal formulas; thus the commercial freedom was detrimental to the least developed nations (hence, the quote "kicking away the ladder").
68 Statement by Representative Ponce, session of August 25, 1845, *El Comercio*, August 26, 1845.
69 Statement by Representative Cavero, session of August 25, 1845, *El Comercio*, August 25, 1845.
70 Ibid.
71 Statement by Representative Cavero, session of August 25, 1845, *El Comercio*, August 25, 1845.
72 This was the most accomplished heterodox economic ideology of the time in the country, according to Gootenberg (1998).

References

Primary Sources

El Comercio Journal (1845–55).
El Peruano Journal (1845–55).

Contemporary monographs

Carrasco, E. 1849. *Calendario y guía de forasteros de la república peruana para el año 1849*, Lima, imprenta Masías.
Casanova, J.N. 1849. *Ensayo económico-político sobre el porvenir de la industria algodonera fabril en el Perú: y demostración de las ventajas que puede tener a su favor sobre los Estados Unidos de NorteAmérica e Inglaterra, mediante la debida protección del gobierno*, Lima, J.M. Masías.
Fuentes, M.A. 1858. *Estadística General de Lima*.

Bibliography

Basadre, J. 2005. *Historia de la República del Perú, t.1*, Lima, El Comercio.
Bastiat, F. 1859. *Sofismas económicos*, Madrid, Imprenta de Manuel Galiano.
Bonilla, Heraclio. 1974. Guano y burguesía en el Perú, Lima, Instituto de Estudios Peruanos.
Borrego, A. 1844. *Principios de economía política con aplicación con aplicación a la reforma de aranceles de aduana, a la situación de la industria fabril de Cataluña, y al mayor y más rápido incremento de la riqueza nacional*, Madrid, Imprenta de la Sociedad de Operarios del mismo arte.

Centeno, M.A. and P. Silva. 1998. "The politics of expertise in Latin America: introduction," in Centeno, M.A. and P. Silva (eds.). *The Politics of Expertise in Latin America*, New York, McMillan Press.

Cheesman, Roxanne. 2011. *El Perú de Lequanda: Economía y comercio a nes del siglo XVIII*, Lima, Instituto de Estudios Peruanos y Fundación Manuel Bustamante de la Fuente.

Chilton, P. and C. Schaffner. 1997. "Discourse and politics," in Van Dijk, T. (ed.). *Discourse as Social Interaction: Discourse Studies, A Multidisciplinary Introduction*, London, California, SAGE.

Collier, D. (ed.). 1979. *The New Authoritarianism in Latin America*, Princeton: Princeton University Press.

Contreras, C. 2004. *El aprendizaje del capitalismo: estudios de historia económica y social del Perú republicano*, Lima, IEP.

Contreras, C. 2011. "Menos plata, pero más papas: consecuencias económicas de la independencia en el Perú," *Histórica*, vol. 35, no. 2, 101–32.

Dancuart, Pedro Emilio. 1903. Anales de la hacienda pública del Peru historia y legislación fiscal de la república, Lima, Librería é imprenta Gil.

Dargent, E. 2014. *Technocracy under democracy: assessing the political autonomy experts in Latin America*, PhD Dissertation, University of Austin at Texas.

Darwin, C. 1890, *Geología de la América Meridional*, Santiago de Chile.

Deustua, J. 1986, *La minería peruana y la iniciación de la República, 1820–1840*, Lima, Instituto de Estudios Peruanos.

Deustua, J. 2011. "Guano, salitre, minería y petróleo en la economía peruana, 1820–1930," in Contreras, C. (ed.). *Compendio de historia económica peruana, t. 4*, Lima, Instituto de Estudios Peruano, Banco Central de Reserva del Perú.

Echenique, J.R. 1952, *Memorias para la historia del Perú (1808–1878)*, Lima, Huascarán.

Fairclough, N. and R. Wodak. 1997. "Critical Discourse Analysis," in Van Dijk, T. (ed.). *Discourse as Social Interaction: Discourse Studies, A Multidisciplinary Introduction*, London, California, SAGE.

Gee, J.P. 1999. *An Introduction to Discourse Analysis: Theory and Method*, London, New York, Routledge.

Gootenberg, P. 1990. "Los orígenes sociales del proteccionismo y libre comercio en Lima del siglo XIX," *Histórica*, vol. 14, no. 2, 235–80.

Gootenberg, P. 1997. *Caudillos y comerciantes: la formación económica del Estado peruano, 1820–1860*, Cusco, Centro Bartolomé de las Casas.

Gootenberg, P. 1998. *Imaginar el desarrollo: las ideas económicas en el Perú postcolonial*, Lima, Instituto de Estudios Peruano, Banco Central de Reserva del Perú.

Hunt, S. 1984. "Guano y crecimiento en el Perú del Siglo XIX," *Hisla: revista latinoamericana de historia económica y social*, vol. 4, 35–92.

Jäger, S. and F. Maier. 2009 "Theoretical and methodological aspects of Foucauldian critical discourse analysis and dispositive analysis," in Wodak, R. and M. Meyer (eds.). *Methods of Critical Discourse Analysis*, London, California, SAGE.

List, F. 1942 [1841]. *Sistema Nacional de Economía Política*, México DF, Fondo de Cultura Económica.

Mathew, William M. 2009. *La firma inglesa Gibbs y el monopolio del guano en el Perù*, Lima, Banco central de reserva del Perù.

O'Phelan, Scarlett. 1988. *Un siglo de rebeliones anticoloniales: Perú y Bolivia 1700–1783*, Cusco, Perú, Centro de Estudios Regionales Andinos "Bartolomé de Las Casas."

Quiroz, A. 1987. *La deuda defraudada: consolidación de 1850 y dominio económico en el Perú*, Lima, Instituto Nacional de Cultura.

Reisigi, M. and R. Wodak. 2009. "The discourse-historical approach," in Wodak, R. and M. Meyer (eds.). *Methods of Critical Discourse Analysis*, London, California, SAGE.

Renkema, J. 2004. *Introduction to Discourse Studies*, Amsterdan, John Benjamins.

Ricardo, D. 1821. *On the Principles of Political Economy and Taxation*, London, John Murray.

Salinas Sánchez, Alejandro. 2009. *La huaneyda: historia del huano, 1840–1879*, Lima, Universidad Nacional Mayor de San Marcos, Seminario de Historia Rural Andina.

Senghaas, Dieter. 1985. *Aprender de Europa. Consideraciones sobre la historia del desarrollo*, Barcelona, Alfa.

Smith, A. 1904 [1776]. *An Inquiry into the Nature and Causes of Wealth of Nations*, London, Methuen & Co.

Tantaleán, J. 2011. *La gobernabilidad y el leviatán guanero: Desarrollo, crisis y guerra con Chile*, Lima, Instituto de Estudios Peruano, Banco Central de Reserva del Perú.

Van Dijk, T. 1993. "Principles of Critical Discourse Analysis," *Discourse & Society*, vol. 4, no. 2, 249–83.

Van Dijk, T. 1997, "Discourse as interaction in society," in Van Dijk, T. (ed.). *Discourse as Social Interaction: Discourse Studies, A Multidisciplinary Introduction*, London, California, SAGE.

Van Dijk, T. 1998. "Opinions and ideologies in the press," in Bell, A. and P. Garret (eds.). *Approaches to Media Discourse*, Oxford, Blackwell.

Van Dijk, T. 2008. *Discourse and Power*, Hampshire, New York, Palgrave Macmillan.

Van Dijk, T. 2009. "Critical discourse studies: a sociocognitive approach," in Wodak, R. and M. Meyer (eds.). *Methods of Critical Discourse Analysis*, London, California, SAGE.

Villalobos, S. and R. Sagredo. 1987. *El proteccionismo económico en Chile siglo XIX*, Santiago de Chile, Instituto Blas Cañas.

Wodak, R. and M. Meyer (eds.). 2009. *Methods of Critical Discourse Analysis*, London, California, SAGE.

Part V

Nationalism and economic development in Latin America

13 Varieties of economic nationalism
Latin America and Europe

Michele Alacevich

The "nation," in its modern meaning of political and territorial unity, is historically very young. A pioneer of studies on the idea of nation, the Italian historian Federico Chabod, pointed out in 1944 that the modern idea of nation emerged as a product of independentist, romantic movements in mid-nineteenth century Europe. The aspiration to "freedom" became an indissoluble companion to the idea of "nation," and, as Chabod wrote, "the Nineteenth century came to know what the Eighteenth century ignored: *national passions.*"[1] In a more recent synthesis, Eric Hobsbawm reports that the *New English Dictionary*, published in 1908, considered the nation, when defined as "political unity and independence," only to be a recent development.[2]

Real though it sometimes became as the outcome of political struggles, the concept of nation is basically an intellectual construction. In fact, the nation derives from other forces – "nationalism," first and foremost – and it is not a specific entity, or a reality, in and of itself. As Ernest Gellner put it, as much as "nationalism is not the awakening of an old, latent, dormant force, though that is how it indeed present itself," likewise "nations as natural, God-given way of classifying men, as an inherent though long-delayed political destiny, are a myth."[3] In the hundred-year period between approximately the 1830s – the beginning of Hobsbawm's Age of Revolution – and the interwar period in the twentieth century, nations emerged as cultural and political artifacts. Still, as should by now be clear, "nationalism" – not "the nation" – was the driving force behind this process. Again in the words of Gellner:

> Nationalism … sometimes takes pre-existing cultures and turns them into nations, sometimes invents them, and often obliterates pre-existing cultures. … Nations are not inscribed into the nature of things …, nor were national states the manifest ultimate destiny of ethnic or cultural groups. What do exist are cultures, often subtly grouped, shading into each other, overlapping, intertwined; and there exist, usually but not always, political units of all shapes and sizes. … Nationalism is not the awakening and assertion of these mythical, supposedly natural and given units. It is, on the contrary, the crystallization of new units.[4]

Even though the primary idea of "nation" insisted on political and territorial concepts – that is, it insisted on the idea of a body of citizens occupying a specific territory – an economic notion of the State soon appeared, too, as formulated for example by John Rae and Alexander Hamilton in North America, and Friedrich List in Europe.[5] Even liberal economists following in the anti-mercantilist footsteps of Adam Smith, arguably less prepared to develop a theory of the economic role of the State, did not abandon "the test of national advantage as a criterion of policy," as Lord Robbins later put it, nor did they refute that there was indeed an "essential continuity of thought in the tradition of economic liberalism concerning the positive nature of the co-operation between the state and the individual" (Robbins 1978, pp. 10 and 38).

The European tradition of economic nationalism, in particular, grew vigorously in parallel to the process of reconfiguration of the political map of the continent that followed World War I, specifically the dismemberment of the Austro-Hungarian and Ottoman empires and the birth of a number of new States. The nation could no longer be described exclusively through the categories of political unity and territorial independence, as the *New English Dictionary* had proposed only a few years before, but acquired a third, fundamental feature: the *national economy*.[6] Yet, if the demise of the Austro-Hungarian and Ottoman empires marked the success of political nationalism, the economic fragility of the new states of Central and Eastern Europe cast a dark shadow on their prospects for long-term independence and economic growth. As Hobsbawm put it, "the European situation now anticipated the situation of the politically decolonized 'Third World' since World War II, and resembled that laboratory of premature neo-colonialism, Latin America."[7] It was clear that without economic development, real political independence would remain a chimera, and this was as true for Central and Eastern European countries in the interwar period as it would have been true for the so-called less developed countries of the postwar period. This same intuition forms the basis of another important book, Joseph Love's *Crafting the Third World*, in which Love shows how ideologies of economic nationalism in Central Europe, and specifically in Rumania, between the late nineteenth century and the interwar period, influenced similar debates in Latin America, and specifically in Brazil, in the post-World War II years.[8]

My purpose in this brief chapter is to start from the work of Hobsbawm and Love and, building on their insights, to discuss a couple of questions that may be useful for comparing economic nationalism in Latin America and Europe in the early postwar period. I will do this by examining two different trajectories taken by a set of ideas on economic nationalism that originated in Central and Eastern Europe in the interwar period. One trajectory, discussed by Love, emphasizes the links between Eastern Europe and Latin America. The other trajectory, which I have discussed elsewhere and will briefly summarize below, shows the links between interwar Eastern Europe and postwar Southern Europe. I will then close the triangle by showing how

Latin American and Southern European scholars and politicians interpreted and reshaped the same set of ideas originally discussed in interwar Eastern Europe. My goal is to highlight some important differences between economic nationalism in Latin America and Europe, with special attention to the role of protectionist policies. This exercise in comparative analysis between Latin America and Europe rests on a consolidated tradition of both academic studies and actual economic reforms that scholars and so-called "money doctors" have conducted in past decades.[9] As has already been argued – without forgetting the importance of local cultural roots and traditions – Latin America can be seen as a sort of "quasi-Europe" or "epigonal Europe" in its formal culture, dominant religion, legal codes, economic institutions, and vision of what constitutes progress.[10] Yet, as we will see, the varieties of economic nationalism that developed in Latin America and Europe, connected though as they were, differed in important ways.

***

Love's *Crafting the Third World*, mentioned above, is particularly important in this respect. This book is a fascinating history of how ideas travel, and how they are transformed, adapted, and eventually adopted in different contexts. Specifically, Love shows how the Central and Eastern European debates on agrarian overpopulation, economic backwardness, industrialization and industrial protectionism, which reached their most mature expressions in the interwar period, directly influenced the development discourse in Latin America in the late 1940s and the 1950s.

Love argues that Rumanian economists, like Latin American economists, had a long-standing tradition of adopting and at the same time deeply transforming classic traditions of economic analysis, whether liberal or socialist. At least since the mid-1880s, even liberal Rumanian economists had abandoned the customary laissez-faire approach in favor of high protectionist tariffs in defense of national production and "infant industries," as famously discussed by Friedrich List in 1841.[11] The Rumanian liberal tradition apparently defined itself in opposition to an ultra-conservative, Eastern European free-trade agrarian party, rather than through any actual resemblance to Western European liberalism.[12]

The same dynamic occurred within other schools of thought. At the beginning of the twentieth century, Constantin Dobrogeanu-Gherea, Marxist by formation, theorized structurally different trajectories for advanced and underdeveloped countries. As is well known, in the Preface to the first volume of *Capital*, Marx claimed that the laws of capitalist production work "with iron necessity towards inevitable results." In other words, he continued, "The country that is more developed industrially only shows, to the less developed, the image of its own future."[13] Even though his analysis was mainly about England, the laws of historical motion that he discussed pertained in fact to all countries, developed and less developed alike. As Marx, quoting Horace, summed it up, "De te fabula narratur!"[14] Leagues away from this view, Gherea considered underdevelopment as a syndrome, and the condition of underdeveloped countries as fundamentally influenced and, ultimately, distorted by advanced countries at the core of the economic system.[15] Far from showing underdeveloped countries their future, Gherea claimed, the conditions of advanced countries were not replicable. England, in particular, was a unique case, which had forever transformed the playing field and made it impossible for late-comers to follow in its footsteps. We might imagine Gherea's response to Marx: "*Non* de nobis fabula narratur!" Only a handful of years earlier, and from different ideological foundations, Rumanian populist Constantin Stere had affirmed basically the same ideas: "Our situation is not only backward, which would be bad enough; it is abnormal, which is much worse."[16]

In particular, most commentators noted how the Rumanian, and more generally Eastern European, economies were characterized at once by a weak and limited industrial sector and by a low-productivity, over-populated agricultural sector. The virtual non-existence, in the region, of a truly laissez-faire liberal tradition made possible a widespread convergence of scholars from different intellectual traditions in favor of some schemes for moving agrarian excess population towards the industrial sector. The concept of an overpopulation problem in the agricultural sector apparently referred to the notion of "disguised unemployment," notably discussed in 1936 by Cambridge economist Joan Robinson.[17] Yet, whereas Robinson introduced the term to describe the adoption of less productive jobs by workers previously employed in higher-productivity industrial sectors – that is, to offer a more realistic description than that offered by the concept of "unemployment" of the effects of a decline in effective demand that would reduce industrial employment – in Eastern Europe, the term could not refer to a "downgraded" industrial workforce, for no strong industrial sector had ever truly existed. Disguised unemployment, in Eastern Europe, was used for the first time to describe an agrarian workforce whose only professional horizon had been a backward agriculture. Two years before Robinson's article, Rumanian economist Constantin Ianculescu had thus summarized the consequences of agrarian backwardness and overpopulation: within a generation, he predicted, "a permanently unemployed agrarian proletariat will be created," which would be forced to migrate towards the urban centers. Industrialization, in Ianculescu's view, was the solution.[18] The two forms of (disguised) unemployment thus originated from two very different problems. Whereas in advanced countries unemployment was based on a lack of effective demand, in backward countries it was based on the lack of capital equipment, in turn due to basic disproportions among factors of production. If Joan Robinson, in other words, analyzed "disguised unemployment" within the Keynesian framework of the "economics of crisis" in advanced countries, Central and Eastern European scholars analyzed it within the framework of an "economics of backwardness."[19]

The necessity of fostering a process of industrialization through active state interventions such as protectionist policies, supports to exports, tax concessions, and the like, was in sum widely agreed upon, based on the revolt against the "unequal exchange," denounced by a number of Rumanian economists, between advanced industrial countries and backward agricultural Eastern European countries. This view had a long pedigree, from at least Alexandru Xenopol in the 1880s, to Mihail Manoilescu, who, in spite of his theoretical vacillations, was considered the most famous and influential Rumanian economist of his era.

Manoilescu, who was active in the 1930s, was an economic nationalist and politician with Fascist and Nazi sympathies. He strongly supported protectionist and corporatist policies to shield the Rumanian national economy from an international scenario detrimental to its economy and labor force. At times supporting the mechanization of the country's agriculture and thus the specialization of Rumania as a high-productivity agrarian country, but more often in favor of policies of import substitution industrialization, Manoilescu remained coherent in focusing on the problem of how to increase the productivity of the country's labor force. Other than in the late 1930s and early 1940s, when his allegiance to the Nazi regime turned him into a supporter of the complementarity of agrarian Rumania with industrial Germany within a *Grossraumwirtschaft* (Greater economic space) framework, Manoilescu was in fact a fervent protectionist in support of the Rumanian national industrial sector. The increasing shift of workforce from low-productivity agriculture to high-productivity manufactures would, in his view, create a convergence between the productivities of the two sectors, which, in the long run, would benefit the agrarian sector as well. This, however, could only happen if the nascent industry were to be allowed to develop behind protectionist policies. Like Xenopol, Manoilescu, too, denounced the "unequal exchange" between agrarian and industrial countries.[20]

As Love has put it, the protectionist tradition discussed above "was reinvented in the postwar era by structuralists and dependency writers in Latin America" (1996, p. 214). In other words, in order to understand national economic policies of postwar Latin America, Love suggests that we look at the economic nationalism of interwar Eastern Europe. Latin America, however, was not the only destination for the migratory flow of the ideas developed within the framework of interwar Central European economic nationalism. To develop our comparative analysis, another route, geographically and intellectually closer to the roots of those ideas, will turn out to be particularly useful. Hence, instead of following how those ideas migrated to Latin America, I will follow them on a different journey, that is, to Southern Europe.

***

As I have discussed elsewhere, the tradition of interwar debates on agrarian overpopulation in Central and Eastern Europe deeply influenced a multi-year study project during World War II by the Royal Institute of International Affairs, also known as Chatham House, on how to reconstruct and develop Central and Eastern Europe at the end of the hostilities.[21] Founded in 1920 by a group of British scholars disappointed with the final outcome of the Paris Peace Treaty that formally ended World War I, Chatham House quickly become the most important British think-tank specialized in the study of international relations. There, they argued that the punitive reparation clauses imposed on Germany, far from reducing that country to impotence and restoring the European balance of powers, would plant the seeds for future and potentially even more destructive tensions.

When World War II erupted, Chatham House committed itself to avoiding the mistakes that had doomed peace after World War I, by discussing the foundations for long-term peace and prosperity in Europe that might be possible once the war was over and, hopefully, Nazism defeated. Central and Eastern Europe were the weakest areas of the continent, and the natural target of the Nazi European imperial project.[22] There was in fact widespread agreement that, as a British geographer wrote, Eastern Europe was a pivotal region for the control of the European continent and, in ever broader perspectives, the Eurasian continent, the entire Mediterranean area (which, considered in Braudelian terms, also entailed the surrounding lands and major mountain chains), and, indeed, eventually the World.[23] In sum, to succeed where the Paris Peace Conference had failed, it would be crucial after World War II to help Eastern Europe overcome its backwardness and reach a condition of political stability and economic prosperity.

During World War II, London became the destination of a huge network of émigré economists from Eastern Europe who were soon recruited, formally and informally, by Chatham House. Through them, the interwar debate on backwardness and industrialization in Eastern Europe (examined by Love in his book) became a fundamental element in Chatham House's study. The organizer of the Chatham House study group was a 40-year-old Polish economist who had studied in Vienna and Italy and moved to London in the early 1930s. A brilliant but not particularly famous economics professor at University College London, he would be later recognized as one of the "pioneers" of development economics. His name was Paul Rosenstein-Rodan, and an article he published in 1943 summarizing the main points of the Chatham House study he directed – "Problems of Industrialisation in Eastern and South-Eastern Europe" – is now often mentioned as a sort of birth certificate of development economics.[24]

In this article, the influence of the interwar debate on economic and social backwardness is absolutely evident: the excess agrarian population plays a central role, as does the need to move this population to an industrial sector that would have to be established from scratch. Yet there is a striking absence in Rosenstein-Rodan's reproposal of the interwar debate: in this article, protectionist policies play no role. Despite Rosenstein-Rodan's acknowledgment that State or regional planning policies would be necessary to trigger economic development in a backward area, which is characterized by strong disincentives to private entrepreneurship, in fact protectionist policies are conspicuously missing.

Major though this difference from the interwar debate was, it should not surprise us. After all, the study took place in Britain at a time when the

United Kingdom intended to maintain a hegemonic role in postwar Central and Eastern Europe. As we know, events unfolded differently from the British script, and the Soviet takeover of Eastern Europe made Chatham House's plans useless. Yet, if *Eastern* Europe disappeared from the picture, the onset of the Cold War made the problem of backwardness a crucial question for *Western* Europe. At that turn of events, and more precisely in 1947, all eyes turned to Italy, whose Southern regions were extremely poor and characterized by social and political instability, and whose Communist Party, the most well-organized among anti-Fascist groups throughout the *Ventennio*, was the largest in Western Europe.[25] For the same reasons that development was to be fostered in Eastern Europe in an anti-Nazi perspective, development was now to be fostered in Southern Europe, and namely Italy, in an anti-Communist perspective.

As a World Bank document put it,

> Italy is a country of extreme contrasts. The Northern part is highly developed …, while the Southern part is poor, underdeveloped and overpopulated, and should probably be regarded as a development rather than a reconstruction area. The Mezzogiorno is the only underdeveloped region of its size in Western Europe. … An area larger than Benelux and Denmark combined, the most vulnerable point of social stability in Western Europe.[26]

The memo was prepared under the supervision of Rosenstein-Rodan, who after leaving Chatham House had joined the Bank, and became the principal architect of its loans to Italy.[27] Building on his previous analysis of the economic problems of Eastern Europe, Rosenstein-Rodan and the Italian economists and civil servants with whom he collaborated insisted – like in the Chatham House study – on the problem of excess agrarian population and on the opportunity of tackling it through a comprehensive plan of industrialization.[28]

As the World Bank's *Articles of Agreement* – in other words, its foundational document – state, the Bank's mandate was to make loans for specific projects, with no focus on macroeconomic questions such as structural imbalances in international trade or the like.[29] Interestingly, however, the Bank's loan to Italy was exclusively aimed at supporting the country's balance of payments. In other words, while Italy implemented a domestic development plan, the World Bank was concerned with making sure that this plan would not adversely impact Italy's foreign trade.

Based on the calculations made by an Italian think-tank specialized in studying the conditions of the Italian South, the World Bank and the Bank of Italy agreed that a multi-year domestic plan of investments would have a direct impact on the balance of payments through an increase in employment and hence in consumption, and thus a decrease of export or increase of imports (see Table 13.1).[30]

Table 13.1 Italy: domestic development and international trade

---

Domestic investment plan of Lira 66 billion p.a. (i.e., $100 million p.a.)
↓
Employment increase = rise in consumption
↓
Rise in imports (and/or decrease in exports)
↓
Plan's impact on the balance of payments
Loan = $10 million p.a.

***

The different trajectories that nationalistic economic ideas originally discussed in interwar Eastern Europe followed in the postwar period deeply transformed those same ideas in different ways. If in their trajectory from Eastern Europe to Latin America the accent was principally on protectionist policies – Joseph Love writes of a "family resemblance" between the theory of industrial protectionism of the Rumanian economist Manoilescu and "at least some varieties of structuralism" – in the path from Eastern to Southern Europe, on the contrary, economic nationalism lost its most protectionist features and adapted to an international system that was built in open opposition to the collapse of interwar international trade.[31] In the European situation, the thinking went, domestic development policies should coexist with international open trade policies.

With some simplifications, we could relate these two approaches to two different visions of the political economy of development (see Table 13.2).[32] One refers to the work of Ha-Joon Chang, and we could refer to it as the "kicking away the ladder" thesis. Chang demonstrates that now-developed countries heavily applied protectionist policies when they were developing their own industrial sectors, only to impose free trade to less developed countries at a later stage. For example, Britain, in the words of Chang, "was an aggressive user, and in certain areas a pioneer, of activist policies intended to promote infant industries" (Chang 2003, p. 24). More precisely, Chang notes that now-developed countries, especially Britain and the United States of America, not only protected but actively *promoted* their infant industries through interventionist industrial, trade, and technology policies (Chang 2003, pp. 24–25) and later shifted to free trade to maintain their global economic primacy and stop industrialization elsewhere by enlarging the markets for primary products. Reporting a comparison originally used by Friedrich List, Chang then concludes that "the British preaching for free trade is equivalent to someone who has already climbed to the top 'kicking away the ladder' with which he/she climbed" (Chang 2003, p. 24). In fact, according to Chang, now-developed countries "actually protected their industries a lot more heavily than the currently developing countries" (Chang 2003, p. 28). If this is the case, the only possible conclusion is that supposedly "good" or orthodox free-trade policies are not the right policies for less developed countries to catch up. While this does not imply that currently

Table 13.2 Different visions of development in Europe and Latin America

Visions of development	
Latin America	*Europe*
Protectionist policies	Domestic development plans
"Kicking away the ladder" vision	"Embedded liberalism" vision
↓	↓
Dependency theory	International trade and domestic development

less developed countries should automatically apply active infant industry promotion strategies like those applied by now-developed countries in their past, the historical record as revisited by Chang suggests that less developed countries have a point in developing strategies that defend them from laissez-faire policies that ultimately reinforce unequal exchange.

The second vision could be called the "embedded liberalism" thesis, after the famous definition by political scientist John Ruggie. Ruggie based his analysis on the dichotomy, proposed by Karl Polanyi in 1944, of embedded and disembedded economies, the latter relating to the classical free-trade era preceding World War I, and the former to the protectionist reaction of the interwar years. According to Ruggie, the period after World War II saw the emergence of an international economic system that was in itself novel, though it combined elements characteristic of previous periods.[33] "Unlike the economic nationalism of the thirties," Ruggie claimed, embedded liberalism "would be multilateral in character; unlike the liberalism of the gold standard and free trade, its multilateralism would be predicated upon domestic interventionism" (Ruggie 1982, p. 393). As even these few references make clear, the accent here is notably different from that in Chang's analysis. The "embedded liberalism" thesis would support state interventionism at the domestic level for development purposes – provided, however, that this did not conflict with international trade flows. Thus, unlike in the "kicking away the ladder" vision, in the "embedded liberalism" vision there is no place for truly protectionist policies.

It may be useful to repeat here that this juxtaposition of visions is possible only if we accept some degree of simplification. Ricardo Bielschowsky, for instance, has rightly pointed out that a division along these lines may become deeply misleading. Latin American economists were depicted as "autarkic," though they were not.[34] Yet, this autarkic characterization – or caricature – of Latin American economists bears some significance. The same ideas, transposed in different contexts, were received differently in Latin America and in Europe, and shaped the debate on their national economic policies in different ways, ultimately influencing the way Latin American policies and their principal proponents were perceived in the broader international debate.

Table 13.3 "Types of Development Theories"

Types of development theories

		Monoeconomics claim	
		asserted	rejected
Mutual-benefit claim:	asserted	Orthodox economics	Development economics
	rejected	Marx?	Neo-Marxist theories

Source: from Hirschman 1981, p. 3.

Consider, for example, how Albert Hirschman, another "pioneer," defined the discipline of development economics in its golden age, and what elements, in his view, differentiated it from other approaches. Hirschman had a deep, first-hand knowledge of the Latin American economic situation and economic policies, having lived in Colombia for four years between 1952 and 1956, first as economic advisor to the Colombian *Consejo Nacional de Planificación* and later as private consultant. The book that made him famous in the development community, *The Strategy of Economic Development* (1958), although rather theoretical and not focused on any specific case study, was based on the observations that Hirschman had put together during his Colombian sojourn.[35] Hirschman was a personal friend of many Latin American structuralists, was highly conversant with their work (see Hirschman 1961), and considered his own analysis close in many respects to Latin American structuralism. Yet, when it came to defining the borders of the discipline of development economics, Hirschman notably excluded the structuralists and dependency theorists from the field.

As he argued in a famous 1981 article, while development economists and dependency scholars agreed on the fact that mainstream economics was unfit to study the specific mechanisms of less developed economies, and was thus a poor basis for the design and implementation of economic policies for them, they differed on a crucial point. Whereas development economists believed that economic relations between advanced and less developed countries could be mutually beneficial, structuralists and especially dependency scholars were highly skeptical about this.

In other words, whereas development economists interpreted international economic relations between developed and less developed countries within the framework of "embedded liberalism," that is, a combination of domestic, state-supported development policies and mutually beneficial international trade, Latin American structuralists and dependency theorists leaned crucially towards a "kicking away the ladder" interpretation of such relations.

***

Although I do not personally agree with Hirschman's somewhat narrow definition of development economics, it certainly resonates with how a cluster of ideas travelled, mixed with autochthonous analyses, and led eventually to rather different interpretations of economic nationalism in Latin America and Europe. Protectionist policies and import-substituting industrialization characterized the Latin American economic nationalism in a way that cannot be applied to Southern European regions. And yet, the picture would remain grossly incomplete if we did not also underscore some important similarities existing between Latin American and European postwar economic policies.

To start with, we should consider the prominent role in fostering a domestic process of development assigned to the state by scholars and practitioners from both sides of the Atlantic. We mentioned this question in a number of passages above, yet without the necessary emphasis it deserves. Pasquale Saraceno, one of the major architects of postwar development planning in Italy, for instance, highlighted the leading role that a state development plan would have in overcoming the Italian economic dualism between the industrialized North and the agrarian and backward South: "The only certainty we had," wrote Saraceno in a later recollection, "was that any economic policy should privilege the regional diffusion of the industrial sector to close the gap between North and South."[36]

As it had been for Eastern Europe a few years earlier, the dichotomy backwardness/development was discussed in terms of (i) overpopulation in the agrarian sector and (ii) industrialization to absorb agrarian disguised unemployment, (iii) within the framework of a state development plan.[37] In this respect, the similarities between Latin America and Southern Europe are remarkably strong. In both cases, there is a rejection of agricultural specialization; the economic role of the state is emphasized; and finally, the process of industrialization is seen as a means for social inclusion and political stabilization.

This connection between economic nationalism and social inclusion is a phenomenon of particular relevance. After World War II, Latin America and Southern Europe saw the recurrence of a specific aspect of the "bourgeois" nation that had already characterized interwar Europe and that we mentioned at the beginning of this chapter: "the nation as a 'national economy'."[38] Industrialization, in other words, became a central element of the process of nation building, and the main vehicle for social inclusion. In Southern Italy this meant the emancipation of large strata of the population from the latifundium, an agrarian quasi-feudal system that had survived Fascism. For the first time, the masses of Southern-Italy agrarian workers obtained access to, and actually participated in, the political life of the newborn Republic. For many Latin American countries, the process of economic development and social inclusion was, if possible, even more formidable, directed as it was both against domestic feudal structures and new forms of foreign economic domination. Postwar commentators have over and over insisted on the fundamental link between the process of economic development and the dynamics of nation building. On the occasion of the centenary of the foundation of the Italian State, for example, Pasquale Saraceno denounced "the failed Italian economic unification one century after its political unification" as the most important problem that Italy had to face. The same perspective has more recently been emphasized by economic sociologist and former Italian Minister of Development Carlo Trigilia: "the effects of this fracture ... can endanger the national unity."[39] In Brazil in the late 1950s, President Juscelino Kubitschek offered a more optimistic view, claiming that economic development will "consolidate a free and powerful nation."[40] The subsequent military dictatorship did not quite keep faith with Kubitschek's promises of freedom and emancipation, but under the Lula government, between 2001 and 2008, the Social Inclusion Index, which includes factors such as job creation, improvements in education, access to media and telecommunications, grew on average at more than twice the rate of economic growth, that is, 5.3 percent and 2.3 percent respectively.[41]

***

The discussion above has offered some elements, I hope, with which to compare the many similarities as well as striking differences among the various forms that economic nationalism took in Latin America and Europe in the years after World War II. One further question, however, remains to be mentioned, if not fully discussed, in order to explain the different shapes that economic nationalism took in Latin America and Europe, namely, the broader historical context of the early postwar period.

In the early postwar years, Europe reemerged from a recent past of aggressive totalitarianisms. Protectionist policies – a major economic weapon of Fascist Italy and Nazi Germany – were completely discredited and politically untenable. Moreover, after five years of immensely destructive war, Europe became the major field of Cold War confrontation. The Marshall Plan, which emerged from this specific context, was thus entangled with longer-term development policies on the continent, especially in the south. The World Bank loans to support the balance of payments can also be explained within this framework. As Cowen pointed out, "Since the late 1940s, many Latin American leaders have called for a 'Marshall Plan for Latin America,' and US Administrations as diverse as the Kennedy's and Reagan's have played with the idea."[42] Leaving aside whether this would have been a sensible solution for the continent, what is certain is that it was never brought to fruition, nor did Latin American countries receive loans in support of their balances of payments. Indeed, one could argue that Latin American scholars and politicians were confirmed in their analysis of being a peripheral area by the state of international economic affairs. Latin American economic nationalism responded to a different set of forces than, and was inevitably different from, the European variant. Latin American structuralists could not help but look for their own solutions.

Notes

1 "Il secolo diciannovesimo conosce, insomma, quel che il Settecento ignorava: *le passioni nazionali*" (Chabod 1961 [1943–44], p. 50, emphasis in the original).
2 As quoted in Hobsbawm 1992, p. 18.

3 Gellner 1983, pp. 48–49.
4 Gellner 1983, p. 49.
5 See, for example, Rae 1905 [1834], pp. 359–447, and List 1966 [1841]. On Rae, see also Schumpeter 1968 [1954], pp. 468–469; on Hamilton's *Report on Manufactures* (1791), and in particular on how it "reveals quite clearly essentials of the analytic framework that was to be made explicit by … F. List," see Schumpeter 1968 [1954], p. 199.
6 Hobsbawm 1992.
7 Hobsbawm 1992, p. 138.
8 Love 1996.
9 See, among others, Drake 1988; 1994; Flandreau 2003.
10 Love 1996, p. 5.
11 List 1966 [1841].
12 See Love 1996, pp. 28–29.
13 Marx 1998 [1867], p. 21.
14 Horace, *Satires I*, as quoted in Marx 1998 [1867], p. 21.
15 See Love 1996, p. 41, referring to Constantin Dobrogeanu-Gherea.
16 As quoted in Love 1996, p. 32.
17 Robinson 1936.
18 As quoted in Love 1996, p. 61.
19 On this, see also the analysis of Love 1996, pp. 65–66. According to Love, the first to use "disguised unemployment" in English in the framework of the economics of backwardness was Michal Kalecki in a 1938 review of the German edition of Rumanian economist Mihail Manoilescu's *Theory of Protectionism*.
20 The life and political economy of Mihail Manoilescu are discussed at length in Love 1996, pp. 71–98.
21 See Alacevich 2013b.
22 On this, see Mazower 2008.
23 Mackinder (1996 [1919]). For Fernand Braudel's vision of the Mediterranean as a much larger region than that actually defined by the Mediterranean Sea and its shores, see Braudel (1972 [1949]).
24 Rosenstein-Rodan 1943. On the importance of this article for the discipline of development economics, see Bhagwati 2000; Krugman 1992, 1994; Murphy et al. 1989; and Pomfret 1992.
25 Aga-Rossi 1990.
26 "Proposed Bank Action Toward Italy," Economic Department at McCloy's request, March 29, 1949, World Bank Group Archives, quoted in Alacevich 2010 and 2014.
27 See Rosenstein-Rodan 1961.
28 On this, see a much more extensive discussion in Alacevich 2013a and 2013b.
29 International Bank for Reconstruction and Development, *Articles of Agreement*, Art. I (i).
30 See also Alacevich 2010.
31 Love 1996, p. 12.
32 I am indebted to Andreas Kakridis for his extremely useful and lucid comments on these different visions.
33 See Polanyi 1944.
34 See Bielschowsky 2009.
35 For an analysis of Hirschman's years in Colombia and early development economics, see Adelman 2013; Alacevich 2009, 2011.
36 Saraceno 1977, p. 139.
37 This was not a completely novel position in the Italian debate, but only in the post-war period the rejection of agricultural specialization for the Italian South reached a vast consensus. See Alacevich 2013a.

266   M. Alacevich

38 Hobsbawm 1992, p. 131.
39 See Saraceno 1961 and Trigilia 2012, p. 47.
40 Juscelino Kubitschek, 1956 message to Congress, as quoted in Wolfe 2009, p. 135.
41 As reported in Freitas de Moraes and Felicio 2013.
42 See the call for an Alliance for Progress by President John F. Kennedy on March 13, 1961, and a comprehensive aid plan for Latin America advocated by the Reagan Administration, mentioned in Cowen 1985.

Bibliography

Adelman, Jeremy (2013), *Worldly Philosopher: The Odyssey of Albert O. Hirschman*, Princeton: Princeton University Press.
Aga-Rossi, Elena (1990), "L'Italia allo scoppio della guerra fredda: fattori nazionali e internazionali," in Ennio di Nolfo, Roman H. Rainero, and Brunello Vigezzi (eds.), *L'Italia e la Politica di Potenza in Europa, 1945–50*, Settimo Milanese: Marzorati, pp. 621–633.
Alacevich, Michele (2009), *The Political Economy of the World Bank. The Early Years*, Stanford, CA: Stanford University Press.
Alacevich, Michele (2010), "The World Bank and the Reconstruction of Italy, 1947–49," mimeo, Columbia University, February 24, 2010 and subsequent revisions.
Alacevich, Michele (2011), "Early Development Economics Debates Revisited," *Journal of the History of Economic Thought*, Vol. 33, No. 2 (Jun.), pp. 145–171.
Alacevich, Michele (2013a), "Postwar Development in the Italian Mezzogiorno. Analyses and Policies," *Journal of Modern Italian Studies*, Vol. 18, No. 1, pp. 90–112.
Alacevich, Michele (2013b), "Planning Peace. Development Policies in Postwar Europe," mimeo, Cambridge University, April 15, 2013 and subsequent revisions.
Alacevich, Michele (2014), "The Making of a Development Economist: Paul Rosenstein-Rodan and the Birth of Development Economics," University of Siena, Italy, 8th Annual Conference on the History of Recent Economics, mimeo, May 24, 2014 and subsequent revisions.
Bhagwati, Jagdish N. (2000), *The Wind of the Hundred Days: How Washington Mismanaged Globalization*, Cambridge, MA: MIT Press.
Bielschowsky, Ricardo (2009). "Sixty Years of ECLAC: Structuralism and Neo-structuralism," CEPAL Review, Vol. 97, p. 171.
Braudel, Fernand (1972 [1949]), *The Mediterranean and the Mediterranean World in the Age of Philip II*, New York: Harper & Row.
Chabod, Federico (1961 [1943–44]), *L'idea di Nazione*, edited by Armando Saitta and Ernesto Sestan, Rome-Bari: Laterza.
Chang, Ha-Joon (2003), "Kicking Away the Ladder: Infant Industry Promotion in Historical Perspective," *Oxford Development Studies*, Vol. 31, No. 1, pp. 21–32.
Cowen, Tyler (1985), "The Marshall Plan: Myths and Realities," in Doug Bandow (ed.), *U.S. Aid to the Developing World: A Free Market Agenda*, Washington, DC: The Heritage Foundation, pp. 61–74.
Drake, Paul W. (1988), *The Money Doctor in the Andes: U.S. Advisors, Investors, and Economic Reform in Latin America from World War I to the Great Depression*, Durham, NC: Duke University Press.
Drake, Paul W., ed. (1994), *Money Doctors, Foreign Debts, and Economic Reforms in Latin America from the 1890s to the Present*, Wilmington, DE: SR Books.
Flandreau, Marc (2003), *Money Doctors: The Experience of International Financial Advising, 1850–2000*, London: Routledge.

Freitas de Moraes, Vagner and João Antonio Felicio (2013), "Growth is Not Enough," *OECD Forum*, www.oecd.org/forum/growth-is-not-enough.htm, accessed on Feb. 2, 2016.

Gellner, Ernest (1983), *Nations and Nationalism*, Ithaca, NY: Cornell University Press.

Hirschman, Albert O. (1958), *The Strategy of Economic Development*, New Haven, CT: Yale University Press.

Hirschman, Albert O. (1961), "Ideologies of Economic Development in Latin America," in Albert O. Hirschman (ed.), *Latin American Issues: Essays and Comments*, New York: Twentieth Century Fund, pp. 3–42.

Hirschman, Albert O. (1981), "The Rise and Decline of Development Economics," in Albert O. Hirschman, *Essays in Trespassing: Economics to Politics and Beyond*, Cambridge: Cambridge University Press.

Hobsbawm, Eric (1992), *Nations and Nationalism Since 1780. Programme, Myth, Reality*, Second edition, Cambridge: Cambridge University Press.

Krugman, Paul (1992), "Toward a Counter-Counterrevolution in Development Theory," in Lawrence H. Summers and Shekhar Shah (eds.), *Proceedings of the World Bank Annual Conference on Development Economics 1992*, Washington, DC: The World Bank, pp. 15–38.

Krugman, Paul (1994), "The Fall and Rise of Development Economics," in Lloyd Rodwin and Donald A. Schön (eds.), *Rethinking the Development Experience. Essays Provoked by the Work of Albert O. Hirschman*, Washington, DC, and Cambridge, MA: The Brookings Institution and the Lincoln Institute of Land Policy, pp. 39–58.

List, Friedrich (1966 [1841]), *The National System of Political Economy*, New York: Augustus M. Kelley Publishers.

Love, Joseph L. (1996), *Crafting the Third World. Theorizing Underdevelopment in Rumania and Brazil*, Stanford: Stanford University Press.

Mackinder, Halford J. (1996 [1919]), *Democratic Ideals and Reality: A Study in the Politics of Reconstruction*, Washington, DC: National Defense University Press.

Marx, Karl (1998 [1867]), *Capital. A Critique of Political Economy. Volume I*, London: ElecBook.

Mazower, Mark (2008), *Hitler's Empire: How the Nazis Ruled Europe*, New York: Penguin.

Murphy, Kevin M., Andrei Shleifer, and Robert W. Vishny (1989), "Industrialization and the Big Push," *Journal of Political Economy*, Vol. 97, No. 5 (Oct.), pp. 1003–1026.

Polanyi, Karl (1944), *The Great Transformation*, New York: Farrar & Rinehart.

Pomfret, Richard (1992), *Diverse Paths of Economic Development*, London: Harvester Wheatsheaf.

Rae, John (1905 [1834]), *The Sociological Theory of Capital. Being a Complete Reprint of the New Principles of Political Economy, 1834*, edited by Charles Whitney Mixter, London: Macmillan.

Robbins, Lionel (1978), *The Theory of Economic Policy in English Classical Political Economy*, Second edition, London: Macmillan.

Robinson, Joan (1936), "Disguised Unemployment," *The Economic Journal*, Vol. 46, No. 182 (Jun.), pp. 225–237.

Rosenstein-Rodan, Paul N. (1943), "Problems of Industrialisation of Eastern and South-Eastern Europe," *The Economic Journal*, Vol. 53, No. 210/211 (Jun.–Sep.), pp. 202–211.

Rosenstein-Rodan, Paul N. (1961), "Interview" by R. Oliver, August 14, 1961, The World Bank/IFC Archives, Oral History Program.

Ruggie, John G. (1982), "International Regimes, Transactions, and Change: Embedded Liberalism in the Postwar Economic Order," *International Organization*, Vol. 36, No. 2, International Regimes (Spring), pp. 379–415.

Saraceno, Pasquale (1961), "La mancata unificazione economica italiana a cento anni dalla unificazione politica," in Pasquale Saraceno, *Sottosviluppo Industriale e Questione Meridionale. Studi degli anni 1952–1963*, Bologna: Il Mulino, 1990.

Saraceno, Pasquale (1977), *Intervista sulla Ricostruzione*, Roma: Laterza.

Schumpeter, Joseph (1968 [1954]), *History of Economic Analysis*. Edited from manuscript by Elizabeth Body Schumpeter, New York: Oxford University Press.

Trigilia, Carlo (2012), *Non c'è Nord senza Sud. Perché la crescita dell'Italia si decide nel Mezzogiorno*, Bologna: Il Mulino.

Wolfe, Joel (2009), *Autos and Progress. The Brazilian Search for Modernity*, New York: Oxford University Press.

14 A note on some historical connections between nationalism and economic development in Latin America[1]

Mauro Boianovsky

Nationalism as a condition for economic growth

In her well-known 2001 book on *The spirit of capitalism: nationalism and economic growth*, Liah Greenfeld argues that the dominant historical factor explaining the motivation for economic growth has been nationalism. This is behind the main feature of modern capitalist economic systems, that is, their orientation to growth, as well as the concept of "economic civilization" as the dominant aspect of social life. As implied by its title, the book is informed by Max Weber's approach to economic sociology. Even if controversial, her thesis has received wide attention (see e.g. Hall 2003; Szlajfer and Chmielewska-Szlajfer 2012, chapter 1). Greenfeld's case studies are formed by a set of industrialized nations (Great Britain, France, Germany, Japan and the United States), with no reference to Latin America or other developing countries. The present note about the Latin American case is largely inspired by Greenfeld's framework, albeit it is not meant to be a full application to Latin America.

Surely, the historical relation between nationalism and growth has attracted as well the attention of Latin American scholars, as illustrated by the 2008 special issue of the Brazilian journal *Estudos Avançados*, with articles by L.C. Bresser-Pereira and João Antonio de Paula, among others. In fact, Dudley Seers (1983) – a British economist who worked at the United Nations Economic Commission for Latin America (CEPAL) in the late 1950s and early 1960s – argued for a strong relation between nationalism and the emergence of development economics as a field in the post-war period. Such links can be traced back to Friedrich List's 1841 German volume *Das nationale System der Politischen Oekonomie* (translated into English in 1856 in the United States and in 1885 in England), which, as indicated by its title, focused on the "national" dimension of economic thought and policy. List's *System* may be regarded as the foremost expression of "economic nationalism" in the nineteenth century (see Hont 2005). The relation between economic development and nationalism is prominent in W.W. Rostow's ([1960] 1990) concepts of growth stages and "reactive nationalism," which had a clear influence on

Greenfeld's approach and on historical accounts of economic development theory and policy (see e.g. Arndt 1987).

As a unique form of social consciousness, nationalism emerged in the sixteenth century in mercantilist England and spread first to the English colonies in America. After that, during the eighteenth century it reached France and Russia, followed in the nineteenth and twentieth centuries by the rest of Europe, Latin America, part of Africa and most of Asia. Such social consciousness corresponds to an inclusive society called the "nation," formed by essentially equal members (Greenfeld, p. 2). In that sense, nationalism has fostered the notion of economic gain as constitutive both of man's nature and of the common good of the society. It implies competition between intrinsically equal individuals within each nation as well as between nations. Nationalism led to an orientation to growth only to the extent that the national economy engaged in competition through international trade. Accordingly, nationalism brought forward an increasing awareness of backwardness and inequality caused by the uneven diffusion of modernization (see also Gellner [1983] 2006).

Reactive nationalism and List

According to Rostow's ([1960] 1990, p. 26) classic *Stages of economic growth*, the main non-economic precondition for the take-off into sustained growth is reactive nationalism, defined as a "reaction against intrusion from more advanced nations." The transition from traditional to modern societies, from that perspective, has been marked primarily not by the profit motive, but by the failure of traditional societies to protect their citizens from humiliation by foreigners. This applied especially to Germany, Russia and China in the nineteenth century. Even Britain, the first industrial nation, may be interpreted as reactive nationalism if its political history in the sixteenth and seventeenth centuries is carefully examined (Rostow [1960] 1990, pp. 34–35; Greenfeld, 2001, chapter 2). In the case of the colonies, nationalism reflected to some extent the demonstration effects caused by the introduction of more advanced technology and institutions by the metropolis, so that "a concept of nationalism, transcending the old ties to clan or region, inevitably crystallized around an accumulating resentment of colonial rule" (Rostow [1960] 1990, p. 28).

James Cypher ([1997] 2014, p. 189) has tested the application of Rostow's hypothesis about the preconditions for take-off to early nineteenth-century Latin America. The breaking of the colonial bonds, however, did not lead to a full rupture with the past. The new nationalist elite classes, as Cypher suggests, "were not interested in, or were not capable of, transforming their newly independent countries along the path that had been followed in Europe and the United States, that is, following a dynamic capitalist and industrial revolution." Rather, they aspired to obtain the class privileges that Iberian colonial policy had reserved for immigrants born in Spain and Portugal. This "backward looking" elite continued the pattern of primary commodities export established by the metropolis. In that they were helped by the favorable terms of trade for primary commodities throughout most of the nineteenth century.

Rostow's thesis about reactive nationalism has been further elaborated by Heinz Arndt (1987, pp. 14–22). According to Arndt, "the prehistory of economic development as a policy objective in the minds of the Third World leaders and writers is very much a history of reactive nationalism," with Meiji Japan providing the clearest case of economic modernization motivated by nationalism (see also Greenfeld, 2001, chapter 5). Nationalism also played a role in India, but there was no consensus about modernization as an economic goal, in contrast with Japan. The role of nationalism as the catalyst of modernization in Japan, China and (to a lesser extent) India influenced other countries in Asia and Africa. In that respect, Latin America represented an exception. Similarly to Cypher (op. cit.), Arndt calls attention to the integration of Latin American countries as suppliers of commodities in the nineteenth-century international economy. Hence, their economies developed as part of the liberal international economic order; their political and economic elites reflected that, with relatively little concern with protectionism. This started to change in the early twentieth century, as the unequal division of the gains from economic growth among different sectors of the population became increasingly clear. As put by Arndt (p. 22), by 1945 Latin America

> had become economically and even more so emotionally and ideologically, part of the Third World. In the following decades, reactive nationalism began to play a part also in Latin America, in the guise of popular anti-imperialism, resentment of *dependencia* and demands for a New International Economic Order.

In fact, already in the end of the nineteenth century economic nationalism started to become visible in Latin America, in part due to the influence of List (1841), the first authoritative formulation of economic nationalism and of the view that nations (rather than individuals) are the real actors in history (Greenfeld, 2001, pp. 199–214; Tribe 1988). List's argument was organized around an extended criticism of the economics of Adam Smith, J.B. Say and other classical economists who formed what he called the "school" of "cosmopolitical economy," which he contrasted with his own "political economy" based on the role of the nation (see List [1841] 1885, ch. 11). The main concern of List's political economy of nationalism was power, not just welfare. The cosmopolitical economists, in giving priority to the markets over the states, and reducing politics to a sum of individual actions, had lost sight of the interconnection between trade and national politics (Hont 2005, p. 150). List's understanding of the national economy and its political and economic growth were based on the concept of a nation's "productive power" as opposed to the emphasis on material "exchange values" he ascribed to the "school" of Smith and Say (and to the Physiocrats before them).

List's "productive powers" are culturally grounded and nationally bounded, as pointed out by David Levi-Faur (1997, p. 165). The economic role of the state is to protect and enlarge the national productive powers mainly through industrial development, since manufacturing is perceived as closely associated with technical progress, art, improved infrastructure, political freedom, urbanization and methods of warfare (List [1841] 1885, ch. 17). Differently from the widespread description of List as a champion of the Third World, the German-American economist often pointed out that his discussion of economic development policy (particularly the famous "infant industry" argument) applied only to a relatively small group of nations, which, among other features, belonged to the temperate climate zone. List's sense of "tropical" and "temperate" areas was not exact, as shown by his treatment of the whole South American continent (including Chile, Uruguay, Argentina and the south of Brazil) as a tropical zone. List's division of the world economy into two broad sets of nations is better rendered by the distinction between the industrialized/industrializing "North" (or "center") and the primary commodities exporters of the "South" (or "periphery").

Tropical nations are deemed "ill-suited for manufactures." Instead, they possess the natural monopoly of agricultural products that are in high demand by the countries of the temperate zone. List identified the exchange of the manufactures of temperate countries for the tropical ("colonial") goods as the dominant form of international trade, which would benefit both groups of nations. Hence, in contrast with classical economists, List understood national economic development in terms of complementary and interdependent economic relations between nations. Such international division of labor would in principle bring about a balanced growth of the world economy he called "civilizing process." Although the tropical zone could benefit from such a process, its pace of economic development would be probably lower than growth in industrialized countries.

List's distinction between "temperate" and "tropical" zones, and his restrictions concerning the industrialization of the latter, were largely ignored by economists who were influenced by his nationalist ideas in Latin America (see Boianovsky 2013). The selective reading of List by the interpretive communities formed by South American economists from the end of the nineteenth to the middle of the twentieth centuries probably reflects the fact that they got from him what they were looking for, regardless of the accuracy of that reading. By doing so, they applied to their own countries ideas that had been originally designed for Germany or the United States.

Development economics and the search for the "formation" of the nation

List's nationalism probably influenced CEPAL, particularly its secretary (1949–1963) Raúl Prebisch, despite the absence of references to List's work in CEPAL documents produced in the post-war period (see Seers 1983, p.

52). Indeed, claimed Seers (chapter 2), nationalism is a necessary constitutive ingredient of development economics and economic theory in general, instead of fundamentally irrational as seen by both neoclassical and Marxian economics. As observed by Jacob Viner (1953, p. 12) in his Brazilian lectures, the emerging field of development economics, with its challenge to classical trade theory, was "quite 'Listian' in character, even when not directly derived from List." In the same vein, Harry Johnson (1967, pp. 131–2) argued that List's nationalist and interventionist ideas were transmitted indirectly to Anglo-Saxon economics by Central European economists who migrated to Britain in the inter-war period (Mandelbaum, Kaldor, Rosentein-Rodan, Balogh and others) and had lived through the adoption of nationalist economic policies in the Balkan states following the breakup of the Austro-Hungarian Empire. The "infiltration" of ideas from Central Europe into the Anglo-Saxon tradition, regretted by Johnson, played an important role in disseminating nationalist instead of cosmopolitan thinking in Western development economics in general – and Latin American development economics in particular – and in establishing the "fictional" (in Johnson's view) concept of the nation as an economic entity. Such perspective was naturally associated with the need for industrialization through protectionism, which became the "conventional wisdom" of development economics.

In Latin American countries, the nationalist content of the study and policy of economic development, especially in the post-war period, should be seen against the background of the search for an interpretation of the broad cultural, historical and political dimensions of Latin American societies, called "national formation" by Latin American intellectuals. National economic development could only be understood after the meaning of national formation was grasped in each country's case (see Paula 2008). This is well illustrated in Brazil by frequent comparisons made between Celso Furtado's (1959, 1963) – director of CEPAL's economic development department between 1950 and 1957 – classic book about Brazilian economic history on one side, and the sociological and historical essays by Sergio Buarque de Holanda ([1936] 2012) and Gilberto Freyre (1933, 1946) on the other. They all dealt with distinct aspects of the formation ("formação") of the country's identity, such as its economic structure, national character and social relations; in that sense, they complement each other. Probably the best-known Latin American essay of that kind is by Octavio Paz (1950, 1961), about the formation of Mexican identity. Latin American nationalism is then associated with a particular political-economic project which features growth as one of its goals, and whose meaning becomes clear only through a study of the historical formation of national socio-cultural-economic structures. The same applies to Latin American novels that have captured essential ingredients of national identities, such as Garcia Marquez's *One Hundred Years of Solitude*. Latin American literature has illustrated the constructed nature of nations as "imagined communities" (see also Corse 1997; Gellner [1983] 2006).

Latin American economic nationalism has much in common with other historical experiences. Its peculiarities come mainly from the fact that it was put forward mostly when development economics was established as a field and, therefore, reflected the overall concern with growth as an explicit objective.

Note

1 This chapter is based on a lecture given at the Latin American meetings of the European Society for the History of Economic Thought, Belo Horizonte, November 2014. Reactions from participants are gratefully acknowledged.

References

Arndt, H.W. 1987. *Economic development – the history of an idea.* Chicago: University of Chicago Press.
Boianovsky, M. 2013. Friedrich List and the economic fate of tropical countries. *History of Political Economy.* 45: 647–91.
Bresser-Pereira, L.C. 2008. Nationalism at the center and periphery of capitalism. *Estudos Avançados.* 22: 171–92.
Corse, S. 1997. *Nationalism and literature.* Cambridge: Cambridge University Press.
Cypher, J.M. [1997] 2014. *The process of economic development,* 4th edition. New York: Routledge.
Freyre, G. 1933. *Casa-Grande & Senzala.* Rio: José Olympio.
Freyre, G. 1946. *The masters and the slaves: a study in the development of Brazilian civilization,* tr. by S. Putnam. New York: Alfred Knopf. Originally published as Freyre 1933.
Furtado, C. 1959. *Formação economica do Brasil.* Rio: Fundo de Cultura.
Furtado, C. 1963. *The economic growth of Brazil – a survey from colonial to modern times,* tr. by R. Aguiar and E. Drysdale. Berkeley: University of California Press. Originally published as Furtado 1959.
Garcia Marquez, G. 1967. *Cien años de soledad.* Buenos Aires: Editorial Sudamericana.
Garcia Marquez, G. 1970. *One hundred years of solitude,* tr. by G. Rabassa. New York: Harper & Row. Originally published as Garcia Marquez 1967.
Gellner, E. [1983] 2006. *Nations and nationalism,* 2nd edition. Oxford: Blackwell.
Greenfeld, L. 2001. *The spirit of capitalism: nationalism and economic growth.* Cambridge (Mass.): Harvard University Press.
Hall, J.A. 2003. Nation-states in history. In *The nation-state in question,* ed. by T.V. Paul, G. John Ikenberry, and John A. Hall. Princeton, NJ: Princeton University Press.
Holanda, S.B. [1936] 2012. *Raizes do Brasil.* Rio: José Olympio.
Holanda, S.B. 2002. *Roots of Brazil,* tr. by G.H. Summ. Notre Dame: University of Notre Dame Press. Originally published as Holanda 1936.
Hont, I. 2005. *Jealously of trade – international competition and the nation-state in historical perspective.* Cambridge (Mass.): The Belknap Press of Harvard University Press.
Johnson, H.G. 1967. The ideology of economic policy in new states. In *Economic nationalism in old and new states,* ed. by H.G. Johnson, pp. 124–42. Chicago: University of Chicago Press.

Levi-Faur, D. 1997. Friedrich List and the political economy of the nation-state. *Review of International Political Economy.* 4: 154–78.

List, F. 1841. *Das nationale System der Politischen Oekonomie.* Stuttgart and Tübingen: J.G. Cotta.

List, F. [1841] 1856. *National system of political economy*, trans. by G.A. Matile. Philadelphia: J.B. Lippincott & Co.

List, F. [1841] 1885. *The national system of political economy*, trans. by S.S. Lloyd. London: Longmans & Co.

Paula, J.A. 2008. The idea of nation in the 19th century and Marxism. *Estudos Avançados.* 22: 219–35.

Paz, O. 1950. *El laberinto de la soledad.* Mexico City: Fondo de Cultura.

Paz, O. 1961. *The labyrinth of solitude*, tr. by L. Kemp. New York: Grove Press. Originally published as Paz 1950.

Rostow, W.W. [1960] 1990. *The stages of economic growth: a non-communist manifesto*, 3rd edition. Cambridge: Cambridge University Press.

Seers, D. 1983. *The political economy of nationalism.* Oxford: Oxford University Press.

Szlajfer, H. and M. Chmielewska-Szlajfer. 2012. *Economic nationalism and globalization: lessons from Latin America and Central Europe.* Leiden: Brill.

Tribe, K. 1988. Friedrich List and the critique of "Cosmopolitical Economy." *Manchester School.* 65: 17–36.

Viner, J. 1953. *International trade and economic development – lectures delivered at the National University of Brazil.* Oxford: Clarendon Press.

15 CEPAL, economic nationalism, and development

Joseph L. Love

This chapter begins with a look at the atheoretical efforts to promote industrialization by Latin American industrialists and their spokesmen in the pre-War era, followed by an examination of the growth and the development of the UN Economic Commission for Latin America[1] (best known by its Spanish acronym, CEPAL). A discussion of CEPAL's activities in the 1950s and 1960s ensues. This was the period of CEPAL's greatest influence on governments, in which the organization developed and propagated a rationale for industrialization led by national states. Beginning in the late 1960s, a series of crises arose not foreseen in the 1950s, followed by a ten-year period of stagnation that forced a reworking of CEPAL's theses in 1990. In the chapter I make special reference to Brazil, the country in which CEPAL's influence in the 1950s and 1960s was arguably greatest, and the country whose economic history I know best.

Economic nationalism had made an appearance in the interwar years with assertions of state control of mineral resources, along with protection and subsidization of manufacturing industry – timid at first – as Latin American states reacted to protectionist trends in the United States and Western Europe. However, tariff protection in Latin America was already higher than that elsewhere before World War I and into the 1920s, although this fact was not widely understood at the time.[2] In the interwar years, with the breakdown of the international trading system following the protectionist Smoot–Hawley Tariff in 1930 in the United States and the failure of the world trade conference in London (1933), independent Third World states – notably those in Eastern Europe – moved more resolutely to state-sponsored industrialization as a response to the breakdown of the international trading system.[3] For the new and enlarged states stretching from the Baltic to the Black Seas, the development of manufacturing industries was seen as both a source of new wealth and the economic basis of a strategic guarantee of the postwar order. Jan Kofman, in Henrik Szlajfer's collection *Economic Nationalism in East-Central Europe and South America: 1918–1939*, holds that "protectionism, autarky and industrialism … along with the dislike of foreign capital" were "the basic ingredients of economic nationalism." A "holistic" economic nationalism for Kofman placed a state-sponsored industrialization program at the center of the development process. "Holistic nationalism" had integrative aspirations, seeking to place a whole society behind the development objective, as opposed to a "particular nationalism only serving a fraction of the local bourgeoisie."[4]

Industry's strategic role in national defense was far less salient in Latin America. One reason was that, unlike Eastern Europe, no states had been created or enlarged recently, nor had existing borders of the large majority of states been changed for a century.[5] This, because of the existence of an informal Pax Americana, under which no state in Latin America posed a threat to existing borders, the only exception being the conflict between Bolivia and Paraguay over the Chaco region in 1932–35.

In Latin America the central issue that economic theory and ideology addressed in the period after 1930 was industrialization, both as fact (at first a consequence of the decline of export-led growth) and as desideratum (for CEPAL, at least at the outset, industrialization was the centerpiece of resolving the problem of economic underdevelopment). In the early years, before 1949, with some notable exceptions, the process of industrialization was defended without the benefit of economic theory and a counterpart coherent ideology. The arguments were often limited in scope to special circumstances, sometimes inconsistent, and frequently apologetic. This was in part, because they "contradicted" neoclassical theory. In particular, they ran afoul of the Ricardian model of the international division of labor, still very much alive in the early years of the Depression of the 1930s, despite a surge of protectionism around the world in the previous decade.

In the 1930s the proponents of industrialization were almost exclusively the industrialists themselves, though by the time of World War II they were joined by government spokesmen, at least in the four most industrialized countries – Argentina, Brazil, Mexico, and Chile. CEPAL, whose analyses legitimized and prescribed industrialization, reached the apogee of its influence in the twenty-year period after 1950. The general absence of theoretical foundations for industrial development notwithstanding, Argentina, Brazil, and Chile had made rapid industrial advances in the 1920s. But after 1929 they faced a sustained crisis in export markets (the dollar value of Argentina's exports in 1933, for example, was one-third the 1929 figure); and despite the importance of incipient industrialization in the 1920s, the following decade can still be understood as a period of significant structural and institutional change. In Argentina, Brazil, Chile, and Mexico, convertibility and the gold standard were abandoned early in the Depression. The rise in prices of importables, because of a fall in the terms of trade and exchange devaluation, encouraged the substitution of domestic manufactures for imported goods, as did expansionary fiscal and monetary policies. By 1935 a North American economist would hazard that "There is probably no major section of the world in which there is a greater industrial activity relative to pre-depression years than in temperate South America," i.e., Argentina, southern Brazil, and Chile.[6] When war came in 1939, manufactures in international trade became scarce again, permitting further industrialization to the extent that capital goods, fuel, and raw materials were available.

During the 1930s spokesmen for industry probably grew bolder, but without any theory to undergird their position with the exception of those Brazilians who had initially followed Mihail Manoilescu, the Romanian trade theorist. In his major economic study, *The Theory of Protectionism* (1929) Manoilescu made a frontal attack on the existing international division of labor, and argued that labor productivity in "agricultural" countries was intrinsically and measurably inferior to that in "industrial" countries – so categorized by the composition of their exports. The Romanian theorist did not hesitate to call agricultural countries "backward," contending that surplus labor in agriculture in such nations should be transferred to industrial activities.[7] Manoilescu denounced the international division of labor and the classical theories of trade which recommended to agricultural nations that they continue to channel their labor force into areas of what he considered inherently inferior productivity. New industries should be introduced as long as their labor productivity remained above the national average. Manoilescu's book was translated into Portuguese, and found champions in the São Paulo industrialists' association (CIESP, later FIESP) and its chief spokesman, Roberto Simonsen. It had lost ground by the beginning of World War II, however, because of the withering attacks on its naïve economic theory by the trade theorists Bertil Ohlin and Jacob Viner. Moreover, the Romanian supported Nazi Germany in the War.

In Brazil and elsewhere in Latin America, industrialists themselves made ad hoc protectionist arguments. Note, for example, the themes chosen by Luis Colombo, the president of Argentina's Union Industrial Argentina: In 1931, he supported a moderate and "rational" protectionism, and defended the manufacturers against the charge of promoting policies inimical to the interests of Argentine consumers; in 1933, he even-handedly justified protection for both industry and agriculture; and by 1940 he was attacking the industrial countries as having themselves violated the rules of the international division of labor by developing large agricultural establishments, only choosing to buy abroad when convenient.[8] Industrialists pointed to the vulnerability of export economies, which they more frequently dubbed "colonial" than before. Gathering war clouds in Europe added another argument: domestic industries were necessary for an adequate national defense.[9] A basic characteristic of the period 1930–45 was an intensification of state intervention in the economy, in Latin America as elsewhere, and industrialists like other economic groups sought state assistance; they asked for subsidies, credits, and increased tariff protection. The state should, they argued, aid in "economic rationalization," i.e., cartelization, a theme of European industrialists in the 1930s.[10]

In Argentina, Brazil, Chile, and Mexico, governments began to heed the importuning of manufacturers. State aid to industry in the form of development loans tended to converge in the early years of the War. The establishment of industrial development banks was an important symbolic act, as we shall see, but changes in tariff structures, which have not yet been thoroughly analyzed, might have been more important for growth.

The reasons for such a shift by governments are clear in retrospect: a decade of wrestling with the intractable problem of reviving traditional export markets; the relative unavailability of foreign industrial goods over virtually a fifteen-year period (1930–45); and the fact that states (and particularly the officer corps) as well as industrialists began to consider the relation between manufacturing and national defense – a process that had already begun in Chile in the late 1920s. Governments, however, moved hesitantly and inconsistently toward addressing the problems of industry. In Argentina, Luis Duhau, the Minister of Agriculture, in 1933 proclaimed the necessity of producing industrial goods that could no longer be imported (for lack of foreign exchange), and he pledged his government's support for the process.[11] But in the same month the Argentine government supported the US initiative for general tariff reductions at the Pan American Union Conference in Montevideo. Earlier that year Argentina had yielded to British pressure in the Roca-Runciman pact, a trade agreement favoring British manufactures in the Argentine market in exchange for a share of the British beef market for Argentina. As late as 1940, Finance Minister Federico Pinedo's Plan for the economic development of Argentina still distinguished between "natural" and "artificial" industries, implying that industrial development would occur in concert with the needs of the agricultural and pastoral sectors. By the time of the colonels' coup in June 1943, intervention for industrial development had become state policy, and an industrial development bank was created in 1944. Yet even at that point support for manufacturing was far from unrestrained: the ministry of agriculture still housed the department of industry, and the minister assured Argentinians that the development of manufacturing would not threaten, but would contribute to the growth of, the country's "mother industries," stockraising and agriculture.[12] In the next few years, however, the Perón government would demonstrably put the interests of industrialists above those of ranchers and farmers.

In Brazil, Getúlio Vargas favored industry – was he not the friend of all established economic interests? – but he had opposed "artificial" industries (manufacturing) in his presidential campaign in 1930. Government loans to "artificial" industries were still prohibited in 1937. Osvaldo Aranha, Vargas's Minister of Finance in 1933, even termed industries "fictitious" if they did not use at least 70 percent domestic raw materials.[13] Vargas only became committed to rapid industrial expansion during his Estado Novo dictatorship (1937–45). Although he said in 1939 that he could not accept the idea of Brazil's remaining a "semi-colonial" economy in 1939, as late as 1940, when the coffee market was still depressed after a decade of attempts to revive it, Vargas wanted to "balance" industrial and agricultural growth. In 1941 a division for industrial development of the Bank of Brazil began to make significant loans, but from 1941 through 1945 the Bank only disbursed an annual average of 17.5 percent of its private sector loans to manufacturing concerns.[14]

In Mexico, industrialization in the 1930s made impressive advances even while agrarian reform was at the top of Lazaro Cardenas' agenda. It was not, however, the result of government policy. Nacional Financiera, a partly government-owned development bank, had been established in 1934, but only became seriously committed to manufacturing after its reorganization at the end of 1940, when the new pro-industry administration of Avila Camacho took office. During World War II, the pace quickened.[15] In Chile, nominal government support for industrial development began with the creation of an Institute of Industrial Credit in 1928. Ten years later the Popular Front government of Pedro Aguirre Cerda established CORFO, the government development corporation. But in 1940 the sum budgeted for the development of manufacturing was less than each of those for agriculture, mining, energy, and public housing.[16]

All the same, government attitudes were changing, as were the views of economists both inside and outside Latin America. Even the economists of the League of Nations, champions of free trade in the 1920s and 1930s, had begun to doubt the advisability of full agricultural specialization for the world's poorer countries. As early as 1937, the League's economic section stated a preference for a modicum of industrialization for agricultural countries, on the practical ground that factor flows remained substantially blocked, seven years after the onset of depression. A League study at the end of the War argued that the poorer agricultural countries had to industrialize to some degree, because of their lack of sufficient agricultural surpluses "to ensure them a plentiful supply of imported manufactures."[17]

In 1943 Paul Rosenstein-Rodan, in an article often considered the point of departure for modern development theory, called for the industrialization of agrarian countries, as did MIT's trade theorist Charles Kindleberger. At a policy level, the Hot Springs conference of the Allied Nations the same year favored a degree of industrialization for the "backward" countries. More boldly, the economist Colin Clark had written in 1942 that future equilibrium in world trade depended on the willingness of Europe and the United States "to accept a large flow of ... exports of manufactured goods" from India and China.[18]

The somewhat "unintended" industrialization of the larger Latin American countries and a partial acceptance of it by United States government was reflected at the Chapultepec conference of the Pan American Union (1945). The meeting's resolutions gave a qualified benediction to the industrialization process in Latin America.[19] At the end of the War it was clear that industrialization had greatly advanced in Latin America, and that was characteristically import-substitution industrialization (ISI) – the replacement of imported goods with domestic manufactures, based on existing patterns of demand. Economists in several countries were noting the trend and searching for a theory to legitimate it.[20]

A more aggressive wave of Latin American nationalism arrived in the 1950s, following the fifteen years of disruption of the international trading system from 1930 to 1945. This movement coincided and interacted with the Cold War; with the incipient professionalization of economics as a discipline in Latin America; and with the arrival of the new subdiscipline of development economics. Economic nationalism benefited from more effective "stateness" through greater revenue extraction and enhanced Weberian rationalization of the state. In Lawrence Whitehead's opinion, "stateness" in terms of government income, outlay, and efficiency rose markedly between the late 1920s and the late 1950s, so that "modernizing" states had replaced "oligarchic" states by the end of the period. Gains were especially notable in direct taxation, as Argentina, Brazil, Chile, and Venezuela, among others, introduced taxes on income. On the outlay side, governments had acquired new obligations in social spending; Brazil, Chile, and Uruguay put social security systems in place before the War, and Argentina and Mexico followed in the 1940s.[21]

Concurrently, a new populism arose, based on rising urbanization, the extension of suffrage to women, the expansion of mass media, and newly created or expanded state-sponsored welfare systems. A phenomenon often confused with CEPAL-derived Structuralism was *desarrollismo* ("developmentalism") a form of populist nationalism that sometimes borrowed arguments for industrialization from CEPAL.

This is the milieu in which the UN Economic Commission for Latin America (better known by its Spanish acronym CEPAL) arose in the late 1940s. The Structuralist school of thought associated with CEPAL was pioneered by the Argentinean Raúl Prebisch, who in 1949 characterized the international economy as a set of relations between an industrialized Center and a Periphery exporting foodstuffs and raw materials. In this CEPAL manifesto, "Latin America and its Principal Problems," Prebisch set forth the principal problems of the Periphery: 1) structural unemployment,[22] owing to the inability of traditional export industries to grow and therefore to absorb excess rural population; 2) external disequilibrium, because of higher propensities to import industrial goods than to export traditional agricultural and mineral goods; and 3) a long-term tendency toward deteriorating terms of trade – all of which a properly implemented policy of industrialization could help eliminate.

In the 1970s CEPAL made clear another basic feature, already implicit in the agency's early conceptions but now made explicit by Anibal Pinto, the characterization of underdevelopment as "structural heterogeneity," in which economic processes of vastly different productivities coexisted in the same national economy.[23] This was the very definition of economic backwardness for CEPAL: Underdevelopment was conceived not as moving labor from a low-productivity subsistence economy to a high-productivity modern economy (as in Arthur Lewis's conception), but rather a situation in which the Periphery was characterized by heterogeneous productivities of economic activities existing side-by-side in both urban and rural areas.

The Structuralist analysis of CEPAL fitted easily into the aspirations of the economic nationalism of the early postwar era. Structuralism[24] was a movement that focused on industrialization and greater independence of national states from the international trading system, in which Latin America in the early postwar years was largely producing agricultural and mineral goods to exchange on the world market for industrial imports. Structuralism wove together a coherent discourse to justify industrialization to replace the ad hoc arguments of industrialists' organization and their spokesmen and to justify this policy in the language of standard economics.

CEPAL was the chief "idea factory" of Latin American Structuralism but the school – one might even say the movement – extended well beyond it. Structuralist economists associated with CEPAL also moved in and out of national governments – e.g., Celso Furtado, Jorge Ahumada, and Victor Urquidi in their respective national governments of Brazil, Chile, and Mexico. Although CEPAL was responsible to the governments of Latin American states, it also developed a form of economic reasoning that was coherent and implicitly nationalist.

CEPAL offered an explanation of Latin American economic backwardness and presented measures that would allegedly quicken the pace of growth and enhance national sovereignty. This occurred against an international background of sustained state interventionism during the Depression and World War II. By the end of the War, planning had become respectable in both Europe and the United States. As early as 1947, the UN Department of Economic Affairs produced a list of dozens of state agencies involved in economic planning and development in large Latin American countries – Argentina, Mexico, Brazil, and Venezuela.[25]

Furthermore, CEPAL, in the view of some social scientists, provided a project for the national bourgeoisie, though its analyses and policy recommendations remained controversial. As a constituent unit of the United Nations bureaucracy, of course, CEPAL could only recommend its measures directly to sovereign governments, but it did provide a rationale for state action to stimulate industry and, by implication, develop a powerful social group of industrial entrepreneurs who could successfully compete with powerful agricultural and commercial interests domestically, and, in the longer term, compete with First World industrial firms internationally.

Perhaps the most effective means of diffusing the Structuralist doctrine was by teaching it in short but formal courses. CEPAL had organized courses in basic economic concepts and techniques, along with Structuralist doctrine, as early as 1952 (when the Chilean Jorge Ahumada directed the teaching program). It also influenced the international master's program ESCOLATINA at the University of Chile later in that decade. These two institutions, often in collaboration with others outside Chile, trained and indoctrinated middle-ranking Latin American personnel in central banks, development and finance ministries, and university faculties. Scores of such men and women studied at CEPAL itself in courses varying from several months' duration to a year's length before the creation of the Instituto Latinoamericano y del Caribe de Planificación Económica y Social (ILPES) in 1962. Instructors in the

1960s included such leading Structuralist economists as Aníbal Pinto, Jorge Ahumada, Antônio Barros de Castro, Maria da Conceição Tavares, Carlos Lessa, Leopoldo Solís, and Osvaldo Sunkel, himself a graduate of the ILPES program. In sociology and political science, Fernando Henrique Cardoso, Torcuato di Tella, Rodolfo Stavenhagen, Aldo Solari, and Francisco Weffort offered courses.

While its instructors were training aspiring civil servants and others in Santiago, ILPES also went on the road, offering short courses in a majority of the Latin American states. Multiple sites were available in several countries, including eight in Brazil alone between 1963 and 1969. In 2004, according to the organization's website, ILPES claimed a total of 15,000 graduates. Moreover, by that time it had published sixty textbooks, many of them in multiple editions. In 1990 the ILPES program in Santiago still included a strong dose of Structuralism along with more technical matters. But it should not be assumed ILPES was only interested in doctrine. As part of CEPAL, it played an important role in diffusing modern economic analysis and statistics, as well as in developing planning agencies and public administration schools. Moreover, much of the day-to-day activity of the CEPAL staff was gathering, ordering, revising, and publishing economic and social data on Latin America and CEPAL's member states.

Structuralism also had an influence beyond Latin America. Although this is a subject that has not been researched adequately, I have written about its influence in Portugal, Spain, and Romania in the 1950s through the 1970s.[26] By the 1970s Europeans were more interested in dependency analysis,[27] but the transition between the two sets of ideas was almost seamless, since former CEPAL social scientists were also leading dependency theorists – notably Furtado, Cardoso, Prebisch, and Sunkel.

Although far from being exclusively Structralist venues, leading publishing houses in Latin America were sympathetic to the movement as were professional journals. Leading the pack was the Fondo de Cultura Economica in Mexico and the professional journals *Trimestre Economico* in Mexico, the *Revista Brasileira de Economia*, and *Desarrollo Economico* in Argentina.

There are many ways to judge the effectiveness of the CEPAL message, addressed to governments, but implicitly seeking the cooperation of industrial leaders. One such method is to look at official endorsements of CEPAL tenets by heads of national states. Surveying this material involves trolling the annual presidential "state of the Union" messages to congress, along with reports from state banks. I have done this for the 1950s and 1960s for five countries – Argentina, Brazil, Chile, Mexico, and Venezuela. Looking at certain concepts and propositions put forth by CEPAL, I found that some items were an easy sell – the recognition of the process of import substitution industrialization, which began long before the "CEPAL manifesto" of 1949, but was now proclaimed as a policy, e.g., by Romulo Betancourt, in his 1962 report to the Venezuelan congress. The thesis of the deterioration of the terms of trade was endorsed by Adolfo Ruíz Cortines in Mexico (1953),

Betancourt in 1962, and by his successor Raul Leoni in 1964. The demand for more "just" prices for primary goods by Leoni (1964) was followed by his support the following year for Prebisch's global agency, the UN Conference on Trade and Development (UNCTAD), created in 1964. The CEPAL objective of "inward-directed development" was adopted by Carlos Ibanez in Chile (1954) and Leoni (1965). Even the objective of exporting manufactures was endorsed by at least two chief executives – Betancourt of Venezuela (1962) and Gustavo Diaz Ordaz of Mexico (1968), though such an aspiration became more significant in the following decade. Regional integration in the form of the Latin American Free Trade Association (LAFTA, or in Spanish, ALALC) was specifically mentioned by several heads of state – Arturo Frondizi of Argentina (1961), Betancourt (1960), Diaz Ordaz in Mexico (1965), in their annual reports. Likewise, the principle of state planning, in the modest form advanced by CEPAL called "programming" – that is, calculating required savings and inputs to meet government-specified development targets, was welcomed by Chilean President Eduardo Frei (1970).

Brazil was probably the country in which the CEPAL program was most influential. President Getulio Vargas saw in CEPAL's program a key to greater national autonomy.[28] CEPAL's emphasis on the creation of infrastructure as the basis for industrialization was for him persuasive, and CEPAL helped train Brazilian economists and *técnicos*. Moreover, in the absence of PhD programs in economics before the mid-1960s, CEPAL provided basic training in formal economics and planning techniques.[29] That fact tended to signify a "depoliticization" of planning techniques, realized by technical experts, state economists, and by CEPAL itself. Thus state participation in the economy in Brazil was increasingly seen as a guarantee, and not a risk, for investors.[30] President Vargas's government hosted the 5th plenary meeting of CEPAL in Petropolis in 1953. On that occasion Celso Furtado presented a "Sketch of a program of development for Brazil," a document presented by the joint team of CEPAL and the Banco Nacional de Desenvolvimento Econômico (Brazilian national development bank) known as the Grupo Misto CEPAL-BNDE.

Vargas's enthusiasm for CEPAL's ideas was matched by that of Brazilian President Juscelino Kubitschek (1956–61), but with a different emphasis – putting growth ahead of independence from the international trading system. With his slogan "Fifty years of progress in five" Kubitschek announced in his 1956 presidential address that CEPAL and the BNDE had devised a five-year development plan. In carrying out the plan Celso Furtado – an economist who worked alternately in the Brazilian government and CEPAL – figured importantly as head of the new regional development commission for Northeast Brazil (SUDENE).[31] Kubitschek endorsed CEPAL's analysis of deteriorating terms of trade and its interpretation of the persistent disequilibrium in Brazil's balance of payments. The Brazilian president asserted the need for industrialization to absorb surplus labor in agriculture, and embraced CEPAL's programming techniques.[32]

However, Kubitschek's interest in *cepalino* doctrine was not strictly nationalist, because he also welcomed the entry of foreign capital in Brazil. The President used CEPAL's recommendations to prioritize growth over national autonomy,[33] and indeed, CEPAL had always seen a major role for foreign capital in Latin American development. Kubitschek also gave growth precedence over greater equity in income distribution,[34] whereas Vargas had to some degree lessened inequality through raising the minimum wage.[35]

Industrialists also welcomed CEPAL's initiatives. Furtado and Prebisch courted Brazilian industrialists, participating in the debates of the National Confederation of Industries (CNI) in 1950. The organization and many individual manufacturers received Prebisch's thesis warmly. In the same year *Estudos Economicos* (Economic Studies), the CNI journal, ran an article explaining and implicitly endorsing CEPAL's position, and in 1953 the Industrialists' Confederation financially supported a regular CEPAL session in Brazil. A later CNI review, *Desenvolvimento e Conjuntura* (Development and the Business Cycle), founded in 1957, endorsed CEPAL's interpretations and proposals in its first editorial. In general, industrial leaders in Furtado's Brazil accepted state intervention and Structuralist doctrines in the 1950s much more readily than did their counterparts in Prebisch's Argentina,[36] though Brazil may have been an outlier in its industrialists' enthusiasm for CEPAL's theses.

The reformism of the 1960s was conditioned by, and for an increasing number of Structuralists, made irrelevant by, a long evolution of CEPAL's views on its initial key policy recommendation – import-substitution industrialization (ISI). An ISI policy had seemed a brilliant success, especially in Brazil in Mexico, during the 1950s, but success owed in part to unusually high commodity prices during the Korean War. In the latter 1950s, CEPAL began to consider the complexities of ISI. In 1956 CEPAL had still assumed the existence of a threshold in structural changes in the economy, beyond which "dependence on external contingencies" would diminish. Yet the following year the agency first suggested that dependence on "events overseas" might even increase as ISI advanced; all the same, it still held that "import substitution" consisted of lowering "the import content of supplies for the home market."[37] CEPAL now distinguished between "horizontal" ISI, an initial process scattered on a broad front of producing simple consumer goods, and "vertical" ISI. This second, more difficult, process involved the production of intermediate goods and consumer durables, an integrated line of production of fewer final goods and their inputs. A third phase, the production of capital goods, would ensue at a later date.

Argentina was Latin America's most industrialized country, and despite its unique political phenomenon of *peronismo*, CEPAL tended to view it in 1957 as a trendsetter for other Latin American nations. Argentina, CEPAL noted, had reduced its imports of finished goods to one-third the total dollar amount. Yet its declining capacity to import had meant that reducing the importation of consumer goods was not sufficient to contain balance-of-payment difficulties; capital goods and fuels also had to be reduced, and this fact was reducing the rate of growth. Chile was seen as facing similar though less dire problems. CEPAL seemed to wonder aloud whether the Argentine experience was the future of Latin America. Two conclusions followed: that primary exports and food production for domestic consumption had to be increased (the latter to relieve pressure on imports), and that a region-wide common market must be developed to assure the future development of efficient manufacturing industries.[38]

Yet in its early years the Latin American Free Trade Area, established in 1960, was only an expression of hope for alleviating the ills associated with ISI. Already in 1959 Prebisch had observed that the more economically advanced Latin American countries were becoming increasingly the hostages of external events, because they had compressed their imports to the absolute essentials for the maintenance of growth. Two years later he wrote, "It remains a paradox that industrialization, instead of helping greatly to soften the internal impact of external fluctuations, is bringing us a new and unknown type of external vulnerability."[39]

The agonizing reappraisal of ISI came in 1964. In that year a CEPAL study, though blaming Latin America's declining rates of growth on deteriorating terms of trade in the 1950s, also noted that 80 percent of regional imports now consisted of fuels, intermediate goods, and capital equipment. Consequently, there was little left to "squeeze" in the region's import profile to favor manufacturing.[40] Meanwhile, two monographs, highly critical of ISI, appeared in the agency's *Economic Bulletin* – one on the Brazilian experience in particular, and the other on Latin America in general.[41] Examining the Brazilian case in the 1950s and early 1960s, Maria da Conceição Tavares argued that ISI had failed because of the lack of dynamism of the export sector, coupled with the fact that ISI had not diminished capital and fuel import requirements. Other problems were apparent ceilings on the domestic market, owing in part to highly skewed income distribution, which also determined the structure of demand; the constellation of productive resources e.g., the lack of skilled labor; and the capital-intensive nature of industrialization in more advanced phases of ISI, which implied little labor absorption. In the advanced stages of ISI, Tavares contended, the low labor absorption of manufacturing tended to exaggerate rather than to terminate the dualism of Brazil's economy.

In the same number of the *Bulletin*, Santiago Macario wrote a blistering critique of the way in which ISI had actually been practiced in Latin America, following up Prebisch's observation the previous year, 1963, that the region had the highest tariffs in the world. Macario observed that the governments of the four most industrialized countries – Argentina, Brazil, Mexico, and Chile – had used ISI as a deliberate strategy to counteract a persistent lack of foreign exchange, and to create employment for expanding populations. But in those four countries, and in most of the others of the region, protectionism, primarily in the form of tariff and exchange policies, had been irrational, in that there was no consistent policy to develop the most viable and efficient manufacturing industries. On the contrary, the most inefficient industries had received the greatest protection; there had been over-diversification of manufacturing in small markets in the "horizontal" phase; and these factors had contributed, in some instances, to real dissavings.[42]

CEPAL had voiced its first doubts in 1956 whether industry, in the world region with the fastest growing population, could absorb surplus labor from agriculture; nine years later its survey of ISI showed that non-agricultural employment in Latin America had increased from 13 to 36 million persons between 1925 and 1960, but that only 5 million of the 23 million additional employees were absorbed in industrial activities.[43] Furtado, writing over his own signature, contemporaneously noted that while Latin America's industrial output in the 1950s had risen 6.2 percent a year, industrial employment had risen only 1.6 percent annually, about half Latin America's average population growth rate. The problem in part was the labor-saving technology which the Periphery had imported from the Center.[44]

Meanwhile, since the publication of "Latin America and its Principal Problems in 1949," CEPAL's classic thesis of deterioration of the terms of trade has continued to be debated, with a sophisticated examination and revision of the deterioration thesis for most of the twentieth century by José Antonio Ocampo, former Executive Secretary of CEPAL, and Mariangela Parra.[45] They hold that "there was an improvement in the barter terms of trade for non-fuel commodities vs. manufactures in the late nineteenth and early twentieth centuries, followed by significant deterioration over the rest of the twentieth century." With the advantage of writing sixty years after Prebisch, they suggest the possibility that real commodity prices might rise again in the twenty-first century in a long-term swing. If true, this trend would invalidate the proposition that there is a tendency toward structural disequilibrium caused by deteriorating terms of trade.

There is also a revisionist view that argues the terms of trade are less important than other factors affecting trade and development. Jeffrey Williamson believes that *volatility* was more important than declining terms of trade in discouraging new investment in peripheral countries.[46]

At the international level State-led economic change lost ground in the 1970s, when Keynesian economics failed to eliminate "stagflation." In the following decade Margaret Thatcher and Ronald Reagan launched successful attacks on the perceived excesses of the welfare state. They also made income taxes more regressive, in Thatcher's case relying more heavily on a value-added tax. Therefore, "neoliberalism" – a return to the values of nineteenth-century economic liberalism – made its appearance on the international scene, and its prestige grew as the Soviet Union collapsed and capitalist globalization intensified. The "Washington consensus" of IMF, World Bank, State Department officials, and members of Washington think tanks produced a document drawn up in 1989 by John Williamson of the Institute for International Economics. He drew up a ten-point agenda for pursuing economic growth through liberalization and privatization. Dubbed the "Washington Consensus" by him, because it reflected the consensus of the World Bank, the IMF, and the State Department, it was "prescribed" to Latin America in 1989, and applied quickly thereafter to Eastern Europe, now freed from Soviet-directed socialism.

Latin America went through a decade of shrinking economies in the 1980s, and CEPAL met the crisis and the assault of neoliberalism with a restructuring of its doctrine formally announced in 1990 as Neostructuralism.[47] The revised doctrine, like neoliberalism, condemned the excesses of protectionism and further argued that growth could only be sustained by progressively introducing high-technology, high-productivity goods for the international market. The goal was to endogenize technological innovation by establishing research and development traditions in Latin America. But the doctrine also called for a greater degree of equity in the distribution of income, consistent with rising levels of productivity in agriculture as well as industry.

To sum up, in this chapter I have surveyed the rise of industrialization in Latin America, with special attention to the Brazilian case. The growth of manufacturing was a process already under way before it became government policy, it became policy before it had a theoretical justification; and CEPAL provided that rationale. The international agency put forth a coherent doctrine and offered new, more rational policy prescriptions that had their greatest impact in the years 1950–70. In addition, CEPAL implicitly offered a justification for building modern national bourgeoisies. The *cepalino* project went into crisis in the latter 1960s, as ISI began to falter because further industrial advances required ever-increasing amounts of industrial imports, unforeseen in the original *cepalino* project. A thorough restructuring of CEPAL doctrine would only arrive with the birth of Neostructuralism in 1990.

Notes

1 Later renamed the Economic Commission for Latin America and the Caribbean. I will use "CEPAL" throughout.
2 John H. Coatsworth and Jeffrey G. Williamson, "Always Protectionist? Latin American Tariffs from Independence to Great Depression," *Journal of Latin American Studies* (May, 2004), pp. 210, 212.
3 See Thomas David, *Nationalisme économique et industrialization: L'éxperience des pays de l'Est (1789–1939)* (Geneva: Droz, 2009), and Love, *Crafting the Third World: Theorizing Development in Rumania and Brazil* (Stanford, CA: Stanford University Press, 1996).
4 Jan Kofman, "How to Define Economic Nationalism? A Critical Review of Some Old and New Standpoints," in Henryk Szlajfer, ed., *Economic Nationalism in East-Central Europe and South America 1981-1939* (Geneva: Libraire Droz, 1990), p. 53.
5 Exceptions: Panama's separation from Colombia (with US backing), and Chile's incorporation of Tacna and Arica at the expense of Peru and Bolivia.
6 D. M. Phelps, "Industrial Expansion in Temperate South America," *American Economic Review*, 25 (1935), p. 281.

7 Mihail Manoilescu, *Théorie du protectionnisme et de l'échange international* (Paris: M. Giard, 1929), pp. 61, 65, 184; *Le siecle du corporatisme: Doctrine du corporatisme intégral et pur* (Paris: M. Giard, 1934), p. 28.

8 See Colombo's speeches in *Anales de la Unión Industrial Argentina*, año 44 (Dec., 1931), pp. 25, 27; ibid., año 46 (July, 1933), p. 37; *Argentina Fabril*, año 53 (Jan., 1940), p. 3.

9 Unión Industrial Argentina, *Revista* ano 57 [sic] (May, 1946), p. 9; Oscar Alvarez Andrews, *Historia del desarrollo industrial de Chile* (Santiago: Imp. y lit. La Ilustración, 1936), pp. 6, 328, 348; "Necesitamos una politica económica de industrialización," [editorial], *Revista de Economía y Finanzas* (Peru), 16, 92 (Aug., 1940), p. 128.

10 Alvarez Andrews, *Historia*, pp. 327–328, 385; Pupo Nogueira, "A propósito da modernizaçáo de uma grande indústria," *Revista Industrial de S. Paulo*, ano 1, 6 (May, 1945), p. 18; "Industrialización," [editorial], *Revista Económica* (Mexico), 8, 10 (Oct., 1945), p. 6. In 1942, Enrique Zañartu Prieto defended "autarky" in Chile, but in vague terms. See his *Tratado de economía política* (Santiago: Zig-Zag, 2d edn, 1946), p. 243.

11 "The Argentine Industrial Exhibition," *Review of the River Plate*, 22 (Dec., 1933), pp. 11, 13, 15.

12 Diego Masón, "Introducción" to Mariano Abarca, *La industrialización de la Argentina* (Bs.As.: Ministerio de agricultura de la nación, Dirección general de industria, 1944), pp. 5–6.

13 Getúlio Vargas, *A nova política do Brasil*, I (Rio: J. Olympio, 1938), pp. 26–27; *O Estado de S. Paulo*, March 8, 1933.

14 Getúlio Vargas, *A nova política*, VI (Rio: J. Olympio, 1940), p. 91; VIII (Rio: J. Olympio, 1941), p. 179; Aníbal Villela and Wilson Suzigan, *Política do governo e crescimento da economia brasileira, 1889–1945* (Rio de Janeiro: IPEA/INPES, 1973), p. 352.

15 Stephen Haber, *Industrialization and Underdevelopment: The Industrialization of Mexico, 1890–1940* (Stanford, Calif.: Stanford University Press, 1989), pp. 176–177; René Villareal, *El desequilibrio externo en la industrialización de México (1929–75): um enfoque estructuralista* (Mexico: Fondo de Cultura Económica, 1976), pp. 43–45; Calvin S. Blair, "Nacional Financiera: Entrepreneurship in a Mixed Economy," in Raymond Vernon, ed., *Public Policy and Private Enterprise in Mexico* (Cambridge, Mass.: Harvard University Press, 1964), pp. 210, 213; Rafael Izquierdo, "Protectionism in Mexico," in *ibid.*, p. 243; Alfredo R. Navarrete, "The Financing of Economic Development," in Enrique Pérez López et al., *Mexico's Recent Economic Growth: The Mexican View*, tr. Marjory Urquidi (Austin: Institute of Latin American Studies by the University of Texas Press, 1967), p. 119.

16 Presidente de la República [de Chile, Pedro Aguirre Cerda], *Mensaje ... en la apertura ... de Congreso Nacional 21 de Mayo de 1940* (Santiago: Impr. Fiscal de la Penitenciaría, 1940), pp. 21–22, 95.

17 S[ergei] Prokopovicz, *L'industrialisation des pays agricoles et la structure de l'économie mondiale après la guerre*, tr. N. Nicolsky (Neuchatel: Éditions de la Baconnière, 1946), p. 276; League of Nations: Economic, Financial and Transit Dept., *Industrialization and Foreign Trade* (n.p., 1945), p. 34.

18 Paul Rosenstein-Rodan, "Problems of Industrialization of Eastern and Southeastern Europe," in A. N. Agarwala and S. P. Singh, eds., *The Economics of Underdevelopment* (London: Oxford University Press, 1958 [orig., 1943]), pp. 246, 253–254; Charles Kindleberger, "Planning for Foreign Investment," *American Economic Review*, 33, 1 (Mar., 1943), Supplement, pp. 347–354; Prokopovicz, *L'industrialisation des pays agricoles*, pp. 278–279; Colin Clark, *The Economics of 1960* (London: Macmillan, 1942), p. 114.

19 *Revista Económica* (Mexico), 8, 1–2 (Feb. 28, 1945), p. 30.
20 Sergio Bagú, "Y mañana, Que?," *Revista de Economía* (Mexico), 7, 5–6 (June 30, 1944), p. 37; Heitor Ferreira Lima, "Evolução industrial de São Paulo," *Revista Industrial de S. Paulo*, ano 1, 7 (June, 1945), p. 17; "Monetary Developments in Latin America," *Federal Reserve Bulletin*, 31, 6 (June, 1945), p. 523; Gonzalo Robles, "Sudamérica y el fomento industrial," *Trimestre Económico*, 14, 1 (April–June, 1947), p. 1.
21 Whitehead, "State Organization in Latin America since 1930," in Leslie Bethell, ed., *Cambridge History of Latin America* Vol. VI, Part 2 (Cambridge: Cambridge University Press, 1994), pp. 76, 90.
22 Note that this is different from Keynesian unemployment which increases cyclically with periods of recession.
23 Ricardo Bielschowsky, "Cincuenta años del Pensamiento de la CEPAL: Una Reseña," in CEPAL, *Cincuenta Años de Pensamiento en la CEPAL. Textos Seleccionados* Vol. 1. (Santiago, Chile: CEPAL, 1998), p. 35. See Aníbal Pinto, *América Latina: una visión estructuralista* (Colección América Latina, Facultad de Economía, Universidad Nacional Autónoma de México, México, 1991), and see especially in that collection, "Notas sobre la estrategia de la distribución y la redistribución del ingreso en América Latina," pp. 535–553 (originally published in 1974).
24 "Structuralism" means a variety of things in economics, as in other disciplines, and my definition is a broad and simple one. Structuralism refers to theoretical efforts to specify, analyze, and correct economic structures that impede or block the "normal," implicitly unproblematic, development and functioning allegedly characteristic of Western economies. Because of these impediments and blockages, standard classical or neoclassical prescriptions were rejected by Structuralists as inappropriate, inapplicable. Some Structuralist theory, in fact, was designed to move the economy to the point where neoclassical economics *would* be applicable.
25 United Nations. Dept. of Economic Affairs. *Economic Development in Selected Countries: Plans, Programmes and Agencies* (Lake Success, NY: [UN], Oct. 1947).
26 Love, "Structuralism and Dependency in Peripheral Europe: Latin American Ideas in Spain and Portugal," *Latin American Research Review*, 39, 2 (June, 2004), pp. 114–139, and "Flux and Reflux: Interwar and Postwar Structuralist Theories of Development in Romania and Latin America," in Helga Schultz and Eduard Kubu, eds., *History and Culture of Economic Nationalism in East-Central Europe* (Berlin: Berliner Wissenschafts-Verlag, 2006), pp. 71–86.
27 Dependency, like Structuralism, posited a Center-Periphery system developing historically, characterized by unequal exchange and a dependence of the Periphery on the Center. But Dependency went beyond Structuralism in asserting that the national bourgeoisie was incapable of developing modern capitalism in Latin America.
28 See Vargas's annual messages to the Brazilian congress in 1951 and 1954, cited in Jacqueline A. H. Haffner, *A CEPAL e a industrialização brasileira (1950–1961)* (Porto Alegre: EDIPUCRS, 2002), p. 45.
29 Haffner, pp. 44, 52. Octavio Ianni, *Estado e planejamento econômico no Brasil (1930–1970)* (Rio: Civ. Brasileira, 1971), p. 131. For more on the creation of graduate programs and elsewhere in Latin America, see Love, "Institutional Foundations of Economic Ideas in Latin America, 1914–1950," in Rosemary Thorp and Valpy Fitzgerald, eds., *Economic Doctrines in Latin America: Origins, Embedding and Evolution* (Houndmills, UK: Palgrave, 2005), pp. 142–156.
30 Haffner, p. 45.
31 In the government of President João Goulart (1961–64), Furtado became minister of planning.

32 Juscelino Kubitschek, *Mensagem ao Congresso Nacional: 1956* (Rio de Janeiro: Imprensa nacional, 1956), pp. 47–48, 54, 275, 278, 362.
33 Ianni, p. 183.
34 Haffner, citing Carlos Lessa, p. 195.
35 For a more detailed treatment of economic and financial policy under Kubitschek, see Maria Antonieta P. Leopoldi, "Crescendo em meio a incerteza: a política econômica do governo JK (1956–60)," in Angela de Castro Gomes, ed., *O Brasil de JK* (Rio: FGV/CPDOC, 1991), pp. 71–99.
36 For documentation on material in this paragraph, see Love, *Crafting*, p. 155.
37 "The Situation in Argentina and the New Economic Policy," *Economic Bulletin*, 1, 1 (Jan., 1956), p. 30; CEPAL, "Preliminary Study of the Effects of Postwar Industrialisation on Import Structures and External Vulnerability in Latin America," in *Economic Survey 1956*, p. 115.
38 CEPAL, "Preliminary Study of the Effects of Postwar Industrialization on Import Structures and External Vulnerability in Latin America," pp. 128, 150, 151.
39 Prebisch, "Economic Development or Monetary Stability: A False Dilemma," *Economic Bulletin for Latin America* 6, 1 (Mar., 1961), p. 5; Prebisch, "Commercial Policy in Underdeveloped Countries," *American Economic Review* 49, 2 (May, 1959), p. 268.
40 CEPAL, *The Economic Development of Latin America in the Postwar Period* (New York: United Nations, 1964), pp. 14, 21.
41 Maria da Conceição Tavares, "The Growth and Decline of Import Substitution in Brazil," and Santiago Macario, "Protectionism and Industrialization in Latin America," in *Economic Bulletin for Latin America*, 9 (1964), pp. 1–59, and 61–101, respectively.
42 Macario, "Protectionism," pp. 65–67, 77, 81.
43 CEPAL, "The Situation in Argentina," p. 42; CEPAL, *The Process of Industrial Development* (New York: United Nations, 1966 [Sp. orig., 1965]), p. 38.
44 Celso Furtado, *Subdesenvolvimento e estagnação na América Latina* (Rio: Civilização Brasileira, 2d edn, 1968 [orig., 1966]), pp. 9–10.
45 Ocampo, J. A. and M. Parra-Lancourt, "The Terms of Trade for Commodities since the Mid-Nineteenth Century," *Revista de Historia Económica – Journal of Iberian and Latin American Economic History* 28 (2010), 1, pp. 11–37.
46 He also argues that improving terms of trade in the nineteenth century up to 1870 in some cases – notably India – resulted in a serious deindustrialization, but that Latin America – notably Mexico, Brazil, and Chile – resisted this trend. J. G. Williamson, *Trade and Poverty: When the Third World Fell Behind* (Cambridge, MA: MIT Press, 2011).
47 See Love, "CEPAL, Economic Nationalism, and Economic Inequality," forthcoming.

Index

disguised unemployment 256
Disraeli, Benjamin 48
Döllinger, Johann Joseph Ignaz von 170
Dom João, King 11, 63, 65
Dom Pedro I, Emperor 11, 58, 63
Dom Pedro II, Emperor 11, 189, 200
Duhau, Luis 279

Echenique, José Rufino 233, 238
"economic civilization" 269
economic ideas, international 8–9, 32, 33, 34–5, 36, 164, 165
economic independence 10–18; and *emerging world order* 8
economic liberalism 20–2, 117; and Brazil 44, 58–77; and Chile 137; and nationalism 254; and Peru xv, 237, 238; Say and 148; and USA 117
economic nationalism 253–64, 269–74, 276–88; European 254
"economic rationalization" 278
economic utilitarianism 153
The Economist (journal) 47
education 24, 148, 149–52, 153
emancipation 7, 8, 15
"embedded liberalism" 261, 262
England *see* Britain
Enlightenment 16, 18, 37–8, 107
Espinosa, A. 205
'*estrangeirado*' 107
Estudos Avançados (journal) 269
ethnic miscegenation 25
export economies, Furtado on 16, 17
exports: Brazil 66–7, 72, 110, 171; Britain 115, 116; Chile 126, 127, 128, 130, 137; Colombia 96, 212, 221; fall in 277–9; and foreign currency 221; Germany 166; growth of 21, 52; Italy 259, 260; Peru 229, 236, 238, 240; of primary products 13, 16, 100, 271, 272, 286; and unemployment 281; US 84, 87, 88, 95, 97

Faria Junior, C. 78n23
fiction, Latin American 273
Fordney–McCumber Act 1922 95, 102n22
Forget, Evelyn L. 38, 148, 151, 152, 153
Forsyth, John 88
Foster, John W. 93, 94
France 8, 13, 115
Franklin, President Benjamin 69
Frederick William I, King 166

free labor 22, 49, 51, 60, 70, 71–5, 174, 230
free trade 43–53; and bilateral trade agreements 81, 116; '*comercio libre*' regulations 14; debate in Chile 125; end of power of 127, 128; Hull on 99; Menadier on 129; as modernizing 53; and nationalism 23; Say on 154
"free trade imperialism" 44
Free Trade Treaty, US–Brazil 164, 165, 176
"free translation" 38
free-banking system: Colombia 206, 209–13, 219, 220–3; USA 199
French language, role of 37
French liberalism 211, 212, 220
French Revolution 13, 115
Freyre, Gilberto 273
Furtado, Celso 27, 28, 273, 284, 285; on consumption patterns 17, 18; *Formação Econômica da América Latina* 16, 17; *Formação Econômica do Brasil* 16; on free trade 44

Galindo, Anibal 147, 205, 207, 208, 212, 213, 219
Gaos, José 2
Garcia del Rio, Juan 215
Garfield, James A. 91
Gavroglu, Kostas et al. 2008 36
Gee, J. P. 235
Gellner, Ernest 253
"Generation of the 1790s" 14, 15, 107–8
German Historical School of economics 26, 27, 163–79
Germany: centres of political economic thought 8; foundation of *Reich* 167; growing competition for trade 50; political unification 163; popularity of Listian economics 126; reactive nationalism 270
Gherea, Constantin Dobrogeanu 255, 256
Gladstone, William 46, 48, 51
Godoy, Manuel 13
gold standard 191, 192, 201, 207, 224, 277
Gonzalez, Florentino 215–16
Gootenberg, P. 231, 232
gradualism 68
Greenfield, Liah, *The spirit of capitalism: nationalism and economic growth* 269

Printed in the United States
By Bookmasters